IMPRACTICAL PYTHON PROJECTS

IMPRACTICAL PYTHON PROJECTS

Playful Programming Activities to Make You Smarter

by Lee Vaughan

San Francisco

Printed in USA

First printing

22 21 20 19 18   1 2 3 4 5 6 7 8 9

ISBN-10: 1-59327-890-X
ISBN-13: 978-1-59327-890-8

Publisher: William Pollock
Production Editor: Janelle Ludowise
Cover Illustration: Josh Ellingson
Interior Design: Octopod Studios
Developmental Editor: Zach Lebowski
Technical Reviewers: Jeremy Kun, Michael Contraveos, and Michele Pratusevich
Copyeditor: Rachel Monaghan
Compositor: David Van Ness
Proofreader: Paula L. Fleming
Indexer: Beth Nauman-Montana

The following images are reproduced with permission: Figure 4-1 courtesy of the Library of Congress; Figure 7-1 created by *vecteezy.com*; rat silhouette in Figure 7-2 created by *vecteezy.com*; door image in Figures 11-1, 11-3, 11-4, 11-5, and 11-6 created by Dooder at *Freepik.com*; goat and moneybag images in Figures 11-1, 11-4, 11-5, and 11-6 created by *Freepik.com*; Figures 10-1, 10-7, 13-1, 14-21, and 15-1 from NASA; satellite images in Figures 14-13 and 14-24 courtesy of *www.aha-soft.com/*; output in Figure 12-5 supplied by *ifa.com*

For information on distribution, translations, or bulk sales, please contact No Starch Press, Inc. directly:
No Starch Press, Inc.
245 8th Street, San Francisco, CA 94103
phone: 1.415.863.9900; info@nostarch.com
www.nostarch.com

Library of Congress Cataloging-in-Publication Data

Names: Vaughan, Lee, author.
Title: Impractical Python projects : playful programming activities to make you smarter / Lee Vaughan.
Description: First edition. | San Francisco : No Starch Press, Inc., [2018] | Includes bibliographical references and index.
Identifiers: LCCN 2018027576 (print) | LCCN 2018029119 (ebook) | ISBN 9781593278915 (epub) | ISBN 1593278918 (epub) | ISBN 9781593278908 (pbk. : alk. paper) | ISBN 159327890X (pbk. : alk. paper) | ISBN 9781593278915 (ebook) | ISBN 1593278918 (ebook)
Subjects: LCSH: Python (Computer program language)
Classification: LCC QA76.73.P98 (ebook) | LCC QA76.73.P98 V38 2018 (print) | DDC 005.13/3--dc23
LC record available at https://lccn.loc.gov/2018027576

2007036190

For the Accidental Programmers,
the Dedicated Non-Specialists,
the Dibblers and Dabblers:
all the non-professionals who find
themselves writing code every day.
May this help you on your way.

About the Author

Lee Vaughan is a geologist with more than 30 years of experience in the petroleum industry. As the Senior Technical Professional for Geological Modeling at a major international oil company, he was involved in the construction and review of computer models; the development, testing, and commercialization of software; and the training of geoscientists and engineers. An advocate for nonprogrammers who must use programming in their careers, he wrote *Impractical Python Projects* to help self-learners hone their skills with the Python language.

About the Technical Reviewer

Jeremy Kun graduated with his PhD in mathematics from the University of Illinois at Chicago. He writes the blog Math ∩ Programming (*https://jeremykun.com/*) and currently works on datacenter optimization at Google.

BRIEF CONTENTS

CONTENTS IN DETAIL

5
ENCODING ENGLISH CIVIL WAR CIPHERS 91

6
WRITING IN INVISIBLE INK 105

7
BREEDING GIANT RATS WITH GENETIC ALGORITHMS 125

8
COUNTING SYLLABLES FOR HAIKU POETRY 145

9
WRITING HAIKU WITH MARKOV CHAIN ANALYSIS 161

10
ARE WE ALONE? EXPLORING THE FERMI PARADOX 187

11
THE MONTY HALL PROBLEM 217

12
SECURING YOUR NEST EGG 239

15
IMPROVING YOUR ASTROPHOTOGRAPHY WITH PLANET STACKING 325

16
FINDING FRAUDS WITH BENFORD'S LAW 347

APPENDIX
PRACTICE PROJECT SOLUTIONS 367

INDEX 389

ACKNOWLEDGMENTS

Writing a book is a family affair, and I couldn't have succeeded without the support of both my real family and my surrogate family at No Starch Press. First, thanks to my wife, Hannah, and daughters, Sarah and Lora, for their understanding, patience, and endless editing support.

At No Starch, thanks to Bill Pollock and Tyler Ortman for accepting my proposal; Zach Lebowski for making sense of what I was trying to say; Janelle Ludowise for a highly professional job of production editing; Rachel Monaghan and Paula Fleming for taking on the difficult job of copyediting and proofing a technical book; David Van Ness for composition; and Serena Yang and Josh Ellingson for the awesome cover design. Thanks also to my technical reviewers, Jeremy Kun, Michael Contraveos, and Michele Pratusevich, for significantly improving the book with invaluable suggestions and corrections.

External to No Starch, Sarah Vaughan, Eric Evenchick, Xiao-Hui Wu, Brooks Clark, Brian Proett, Brent Francis, and Glenn Krum provided significant technical support.

Finally, thanks to Mark Nathern for introducing me to Python, and to Guido van Rossum for inventing the thing in the first place!

INTRODUCTION

Welcome to *Impractical Python Projects*! Here, you'll use the Python programming language to explore Mars, Jupiter, and the farthest reaches of the galaxy; the souls of poets; the world of high finance; the underworld of espionage and vote tampering; the trickery of game shows; and more. You'll use techniques such as Markov chain analysis to write haiku, Monte Carlo simulation to model financial markets, image stacking to improve your astrophotography, and genetic algorithms to breed an army of gigantic rats, all while gaining experience with modules like `pygame`, Pylint, pydocstyle, `tkinter`, `python-docx`, `matplotlib`, and `pillow`. And most of all, you'll have fun.

Who This Book Is For

You can think of this as your second Python book. It's designed to follow and complement either a complete beginner's book or an introductory class. You'll be able to continue self-training using a project-based approach, without wasting your money or shelf space on a thorough rehashing of concepts you've already learned. But don't worry, I won't leave you hanging; all the code is annotated and explained.

These projects are for anyone who wants to use programming to conduct experiments, test theories, simulate nature, or just have fun. This includes people who use programming as part of their jobs (like scientists and engineers) but who aren't programmers per se, as well as those I call the "determined non-specialists"—dilettantes and dabblers who enjoy programming problems as a fun pastime. If you've wanted to toy with the concepts presented here but found starting potentially complicated projects from scratch too daunting or time-consuming, this book is for you.

What's in This Book

As you work through the projects, you'll increase your knowledge of useful Python libraries and modules; learn more shortcuts, built-in functions, and helpful techniques; and practice designing, testing, and optimizing programs. Additionally, you'll be able to relate what you're doing to real-world applications, datasets, and issues.

To quote Ralph Waldo Emerson, "Nothing great was ever achieved without enthusiasm." This includes the learning experience. The ultimate goal of this book is to spark your imagination and lead you to develop interesting projects of your own. Don't worry if they seem too ambitious at first; a little diligence and a lot of googling can work miracles—and faster than you think.

The following is an overview of the chapters in this book. You don't have to work through them sequentially, but the easiest projects are at the beginning, and I explain new concepts, modules, and techniques more thoroughly when they're first introduced.

Chapter 1: Silly Name Generator This warm-up project introduces the Python PEP 8 and PEP 257 style guides as well as the Pylint and pydocstyle modules, which analyze your code's conformance to these guidelines. The end product is a goofy-name generator inspired by the USA Network TV show *Psych*.

Chapter 2: Finding Palingram Spells Learn how to profile your code while saving DC Comics sorceress Zatanna from a painful death. Search online dictionaries for the magical palingrams that Zatanna needs to beat a time-reversing villain.

Chapter 3: Solving Anagrams Write a program that helps a user create a phrase anagram from their name; for example, *Clint Eastwood* yields *old west action*. Then help Tom Marvolo Riddle derive his anagram, "I am Lord Voldemort," using linguistic sieves.

Chapter 4: Decoding American Civil War Ciphers Investigate and crack one of the most successful military ciphers in history, the Union route cipher. Then help spies on both sides send and decode secret messages using the zig-zagging rail fence cipher.

Chapter 5: Encoding English Civil War Ciphers Read a message hidden in plain sight by decoding a null cipher from the English Civil War. Then save the head of Mary, Queen of Scots, by designing and implementing code to accomplish the more difficult task of *writing* a null cipher.

Chapter 6: Writing in Invisible Ink Help a corporate mole betray Sherlock Holmes's dad and evade detection with invisible electronic ink. This chapter is based on an episode of the CBS television show *Elementary*.

Chapter 7: Breeding Giant Rats with Genetic Algorithms Use genetic algorithms—inspired by Darwinian evolution—to breed a race of super-rats the size of female bullmastiffs. Then help James Bond crack a safe with 10 billion possible combinations in the blink of an eye.

Chapter 8: Counting Syllables for Haiku Poetry Teach your computer to count syllables in English as a prelude to writing Japanese poetry, or haiku, in the next chapter.

Chapter 9: Writing Haiku with Markov Chain Analysis Teach your computer to write *haiku* by combining the syllable-counting module from Chapter 8 with Markov chain analysis and a training corpus of several hundred ancient and modern haiku.

Chapter 10: Are We Alone? Exploring the Fermi Paradox Investigate the absence of alien radio signals using Drake's equation, the dimensions of the Milky Way galaxy, and assumptions about the size of detectable "emissions bubbles." Learn and use the popular `tkinter` module to build a graphical display of the galaxy and Earth's own radio bubble.

Chapter 11: The Monty Hall Problem Help the world's smartest woman win the Monty Hall problem argument. Then use object-oriented programming (OOP) to build a version of Monty's famous game with a fun graphical interface.

Chapter 12: Securing Your Nest Egg Plan your (or your parents') secure retirement using a Monte Carlo–based financial simulation.

Chapter 13: Simulating an Alien Volcano Use `pygame` to simulate a volcanic eruption on Io, one of Jupiter's moons.

Chapter 14: Mapping Mars with the Mars Orbiter Build a gravity-based arcade game and nudge a satellite into a circular mapping orbit without running out of fuel or burning up in the atmosphere. Display readouts of key parameters, track orbital paths, add the planet's shadow, and spin Mars slowly on its axis, all while learning orbital mechanics!

Chapter 15: Improving Your Astrophotography with Planet Stacking Reveal Jupiter's cloud bands and Great Red Spot by optically stacking poor-quality video images using the Python imaging library. Learn how to work with files, folders, and directory paths using the built-in `os` and `shutil` modules.

Chapter 16: Finding Frauds with Benford's Law Use *Benford's law* to investigate vote tampering in the 2016 presidential election. Use `matplotlib` to summarize the results in a chart.

Each chapter ends with at least one Practice Project or Challenge Project. Each Practice Project comes with a solution. That doesn't mean it's the *best* solution—you may come up with a better one on your own, so don't peek ahead!

With the Challenge Projects, however, you're truly on your own. When Cortez invaded Mexico in 1519, he burned his caravels so that his conquistadors would realize there was no going back; they would have to face the Aztecs with grim and unwavering determination. Thus, the expression "burn your boats" has come to represent wholeheartedness or full commitment to a task. This is how you should face the Challenge Projects—as if your boat were burned—and if you do, you're likely to learn more from these exercises than from any other part of the book!

Python Version, Platform, and IDE

I constructed each of the projects in this book with Python v3.5 in a Microsoft Windows 10 environment. If you're using a different operating system, no problem: I suggest compatible modules for other platforms, where appropriate.

The code examples and screen captures in this book are from either the Python IDLE text editor or the interactive shell. IDLE stands for *integrated development and learning environment*. It's an *integrated development environment (IDE)* with an *L* added so that the acronym references Eric Idle of *Monty Python* fame. The interactive shell, also called the *interpreter*, is a window that lets you immediately execute commands and test code without needing to create a file.

IDLE has numerous drawbacks, such as the lack of a line-number column, but it is free and bundled with Python, so everyone has access to it. You are welcome to use whichever IDE you wish. There are many choices available online, such as Geany (pronounced *genie*), PyCharm, and PyScripter. Geany works with a wide range of operating systems, including Unix, macOS, and Windows. PyCharm works with Linux, Windows, and macOS. PyScripter works with Windows. For an extensive listing of available Python development tools and compatible platforms, visit *https://wiki.python.org/moin/DevelopmentTools/*.

The Code

Every line of code is provided for each project in this book, and I recommend you enter it by hand whenever possible. A college professor once told me that we "learn through our hands," and I have to agree that keying in code forces you to pay maximum attention to what's going on.

But if you want to complete a project quickly or you accidentally delete all your work, you can download all of the code, including solutions to the Practice Projects, from *https://www.nostarch.com/impracticalpython/.*

Coding Style

This book is about problem solving and beginner-level fun, so the code may deviate at times from best practices and peak efficiency. Occasionally, you may use list comprehension or a special operator, but for the most part, you'll focus on simple, approachable code that's easy to learn.

Keeping things simple is important for the programming nonprogrammers who read this book. Much of their code may be "Kleenex code"—used once or twice for a specific purpose and then thrown away. This is the type of code that might be shared with colleagues, or thrust upon them during staff changes, so it should be easy to pick up and understand.

All of the main project code is annotated and explained in a standalone manner, and it generally follows the style recommendations from *Python Enhancement Proposal 8*, otherwise known as *PEP 8*. Details on PEP 8, and software to help you honor these guidelines, are in Chapter 1.

Where to Get Help

Taking on a programming challenge can be, well, challenging. Coding isn't always something that you can intuitively figure out—even with a language as friendly as Python. Throughout the following chapters, I will provide links and references to useful sources of information, but for projects you formulate on your own, nothing can beat online searches.

The key to successful searching is knowing what to ask. This can be quite frustrating at first, but think of it as a game of Twenty Questions. Keep honing your keywords with each successive search until you find an answer or reach a point of diminishing returns.

If books and online searches fail, then the next step is to ask someone. You can do this online, either for a fee or at free forums like Stack Overflow (*https://stackoverflow.com/*). But be warned: the members of these sites don't suffer fools gladly. Be sure to read their "How do I ask a good question?" pages before posting; for example, you can find the one for Stack Overflow at *http://stackoverflow.com/help/how-to-ask/.*

Onward!

Thanks for taking the time to read the Introduction! You clearly want to get as much as possible from this book, and you're off to a good start. When you reach the other end, you'll be more adept at Python and better prepared to solve challenging real-world problems. Let's get to work.

1

SILLY NAME GENERATOR

The USA Network television channel once ran a detective dramedy called *Psych*, in which hyper-observant amateur sleuth Sean Spencer solved cases while pretending to use psychic abilities. A trademark of the show was the way he would introduce his sidekick, Gus, with goofy names made up on the fly, like Galileo Humpkins, Lavender Gooms, and Bad News Marvin Barnes. This made an impression on me because, years ago, someone who worked at the Census Bureau gave me a list of real names every bit as strange as those invented by Sean.

Project #1: Generating Pseudonyms

In this warm-up project, you'll write a simple Python program that generates nutty names by randomly combining first names and surnames. With any luck, you'll produce a plethora of aliases that would make any sidekick proud. You'll also review best-practice coding guidelines and apply external programs that will help you write code that conforms to those guidelines.

Psych not your thing? Replace the names in my list in the code with your own jokes or theme. You could just as easily turn this project into a *Game of Thrones* name generator, or perhaps you want to discover your very own "Benedict Cumberbatch" name; my favorite is Bendylick Cricketbat.

THE OBJECTIVE

Randomly generate funny sidekick names using Python code that conforms to established style guidelines.

Planning and Designing a Project

Planning time is never wasted time. It doesn't matter whether you're programming for fun or profit; at some point, you'll need to estimate—fairly accurately—how long the project will take, what obstacles you may encounter, and what tools and resources you'll need to do the work. And to accomplish that, you'll need to know what you're trying to create in the first place!

A successful manager once told me that his secret was simply to ask lots of questions: *What* are you trying to do? *Why* are you doing it? Why are you doing it *this way*? How much *time* do you have? How much *money*? Answering these questions is extremely helpful to the design process and gives you a clear line of sight.

In his book *Think Python, 2nd Edition* (O'Reilly, 2015), Allen Downey describes two types of software development plans: "prototype and patch" and "designed development." With prototype and patch, you start with a simple program and then use *patches*, or edited code, to handle problems encountered in testing. This can be a good approach when you're working through a complex problem you don't understand very well. But it can also produce complicated and unreliable code. If you have a clear view of the problem and how you want to solve it, you should use a designed development plan to avoid future issues and their subsequent patches. This approach can make coding easier and more efficient, and it typically leads to stronger and more reliable code.

For all the projects in this book, you'll start with a clearly defined problem or goal that will form the basis of your design decisions. Then we'll discuss strategy to better understand the issues and create a designed development plan.

The Strategy

You'll start with two lists—first and last—of funny names. The lists will be relatively short, so they won't be memory intensive, won't need to be dynamically updated, and shouldn't present any runtime issues. Since all you'll need to do is read names from the list, you'll use a tuple as a container.

With your two tuples of names, you'll generate new names—pairing a first name with a last—at the touch of a button. That way, the user can easily repeat the process until a sufficiently funny name appears.

You should also highlight the name in the interpreter window somehow so it stands out from the command prompts. The IDLE shell doesn't provide many font options, but you probably know—all too well—that errors appear in red. The default for the `print()` function is the standard output, but with the sys module loaded, you can redirect the output to the error channel, with its trademark red coloring, using the `file` parameter: `print(something, file=sys.stderr)`.

Finally, you'll determine what style recommendations exist for Python programming. These guidelines should address not only the code but also documentation embedded within the code.

The Pseudocode

"You can always count on the Americans to do the right thing after they have tried everything else." That quote, weakly linked to Winston Churchill, sums up the way many people approach writing pseudocode.

Pseudocode is a high-level, informal way to describe computer programs using structured English or any human language. It should resemble a simplified programming language and include keywords and proper indentations. Developers use it to ignore all the arcane syntax of true programming languages and focus on the underlying logic. Despite its widespread use, pseudocode has no official standards—only guidelines.

If you find you've hacked your way into frustration, it may be because you didn't take the time to write pseudocode. I am a true believer in it, as pseudocode has—without fail—guided me to solutions when I was otherwise lost in the woods. Consequently, you'll use some form of pseudocode in most of the projects in this book. At the very least, I hope you'll see its utility, but I also hope you'll develop the discipline to write it in your own projects.

A very high-level pseudocode for our funny name generator could look like this:

```
Load a list of first names
Load a list of surnames
Choose a first name at random
Assign the name to a variable
Choose a surname at random
Assign the name to a variable
```

```
Print the names to the screen in order and in red font
Ask the user to quit or play again
If user plays again:
    repeat
If user quits:
    end and exit
```

Unless you're trying to pass a programming class or provide clear instructions to others, focus on the *purpose* of the pseudocode; don't worry about slavishly complying with the (nonstandard) guidelines for writing it. And don't stop with programming—you can apply the pseudocode process to much more. Once you get the hang of it, you might find it helps you complete other tasks like doing your taxes, planning your investments, building a house, or getting ready for a camping trip. It's a great way to focus your thinking and carry programming successes over into real life. If only Congress would use it!

The Code

Listing 1-1 is the code for the funny name generator, *pseudonyms.py*, which compiles and prints a list of pseudonyms from two tuples of names. If you don't want to type all the names, you can type a subset or download the code from *https://nostarch.com/impracticalpython/*.

pseudonyms.py

```
❶ import sys, random

❷ print("Welcome to the Psych 'Sidekick Name Picker.'\n")
  print("A name just like Sean would pick for Gus:\n\n")

  first = ('Baby Oil', 'Bad News', 'Big Burps', "Bill 'Beenie-Weenie'",
           "Bob 'Stinkbug'", 'Bowel Noises', 'Boxelder', "Bud 'Lite' ",
           'Butterbean', 'Buttermilk', 'Buttocks', 'Chad', 'Chesterfield',
           'Chewy', 'Chigger", "Cinnabuns', 'Cleet', 'Cornbread', 'Crab Meat',
           'Crapps', 'Dark Skies', 'Dennis Clawhammer', 'Dicman', 'Elphonso',
           'Fancypants', 'Figgs', 'Foncy', 'Gootsy', 'Greasy Jim', 'Huckleberry',
           'Huggy', 'Ignatious', 'Jimbo', "Joe 'Pottin Soil'", 'Johnny',
           'Lemongrass', 'Lil Debil', 'Longbranch', '"Lunch Money"',
           'Mergatroid', '"Mr Peabody"', 'Oil-Can', 'Oinks', 'Old Scratch',
           'Ovaltine', 'Pennywhistle', 'Pitchfork Ben', 'Potato Bug',
           'Pushmeet','Rock Candy', 'Schlomo', 'Scratchensniff', 'Scut',
           "Sid 'The Squirts'", 'Skidmark', 'Slaps', 'Snakes', 'Snoobs',
           'Snorki', 'Soupcan Sam', 'Spitzitout', 'Squids', 'Stinky',
           'Storyboard', 'Sweet Tea', 'TeeTee', 'Wheezy Joe',
           "Winston 'Jazz Hands'", 'Worms')

  last = ('Appleyard', 'Bigmeat', 'Bloominshine', 'Boogerbottom',
          'Breedslovetrout', 'Butterbaugh', 'Clovenhoof', 'Clutterbuck',
          'Cocktoasten', 'Endicott', 'Fewhairs', 'Gooberdapple', 'Goodensmith',
          'Goodpasture', 'Guster', 'Henderson', 'Hooperbag', 'Hoosenater',
          'Hootkins', 'Jefferson', 'Jenkins', 'Jingley-Schmidt', 'Johnson',
```

```
        'Kingfish', 'Listenbee', "M'Bembo", 'McFadden', 'Moonshine', 'Nettles',
        'Noseworthy', 'Olivetti', 'Outerbridge', 'Overpeck', 'Overturf',
        'Oxhandler', 'Pealike', 'Pennywhistle', 'Peterson', 'Pieplow',
        'Pinkerton', 'Porkins', 'Putney', 'Quakenbush', 'Rainwater',
        'Rosenthal', 'Rubbins', 'Sackrider', 'Snuggleshine', 'Splern',
        'Stevens', 'Stroganoff', 'Sugar-Gold', 'Swackhamer', 'Tippins',
        'Turnipseed', 'Vinaigrette', 'Walkingstick', 'Wallbanger', 'Weewax',
        'Weiners', 'Whipkey', 'Wigglesworth', 'Wimplesnatch', 'Winterkorn',
        'Woolysocks')

❸ while True:
    ❹ firstName = random.choice(first)

    ❺ lastName = random.choice(last)

      print("\n\n")
    ❻ print("{} {}".format(firstName, lastName), file=sys.stderr)
      print("\n\n")

    ❼ try_again = input("\n\nTry again? (Press Enter else n to quit)\n ")
      if try_again.lower() == "n":
          break

❽ input("\nPress Enter to exit.")
```

Listing 1-1: Generates silly pseudonyms from tuples of names

First, import the sys and random modules ❶. You'll use sys to access the system-specific error message functionality, so you can color your output an eye-catching red in the IDLE window. And random lets you pick, at random, items from your name lists.

The print statements at ❷ introduce the program to the user. The newline command \n forces a new line, and single quotes '' allow you to use quotes in the printout without having to resort to the backslash escape character, which would reduce code readability.

Next, define your tuples of names. Then initiate the while loop ❸. Setting while = True basically means "Keep running until I tell you to stop." Eventually, you'll use a break statement to end the loop.

The loop starts by choosing a name from the first tuple at random and then assigns that name to the variable firstName ❹. It uses the random module's choice method to return a random element from a nonempty sequence—in this case, the tuple of first names.

Next, choose a surname at random from the last tuple and assign it to the variable lastName ❺. Now that you have both names, print them and trick IDLE into using the red "error" font by supplying the optional argument file=sys.stderr to the print statement ❻. Use the newer string format *method*, rather than the older string format *operator* (%), to convert the name variables to a string. To read more about the new method, see *https://docs.python.org/3.7/library/string.html.*

Once the name is displayed, ask the user to choose to play again or quit, using input to provide the instruction in quotes. In this case, include a few blank lines as well to make the funny name more obvious in the IDLE window. If the user responds by pressing the ENTER key, nothing is returned to the `try_again` variable ❼. With nothing returned, the condition on the `if` statement isn't met, the `while` loop continues, and a new name is printed. If the user instead presses the N key, the `if` statement results in a `break` command, and the loop ends because the `while` statement no longer evaluates to `True`. Use the lowercase string method `.lower()` to mitigate the player's CAPS LOCK key being engaged. In other words, it doesn't matter whether the user inputs a lowercase or uppercase N, because the program will always read it as lowercase.

Finally, ask the user to exit by pressing the ENTER key ❽. Pressing ENTER doesn't assign the return value of `input()` to a variable, the program ends, and the console window closes. Pressing F5 in the IDLE editor window executes the completed program.

This code works, but working isn't enough—programs in Python should work with *style*.

Using the Python Community's Style Guide

According to the *Zen of Python* (*https://www.python.org/dev/peps/pep-0020/*), "There should be one—and preferably only one—obvious way to do something." In the spirit of providing a single obvious "right way" of doing things and building consensus around these practices, the Python community releases *Python Enhancement Proposals*, which are coding conventions for the Python code comprising the standard library in the main Python distribution. The most important of these is *PEP 8*, a style guide for Python programming. PEP 8 evolves over time as new conventions are identified and past ones are rendered obsolete by changes in the language.

PEP 8 (*https://www.python.org/dev/peps/pep-0008/*) sets standards for naming conventions; use of blank lines, tabs, and spaces; maximum line length; comments; and so on. The goal is to improve the readability of code and make it consistent across a wide spectrum of Python programs. When you start programming, you should strive to learn and follow the accepted conventions, before bad habits become engrained. The code in this book will conform closely to PEP 8, but I have overridden some conventions (by using less commented code, fewer blank lines, and shorter docstrings, for example) in deference to the publishing industry.

Standardized names and procedures are especially important when you're working in cross-functional teams. A lot can get lost in translation between scientists and engineers, as in 1999, when engineers lost the Mars Climate Orbiter because different teams used different measurement units. For almost two decades, I built computer models of the earth that were transferred to an engineering function. The engineers used scripts to load these models into their own proprietary software. They would share these scripts among projects for efficiency and to help the inexperienced. Since these "command files" were customized to each project, the engineers were understandably annoyed when attribute names changed during model updates. In fact, one of their internal guidelines was "Beg, bribe, or bully your modeler into using consistent property names!"

Checking Your Code with Pylint

You should become familiar with PEP 8, but you'll still make mistakes, and comparing your code to the guide is a major drag. Luckily, programs such as Pylint, pycodestyle, and Flake8 can help you easily follow the PEP 8 style recommendations. For this project, you'll use Pylint.

Installing Pylint

Pylint is a source code, bug, and quality checker for the Python programming language. To download a free copy, go to *https://www.pylint.org/#install* and find the install button for your platform. This button will show the command for installing Pylint. For example, in Windows, go to the folder that contains your copy of Python (such as *C:\Python35*), use SHIFT-right-click to open a context menu, and then click either **open command window here** or **open PowerShell window here**, depending on which version of Windows you're using. In the window, run **`pip install pylint`**.

Running Pylint

In Windows, Pylint is run from a command window or, for newer systems, the PowerShell (you open both by using SHIFT-right-click in the folder containing the Python module you want to check). Type **`pylint`** ***`filename`*** to run the program (see Figure 1-1). The *.py* extension is optional, and your directory path will vary from the one shown. On macOS or another Unix-based system, use the terminal emulator.

Figure 1-1: The Windows command window with the command to run Pylint

The command window will display the Pylint results. Here's a sample of a useful output:

```
C:\Python35\Python 3 Stuff\Psych>pylint pseudonyms.py
No config file found, using default configuration
************* Module pseudonyms
C: 45, 0: No space allowed around keyword argument assignment
    print(firstName, lastName, file = sys.stderr)
                                    ^ (bad-whitespace)
C:  1, 0: Missing module docstring (missing-docstring)
C:  2, 0: Multiple imports on one line (sys, random) (multiple-imports)
C:  7, 0: Invalid constant name "first" (invalid-name)
C: 23, 0: Invalid constant name "last" (invalid-name)
C: 40, 4: Invalid constant name "firstName" (invalid-name)
C: 42, 4: Invalid constant name "lastName" (invalid-name)
C: 48, 4: Invalid constant name "try_again" (invalid-name)
```

The capital letter at the start of each line is a message code. For example, `C: 15, 0` refers to a coding standard violation in line 15, column 0. You can reference the following key for the various Pylint message codes:

- **R** Refactor for a "good practice" metric violation
- **C** Convention for coding standard violation
- **W** Warning for stylistic problems or minor programming issues
- **E** Error for important programming issues (i.e., most probably a bug)
- **F** Fatal for errors that prevent further processing

Pylint will end its report by grading your program's conformance to PEP 8. In this case, your code received a 4 out of 10:

```
Global evaluation
-----------------
Your code has been rated at 4.00/10 (previous run: 4.00/10, +0.00)
```

Handling False Constant Name Errors

You might have noticed that Pylint incorrectly assumes all variable names in the global space refer to constants, and should therefore be in all caps. You can work around this shortcoming in a number of ways. The first is to embed your code in a `main()` function (as shown in Listing 1-2); that way, it's out of the global space.

```
def main():
    some indented code
    some indented code
    some indented code
❶ if __name__ == "__main__":
  ❷ main()
```

Listing 1-2: Defines and calls a `main()` function

The `__name__` variable is a special built-in variable that you can use to evaluate whether a program is being run in stand-alone mode or as an imported module; remember that a module is just a Python program used inside of another Python program. If you run the program directly, `__name__` is set to `__main__`. In Listing 1-2 `__name__` is used to ensure that, when the program is imported, the `main()` function isn't run until you intentionally call it, but when you run the program directly, the condition in the `if` statement is met ❶ and `main()` is automatically called ❷. You don't always need this convention. For example, if your code just defines a function, you can load it as a module and call it without the need for `__name__`.

Let's embed everything in *pseudonyms.py*, except for the `import` statement, under a `main()` function and then embed the `main()` function call under an `if` statement, as in Listing 1-2. You can make the changes yourself or download the *pseudonyms_main.py* program from the website. Rerun Pylint. You should get the following results in your command window.

```
C:\Python35\Python 3 Stuff\Psych>pylint pseudonyms_main
No config file found, using default configuration
************* Module pseudonyms_main
C: 47, 0: No space allowed around keyword argument assignment
        print(firstName, lastName, file = sys.stderr)
                                        ^ (bad-whitespace)
C:  1, 0: Missing module docstring (missing-docstring)
C:  2, 0: Multiple imports on one line (sys, random) (multiple-imports)
C:  4, 0: Missing function docstring (missing-docstring)
C: 42, 8: Invalid variable name "firstName" (invalid-name)
C: 44, 8: Invalid variable name "lastName" (invalid-name)
```

Now those annoying comments about invalid constant names have disappeared, but you aren't out of the woods yet. As much as I like them, Python conventions don't allow for *camel case* names, like `firstName`.

Configuring Pylint

When evaluating small scripts, I prefer to use the Pylint defaults and ignore the false "constant name" errors. I also like to run the option `-rn` (short for `-reports=n`) to suppress the large volume of extraneous statistics that Pylint returns:

```
C:\Python35\Python 3 Stuff\Psych>pylint -rn pseudonyms_main.py
```

Note that using `-rn` will disable the code-grading option.

Another issue with Pylint is that its maximum line length default is 100 characters but PEP 8 recommends 79 characters. To comply with PEP 8, you can run Pylint with the following option:

```
C:\Python35\Python 3 Stuff\Psych>pylint --max-line-length=79 pseudonyms_main
```

Now you'll see that indenting the names for the `main()` function caused some lines to exceed the guidelines:

```
C: 12, 0: Line too long (80/79) (line-too-long)
C: 14, 0: Line too long (83/79) (line-too-long)
--snip--
```

You probably don't want to configure Pylint every time you run it, and fortunately, you don't have to. Instead, you can make your own customized configuration file using the command `--generate-rcfile`. For example, to suppress reporting and set the maximum line length to 79, enter the following into your command prompt:

```
your pathname>pylint -rn --max-line-length=79 --generate-rcfile > name.pylintrc
```

Put the changes you want before the `--generate-rcfile > name.pylintrc` statement and provide your own name before the `.pylintrc` extension. You can create a configuration file either stand-alone, as just shown, or at the same time you evaluate a Python program. The *.pylintrc* file is automatically saved in your current working directory, though there is an option for adding a directory path (see *https://pylint.org* and *https://pylint.readthedocs.io/en/latest/user_guide/run.html* for more details).

To reuse your custom configuration file, use the `--rcfile` option followed by the name of your personal configuration file and the name of the program you're evaluating. For example, to run *myconfig.pylintrc* on the *pseudonyms_main.py* program, enter the following:

```
C:\Python35\Python 3 Stuff\Psych>pylint --rcfile myconfig.pylintrc pseudonyms_main
```

Describing Your Code with Docstrings

Pylint identifies that the *pseudonyms_main.py* program is missing a docstring. According to the PEP 257 style guide (*https://www.python.org/dev/peps/pep-0257/*), a *docstring* is a string literal that occurs as the first statement in a module, function, class, or method definition. A docstring is basically a short description of what your code does, and it may include specifics on aspects of the code such as required inputs. Here, in triple quotes, is an example of a single-line docstring for a function:

```
def circ(r):
    """Return the circumference of a circle with radius of r."""
    c = 2 * r * math.pi
    return c
```

The preceding docstring simply states what the function does, but docstrings can be longer and include more information. For instance, the following is a multiline docstring for the same function that displays information about the function's input and output:

```
def circ(r):
    """Return the circumference of a circle with radius of r.

    Arguments:
    r - radius of circle

    Returns:
        float: circumference of circle
    """
    c = 2 * r * math.pi
    return c
```

Unfortunately, docstrings are person-, project-, and company-specific things, and you can find a lot of conflicting guidance. Google has its own format and an excellent style guide. Some members of the scientific community use a `NumPy` docstring standard. And *reStructuredText* is a popular format used mainly in conjunction with Sphinx—a tool that uses docstrings to generate documentation for Python projects in formats such as HTML and PDF. If you've ever read the docs (*https://readthedocs.org/*) for a Python module, then you've seen Sphinx in action. You can find links to guides for some of these different styles in "Further Reading" on page 14.

You can check how well your docstrings conform to the PEP 257 conventions with a free tool called pydocstyle. To install it in Windows or any other operating system, open a command window and run **pip install pydocstyle** (use pip3 if both Python 2 and 3 are installed).

To run pydocstyle, open a command window in the folder containing the code you want to check. If you don't specify a filename, pydocstyle will run on *all* the Python programs in the folder and give you feedback:

```
C:\Python35\Python 3 Stuff\Psych>pydocstyle
.\OLD_pseudonyms_main.py:1 at module level:
        D100: Missing docstring in public module
.\OLD_pseudonyms_main.py:4 in public function `main`:
        D103: Missing docstring in public function
.\ pseudonyms.py:1 at module level:
        D100: Missing docstring in public module
.\ pseudonyms_main_broken.py:1 at module level:
        D200: One-line docstring should fit on one line with quotes (found 2)
.\ pseudonyms_main_broken.py:6 in public function `main`:
        D205: 1 blank line required between summary line and description
(found 0)
```

If you specify a file with no docstring issues, pydocstyle will return nothing:

```
C:\Python35\Python 3 Stuff\Psych>pydocstyle pseudonyms_main_fixed.py

C:\Python35\Python 3 Stuff\Psych>
```

I'll use fairly simple docstrings in all of the projects in this book in order to reduce visual noise in the annotated code. Feel free to expand on these if you wish to practice. You can always check your results with pydocstyle.

Checking Your Code Style

When I was growing up, my uncle would drive from our rural town to a larger city to have his hair "styled." I never understood how that was different from a regular haircut, but I do know how to "style" our funny name generator code so that it complies with PEP 8 and PEP 257.

Make a copy of *pseudonyms_main.py* called *pseudonyms_main_fixed.py* and immediately evaluate it with Pylint using this command:

```
your_path>pylint --max-line-length=79 pseudonyms_main_fixed
```

Don't suppress the report using -rn. You should see this output at the bottom of the command window:

```
Global evaluation
-----------------
Your code has been rated at 3.33/10
```

Now correct the code based on the Pylint output. In the following example, I have provided the corrections in **bold**. I made changes to the name tuples to correct for line-length issues. You can also download the corrected code, *pseudonyms_main_fixed.py*, from the book's resources at *https://www.nostarch.com/impracticalpython/*.

pseudonyms_main_fixed.py

```
"""Generate funny names by randomly combining names from 2 separate lists."""
import sys
import random

def main():
    """Choose names at random from 2 tuples of names and print to screen."""
    print("Welcome to the Psych 'Sidekick Name Picker.'\n")
    print("A name just like Sean would pick for Gus:\n\n")

    first = ('Baby Oil', 'Bad News', 'Big Burps', "Bill 'Beenie-Weenie'",
             "Bob 'Stinkbug'", 'Bowel Noises', 'Boxelder', "Bud 'Lite'",
             'Butterbean', 'Buttermilk', 'Buttocks', 'Chad', 'Chesterfield',
             'Chewy', 'Chigger', 'Cinnabuns', 'Cleet', 'Cornbread',
             'Crab Meat', 'Crapps', 'Dark Skies', 'Dennis Clawhammer',
             'Dicman', 'Elphonso', 'Fancypants', 'Figgs', 'Foncy', 'Gootsy',
             'Greasy Jim', 'Huckleberry', 'Huggy', 'Ignatious', 'Jimbo',
             "Joe 'Pottin Soil'", 'Johnny', 'Lemongrass', 'Lil Debil',
             'Longbranch', '"Lunch Money"', 'Mergatroid', '"Mr Peabody"',
             'Oil-Can', 'Oinks', 'Old Scratch', 'Ovaltine', 'Pennywhistle',
             'Pitchfork Ben', 'Potato Bug', 'Pushmeet', 'Rock Candy',
             'Schlomo', 'Scratchensniff', 'Scut', "Sid 'The Squirts'",
             'Skidmark', 'Slaps', 'Snakes', 'Snoobs', 'Snorki', 'Soupcan Sam',
             'Spitzitout', 'Squids', 'Stinky', 'Storyboard', 'Sweet Tea',
             'TeeTee', 'Wheezy Joe', "Winston 'Jazz Hands'", 'Worms')

    last = ('Appleyard', 'Bigmeat', 'Bloominshine', 'Boogerbottom',
            'Breedslovetrout', 'Butterbaugh', 'Clovenhoof', 'Clutterbuck',
            'Cocktoasten', 'Endicott', 'Fewhairs', 'Gooberdapple',
            'Goodensmith', 'Goodpasture', 'Guster', 'Henderson', 'Hooperbag',
            'Hoosenater', 'Hootkins', 'Jefferson', 'Jenkins',
            'Jingley-Schmidt', 'Johnson', 'Kingfish', 'Listenbee', "M'Bembo",
            'McFadden', 'Moonshine', 'Nettles', 'Noseworthy', 'Olivetti',
            'Outerbridge', 'Overpeck', 'Overturf', 'Oxhandler', 'Pealike',
            'Pennywhistle', 'Peterson', 'Pieplow', 'Pinkerton', 'Porkins',
            'Putney', 'Quakenbush', 'Rainwater', 'Rosenthal', 'Rubbins',
            'Sackrider', 'Snuggleshine', 'Splern', 'Stevens', 'Stroganoff',
            'Sugar-Gold', 'Swackhamer', 'Tippins', 'Turnipseed',
```

```
            'Vinaigrette', 'Walkingstick', 'Wallbanger', 'Weewax', 'Weiners',
            'Whipkey', 'Wigglesworth', 'Wimplesnatch', 'Winterkorn',
            'Woolysocks')

    while True:
        first_name = random.choice(first)
        last_name = random.choice(last)

        print("\n\n")
        # Trick IDLE by using "fatal error" setting to print name in red.
        print("{} {}".format(first_name, last_name), file=sys.stderr)
        print("\n\n")

        try_again = input("\n\nTry again? (Press Enter else n to quit)\n ")

        if try_again.lower() == "n":
            break

    input("\nPress Enter to exit.")

if __name__ == "__main__":
    main()
```

Pylint gives the revised code a grade of 10 out of 10:

```
Global evaluation
-----------------
Your code has been rated at 10.00/10 (previous run: 3.33/10, +6.67)
```

As you saw in the previous section, running pydocstyle on *pseudonyms_main_fixed.py* yields no errors, but don't be fooled into thinking that means it's good or even adequate. For example, this docstring also passes: `"""ksjkdls lskjds kjs jdi wllk sijkljs dsdw noiu sss."""`

It's hard to write sparse, succinct, and truly useful docstrings and comments. PEP 257 will help with docstrings, but comments are more freestyle and "open range." Too many comments create visual noise, can be off-putting to the user, and shouldn't be needed, as well-written code is largely self-documenting. Good reasons for adding comments include clarifying intent and heading off potential user errors, such as when specific measurement units or input formats are required. To find the right balance in commenting, take note of good examples when you run across them. Also, think about what you would want to see if you had to pick up your own code after a five-year hiatus!

Pylint and pydocstyle are easy to install, are easy to run, and will help you learn and comply with the accepted coding standards of the Python community. Running your code through Pylint prior to posting it on web forums is also a good practice when you're seeking help and should prompt "kinder, gentler" responses!

Summary

You should now know how to write code and documentation that conforms to the Python community's expectations. More importantly, you've generated some seriously funny names for a sidekick, gangster, informant, whoever. Here are a few of my favorites:

Pitchfork Ben Pennywhistle	'Bad News' Bloominshine
Chewy Stroganoff	'Sweet Tea' Tippins
Spitzitout Winterkorn	Wheezy Joe Jenkins
'Big Burps' Rosenthal	Soupcan Sam Putney
Bill 'Beenie-Weenie' Clutterbuck	Greasy Jim Wigglesworth
Dark Skies Jingley-Schmidt	Chesterfield Walkingstick
Potato Bug Quakenbush	Jimbo Woolysocks
Worms Endicott	Fancypants Pinkerton
Cleet Weiners	Dicman Overpeck
Ignatious Outerbridge	Buttocks Rubbins

Further Reading

For a clickable version of these resources, visit *https://www.nostarch.com/impracticalpython/*.

Pseudocode

Descriptions of some fairly formal pseudocode standards can be found at *http://users.csc.calpoly.edu/~jdalbey/SWE/pdl_std.html* and *http://www.slideshare.net/sabiksabz/pseudo-code-basics/*.

Style Guides

Here's a list of style guides you can reference when creating Python programs.

- The PEP 8 style guide can be found at *https://www.python.org/dev/peps/pep-0008/*.
- The PEP 257 guidelines can be found at *https://www.python.org/dev/peps/pep-0257/*.
- Google has its own format and style guide at *https://google.github.io/styleguide/pyguide.html.*
- Examples of Google style can be found at *https://sphinxcontrib-napoleon.readthedocs.io/en/latest/example_google.html.*

- NumPy docstring standards are at *https://numpydoc.readthedocs.io/en/latest/*.
- NumPy docstrings examples can be found at *https://sphinxcontrib-napoleon.readthedocs.io/en/latest/example_numpy.html*.
- You can find out about reStructuredText at *https://docs.python.org/devguide/documenting.html*, *https://docs.python.org/3.1/documenting/rest.html*, and *https://wiki.python.org/moin/reStructuredText/*.
- *The Hitchhiker's Guide to Python* (*http://docs.python-guide.org/en/latest/writing/style/*) contains a section on code styles and *autopep8*, which will automatically reformat code for PEP 8 (to a point).
- *Effective Python* by Brett Slatkin (Addison-Wesley, 2015) contains a useful section on documenting programs.

Third-Party Modules

The following are some resources for using third-party modules.

- Details on Pylint are at *https://docs.pylint.org/en/1.8/tutorial.html*.
- Details on pydocstyle can be found at *http://www.pydocstyle.org/en/latest/*.

Practice Projects

Try out these projects for working with strings. My own solutions are available in the appendix.

Pig Latin

To form Pig Latin, you take an English word that begins with a consonant, move that consonant to the end, and then add "ay" to the end of the word. If the word begins with a vowel, you simply add "way" to the end of the word. One of the most famous Pig Latin phrases of all time is "ixnay on the ottenray," uttered by Marty Feldman in Mel Brooks's comedic masterpiece *Young Frankenstein*.

Write a program that takes a word as input and uses indexing and slicing to return its Pig Latin equivalent. Run Pylint and pydocstyle on your code and correct any style mistakes. You can find a solution in the appendix or download *pig_latin_practice.py* from *https://www.nostarch.com/impracticalpython/*.

Poor Man's Bar Chart

The six most commonly used letters in the English language can be remembered with the mnemonic "etaoin" (pronounced *eh-tay-oh-in*). Write a Python script that takes a sentence (string) as input and returns a simple bar chart–type display as in Figure 1-2. Hint: I used a dictionary data structure and two modules that I haven't covered yet, `pprint` and `collections/defaultdict`.

```
Python 3.5.2 Shell
File Edit Shell Debug Options Window Help
You may need to stretch console window if text wrapping occurs.

text = Like the castle in its corner in a medieval game, I foresee terrible trouble and I stay here just
the same.

defaultdict(<class 'list'>,
            {'a': ['a', 'a', 'a', 'a', 'a', 'a', 'a'],
             'b': ['b', 'b'],
             'c': ['c', 'c'],
             'd': ['d', 'd'],
             'e': ['e', 'e', 'e', 'e', 'e', 'e', 'e', 'e', 'e', 'e', 'e', 'e', 'e', 'e', 'e', 'e', 'e'],
             'f': ['f'],
             'g': ['g'],
             'h': ['h', 'h', 'h'],
             'i': ['i', 'i', 'i', 'i', 'i', 'i', 'i', 'i'],
             'j': ['j'],
             'k': ['k'],
             'l': ['l', 'l', 'l', 'l', 'l'],
             'm': ['m', 'm', 'm'],
             'n': ['n', 'n', 'n', 'n'],
             'o': ['o', 'o', 'o'],
             'r': ['r', 'r', 'r', 'r', 'r', 'r', 'r'],
             's': ['s', 's', 's', 's', 's', 's'],
             't': ['t', 't', 't', 't', 't', 't', 't', 't'],
             'u': ['u', 'u'],
             'v': ['v'],
             'y': ['y']})
>>>
                                                                                        Ln: 23 Col: 34
```

Figure 1-2: Bar chart–like output of the ETAOIN_practice.py *program in the appendix*

Challenge Projects

No solutions are provided for challenge projects. You're on your own with these!

Poor Foreign Man's Bar Chart

Use an online translator to change your text into another Latin-based writing system (such as Spanish or French), rerun your code from the Poor Man's Bar Chart, and compare the results. For example, a Spanish version of the text in Figure 1-2 yields the results in Figure 1-3.

```
Python 3.5.2 Shell
File Edit Shell Debug Options Window Help
You may need to stretch console window if text wrapping occurs.

text = Al igual que el castillo en la esquina en un juego medieval, preveo terribles problemas y me quedo
aquí lo mismo.

defaultdict(<class 'list'>,
            {'a': ['a', 'a', 'a', 'a', 'a', 'a', 'a', 'a'],
             'b': ['b', 'b'],
             'c': ['c'],
             'd': ['d', 'd'],
             'e': ['e', 'e', 'e', 'e', 'e', 'e', 'e', 'e', 'e', 'e', 'e', 'e', 'e', 'e', 'e'],
             'g': ['g', 'g'],
             'i': ['i', 'i', 'i', 'i', 'i', 'i'],
             'j': ['j'],
             'l': ['l', 'l', 'l', 'l', 'l', 'l', 'l', 'l', 'l', 'l'],
             'm': ['m', 'm', 'm', 'm', 'm'],
             'n': ['n', 'n', 'n', 'n'],
             'o': ['o', 'o', 'o', 'o', 'o', 'o', 'o'],
             'p': ['p', 'p'],
             'q': ['q', 'q', 'q', 'q'],
             'r': ['r', 'r', 'r', 'r'],
             's': ['s', 's', 's', 's', 's'],
             't': ['t', 't'],
             'u': ['u', 'u', 'u', 'u', 'u', 'u', 'u'],
             'v': ['v', 'v'],
             'y': ['y']})
>>>
                                                                                        Ln: 31 Col: 4
```

Figure 1-3: The results of running EATOIN_challenge.py *on a Spanish translation of the text in Figure 1-2*

Twice as many *Ls* and three times as many *Us* appear in the Spanish sentence. To make the bar charts for different inputs directly comparable, change the code so every letter of the alphabet has a key and is displayed even if there are no values.

The Middle

Rewrite the funny name generator code to include middle names. First, create a new `middle_name` tuple, then split apart existing first name–middle name pairs (such as "Joe 'Pottin Soil'" or "Sid 'The Squirts'") and add them to the tuple. You should also move some obvious nicknames (like "Oil Can") to your `middle_name` tuple. Finally, add some new middle names (such as "The Big News," or "Grunts," or "Tinkie Winkie"). Use Python's `random` module so that a middle name is chosen only one-half or one-third of the time.

Something Completely Different

Start your own list of funny names and add to the funny name generator. Hint: movie credits are a rich hunting ground!

2

FINDING PALINGRAM SPELLS

Radar. Kayak. Rotator. Sexes. What do these words all have in common? They're *palindromes*, words that are spelled the same forward and backward. Even better are *palingrams*, whole phrases that behave the same way. Napoleon is the author of the most famous palingram. When he first saw Elba, the island of his exile, he said, "Able was I ere I saw Elba."

In 2011, DC Comics published an interesting story that made clever use of palingrams. The superhero sorceress Zatanna was cursed so that she could cast spells only by speaking palindromically. She managed to think up just enough two-word phrases like *nurses run*, *stack cats*, and *puff up* to defeat her sword-wielding attacker. This got me wondering: just how many "combative" palingrams are there? And are there better choices for Zatanna?

In this chapter, you'll load dictionary files from the internet and use Python to discover first palindromes and then the more complex palingrams in those files. Then you'll use a tool called `cProfile` to analyze your palingram code so that you can make it more performant. Finally, you'll sift through the palingrams to see how many have an "aggressive" nature.

Finding and Opening a Dictionary

All the projects in this chapter require a listing of words in a text file format, commonly referred to as a *dictionary file*, so let's start by learning how to load one.

Despite their name, dictionary files contain only words—no pronunciation, syllable count, definitions, and so on. This is good news, as those things would just get in our way. And even better, dictionary files are available online for free.

You can find suitable dictionary files at the locations listed in Table 2-1. Download one of the files or, if it opens directly, copy and paste the contents into a text editor like Notepad or WordPad (TextEdit on macOS) and save it as a *.txt* file. Keep the dictionary in the same folder as the Python code. I used the *2of4brif.txt* file to prepare this project. It can be found in the downloadable *12dicts-6.0.2.zip* file on the website listed first in Table 2-1.

Table 2-1: Downloadable Dictionary Files

File	Number of words
http://wordlist.aspell.net/12dicts/	60,388
https://inventwithpython.com/dictionary.txt	45,000
http://www-personal.umich.edu/~jlawler/wordlist.html	69,903
http://greenteapress.com/thinkpython2/code/words.txt	113,809

In addition to the files in Table 2-1, Unix and Unix-like operating systems come packaged with a large newline-delimited word file of more than 200,000 words. It is usually stored in */usr/share/dict/words* or */usr/dict/words.* On Debian GNU/Linux, word lists are in */usr/share/opendict/dictionaries.* The macOS dictionaries are generally found in */Library/Dictionaries*, and non-English dictionaries are included. You may need to do an online search for your operating system and version to find the exact directory path if you want to use one of these files.

Some dictionary files exclude *a* and *I* as words. Others may include every letter in the dictionary as a single word "header" (such as *d* at the start of words beginning with *d*). We'll ignore one-letter palindromes in these projects, so these issues shouldn't be a problem.

Handling Exceptions When Opening Files

Whenever you load an external file, your program should automatically check for I/O issues, like missing files or incorrect filenames, and let you know if there is a problem.

Use the following try and except statements to catch and handle *exceptions*, which are errors detected during execution:

```
❶ try:
    ❷ with open(file) as in_file:
          do something
  except IOError❸ as e:
    ❹ print("{}\nError opening {}. Terminating program.".format(e, file),
              file=sys.stderr)
    ❺ sys.exit(1)
```

The try clause is executed first ❶. The with statement will automatically close the file after the nested block of code, regardless of how the block exits ❷. Closing files prior to terminating a process is a good practice. If you don't close those files, you could run out of file descriptors (mainly a problem with large scripts that run for a long time), lock the file from further access in Windows, corrupt the files, or lose data if you are writing to the file.

If something goes wrong and if the type of error matches the exception named after the except keyword ❸, the rest of the try clause is skipped, and the except clause is executed ❹. If nothing goes wrong, the try clause is executed, and the except clause is skipped. The print statement in the except clause lets you know there's a problem, and the file=sys.stderr argument colors the error statement red in the IDLE interpreter window.

The sys.exit(1) ❺ statement is used to terminate the program. The 1 in sys.exit(1) indicates that the program experienced an error and did not close successfully.

If an exception occurs that *doesn't* match the named exception in the except clause, it is passed to any outer try statements or the main program execution. If no handler is found, the *unhandled exception* causes the program to stop with a standard "traceback" error message.

Loading the Dictionary File

Listing 2-1 loads a dictionary file as a list. Manually enter this script or download it as *load_dictionary.py* from *https://nostarch.com/impracticalpython/*.

You can import this file into other programs as a module and run it with a one-line statement. Remember, a module is simply a Python program that can be used in another Python program. As you're probably aware, modules represent a form of *abstraction*. Abstraction means you don't have to worry about all the coding details. A principle of abstraction is *encapsulation*, the act of hiding the details. We encapsulate the file-loading code in a module so you don't have to see or worry about the detailed code in another program.

load_dictionary.py

```
"""Load a text file as a list.

Arguments:
-text file name (and directory path, if needed)

Exceptions:
-IOError if filename not found.

Returns:
-A list of all words in a text file in lower case.

Requires-import sys

"""
❶ import sys

❷ def load(file):
    """Open a text file & return a list of lowercase strings."""
    try:
        with open(file) as in_file:
          ❸ loaded_txt = in_file.read().strip().split('\n')
          ❹ loaded_txt = [x.lower() for x in loaded_txt]
            return loaded_txt
    except IOError as e:
      ❺ print("{}\nError opening {}. Terminating program.".format(e, file),
            file=sys.stderr)
        sys.exit(1)
```

Listing 2-1: The module for loading a dictionary file as a list

After the docstring, we import system functions with sys so that our error-handling code will work ❶. The next block of code defines a function based on the previous file-opening discussion ❷. The function takes a file-name as an argument.

If no exceptions are raised, the text file's whitespace is removed, and its items are split into separate lines and added to a list ❸. We want each word to be a separate item in the list, before the list is returned. And since case matters to Python, the words in the list are converted to lowercase via *list comprehension* ❹. List comprehension is a shorthand way to convert a list, or other iterable, into another list. In this case, it replaces a `for` loop.

If an I/O error is encountered, the program displays the standard error message, designated by the `e`, along with a message describing the event and informing the user that the program is ending ❺. The `sys.exit(1)` command then terminates the program.

This code example is for illustrative purposes, to show how these steps work together. Generally, you wouldn't call `sys.exit()` from a module, as you may want your program to do something—like write a log file—prior to terminating. In later chapters, we'll move both the `try-except` blocks and `sys.exit()` into a `main()` function for clarity and control.

Project #2: Finding Palindromes

You'll start by finding single-word palindromes in a dictionary and then move on to the more difficult palindromic phrases.

THE OBJECTIVE

Use Python to search an English language dictionary file for palindromes.

The Strategy and Pseudocode

Before you get into the code, step back and think about what you want to do conceptually. Identifying palindromes is easy: simply compare a word to itself sliced backward. Here is an example of slicing a word front to back and then back to front:

```
>>> word = 'NURSES'
>>> word[:]
'NURSES'
>>> word[::-1]
'SESRUN'
```

If you don't provide values when slicing a string (or any sliceable type), the default is to use the start of the string, the end of the string, and a positive step equal to `1`.

Figure 2-1 illustrates the reverse slicing process. I've provided a starting position of `2` and a step of `-1`. Because no end index is provided (there is no index or space between the colons), the implication is to go backward (because the index step is `-1`) until there are no more characters left.

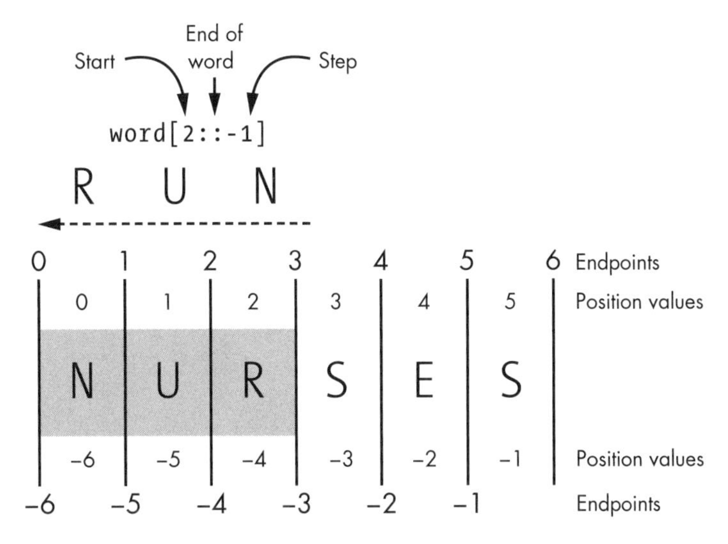

Figure 2-1: An example of negative slicing for `word = 'NURSES'`

Negative slicing doesn't behave exactly the same way as forward slicing, and the positive and negative position values and endpoints are asymmetrical. This can lead to confusion, so let's restrict our negative slicing to the simple `[::-1]` format.

Finding palindromes in the dictionary will take fewer lines of code than loading the dictionary file! Here's the pseudocode:

```
Load digital dictionary file as a list of words
Create an empty list to hold palindromes
Loop through each word in the word list:
    If word sliced forward is the same as word sliced backward:
        Append word to palindrome list
Print palindrome list
```

The Palindrome Code

Listing 2-2, *palindromes.py*, reads in an English dictionary file, identifies which words are palindromes, saves them to a list, and prints the list as stacked items. You can download this code from the book's resources at *https://www.nostarch.com/impracticalpython/*. You will also need *load_dictionary.py* and a dictionary file; save all three files in the same folder.

palindromes.py

```
"""Find palindromes (letter palingrams) in a dictionary file."""
❶ import load_dictionary
❷ word_list = load_dictionary.load('2of4brif.txt')
❸ pali_list = []

❹ for word in word_list:
    if len(word) > 1 and word == word[::-1]:
        pali_list.append(word)

print("\nNumber of palindromes found = {}\n".format(len(pali_list)))
❺ print(*pali_list, sep='\n')
```

Listing 2-2: Finds palindromes in loaded dictionary file

Start by importing *load_dictionary.py* as a module ❶. Note that the *.py* extension is not used for importing. Also, the module is in the same folder as this script, so we don't have to specify a directory path to the module. And since the module contains the required `import sys` line, we don't need to repeat it here.

To populate our word list with words from the dictionary, call the `load()` function in the `load_dictionary` module with dot notation ❷. Pass it the name of the external dictionary file. Again, you don't need to specify a path if the dictionary file is in the same folder as the Python script. The filename you use may be different depending on the dictionary you downloaded.

Next, create an empty list to hold the palindromes ❸ and start looping through every word in `word_list` ❹, comparing the forward slice to the reverse slice. If the two slices are identical, append the word to `pali_list`. Notice that only words with more than one letter are allowed (`len(word) > 1`), which follows the strictest definition of a palindrome.

Finally, print the palindromes in an attractive way—stacked and with no quotation marks or commas ❺. You can accomplish this by looping through every word in the list, but there is a more efficient way to do it. You can use the *splat* operator (designated by the *), which takes a list as input and expands it into positional arguments in the function call. The last argument is the separator used between multiple list values for printing. The default separator is a space (`sep=' '`), but instead, print each item on a new line (`sep='\n'`).

Single-word palindromes are rare, at least in English. Using a 60,000-word dictionary file, you'll be lucky to find about 60, or only 0.1 percent of all the words. Despite their rarity, however, they're easy enough to find with Python. So, let's move on to the more interesting, and more complicated, palingrams.

Project #3: Finding Palingrams

Finding palingrams requires a bit more effort than finding one-word palindromes. In this section, we'll plan and write code to find word-pair palingrams.

THE OBJECTIVE

Use Python to search an English language dictionary for two-word palingrams. Analyze and optimize the palingram code using the cProfile tool.

The Strategy and Pseudocode

Example word-pair palingrams are *nurses run* and *stir grits.* (In case you're wondering, grits are a ground-corn breakfast dish, similar to Italian polenta.)

Like palindromes, palingrams read the same forward and backward. I like to think of these as a *core* word, like *nurses,* from which a *palindromic sequence* and *reversed word* are derived (see Figure 2-2).

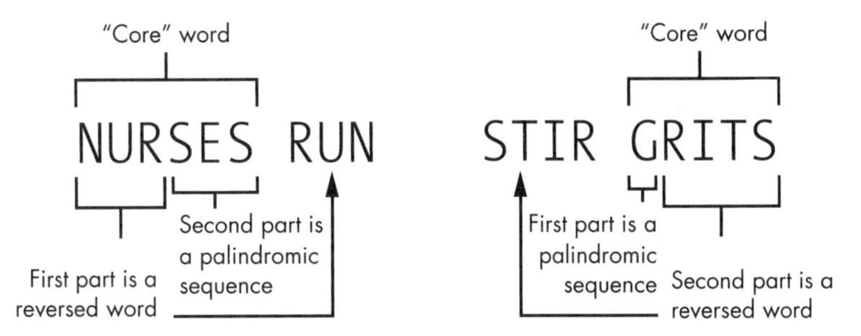

Figure 2-2: Dissecting word-pair palingrams

Our program will examine the core word. Based on Figure 2-2, we can make the following inferences about the core word:

1. It can have either an odd or even number of letters.
2. One contiguous part of the word spells a real word when read backward.
3. This contiguous part can occupy part or all of the core word.
4. The other contiguous part contains a palindromic sequence of letters.
5. The palindromic sequence can occupy part or all of the core word.
6. The palindromic sequence does not have to be a real word (unless it occupies the *whole* word).
7. The two parts cannot overlap or share letters.
8. The sequence is reversible.

NOTE *If the reversed word occupies the whole core word and is not a palindrome, it's called a* semordnilap. *A semordnilap is similar to a palindrome except for one key difference: rather than spelling the* same *word when read backward, it spells a* different *word. Examples are* bats *and* stab, *and* wolf *and* flow. *Semordnilap, by the way, is* palindromes *spelled backward.*

Figure 2-3 represents an arbitrary word of six letters. The Xs represent the part of the word that *might* form a real word when read backward (like *run* in *nurses*). The Os represent the *possible* palindromic sequence (like *ses* in *nurses*). The word represented in the left column in Figure 2-3 behaves like *nurses* in Figure 2-2, with the reversed word at the start. The word represented by the right column behaves like *grits*, with the reversed word at the end. Note that the number of combinations in each column is the total number of letters in the word plus one; note too that the top and bottom rows represent an identical circumstance.

The top row in each column represents a semordnilap. The bottom row in each represents a palindrome. These are both reversed words, just different *types* of reversed words. Hence, they count as one entity and both can be identified with a single line of code in a single loop.

To see the diagram in action, consider Figure 2-4, which shows the palingrams *devils lived* and *retro porter. Devils* and *porter* are both core words and mirror images of each other with respect to palindromic sequences and reversed words. Compare this to the semordnilap *evil* and the palindrome *kayak*.

```
XXXXXX   XXXXXX
XXXXXO   OOOOOX
XXXXOO   OOOOXX
XXXOOO   OOOXXX
XXOOOO   OOXXXX
XOOOOO   OXXXXX
OOOOOO   OOOOOO
```

Figure 2-3: Possible positions for letters of the reversed word (X) and the palindromic sequence (O) in a six-letter core word

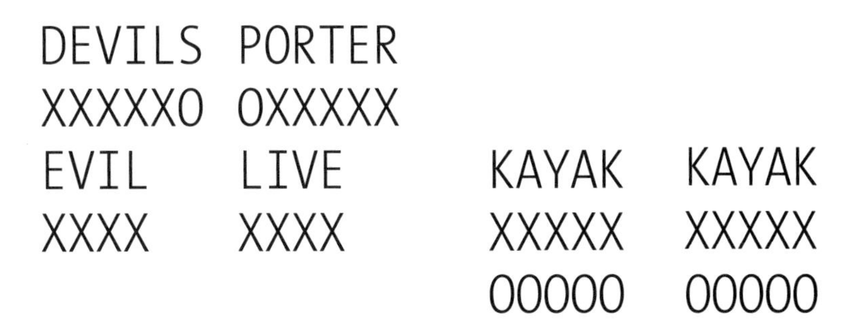

Figure 2-4: Reversed words (Xs) and palindromic sequences (Os) in words, semordnilaps, and palindromes.

Palindromes are both reversed words *and* palindromic sequences. Since they have the same pattern of Xs as in semordnilaps, they can be handled with the same code used for semordnilaps.

From a strategy perspective, you'll need to loop through each word in the dictionary and evaluate it for *all of the combinations* in Figure 2-3. Assuming a 60,000-word dictionary, the program will need to take about 500,000 passes.

To understand the loops, take a look at the core word for the palingram *stack cats* in Figure 2-5. Your program needs to loop through the letters in the word, starting with an end letter and adding a letter with each iteration. To find palingrams like *stack cats*, it will simultaneously evaluate the word for the presence of a palindromic sequence at the end of the core word, *stack*, and a reversed word at the start. Note that the first loop in Figure 2-5 will be successful, as a single letter (*k*) can serve as a palindrome in this situation.

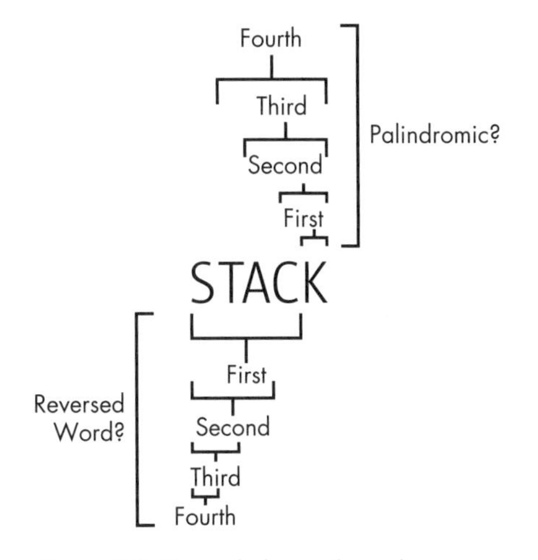

Figure 2-5: Example loops through a core word, simultaneously looking for palindromes and reversed words

But you're not through yet. To capture the "mirror image" behavior in Figure 2-3, you have to run the loops in reverse, looking for palindromic sequences at the start of the word and reversed words at the end. This will allow you to find palingrams like *stir grits.*

Here is the pseudocode for a palingram-finding algorithm:

```
Load digital dictionary as a list of words
Start an empty list to hold palingrams
For word in word list:
    Get length of word
    If length > 1:
        Loop through the letters in the word:
            If reversed word fragment at front of word is in word list and letters
            after form a palindromic sequence:
               Append word and reversed word to palingram list
            If reversed word fragment at end of word is in word list and letters
            before form a palindromic sequence:
               Append reversed word and word to palingram list
Sort palingram list alphabetically
Print word-pair palingrams from palingram list
```

The Palingrams Code

Listing 2-3, *palingrams.py*, loops through a word list, identifies which words form word-pair palingrams, saves those pairs to a list, and prints the list as stacked items. You can download the code from *https://www.nostarch.com/impracticalpython/*. I suggest you use the *2of4brif.txt* dictionary file to start so that your results will match mine. Store your dictionary and *load_dictionary.py* in the same folder as the palingrams script.

palingrams.py

```
"""Find all word-pair palingrams in a dictionary file."""
import load_dictionary

word_list = load_dictionary.load('2of4brif.txt')

# find word-pair palingrams
❶ def find_palingrams():
    """Find dictionary palingrams."""
    pali_list = []
    for word in word_list:
      ❷ end = len(word)
      ❸ rev_word = word[::-1]
      ❹ if end > 1:
          ❺ for i in range(end):
              ❻ if word[i:] == rev_word[:end-i]and rev_word[end-i:]in word_list:
                    pali_list.append((word, rev_word[end-i:]))
              ❼ if word[:i] == rev_word[end-i:]and rev_word[:end-i]in word_list:
                    pali_list.append((rev_word[:end-i], word))
  ❽ return pali_list

❾ palingrams = find_palingrams()
```

```
    # sort palingrams on first word
    palingrams_sorted = sorted(palingrams)

    # display list of palingrams
❿ print("\nNumber of palingrams = {}\n".format(len(palingrams_sorted)))
    for first, second in palingrams_sorted:
        print("{} {}".format(first, second))
```

Listing 2-3: Finds and prints word-pair palingrams in loaded dictionary

After repeating the steps you used in the *palindromes.py* code to load a dictionary file, define a function to find palingrams ❶. Using a function will allow you to isolate the code later and time how long it takes to process all the words in the dictionary.

Immediately start a list called `pali_list` to hold all the palingrams the program discovers. Next, start a `for` loop to evaluate the words in `word_list`. For each word, find its length and assign its length to the variable `end` ❷. The word's length determines the indexes the program uses to slice through the word, looking for every possible reversed word-palindromic sequence combination, as in Figure 2-3.

Next, negatively slice through the word and assign the results to the variable `rev_word` ❸. An alternative to `word[::-1]` is `''.join(reversed(word))`, which some consider more readable.

Since you are looking for word-pair palingrams, exclude single-letter words ❹. Then nest another `for` statement to loop through the letters in the current word ❺.

Now, run a conditional requiring the back end of the word to be palindromic and the front end to be a reverse word in the word list (in other words, a "real" word) ❻. If a word passes the test, it is appended to the palingram list, immediately followed by the reversed word.

Based on Figure 2-3, you know you have to repeat the conditional, but change the slicing direction and word order to reverse the output. In other words, you must capture palindromic sequences at the start of the word rather than at the end ❼. Return the list of palingrams to complete the function ❽.

With the function defined, call it ❾. Since the order in which dictionary words are added to the palingram list switches during the loop, the palingrams won't be in alphabetical order. So, sort the list so that the first words in the word pair are in alphabetical order. Print the length of the list ❿, then print each word-pair on a separate line.

As written, *palingrams.py* will take about three minutes to run on a dictionary file with about 60,000 words. In the next sections, we'll investigate the cause of this long runtime and see what we can do to fix it.

Palingram Profiling

Profiling is an analytical process that gathers statistics on a program's behavior—for example, the number and duration of function calls—as the program executes. Profiling is a key part of the optimization process. It tells you exactly what parts of a program are taking the most time or memory. That way, you'll know where to focus your efforts to improve performance.

Profiling with cProfile

A *profile* is a measurement output—a record of how long and how often parts of a program are executed. The Python standard library provides a handy profiling interface, `cProfile`, which is a C extension suitable for profiling long-running programs.

Something in the `find_palingrams()` function probably accounts for the relatively long runtime of the *palingrams.py* program. To confirm, let's run `cProfile`.

Copy the following code into a new file named *cprofile_test.py* and save it in the same folder as *palingrams.py* and the dictionary file. This code imports `cProfile` and the palingrams program, and it runs `cProfile` on the `find_palingrams()` function—called with dot notation. Note again that you don't need to specify the *.py* extension.

```
import cProfile
import palingrams
cProfile.run('palingrams.find_palingrams()')
```

Run *cprofile_test.py* and, after it finishes (you will see the >>> in the interpreter window), you should see something similar to the following:

```
         62622 function calls in 199.452 seconds

   Ordered by: standard name

   ncalls  tottime  percall  cumtime  percall filename:lineno(function)
        1    0.000    0.000  199.451  199.451 <string>:1(<module>)
        1  199.433  199.433  199.451  199.451 palingrams.py:7(find_palingrams)
        1    0.000    0.000  199.452  199.452 {built-in method builtins.exec}
    60388    0.018    0.000    0.018    0.000 {built-in method builtins.len}
     2230    0.001    0.000    0.001    0.000 {method 'append' of 'list' objects}
```

All that looping, slicing, and searching took 199.452 seconds on my machine, but of course your times may differ from mine. You also get additional information on some of the built-in functions, and since each palingram called the built-in `append()` function, you can even see the number of palingrams found (2,230).

NOTE *The most common way to run* `cProfile` *is directly in the interpreter. This lets you dump your output to a text file and view it with a web viewer. For more information, visit* https://docs.python.org/3/library/profile.html.

Profiling with time

Another way to time the program is to use `time.time()`, which returns an *epoch timestamp*—the number of seconds since 12 AM on January 1, 1970 UTC (the *Unix epoch*). Copy *palingrams.py* to a new file, save it as *palingrams_timed.py*, and insert the following code at the very top:

```
import time
start_time = time.time()
```

Now go to the end of the file and add the following code:

```
end_time = time.time()
print("Runtime for this program was {} seconds.".format(end_time - start_time))
```

Save and run the file. You should get the following feedback at the bottom of the interpreter window—give or take a few seconds:

```
Runtime for this program was 222.73954558372498 seconds.
```

The runtime is longer than before, as you are now evaluating the whole program, including printing, rather than just the `find_palingrams()` function.

Unlike `cProfile`, `time` doesn't provide detailed statistics, but like `cProfile`, it can be run on individual code components. Edit the file you just ran, moving the start and end time statements (as shown below in bold) so they bracket our long-running `find_palingrams()` function. Leave the `import` and `print` statements unchanged at the top and bottom of the file, respectively.

```
start_time = time.time()
palingrams = find_palingrams()
end_time = time.time()
```

Save and run the file. You should get the following feedback at the bottom of the interpreter window:

```
Runtime for this program was 199.42786622047424 seconds.
```

This now matches the initial results using `cProfile`. You won't get the exact same time if you rerun the program or use a different timer, but don't get hung up on it. It's the *relative* times that are important for guiding code optimization.

Palingram Optimization

I'm sorry, but three minutes of my life is too long to wait for palingrams. Armed with our profiling results, we know that the `find_palingrams()` function accounts for most of the processing time. This probably has something to do with reading and writing to lists, slicing over lists, or searching in lists. Using an alternative data structure to lists—like tuples, sets, or dictionaries—might speed up the function. Sets, in particular, are significantly faster than lists when using the in keyword. Sets use a hashtable for very fast lookups. With hashing, strings of text are converted to unique numbers that are much smaller than the referenced text and much more efficient to search. With a list, on the other hand, you have to do a linear search through each item.

Think of it this way: if you're searching your house for your lost cell phone, you could emulate a list by looking through every room before finding it (in the proverbial last place you look). But by emulating a set, you can basically dial your cell number from another phone, listen for the ringtone, and go straight to the proper room.

A downside to using sets is that the order of the items in the set isn't controllable and duplicate values aren't allowed. With lists, the order is preserved and duplicates are allowed, but lookups take longer. Fortunately for us, we don't care about order or duplicates, so sets are the way to go!

Listing 2-4 is the `find_palingrams()` function from the original *palingrams.py* program, edited to use a set of words rather than a list of words. You can find it in a new program named *palingrams_optimized.py*, which you can download from *https://www.nostarch.com/impracticalpython/*, or just make these changes to your copy of *palingrams_timed.py* if you want to check the new runtime yourself.

palingrams_optimized.py

```
def find_palingrams():
    """Find dictionary palingrams."""
    pali_list = []
  ❶ words = set(word_list)
  ❷ for word in words:
        end = len(word)
        rev_word = word[::-1]
        if end > 1:
            for i in range(end):
              ❸ if word[i:] == rev_word[:end-i]and rev_word[end-i:]in words:
                    pali_list.append((word, rev_word[end-i:]))
              ❹ if word[:i] == rev_word[end-i:]and rev_word[:end-i]in words:
                    pali_list.append((rev_word[:end-i], word))
    return pali_list
```

Listing 2-4: The `find_palingrams()` function optimized with sets

Only four lines change. Define a new variable, `words`, which is a set of `word_list` ❶. Then loop through the set ❷, looking for membership of word slices in this set ❸❹, rather than in a list as before.

Here's the new runtime for the `find_palingrams()` function in *palingrams_optimized.py*:

```
Runtime for this program was 0.4858267307281494 seconds.
```

Wow! From over three minutes to under a second! *That's* optimization! And the difference is in the data structure. Verifying the membership of a word in a *list* was the thing that was killing us.

Why did I first show you the "incorrect" way to do this? Because that's how things happen in the real world. You get the code to work, and then you optimize it. This is a simple example that an experienced programmer would have gotten right from the start, but it is emblematic of the overall concept of optimization: get it to work as best as you can, then make it better.

dnE ehT

You've written code to find palindromes and palingrams, profiled code using `cProfile`, and optimized code by using the appropriate data structure for the task. So how did we do with respect to Zatanna? Does she have a fighting chance?

Here I've listed some of the more "aggressive" palingrams found in the *2of4brif* dictionary file—everything from the unexpected *sameness enemas* to the harsh *torsos rot* to my personal favorite as a geologist: *eroded ore.*

dump mud	drowsy sword	sameness enemas
legs gel	denims mined	lepers repel
sleet eels	dairy raid	slam mammals
eroded ore	rise sir	pots nonstop
strafe farts	torsos rot	swan gnaws
wolfs flow	partner entrap	nuts stun
slaps pals	flack calf	knobs bonk

Further Reading

Think Python, 2nd Edition (O'Reilly, 2015) by Allen Downey has a short and lucid description of hashtables and why they are so efficient. It's also an excellent Python reference book.

Practice Project: Dictionary Cleanup

Data files available on the internet are not always "plug and play." You may find you need to massage the data a bit before applying it to your project. As mentioned earlier, some online dictionary files include each letter of the alphabet as a word. These will cause problems if you want to permit the use of one-letter words in palingrams like *acidic a*. You could always remove them by directly editing the dictionary text file, but this is tedious and for losers. Instead, write a short script that removes these after the dictionary has been loaded into Python. To test that it works, edit your dictionary file to include a few one-letter words like *b* and *c*. For a solution, see the appendix, or find a copy (*dictionary_cleanup_practice.py*) online at *https://www.nostarch.com/impracticalpython/*.

Challenge Project: Recursive Approach

With Python, there is usually more than one way to skin a cat. Take a look at the discussion and pseudocode at the Khan Academy website (*https://www.khanacademy.org/computing/computer-science/algorithms/recursive-algorithms/a/using-recursion-to-determine-whether-a-word-is-a-palindrome/*). Then rewrite the *palindrome.py* program so that it uses recursion to identify palindromes.

3

SOLVING ANAGRAMS

An *anagram* is a word formed by rearranging the letters of another word. For example, *Elvis* yields the eerie trio *evils*, *lives*, and *veils*. Does this mean Elvis still lives but veils his evil existence? In the book *Harry Potter and the Chamber of Secrets*, "I am Lord Voldemort" is an anagram of the evil wizard's real name, Tom Marvolo Riddle. "Lord Earldom Vomit" is also an anagram of Tom Marvolo Riddle, but author J.K. Rowling had the good sense to pass on that one.

In this chapter, first you'll find all the anagrams for a given word or name. Then, you'll write a program that lets a user interactively build an anagram phrase from their own name. Finally, you'll play computer wizard and see what it takes to extract "I am Lord Voldemort" from "Tom Marvolo Riddle."

Project #4: Finding Single-Word Anagrams

You'll start by analyzing simple single-word anagrams and figuring out how to identify them programmatically. Having accomplished this, you'll be ready to take on anagram phrases in the following section.

THE OBJECTIVE

Use Python and a dictionary file to find all the single-word anagrams for a given English word or single name. You can read instructions for finding and loading dictionary files at the start of Chapter 2.

The Strategy and Pseudocode

More than 600 newspapers and 100 internet sites carry an anagram game called *Jumble*. Created in 1954, it's now the most recognized word-scramble game in the world. *Jumble* can be really frustrating, but finding anagrams is almost as easy as finding palindromes—you just need to know the common characteristic of all anagrams: they must have the same number of the same letters.

Identifying an Anagram

Python doesn't contain a built-in anagram operator, but you can easily write one. For the projects in this chapter, you'll load the dictionary file from Chapter 2 as a list of strings. So the program needs to verify that two strings are anagrams of each other.

Let's look at an example. *Pots* is an anagram of *stop*, and you can verify that *stop* and *pots* have the same number of letters with the `len()` function. But there's no way for Python to know whether two strings have the same number of any single character—at least not without converting the strings to another data structure or using a counting function. So, instead of looking at these two words simply as strings, you can represent them as two lists containing single-character strings. Create these lists in a shell, like IDLE, and name them `word` and `anagram`, as I've done here:

```
>>> word = list('stop')
>>> word
['s', 't', 'o', 'p']
>>> anagram = list('pots')
>>> anagram
['p', 'o', 't', 's']
```

These two lists match our description of an anagram pair; that is, they contain the same number of the same letters. But if you try to equate them with the comparison operator `==`, the result is `False`.

```
>>> anagram == word
False
```

The problem is that the operator (==) considers two lists equivalent only if they have the same number of the same list items and those items occur in the same order. You can easily solve this problem with the built-in function `sorted()`, which can take a list as an argument and reorder its contents alphabetically. So, if you call `sorted()` twice—once for each of the lists—and then compare the sorted lists, they will be equivalent. In other words, == returns `True`.

```
>>> word = sorted(word)
>>> word
['o', 'p', 's', 't']
>>> anagram = sorted(anagram)
>>> anagram
['o', 'p', 's', 't']
>>> anagram == word
True
```

You can also pass a string to `sorted()` to create a sorted list like the ones in the preceding code snippet. This will be useful for converting the words from the dictionary file into sorted lists of single-character strings.

Now that you know how to verify that you've found an anagram, let's design the script in its entirety—from loading a dictionary and prompting the user for a word (or name) to searching for and printing all the anagrams.

Using Pseudocode

Remember that planning with pseudocode will help you spot potential issues and spotting those issues early will save you time. The following pseudocode should help you better understand the script we'll write in the next section, *anagrams.py*.

```
Load digital dictionary file as a list of words
Accept a word from user
Create an empty list to hold anagrams
Sort the user-word
Loop through each word in the word list:
    Sort the word
    if word sorted is equal to user-word sorted:
        Append word to anagrams list
Print anagrams list
```

The script will start by loading words from a dictionary file into a list as strings. Before you loop through the dictionary in search of anagrams, you need to know which word you want anagrams of, and you need a place to store anagrams when you find them. So, first ask the user to input a word and then create an empty list to store the anagrams. Once the program has looped through every word in the dictionary, it will print that list of anagrams.

Anagram-Finder Code

Listing 3-1 loads a dictionary file, accepts a word or name *specified within the program*, and finds all the anagrams in the dictionary file for that word or name. You'll also need the dictionary-loading code from Chapter 2. You can download these from *https://www.nostarch.com/impracticalpython/* as *anagrams.py* and *load_dictionary.py*, respectively. Keep both files in the same folder. You can use the same dictionary file you used in Chapter 2 or download another one (see Table 2-1 on page 20 for suggestions).

anagrams.py

```
❶ import load_dictionary

❷ word_list = load_dictionary.load('2of4brif.txt')

❸ anagram_list = []

  # input a SINGLE word or SINGLE name below to find its anagram(s):
❹ name = 'Foster'
  print("Input name = {}".format (name))
❺ name = name.lower()
  print("Using name = {}".format(name))

  # sort name & find anagrams
❻ name_sorted = sorted(name)
❼ for word in word_list:
      word = word.lower()
      if word != name:
          if sorted(word) == name_sorted:
              anagram_list.append(word)

  # print out list of anagrams
  print()
❽ if len(anagram_list) == 0:
      print("You need a larger dictionary or a new name!")
  else:
    ❾ print("Anagrams =", *anagram_list, sep='\n')
```

Listing 3-1: Given a word (or name) and a dictionary file, this program searches for and prints a list of anagrams.

You start by importing the `load_dictionary` module you created in Chapter 2 ❶. This module will open a dictionary text file and, with its `load()` function, load all the words into a list ❷. The **.txt* file you use may be different, depending on which dictionary file you downloaded (see "Finding and Opening a Dictionary" on page 20).

Next, create an empty list, called `anagram_list`, to hold any anagrams you find ❸. Have the user add a *single* word, such as their first name ❹. This doesn't have to be a proper name, but we'll refer to it as `name` in the code to distinguish it from a dictionary `word`. Print this name so the user can see what was entered.

The next line anticipates a problematic user action. People tend to type their name with an uppercase first letter, but dictionary files may not include uppercase letters, and that matters to Python. So, first convert all letters to lowercase with the `.lower()`string method ❺.

Now sort the name ❻. As mentioned previously, you can pass `sorted()` a string as well as a list.

With the input sorted alphabetically in a list, it's time to find anagrams. Start a loop through each word in the dictionary word list ❼. To be safe, convert the word to lowercase, as comparison operations are case-sensitive. After the conversion, compare the word to the unsorted name, because a word can't be an anagram of itself. Next, sort the dictionary word and compare it to the sorted name. If it passes, append that dictionary word to `anagram_list`.

Now display the results. First, check whether the anagram list is empty. If it is, print a whimsical reply so you don't just leave the user hanging ❽. If the program found at least one anagram, print the list using the splat (`*`) operator. Remember from Chapter 2 that splat lets you print each member of a list on a separate line ❾.

The following is example output for this program, using the input name *Foster*:

```
Input name = Foster
Using name = foster

Anagrams =
forest
fortes
softer
```

If you'd like to use another input, change the value of the `name` variable in the source code. As an exercise, try to adjust the code so that the user is prompted to input the name (or word); you can do this with the `input()` function.

Project #5: Finding Phrase Anagrams

In the previous project, you took a single name or word and rearranged all the letters to find single-word anagrams. Now you will derive multiple words from a name. The words in these *phrase anagrams* form only part of the input name, and you will need several words to exhaust the available letters.

THE OBJECTIVE

Write a Python program that lets a user interactively build an anagram phrase from the letters in their name.

The Strategy and Pseudocode

The very best phrase anagrams are those that describe some well-known characteristic or action associated with the name bearer. For example, the letters in Clint Eastwood can be rearranged to form *old west action*, Alec Guinness yields *genuine class*, Madam Curie produces *radium came*, George Bush gives *he bugs Gore*, and Statue of Liberty contains *built to stay free*. My own name yields *a huge navel*, which is not really one of my characteristics.

At this point, you may see a strategic challenge ahead: how does a computer handle contextual content? The folks at IBM who invented Watson seem to know, but for the rest of us, that boulder is a little hard to lift.

The *brute-force method* is a common approach used in online anagram generators. These algorithms take a name and return lots of random anagram phrases (generally, 100s to 10,000+). Most of the returned phrases are nonsense, and scrolling through hundreds of these can be a chore.

An alternative approach is to acknowledge that humans are best at contextual issues and write a program that helps the human work through the problem. The computer can take the initial name and provide words that can be made from some (or all) the letters in it; the user can then choose a word that "makes sense." The program will then recalculate the word choices from the remaining letters in the name, repeating the process until every letter is used or the possible word choices are exhausted. This design plays to the strengths of both participants.

You'll need a simple interface that prompts the user to input the initial name, displays potential word choices, and displays any remaining letters. The program will also need to keep track of the growing anagram phrase and let the user know when every letter has been used. There will likely be lots of failed attempts, so the interface should allow the user to restart the process at any time.

Since anagrams have the same number of the same letters, another way to identify them is to count individual letters. If you think of your name as a collection of letters, then a word can be built from your name if (1) all its letters occur in your name and (2) they occur *at the same frequency or less*. Obviously, if *e* occurs three times in a word and twice in your name, the word can't be derived from your name. So, if the collection of letters that make up a word is not a subset of the collection of letters in your name, then that word cannot be part of your name anagram.

Using Counter to Tally Letters

Fortunately for us, Python ships with a module named `collections` that includes several container data types. One of these types, `Counter`, counts the occurrences of an item. Python stores the items as dictionary keys and the counts as dictionary values. For example, the following code snippet counts how many of each bonsai tree type is in a list.

```
  >>> from collections import Counter
❶ >>> my_bonsai_trees = ['maple', 'oak', 'elm', 'maple', 'elm', 'elm', 'elm', 'elm']
❷ >>> count = Counter(my_bonsai_trees)
```

```
>>> print(count)
❸ Counter({'elm': 5, 'maple': 2, 'oak': 1})
```

The `my_bonsai_trees` list contains multiples of the same type of tree ❶. `Counter` tallies up the trees ❷ and creates an easy-to-reference dictionary ❸. Note that the `print()` function is optional and is used here for clarity. Entering `count`, alone, will also display the dictionary contents.

You can use `Counter`, instead of the `sorted()` method, to find single-word anagrams. Rather than two sorted lists, the output will be two dictionaries, which can also be directly compared with `==`. Here's an example:

```
>>> name = 'foster'
>>> word = 'forest'
>>> name_count = Counter(name)
>>> print(name_count)
❶ Counter({'f': 1, 't': 1, 'e': 1, 'o': 1, 'r': 1, 's': 1})
>>> word_count = Counter(word)
>>> print(word_count)
❷ Counter({'f': 1, 't': 1, 'o': 1, 'e': 1, 'r': 1, 's': 1})
```

`Counter` produces a dictionary for each word that maps each letter in the word to the number of times it occurs ❶❷. The dictionaries are unsorted, but despite the lack of sorting, Python correctly identifies each dictionary as being equal if the dictionaries contain the same letters and the same counts:

```
>>> if word_count == name_count:
        print("It's a match!")

It's a match!
```

A `Counter` gives you a wonderful way to find words that "fit" in a name. If the count for each letter in a word is less than or equal to the count for the same letter in the name, then the word can be derived from the name!

The Pseudocode

We've now made two important design decisions: (1) let the user interactively build their anagram one word at a time and (2) use the `Counter` method to find anagrams. This is enough to start thinking about high-level pseudocode:

```
Load a dictionary file
Accept a name from user
Set limit = length of name
Start empty list to hold anagram phrase
While length of phrase < limit:
    Generate list of dictionary words that fit in name
    Present words to user
    Present remaining letters to user
    Present current phrase to user
    Ask user to input word or start over
```

```
    If user input can be made from remaining letters:
        Accept choice of new word or words from user
        Remove letters in choice from letters in name
        Return choice and remaining letters in name
    If choice is not a valid selection:
        Ask user for new choice or let user start over
    Add choice to phrase and show to user
    Generate new list of words and repeat process
When phrase length equals limit value:
    Display final phrase
    Ask user to start over or to exit
```

Divvying Up the Work

As procedural code becomes more complex, it becomes necessary to encapsulate much of it in functions. This makes it easier to manage input and output, perform recursion, and read the code.

A *main function* is where a program starts its execution, and enables high-level organization, such as managing all the bits and pieces of the code, including dealing with the user. In the phrase anagram program, the main function will wrap all the "worker bee" functions, take *most* of the user input, keep track of the growing anagram phrase, determine when the phrase is complete, and show the user the result.

Sketching out the tasks and their flow with pencil and paper is a great way to figure out what you want to do and where (like "graphical pseudocode"). Figure 3-1 is a flowchart with function assignments highlighted. In this case, three functions should be sufficient: `main()`, `find_anagrams()`, and `process_choice()`.

The `main()` function's primary task is to set the letter count limit and manage the `while` loop responsible for the general phrase anagram build. The `find_anagrams()` function will take the current collection of letters remaining in a name and return all possible words that can be made from those letters. The words are then displayed for the user, along with the current phrase, which is "owned" and displayed by the `main()` function. Then, the `process_choice()` function prompts the user to start over or choose a word for the anagram phrase. If the user makes a choice, this function determines whether the letters in the choice are available. If they aren't, the user is prompted to choose again or start over. If the user makes a valid choice, the letters in the user's choice are removed from the list of remaining letters, and both the choice and list of leftovers are returned. The `main()` function adds the returned choice to the existing phrase. If the limit is reached, the completed phrase anagram is displayed, and the user is asked to start over or exit.

Note that you ask for the initial name in the *global* scope, rather than in the `main()` function. This allows the user to start over fresh at any time without having to re-enter their name. For now, if the user wants to choose a brand-new name, they'll have to exit the program and start over. In Chapter 9, you'll use a menu system that lets users completely reset what they're doing without exiting.

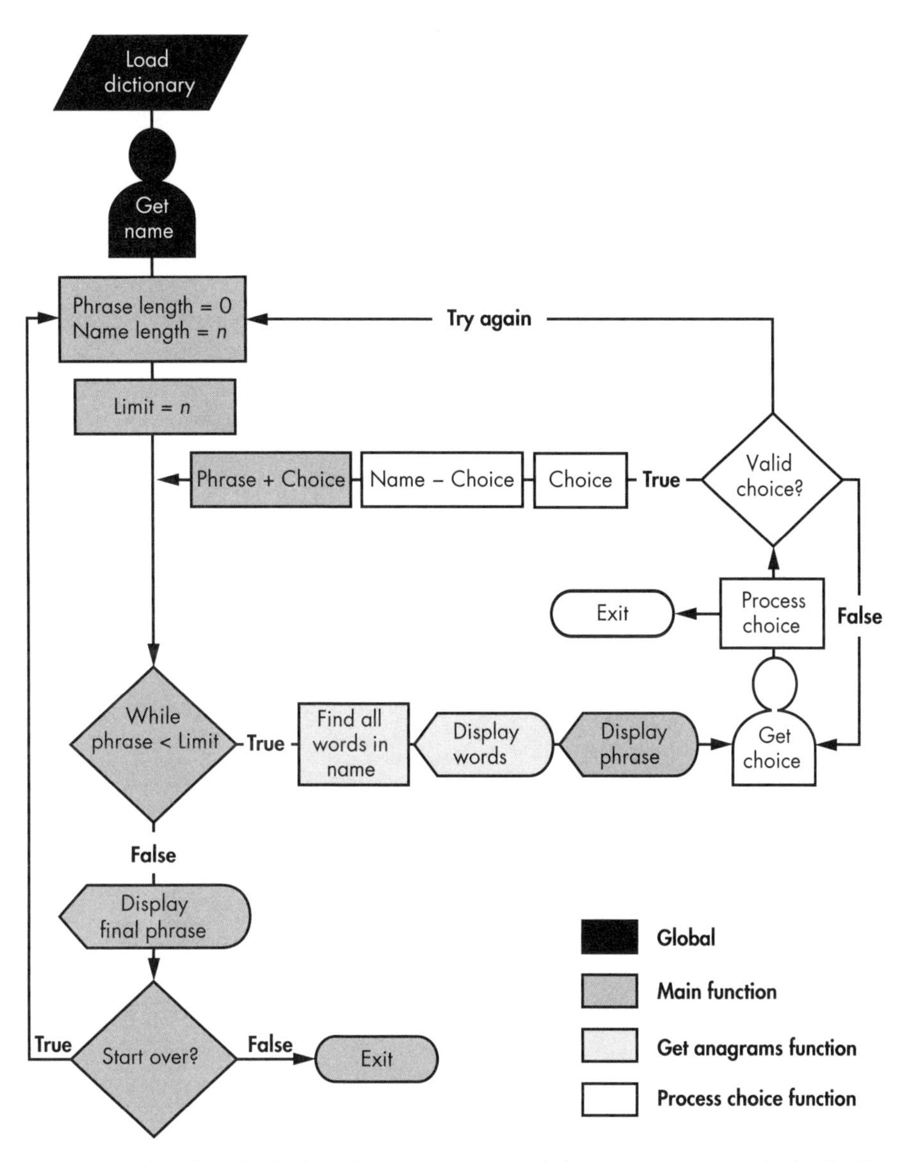

Figure 3-1: Flowchart for finding phrase anagrams with function assignments highlighted

The Anagram Phrase Code

The code in this section takes a name from a user and helps them build an anagram phrase of that name. You can download the entire script from *https://www.nostarch.com/impracticalpython/* as *phrase_anagrams.py*. You'll also need to download the *load_dictionary.py* program. Save both files in the same folder. You can use the same dictionary file you used in "Project #4: Finding Single-Word Anagrams" on page 36.

Setting Up and Finding Anagrams

Listing 3-2 imports the modules that *phrase_anagrams.py* uses, loads a dictionary file, asks the user for an input name, and defines the `find_anagrams()` function, which does most of the work related to finding anagrams.

phrase_anagrams.py, part 1

```
❶ import sys
  from collections import Counter
  import load_dictionary

❷ dict_file = load_dictionary.load('2of4brif.txt')
  # ensure "a" & "I" (both lowercase) are included
  dict_file.append('a')
  dict_file.append('i')
  dict_file = sorted(dict_file)

❸ ini_name = input("Enter a name: ")

❹ def find_anagrams(name, word_list):
      """Read name & dictionary file & display all anagrams IN name."""
    ❺ name_letter_map = Counter(name)
      anagrams = []
    ❻ for word in word_list:
        ❼ test = ''
        ❽ word_letter_map = Counter(word.lower())
        ❾ for letter in word:
              if word_letter_map[letter] <= name_letter_map[letter]:
                  test += letter
          if Counter(test) == word_letter_map:
              anagrams.append(word)
    ❿ print(*anagrams, sep='\n')
      print()
      print("Remaining letters = {}".format(name))
      print("Number of remaining letters = {}".format(len(name)))
      print("Number of remaining (real word) anagrams = {}".format(len(anagrams)))
```

Listing 3-2: Imports modules, loads dictionary, and defines the `find_anagrams()` function

Start with the `import` statements ❶, using the recommended order of Python Standard Library, third-party modules, and then locally developed modules. You need sys for coloring specific outputs red in the IDLE window and for letting the user exit the program with a keystroke. You'll use `Counter` to help identify anagrams of the input name.

Next load the dictionary file using the imported module ❷. The filename argument should be the filename of the dictionary you're using. Because some dictionary files omit *a* and *I*, append these (if needed), and sort the list so that they can be found at the proper alphabetical locations, rather than at the end of the list.

Now get a name from the user and assign it to the variable `ini_name` (or "initial name") ❸. You'll derive a `name` variable from this initial name, and name will be progressively changed as the user builds up the name anagram. Preserving the initial name as a separate variable will let you reset everything if the user wants to start over or try again.

The next block of code is find_anagrams() ❹, the function for finding anagrams in the name. The parameters for this function consist of a name and a word list. The function starts by using Counter to count the number of times a given letter appears in the name and then assigns the count to the variable name_letter_map ❺; Counter uses a dictionary structure with the letter as the key and the count as the value. The function then creates an empty list to hold the anagrams and starts a for loop through each word in the dictionary file ❻.

The for loop starts by creating an empty string called test ❼. Use this variable to accumulate all the letters in the word that "fit" in name. Then make a Counter for the current word, as you did for name, and call it word_letter_map ❽. Loop through the letters in word ❾, checking that the count of each letter is the same as, or less than, the count in name. If the letter meets this condition, then it is added to the test string. Since some letters might get rejected, end the loop by running Counter on test and comparing it to word_letter_map. If they match, append the word to the anagrams list.

The function ends by displaying the list of words, using the splat operator with print, along with some statistics for the user ❿. Note that find_anagrams() doesn't return anything. This is where the human interaction part comes in. The program will continue to run, but nothing will happen until the user chooses a word from the displayed list.

Processing the User's Choice

Listing 3-3 defines process_choice(), the function in *phrase_anagrams.py* that takes the user's choice of word (or words), checks it against the remaining letters in the name variable, and returns acceptable choices—along with any leftover letters—to the main() function. Like main(), this function gets to talk directly to the user.

phrase_anagrams.py, part 2

```
❶ def process_choice(name):
      """Check user choice for validity, return choice & leftover letters."""
      while True:
        ❷ choice = input('\nMake a choice else Enter to start over or # to end: ')
          if choice == '':
              main()
          elif choice == '#':
              sys.exit()
          else:
            ❸ candidate = ''.join(choice.lower().split())
        ❹ left_over_list = list(name)
        ❺ for letter in candidate:
              if letter in left_over_list:
                  left_over_list.remove(letter)
        ❻ if len(name) - len(left_over_list) == len(candidate):
              break
```

```
        else:
            print("Won't work! Make another choice!", file=sys.stderr)
❼ name = ''.join(left_over_list)  # makes display more readable
❽ return choice, name
```

Listing 3-3: Defines the `process_choice()` function

Start by defining the function with one parameter called `name` ❶. The first time the program is run, this parameter will be the same as the `ini_name` variable—the full name entered by the user when the program starts up. After the user has chosen a word (or words) to use in the anagram phrase, it will represent the remaining letters in the name.

Start the function with a `while` loop that will run until the user makes a valid choice and then get input from the user ❷. The user has a choice of entering one or more words from the current anagram list, pressing ENTER to start over, or pressing # to quit. Use #, rather than a word or letter, so that it can't be confused for a valid choice.

If the user makes a choice, the string is assigned to the variable `candidate`, stripped of whitespace, and converted to all lowercase ❸. This is so it can be directly compared to the `name` variable. After that, a list is built from the `name` variable to hold any remaining letters ❹.

Now begin a loop to subtract the letters used in `candidate` ❺. If a chosen letter is present in the list, it's removed.

If the user entered a word that isn't in the displayed list, or entered multiple words, a letter may not be present in the list. To check for this, subtract the leftover letters from `name` and, if the result is the number of letters in `candidate`, determine that the input is valid and break out of the `while` loop ❻. Otherwise, display a warning and color it red for those using the IDLE window. The `while` loop will keep prompting the user until an acceptable choice is made.

If all the letters in the user's choice pass the test, the list of leftovers is converted back into a string and used to update the `name` variable ❼. Converting the list into a string isn't strictly necessary, but it keeps the `name` variable type consistent and lets you display the remaining letters in a clearly readable format without the need for additional `print` arguments.

Finish by returning both the user's choice and the string of remaining letters (`name`) to the `main()` function ❽.

Defining the main() Function

Listing 3-4 defines the `main()` function in *phrase_anagrams.py*. This function wraps the previous functions, runs a `while` loop, and determines when the user has successfully created an anagram phrase.

phrase_anagrams.py, part 3

```
def main():
    """Help user build anagram phrase from their name."""
❶ name = ''.join(ini_name.lower().split())
    name = name.replace('-', '')
```

```
❷ limit = len(name)
   phrase = ''
   running = True

❸ while running:
    ❹ temp_phrase = phrase.replace(' ', '')
    ❺ if len(temp_phrase) < limit:
           print("Length of anagram phrase = {}".format(len(temp_phrase)))

        ❻ find_anagrams(name, dict_file)
           print("Current anagram phrase =", end=" ")
           print(phrase, file=sys.stderr)

        ❼ choice, name = process_choice(name)
           phrase += choice + ' '

    ❽ elif len(temp_phrase) == limit:
           print("\n*****FINISHED!!!*****\n")
           print("Anagram of name =", end=" ")
           print(phrase, file=sys.stderr)
           print()
        ❾ try_again = input('\n\nTry again? (Press Enter else "n" to quit)\n ')
           if try_again.lower() == "n":
               running = False
               sys.exit()
           else:
               main()

❿ if __name__ == '__main__':
    main()
```

Listing 3-4: Defines and calls `main()` *function*

The first order of business is to turn the `ini_name` variable into a continuous string of lowercase characters with no whitespace ❶. Remember, case matters to Python, so convert all strings to lowercase wherever they occur; that way, comparisons will work as intended. Python also recognizes spaces as characters, so you need to remove these, as well as hyphens in hyphenated names, before doing any letter counts. By declaring this new `name` variable, you preserve the initial name in case the user wants to start over. Only `name` will be altered in the `process_choice()` function.

Next, get the length of the name ❷ to use as a limit in the `while` loop. This will let you know when the anagram phrase has used all the letters in the name and it's time to end the loop. Do this outside the `while` loop to ensure you are using the full initial name. Then assign a variable to hold the anagram phrase and set a `running` variable to `True` to control the `while` loop.

Now begins the big loop that lets you iterate over the name and build an anagram phrase ❸. First, prepare a string to hold the growing phrase and strip it of whitespace ❹. Spaces will count as letters and throw off the operator when the length of the phrase is compared to the `limit` variable.

Next, make the comparison, and if the length of the phrase is less than the limit, display the current length of the phrase as a prelude to engaging with the user ❺.

It's time to put the other functions to work. Call `find_anagrams()` ❻ and pass it the name and dictionary file to get the list of anagrams in the name. At the bottom of the displayed list, show the user the current phrase. Use the `print()` function's `end` parameter to display two `print` statements on the same line. This way, you can use a red font on the phrase in the IDLE window to distinguish it from all the other information in the display.

Next, call the `process_choice()` function ❼ to get the user's word choice and add it to the growing anagram phrase. This also gets the updated version of the `name` variable so that the program can use it again in the `while` loop in the event that the phrase isn't complete.

If the length of the phrase is equal to the `limit` variable ❽, the name anagram is complete. Let the user know they're finished and present the phrase using red font. Note that you don't have a conditional for the length of the phrase being greater than the `limit` variable. That's because the `process_choice()` function is already handling this outcome (choosing more letters than are available would not pass the validation criterion).

The `main()` function ends by asking the user whether they want to try again. If they type `n`, the program ends; if they press ENTER, the `main()` function is called again ❾. As stated earlier, the only way for the user to change the initial name is to exit and relaunch the program.

Outside of the `main()` function, end with the standard two lines for calling the `main()` function when the program is not imported as a module ❿.

Running an Example Session

In this section, I've included an example interactive session, using *phrase_anagrams.py* and the name *Bill Bo*. **Bold** font indicates user input, and ***italic bold*** font indicates where red font is used in the display.

```
Enter a name: Bill Bo
Length of anagram phrase = 0
bib
bill
blob
bob
boil
boll
i
ill
lib
lilo
lo
lob
oi
oil
```

```
Remaining letters = billbo
Number of remaining letters = 6
Number of remaining (real word)anagrams = 14
Current anagram phrase =

Make a choice else Enter to start over or # to end: ill
Length of anagram phrase = 3
bob

Remaining letters = bbo
Number of remaining letters = 3
Number of remaining (real word)anagrams = 1
Current anagram phrase = ill

Make a choice else Enter to start over or # to end: Bob

***** FINISHED!!! *****

Anagram of name = ill Bob


Try again? (Press Enter else "n" to quit)
```

The number of anagrams found depends on the dictionary file you use. If you're having a hard time building anagram phrases, try using a larger dictionary.

Project #6: Finding Voldemort: The Gallic Gambit

Did you ever wonder how Tom Riddle came up with the anagram "I am Lord Voldemort"? Did he put quill to parchment or just wave a wand? Could the magic of Python have helped?

Let's pretend for a moment that you're the professor of computer wizardry at Hogwarts, and Tom Riddle, school prefect and model student, has come to you for help. Using your *phrase_anagrams.py* spell from the previous section, he could find *I am Lord* in the very first list of anagrams, much to his delight. But the remaining letters, *tmvoordle*, yield only trivial words like *dolt*, *drool*, *looter*, and *lover*. Riddle would not be pleased.

In hindsight, the problem is apparent: *Voldemort* is French and won't be found in any English dictionary file. *Vol de la mort* means "flight of death" in French, so Voldemort is loosely "death flight." But Riddle is 100 percent English, and so far, you have been working with English. Without reverse engineering, you have no more reason to suddenly switch out your English dictionary for a French one than you have to use Dutch, German, Italian, or Spanish.

You *could* try randomly shuffling the remaining letters and seeing what falls out. Unfortunately, the number of possible combinations is the factorial of the number of letters divided by the factorial of the number of repeats (*o* occurs twice): 9! / 2! = 181,440. If you were to scroll through all those permutations, taking only one second to review each, it would take you over two days to complete the list! And if you asked Tom Riddle to do this, he would probably use you to make a horcrux!

At this point, I would like to explore two logical paths ahead. One I call the "Gallic Gambit" and the other the "British Brute-Force." We'll look at the first one here and the second one in the next section.

NOTE Marvolo *is clearly a* fabricated word *used to make the Voldemort anagram work. J.K. Rowling could have gained additional latitude by using* Thomas *for* Tom *or by leaving off the* Lord *or* I am *parts. Tricks like these are used when the book is translated into non-English languages. In some languages, one or both names may need to be changed. In French, the anagram is "I am Voldemort." In Norwegian, "Voldemort the Great." In Dutch, "My name is Voldemort." In others, like Chinese, the anagram can't be used at all!*

Tom Riddle was obsessed with beating death, and if you go looking for death in *tmvoordle,* you will find both the old French *morte* (as in the famous book *Le Morte d'Arthur* by Sir Thomas Malory) and the modern French *mort.* Removing *mort* leaves *vodle,* five letters with a very manageable number of permutations. In fact, you can easily find *volde* right in the interpreter window:

```
❶ >>> from itertools import permutations
  >>> name = 'vodle'
❷ >>> perms = [''.join(i) for i in permutations(name)]
❸ >>> print(len(perms))
  120
❹ >>> print(perms)
  ['vodle', 'vodel', 'volde', 'voled', 'voedl', 'voeld', 'vdole', 'vdoel',
  'vdloe', 'vdleo', 'vdeol', 'vdelo', 'vlode', 'vloed', 'vldoe', 'vldeo',
  'vleod', 'vledo', 'veodl', 'veold', 'vedol', 'vedlo', 'velod', 'veldo',
  'ovdle', 'ovdel', 'ovlde', 'ovled', 'ovedl', 'oveld', 'odvle', 'odvel',
  'odlve', 'odlev', 'odevl', 'odelv', 'olvde', 'olved', 'oldve', 'oldev',
  'olevd', 'oledv', 'oevdl', 'oevld', 'oedvl', 'oedlv', 'oelvd', 'oeldv',
  'dvole', 'dvoel', 'dvloe', 'dvleo', 'dveol', 'dvelo', 'dovle', 'dovel',
  'dolve', 'dolev', 'doevl', 'doelv', 'dlvoe', 'dlveo', 'dlove', 'dloev',
  'dlevo', 'dleov', 'devol', 'devlo', 'deovl', 'deolv', 'delvo', 'delov',
  'lvode', 'lvoed', 'lvdoe', 'lvdeo', 'lveod', 'lvedo', 'lovde', 'loved',
  'lodve', 'lodev', 'loevd', 'loedv', 'ldvoe', 'ldveo', 'ldove', 'ldoev',
  'ldevo', 'ldeov', 'levod', 'levdo', 'leovd', 'leodv', 'ledvo', 'ledov',
  'evodl', 'evold', 'evdol', 'evdlo', 'evlod', 'evldo', 'eovdl', 'eovld',
  'eodvl', 'eodlv', 'eolvd', 'eoldv', 'edvol', 'edvlo', 'edovl', 'edolv',
  'edlvo', 'edlov', 'elvod', 'elvdo', 'elovd', 'elodv', 'eldvo', 'eldov']
  >>>
❺ >>> print(*perms, sep='\n')
  vodle
  vodel
  volde
  voled
  voedl
  --snip--
```

Start by importing `permutations` from `itertools` ❶. The `itertools` module is a group of functions in the Python Standard Library that create iterators for efficient looping. You generally think of permutations of *numbers*, but the `itertools` version works on *elements* in an iterable, which includes letters.

After entering the name or, in this case, the remaining letters in the name, use list comprehension to create a list of permutations of the name ❷. Join each element in a permutation so each item in the final list will be a unique permutation of *vodle*. Using `join` yields the new name as an element, `'vodle'`, versus a hard-to-read tuple of single-character elements,`('v', 'o', 'd', 'l', 'e')`.

Get the length of the permutations as a check; that way, you can confirm that it is, indeed, the factorial of 5 ❸. At the end, no matter how you print it ❹❺, *volde* is easy to find.

Project #7: Finding Voldemort: The British Brute-Force

Now let's assume Tom Riddle is bad at anagrams (or French). He doesn't recognize *mort* or *morte*, and you're back to shuffling the remaining nine letters thousands and thousands of times, looking for a combination of letters that he would find pleasing.

On the bright side, this is a more interesting problem programmatically than the interactive solution you just saw. You just need to whittle down all the permutations using some form of filtering.

THE OBJECTIVE

Reduce the number of anagrams of *tmvoordle* to a manageable number that will still contain *Voldemort*.

Strategy

Per the *Oxford English Dictionary, 2nd Edition*, there are 171,476 English words currently in use, which is fewer than the total number of permutations in *tmvoordle*! Regardless of the language, you can surmise that most of the anagrams generated by the `permutations()` function are nonsense.

With *cryptography*, the science of codes and ciphers, you can safely eliminate many useless, unpronounceable combinations, such as *ldtmvroeo*, and you won't even have to inspect them visually. Cryptographers have long studied languages and compiled statistics on recurring patterns of words and letters. We can use many cryptanalytical techniques for this project, but let's focus on three: consonant-vowel mapping, trigram frequency, and digram frequency.

Filtering with Consonant-Vowel Mapping

A *consonant-vowel map* (*c-v map*) simply replaces the letters in a word with a *c* or a *v*, as appropriate. *Riddle*, for example, becomes *cvcccv*. You can write a program that goes through a dictionary file and creates c-v maps for each word. By default, impossible combinations, like *ccccccvvv*, will be excluded. You can further exclude membership by removing words with c-v maps that are *possible* but that have a low frequency of occurrence.

C-v maps are fairly inclusive, but that's good. An option for *Riddle* at this point is to make up a new proper name, and proper names don't have to be words that occur in a dictionary. So you don't want to be *too* exclusive early in the process.

Filtering with Trigrams

Since the initial filter needs a relatively wide aperture, you'll need to filter again at a lower level to safely remove more anagrams from the permutations. *Trigrams* are triplets comprising three consecutive letters. It should come as no surprise that the most common trigram in English is the word *the*, followed closely by *and* and *ing*. At the other end of the scale are trigrams like *zvq*.

You can find statistics on the frequency of occurrence of trigrams online at sites like *http://norvig.com/ngrams/count_3l.txt*. For any group of letters, like *tmvoordle*, you can generate and use a list of the least common trigrams to further reduce the number of permutations. For this project, you can use the *least-likely_trigrams.txt* file, downloadable from *https://www.nostarch.com/impracticalpython/*. This text file contains the trigrams in *tmvoordle* that occur in the bottom 10 percent of trigrams in the English language, based on frequency of occurrence.

Filtering with Digrams

Digrams (also called *bigrams*) are letter pairs. Commonly occurring digrams in English include *an*, *st*, and *er*. On the other hand, you rarely see pairs like *kg*, *vl*, or *oq*. You can find statistics on the frequency of occurrence of digrams at websites such as *https://www.math.cornell.edu/~mec/2003-2004/cryptography/subs/digraphs.html* and *http://practicalcryptography.com/*.

Table 3-1 was built from the *tmvoordle* collection of letters and a 60,000-word English dictionary file. The letters along the left side of the chart are the starting letters for the digrams; those along the top represent the end letter. For example, to find *vo*, start with the *v* on the left and read across to the column beneath the *o*. For the digrams found in *tmvoordle*, *vo* occurs only 0.8 percent of the time.

Table 3-1: Relative Frequency of Digrams from the Letters *tmvoordle* in a 60,000-Word Dictionary (Black Squares Indicate No Occurrences)

	d	e	l	m	o	r	t	v
d		3.5%	0.5%	0.1%	1.7%	0.5%	0.0%	0.1%
e	6.6%		2.3%	1.4%	0.7%	8.9%	2.0%	0.6%
l	0.4%	4.4%		0.1%	4.2%	0.0%	0.4%	0.1%
m	0.0%	2.2%	0.0%		2.8%	0.0%	0.0%	0.0%
o	1.5%	0.5%	3.7%	3.2%	5.3%	7.1%	2.4%	1.4%
r	0.9%	6.0%	0.4%	0.7%	5.7%		1.3%	0.3%
t	0.0%	6.2%	0.6%	0.1%	3.6%	2.3%		0.0%
v	0.0%	2.5%	0.0%	0.0%	0.8%	0.0%	0.0%	

Assuming you're looking for "English-like" letter combinations, you can use frequency maps like this to exclude letter pairs that are unlikely to occur. Think of it as a "digram sieve" that lets only the unshaded squares pass.

To be safe, just exclude digrams that occur less than 0.1 percent of the time. I've shaded these in black. Notice that it would be very easy to eliminate the required *vo* pairing in *Voldemort*, if you cut too close to the bone!

You can design your filter to be even more selective by tagging digrams that are unlikely to occur at the start of a word. For example, while it's not unusual for the digram *lm* to occur *within* a word (as in *almanac* and *balmy*), you'll need a lot of luck finding a word that *starts* with *lm*. You don't need cryptography to find these digrams; just try to pronounce them! Some starting-point choices for these are shaded gray in Table 3-2.

Table 3-2: Update of Table 3-1, Where Gray-Shaded Squares Indicate Digrams Unlikely to Occur at the Start of a Word

	d	e	l	m	o	r	t	v
d		3.5%	0.5%	0.1%	1.7%	0.5%	0.0%	0.1%
e	6.6%		2.3%	1.4%	0.7%	8.9%	2.0%	0.6%
l	0.4%	4.4%		0.1%	4.2%	0.0%	0.4%	0.1%
m	0.0%	2.2%	0.0%		2.8%	0.0%	0.0%	0.0%
o	1.5%	0.5%	3.7%	3.2%	5.3%	7.1%	2.4%	1.4%
r	0.9%	6.0%	0.4%	0.7%	5.7%		1.3%	0.3%
t	0.0%	6.2%	0.6%	0.1%	3.6%	2.3%		0.0%
v	0.0%	2.5%	0.0%	0.0%	0.8%	0.0%	0.0%	

You now have three filters you can use on the 181,440 permutations of *tmvoordle*: c-v maps, trigrams, and digrams. As a final filter, you should give the user the option of viewing only anagrams that start with a given letter. This will let the user divide the remaining anagrams into more manageable "chunks," or focus on the more intimidating-sounding anagrams, like those that begin with *v*!

The British Brute-Force Code

The upcoming code generates permutations of *tmvoordle* and passes them through the filters just described. It then gives the user the option to view either all the permutations or only those starting with a given letter.

You can download all the programs you'll need from *https://www.nostarch.com/impracticalpython/*. The code in this section is one script named *voldemort_british.py*. You'll also need the *load_dictionary.py* program in the same folder, along with the same dictionary file you used for the projects earlier in this chapter. Finally, you'll need a new file named *least-likely_trigrams.txt*, a text file of trigrams with a low frequency of occurrence in English. Download all these files into the same folder.

Defining the main() Function

Listing 3-5 imports the modules that *voldemort_british.py* needs and defines its `main()` function. In the *phrase_anagrams.py* program, you defined the `main()` function at the end of the code. Here we put it at the start. The advantage is that you can see what the function is doing—how it's running the program—from the start. The disadvantage is that you don't know what any of the helper functions do yet.

voldemort_british.py, part 1

```
❶ import sys
  from itertools import permutations
  from collections import Counter
  import load_dictionary

❷ def main():
      """Load files, run filters, allow user to view anagrams by 1st letter."""
    ❸ name = 'tmvoordle'
      name = name.lower()

    ❹ word_list_ini = load_dictionary.load('2of4brif.txt')
      trigrams_filtered = load_dictionary.load('least-likely_trigrams.txt')

    ❺ word_list = prep_words(name, word_list_ini)
      filtered_cv_map = cv_map_words(word_list)
      filter_1 = cv_map_filter(name, filtered_cv_map)
      filter_2 = trigram_filter(filter_1, trigrams_filtered)
      filter_3 = letter_pair_filter(filter_2)
      view_by_letter(name, filter_3)
```

Listing 3-5: Imports modules and defines the `main()` *function*

Start by importing modules you've used in the previous projects ❶. Now define the main() function ❷. The name variable is a string of the remaining letters *tmvoordle* ❸. Set it to lowercase to guard against a user input error. Next, use the load_dictionary module to load your dictionary file and the trigrams file as lists ❹. Your dictionary filename may be different from that shown.

Finally, call all the various functions in order ❺. I'll describe each of these functions momentarily, but basically, you need to prepare the word list, prepare the c-v maps, apply the three filters, and let the user view all the anagrams at once or view a subset based on the anagram's first letter.

Preparing the Word List

Listing 3-6 prepares the word list by including just the words that have as many letters as in the name variable (in this case, nine). You should also ensure that all the words are lowercase, to be consistent.

voldemort_british.py, part 2

```
❶ def prep_words(name, word_list_ini):
      """Prep word list for finding anagrams."""
    ❷ print("length initial word_list = {}".format(len(word_list_ini)))
      len_name = len(name)
    ❸ word_list = [word.lower() for word in word_list_ini
                   if len(word) == len_name]
    ❹ print("length of new word_list = {}".format(len(word_list)))
    ❺ return word_list
```

Listing 3-6: Creates lists of words that are equal in length to the name variable

Define the prep_words() function to take a name string and list of dictionary words as arguments ❶. I suggest that you print the lengths of your various word lists before and after they've gone through a filter; that way, you can track how much impact the filters are having. So print the length of the dictionary ❷. Assign a variable to hold the length of the name and then use list comprehension to create a new list by looping through the words in word_list_ini, keeping those whose length is the same as the number of letters in name, and converting them to lowercase ❸. Next, print the length of this new word list ❹, and finally, return this new list for use in the next function ❺.

Generating the C-V Map

You need to convert the prepared word list to a c-v map. Remember that you're no longer interested in actual words in the dictionary; those have been reviewed and rejected. Your goal is to shuffle the remaining letters until they form something that resembles a proper noun.

Listing 3-7 defines a function that generates c-v maps for each word in word_list. The program, *voldemort_british.py*, will use the c-v map to judge whether a shuffled letter combination is reasonable based on consonant-vowel patterns in the English language.

voldemort_british.py, part 3

```
❶ def cv_map_words(word_list):
      """Map letters in words to consonants & vowels."""
    ❷ vowels = 'aeiouy'
    ❸ cv_mapped_words = []
    ❹ for word in word_list:
          temp = ''
          for letter in word:
              if letter in vowels:
                  temp += 'v'
              else:
                  temp += 'c'
          cv_mapped_words.append(temp)

      # determine number of UNIQUE c-v patterns
    ❺ total = len(set(cv_mapped_words))
      # target fraction to eliminate
    ❻ target = 0.05
      # get number of items in target fraction
    ❼ n = int(total * target)
    ❽ count_pruned = Counter(cv_mapped_words).most_common(total - n)
    ❾ filtered_cv_map = set()
      for pattern, count in count_pruned:
          filtered_cv_map.add(pattern)
      print("length filtered_cv_map = {}".format(len(filtered_cv_map)))
    ❿ return filtered_cv_map
```

Listing 3-7: Generates c-v maps from the words in `word_list`

Define the `cv_map_words()` function to take the prepped word list as an argument ❶. Since consonants and vowels form a binary system, you can define the vowels with a string ❷. Create an empty list to hold the maps ❸. Then loop through the words and the letters in each word, converting the letters to either a *c* or *v* ❹. Use a variable called `temp` to accumulate the map; then append it to the list. Note that `temp` is reinitialized each time the loop repeats.

You want to know the frequency of occurrence of a given c-v map pattern (for example, *cvcv*), so you can remove those with a low likelihood of occurrence. Before calculating the frequency, you need to collapse your list down to unique c-v maps—as it is now, *cvcv* may be repeated many, many times. So, turn the `cv_mapped_words` list into a set, to remove duplicates, and get its length ❺. Now you can define a target percentage to eliminate, using fractional values ❻. Start with a low number like `0.05`—equivalent to 5 percent—so you're less likely to eliminate anagrams that can form usable proper names. Multiply this target value by the total length of the `cv_mapped_words` set and assign the result to the variable `n` ❼. Be sure to convert `n` to an integer; since it will represent a count value, it can't be a float.

The `Counter` module data type has a handy method, `most_common()`, that will return the most common items in a list based on a *count* value that you provide; in this case, that value will be the length of the c-v map list, `total`, minus `n`. The value you pass `most_common()` must be an integer. If you pass the most_common() function the length of the list, it will return all the items in the list. If you subtract the count for the least likely 5 percent, you will effectively eliminate these c-v maps from the list ❽.

Remember, Counter returns a dictionary, but all you need are the final c-v maps, not their associated frequency counts. So initialize an empty set called filtered-cv-map ❾ and loop through each key-value pair in count_pruned(), adding only the key to the new set. Print the length of this set, so you can see the impact of the filter. Then finish by returning the filtered c-v map for use in the next function ❿.

Defining the C-V Map Filter

Listing 3-8 applies the c-v map filter: anagrams are generated based on permutations of the letters in the name variable, and then the program converts them to c-v maps and compares those anagrams to the filtered c-v maps built with the cv_map_words() function. If an anagram's c-v map is found in filtered_cv_map, then the program stores the anagram for the next filter.

voldemort_british.py, part 4

```
❶ def cv_map_filter(name, filtered_cv_map):
      """Remove permutations of words based on unlikely cons-vowel combos."""
    ❷ perms = {''.join(i) for i in permutations(name)}
      print("length of initial permutations set = {}".format(len(perms)))
      vowels = 'aeiouy'
    ❸ filter_1 = set()
    ❹ for candidate in perms:
          temp = ''
          for letter in candidate:
              if letter in vowels:
                  temp += 'v'
              else:
                  temp += 'c'
        ❺ if temp in filtered_cv_map:
              filter_1.add(candidate)
      print("# choices after filter_1 = {}".format(len(filter_1)))
    ❻ return filter_1
```

Listing 3-8: Defines cv_map_filter() function

Define the function cv_map_filter() to take two arguments: the name, followed by the set of c-v maps returned by cv_map_words() ❶. Use set comprehension and the permutations module to generate the set of permutations ❷. I described this process in "Project #6: Finding Voldemort: The Gallic Gambit" on page 49. Use a set here to permit later use of set operations, like taking the difference between two filter sets. This also removes duplicates, as permutations treats each *o* as a separate item, and returns 9!, rather than 9! / 2!. Note that permutations considers *tmv**o**o**rdle* and *tmv**oo**rdle* different strings.

Now initialize an empty set to hold the contents of the first filter ❸ and begin looping through the permutations ❹. Use the term *candidate*, as most of these aren't words but just strings of random letters. For each candidate, loop through the letters and map them to a *c* or a *v*, as you did with the `cv_words()` function. Check each c-v map, `temp`, for membership in `filtered_cv_map`. This is one reason for using sets: membership checks are very fast. If the candidate meets the condition, add it to `filter_1` ❺. Finish by returning your new anagram set ❻.

Defining the Trigram Filter

Listing 3-9 defines the trigram filter, which removes the permutations with unlikely three-letter triplets. It uses a text file derived from various cryptography websites that has been tailored to the letters in *tmvoordle*. This function will return only permutations that include one of these trigrams; the `main()` function will pass the new set to the next filter function.

voldemort_british.py, part 5

```
❶ def trigram_filter(filter_1, trigrams_filtered):
      """Remove unlikely trigrams from permutations."""
    ❷ filtered = set()
    ❸ for candidate in filter_1:
        ❹ for triplet in trigrams_filtered:
              triplet = triplet.lower()
              if triplet in candidate:
                  filtered.add(candidate)
    ❺ filter_2 = filter_1 - filtered
      print("# of choices after filter_2 = {}".format(len(filter_2)))
    ❻ return filter_2
```

Listing 3-9: Defines the `trigram_filter()` function

Parameters for the trigram filter include the output from the c-v map filter and the external list of unlikely trigrams, `trigrams_filtered` ❶.

Initialize an empty set to hold permutations that contain one of the forbidden trigrams ❷. Then start another `for` loop that looks through the candidates that survived the last filter ❸. A nested `for` loop looks at each triplet in the trigrams list ❹. If the triplet is in the candidate, it is added to the filter.

Now you can use set operations to subtract the new filter from `filter_1` ❺ and then return the difference for use with the next filter ❻.

Defining the Digram Filter

Listing 3-10 defines the digram filter, which removes unlikely letter pairs. Some will trigger the filter if they occur anywhere within the permutation; others will do so only if they occur at the start of the permutation. The disallowed digrams are based on the shaded cells in Table 3-2. The function returns the results of this filter for use in the final filter function.

voldemort_british.py, part 6

```
❶ def letter_pair_filter(filter_2):
      """Remove unlikely letter-pairs from permutations."""
    ❷ filtered = set()
    ❸ rejects = ['dt', 'lr', 'md', 'ml', 'mr', 'mt', 'mv',
                 'td', 'tv', 'vd', 'vl', 'vm', 'vr', 'vt']
```

```
❹ first_pair_rejects = ['ld', 'lm', 'lt', 'lv', 'rd',
                          'rl', 'rm', 'rt', 'rv', 'tl', 'tm']
❺ for candidate in filter_2:
    ❻ for r in rejects:
          if r in candidate:
              filtered.add(candidate)
    ❼ for fp in first_pair_rejects:
          if candidate.startswith(fp):
              filtered.add(candidate)
❽ filter_3 = filter_2 - filtered
  print("# of choices after filter_3 = {}".format(len(filter_3)))
❾ if 'voldemort' in filter_3:
      print("Voldemort found!", file=sys.stderr)
❿ return filter_3
```

Listing 3-10: Defines the `letter_pair_filter()` function

This filter accepts the results of the previous filter as an argument ❶. An empty set is initialized to hold any discarded permutations ❷. Then two lists of rejected pairs are assigned to the variables `rejects` ❸ and `first_pair_rejects` ❹. Both lists were entered manually. The first represents cells shaded black in Table 3-2; the second references cells shaded gray. Any permutation that contains a member of the first list—anywhere—will be discarded; permutations that *start with* a member of the second list will not be allowed. You can add or remove digrams to these lists to change how the filter behaves.

Begin looping through the permutations—continue to refer to these as "candidates," as they aren't necessarily words ❺. A nested `for` loop goes through the pairs in `rejects`, determines whether any are in `candidate`, and adds them to the `filtered` set ❻. A second nested `for` loop repeats this process for the `first_pair_rejects` ❼. Subtract `filtered` from the set returned from the previous function, `filter_2` ❽.

For fun *and* to ensure you haven't filtered too far, check whether *voldemort* is included in `filter_3` ❾ and print an announcement to highlight the discovery, using eye-catching red font for IDLE users. Then finish by returning the final filtered set ❿.

Letting the User Choose the Starting Letter

You don't know ahead of time whether your filtering will be successful. You may still end up with thousands of permutations. Providing the option to look at only a subset of the output won't reduce the overall number, but it will make it *psychologically* easier to face. Listing 3-11 adds, to *voldemort_british.py*, the ability to view a list of anagrams that begin with a certain input letter.

voldemort_british.py, part 7

```
❶ def view_by_letter(name, filter_3):
      """Filter to anagrams starting with input letter."""
    ❷ print("Remaining letters = {}".format(name))
    ❸ first = input("select a starting letter or press Enter to see all: ")
    ❹ subset = []
```

```
❺ for candidate in filter_3:
       if candidate.startswith(first):
           subset.append(candidate)
❻ print(*sorted(subset), sep='\n')
   print("Number of choices starting with {} = {}".format(first, len(subset)))
❼ try_again = input("Try again? (Press Enter else any other key to Exit):")
   if try_again.lower() == '':
    ❽ view_by_letter(name, filter_3)
   else:
    ❾ sys.exit()
```

Listing 3-11: Defines the `view_by_letter()` function

Define the `view_by_letter()` function to take both the `name` variable and `filter_3` as arguments ❶. You need the name so you can show the user the available letter choices on which to filter ❷. Get the user's input on whether they want to see all the remaining permutations or just those beginning with a certain letter ❸. Then start an empty list to hold the latter subset ❹.

A `for` loop, with a conditional, checks whether a candidate starts with the chosen letter and appends those letters that pass to `subset` ❺. This list is printed with the splat operator ❻. Then the program asks the user whether they want to try again or exit ❼. If they press ENTER, then `view_by_letter()` is called, recursively, and runs again from the start ❽. Otherwise, the program exits ❾. Note that Python has a default recursion depth limit of 1,000, which we'll ignore in this project.

Running the main() Function

Back in the global space, Listing 3-12 completes the code by calling the `main()` function if the user runs the program in stand-alone mode versus importing into another program.

voldemort_british.py, part 8

```
if __name__ == '__main__':
    main()
```

Listing 3-12: Calls the `main()` function

Example output from the completed program is shown below. After the program applies the third filter, there are 248 permutations remaining, of which a very manageable 73 start with *v*. I've omitted the printout of the permutations for brevity. As noted in the output, *voldemort* survives the filtering.

```
length initial word_list = 60388
length of new word_list = 8687
length filtered_cv_map = 234
length of initial permutations set = 181440
# choices after filter_1 = 123120
# of choices after filter_2 = 674
```

```
# of choices after filter_3 = 248
Voldemort found!
Remaining letters = tmvoordle
select a starting letter or Enter to see all: v
```

Interestingly, another surviving permutation is *lovedmort*. Given how many people Voldemort killed—or had killed—this may be the most appropriate moniker of all.

Summary

In this chapter, you first wrote code that found the anagrams for a given word or name. You then expanded on this to find phrasal name anagrams, working interactively with the user. Finally, you employed cryptanalytical techniques to tease *Voldemort* out of almost 200,000 possible anagrams. Along the way, you applied useful functionality in the `collections` and `itertools` modules.

Further Reading

The *Jumble* website is *http://www.jumble.com/*.

You can find some representative online anagram generators at the following sites:

- *http://wordsmith.org/anagram/*
- *https://www.dcode.fr/anagram-generator*
- *http://www.wordplays.com/anagrammer/*

More anagram programs are found in *Think Python, 2nd Edition* (O'Reilly, 2015) by Allen Downey.

Cracking Codes with Python (No Starch Press, 2017) by Al Sweigart provides more code for computing word patterns, such as those used for filtering in the *voldemort_british.py* program.

Practice Project: Finding Digrams

You *could* comb through cryptography websites looking for frequency statistics, or you could derive them for yourself. Write a Python program that finds all the digrams in *tmvoordle* and then counts their frequency of occurrence in a dictionary file. Be sure to test your code on words like *volvo*, so you don't overlook repeating digrams in the same word. You can find a solution in the appendix or download *count_digrams_practice.py* from *https://www.nostarch.com/impracticalpython/*.

Challenge Project: Automatic Anagram Generator

Look at the online anagram generators I just referenced in "Further Reading" and write a Python program that mimics one of these. Your program should automatically generate phrase anagrams from an input name and display a subset (for example, the first 500) for the user to review.

4

DECODING AMERICAN CIVIL WAR CIPHERS

Cryptography is the science of secure communication through the use of *codes* and *ciphers*. A code replaces whole words with other words; a cipher scrambles or replaces the letters in words (so technically, Morse code is really Morse cipher). One goal of cryptography is to use a *key* to both *encrypt* readable *plaintext* into unreadable *ciphertext* and then *decrypt* it back to plaintext. The goal of *cryptanalysis* is to decode ciphers and codes without knowing their key or encryption algorithm.

In this chapter, we'll investigate two ciphers used in the American Civil War: the route cipher, used by the North, and the rail fence cipher, used by both sides. We'll also look at what made one so successful and how we can use lessons learned from its application to better write programs for inexperienced users and those unfamiliar with your Python code.

Project #8: The Route Cipher

In the American Civil War, the Union had just about every advantage over the Confederacy, including the field of cryptography. The Union had better codes, better ciphers, and better-trained personnel. But perhaps its biggest advantage was in leadership and organization.

The head of the US Military Telegraph Department was Anson Stager (Figure 4-1). As the cofounder of Western Union, Stager knew from experience that telegraph operators made fewer mistakes when sending whole words, as opposed to the strings of random letters and numbers common to most ciphertext. He also knew that military dispatches only needed to stay secret long enough for orders to be carried out. His secure solution was a hybrid cryptosystem called the *route transposition cipher*, a combination of transposed real words and code words that became one of the most successful military ciphers of all time.

Figure 4-1: General Anson Stager, US Telegraph Corps, 1865

Transposition ciphers *scramble* the arrangement of letters or words, unlike substitution ciphers, which *replace* the letters in the plaintext with different characters or symbols. Figure 4-2 shows an example of a route transposition cipher. The message is written left to right over a number of predetermined columns and rows, important plaintext words are replaced by code words, and the last row is filled with dummy placeholder words. The reader determines the order of the rearranged words by traversing up and down these columns, as shown. The starting word is *REST,* and then the encryption route is shown with arrows.

Code Words

VILLAGE = Enemy	**ROANOKE** = Cavalry
GODWIN = Tennessee	**SNOW** = Rebels

Original Message in Encryption Matrix

Enemy	calvary	heading	to
Tennessee	With	Rebels	gone
you	are	free	to
transport	your	supplies	south

Encryption Route + Code & Dummy Words

VILLAGE	**ROANOKE**	heading	to
GODWIN	With	**SNOW**	gone
you	are	free	to
transport	your	supplies	south
REST	**IS**	**JUST**	**FILLER**

Cyphertext

```
REST TRANSPORT YOU GODWIN VILLAGE
ROANOKE WITH ARE YOUR IS JUST SUPPLIES FREE
SNOW HEADING TO GONE TO SOUTH FILLER
```

Figure 4-2: A route cipher using actual Union code words

To fully decode this message, you need to know both the starting point and route used to traverse the message and create the final ciphertext *and* the meaning of the code words.

In the early 20th century, the distinguished military cryptanalyst William Friedman disparaged Stager's route cipher. He considered it too unsophisticated and found it highly improbable that the Confederates never cracked it. But the fact remains that hundreds of thousands of route ciphers sent during the war were apparently never decoded, and not from lack of trying. In an early example of crowdsourcing, the Confederates published the coded messages in newspapers, hoping for some help with the decryption, but to no avail. While some historians speculate that this cipher was broken at times, Stager's design teaches several important lessons:

Design for human error. Military ciphers have to be simple, as hundreds might be sent in a day. The real words used in the route cipher made it much less likely to be garbled by telegraph operators. Stager knew his customer and designed for them. He recognized the limitations of his workforce and tailored his product accordingly. The Confederates, by contrast, had great difficulty deciphering their own complex messages, sometimes giving up and riding around enemy lines to talk face-to-face!

Innovation trumps invention. Sometimes you don't need to invent something new; you just need to rediscover something old. The short word-transposition ciphers suitable for telegraph transmission were too weak to use on their own, but combined with code names and disruptive dummy words, they confounded the Confederates.

Share learning. Because everyone in the Telegraph Corps used the same methodology, it was easy to build on existing techniques and share lessons learned. This allowed the route cipher to evolve over time with the introduction of slang and intentional misspellings, as well as a growing number of code words for places, people, and dates.

Stager's practical cipher may not have pleased later "purists," but it was the perfect design for the time. The concepts behind it are timeless and easily transferable to modern-day applications.

THE OBJECTIVE

In Harry Turtledove's award-winning 1992 novel *Guns of the South*, time travelers provide Confederate armies with modern weaponry, changing the course of history. Instead of AK-47s, let's pretend you've traveled back to 1864 with your laptop, a few extra batteries, and Python to design an algorithm that will decrypt a route cipher based on an assumed encryption matrix and path. In the spirit of Stager, you'll write a user-friendly program that will reduce human error.

The Strategy

When it comes to solving ciphers, it's a lot easier if you know what type you're dealing with. In this case, you know it's a transposition cipher, because it's composed of real words that are jumbled. You also know there are code words and null words present. Your job is to figure out ways to decrypt the *transposition* part of the route cipher and let someone else worry about code words while you go have a well-deserved mint julep.

Creating a Control Message

To understand how to do this, create your own message and route cipher. Call this your *control message*:

- Number of columns = 4
- Number of rows = 5
- Start position = Bottom left
- Route = Alternating up and down columns
- Plaintext = 0 1 2 3 4 5 6 7 8 9 10 11 12 13 14 15 16 17 18 19
- Ciphertext = 16 12 8 4 0 1 5 9 13 17 18 14 10 6 2 3 7 11 15 19
- Key = –1 2 –3 4

Using a numeric progression for the plaintext allows you to instantly tell whether you've gotten all or part of the decryption correct, at any place within the message.

The transposition matrix is shown in Figure 4-3. The gray arrows indicate the encryption route.

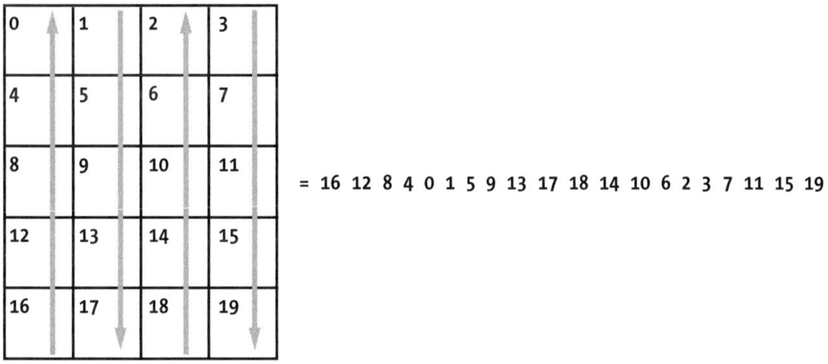

0	1	2	3
4	5	6	7
8	9	10	11
12	13	14	15
16	17	18	19

= 16 12 8 4 0 1 5 9 13 17 18 14 10 6 2 3 7 11 15 19

Figure 4-3: The transposition matrix for the control message with the route cipher path and resulting ciphertext

The key keeps track of both the *order* and *direction* of the route through the columns. The route doesn't have to move through the columns in order. For instance, it can move down the first column, up the third, down the fourth, and finally up the second. Negative numbers mean you start at the bottom and read up a column; positive numbers mean the reverse. For the control message, the final key used in the program will be a list: [–1, 2, –3, 4]. This list will instruct the program to start reading up from the bottom of column 1, move to the top of column 2 and read down, move to the bottom of column 3 and read up, and move to the top of column 4 and read down.

Note that you shouldn't use 0 in keys because the users, being human, prefer to start counting at 1. Of course, Python prefers to start counting at 0, so you'll need to subtract 1 from the key values behind the scenes. Everybody wins!

Later, in "Route Transposition Cipher: Brute-Force Attack" on page 88, you can use this compact key structure to brute-force your way through a route cipher, automatically trying hundreds of keys until the plaintext is restored.

Designing, Populating, and Depopulating the Matrix

You'll input the ciphertext as a continuous string. For your program to unravel the route through this string, you'll first need to build and populate a translation matrix. The ciphertext string is just the columns in the transposition matrix in Figure 4-3 laid end to end, in the order they were read. And as there are five rows in the transposition matrix, every group of five elements in the ciphertext represents a separate column. You can represent this matrix with a list of lists:

```
>>> list_of_lists = [['16', '12', '8', '4', '0'], ['1', '5', '9', '13', '17'],
['18', '14', '10', '6', '2'], ['3', '7', '11', '15', '19']]
```

The items in this new list now represent lists—with each list representing a column—and the five elements in each list represent the rows that comprise that column. This is a little hard to see, so let's print each of these nested lists on a separate line:

```
>>> for i in range(len(list_of_lists)):
        print(list_of_lists[i])
[16, 12, 8, 4, 0]
[1, 5, 9, 13, 17]
[18, 14, 10, 6, 2]
[3, 7, 11, 15, 19]
```

If you read each list left to right, starting at the top, you follow the transposition route, which was up and down alternate columns (see Figure 4-3). From Python's point of view, the first column read is `list-of-lists[0]`, and the starting point is `list-of-lists[0][0]`.

Now, normalize the route by reading all columns in the same direction as the starting column (up). This requires reversing the order of elements in every other list, as shown in bold here:

```
[16, 12, 8, 4, 0]
[17, 13, 9, 5, 1]
[18, 14, 10, 6, 2]
[19, 15, 11, 7, 3]
```

A pattern emerges. If you start at the upper right and read down each column, ending at the lower left, the numbers are in numerical order; you've restored the plaintext!

To replicate this, your script can loop through every nested list, removing the last item in that list and adding the item to a new string, until the translation matrix has been emptied. The script will know from the key which nested lists it needs to reverse and the order in which to depopulate the matrix. The output will be a string of the restored plaintext:

```
'0 1 2 3 4 5 6 7 8 9 10 11 12 13 14 15 16 17 18 19'
```

You should now have a very general view of the strategy. Let's get more descriptive and write the pseudocode next.

The Pseudocode

The script can be broken up into three major parts: user input, translation matrix population, and decryption to plaintext. You should be able to see these parts in the following pseudocode:

```
Load the ciphertext string.
Convert ciphertext into a cipherlist to split out individual words.
Get input for the number of columns and rows.
Get input for the key.
Convert key into a list to split out individual numbers.
Create a new list for the translation matrix.
For every number in the key:
    Create a new list and append every n items (n = # of rows) from the cipherlist.
    Use the sign of key number to decide whether to read the row forward or backward.
    Using the chosen direction, add the new list to the matrix. The index of each
    new list is based on the column number used in the key.
Create a new string to hold translation results.
For range of rows:
    For the nested list in translation matrix:
          Remove the last word in nested list
          Add the word to the translation string.
Print the translation string.
```

Everything before the first loop is essentially just collecting and reformatting the cipher data. The first loop is responsible for building and populating the matrix, and the second loop creates a translation string from that matrix. Finally, the translation string is printed.

The Route Cipher Decryption Code

Listing 4-1 takes a message encrypted with the route cipher, the number of columns and rows in the transposition matrix, and a key and then displays the translated plaintext. It will decrypt all "common" route ciphers, where the route starts at the top or bottom of a column and continues up and/or down columns.

This is the prototype version; once you're sure it's working, you'll package it for others to use. You can download this code at *https://www.nostarch.com/impracticalpython/*.

route_cipher_decrypt_prototype.py

```
❶ ciphertext = "16 12 8 4 0 1 5 9 13 17 18 14 10 6 2 3 7 11 15 19"

  # split elements into words, not letters
```

```
❷ cipherlist = list(ciphertext.split())

❸ # initialize variables
  COLS = 4
  ROWS = 5
  key = '-1 2 -3 4'  # neg number means read UP column vs. DOWN
  translation_matrix = [None] * COLS
  plaintext = ''
  start = 0
  stop = ROWS

  # turn key_int into list of integers:
❹ key_int = [int(i) for i in key.split()]

  # turn columns into items in list of lists:
❺ for k in key_int:
    ❻ if k < 0:  # reading bottom-to-top of column
          col_items = cipherlist[start:stop]
      elif k > 0:  # reading top-to-bottom of columnn
          col_items = list((reversed(cipherlist[start:stop])))
      translation_matrix[abs(k) - 1] = col_items
      start += ROWS
      stop += ROWS

  print("\nciphertext = {}".format(ciphertext))
  print("\ntranslation matrix =", *translation_matrix, sep="\n")
  print("\nkey length= {}".format(len(key_int)))

  # loop through nested lists popping off last item to new list:
❼ for i in range(ROWS):
      for col_items in translation_matrix:
        ❽ word = str(col_items.pop())
        ❾ plaintext += word + ' '

  print("\nplaintext = {}".format(plaintext))
```

Listing 4-1: Code for route_cipher_decrypt_prototype.py

Start by loading the ciphertext ❶ as a string. You want to deal with words, not letters, so split the string apart based on empty spaces using the `split()` string method to create a new list named `cipherlist` ❷. The `split()` method is the inverse of the `join()` method, which you've seen before. You can split on any string; the method just defaults to runs of consecutive whitespace, deleting each whitespace before it moves to the next.

Now it's time to input what you know about the cipher ❸: the columns and rows, which form the matrix, and the key, which contains the route. Initialize the column and row numbers as constants. Then make an empty list named `translation_matrix` to hold the contents of each column as a (nested) list. Assign placeholders by multiplying the value `None` by the number of columns. You can use the indexes of these empty items to put columns back in their correct order for keys that are not in numerical order.

An empty string named `plaintext` will hold the decrypted message. Next are some slicing parameters. Note that some of these are derived from the number of rows, which equates to the number of items in each column.

Now, convert the key variable, which is a string, into a list of integers using *list comprehension*—a shorthand way of performing operations on lists ❹. You'll use the numbers in the key as indexes later, so they need to be integers.

The next block of code is a `for` loop that populates the `translation_matrix`, which is just a list of lists ❺. Since each column becomes a nested list and the length of the `key_int` list is equal to the number of columns, the range for the loop is the key, which also describes the route.

Inside the loop, use a conditional to check whether the key is positive or negative ❻; if the key is positive, then the direction of the slice is reversed. Assign the slice to the correct position in `translation_matrix` based on the absolute key value and subtract 1 (since the keys don't include 0, but the list indexes do). Finish the loop by advancing the slice endpoints by the number of rows and printing some useful information.

The final block ❼ loops through the number of rows—which is equivalent to the number of words in one of the nested lists—and through each nested list. The first two of these loops are shown in Figure 4-4. As you stop in each nested list, you get to employ one of my favorite Python functions, the list `pop()` method ❽. The `pop()` method removes and returns the last item from a list, unless a specific index is provided. It destroys the nested list, but you're done with it anyway.

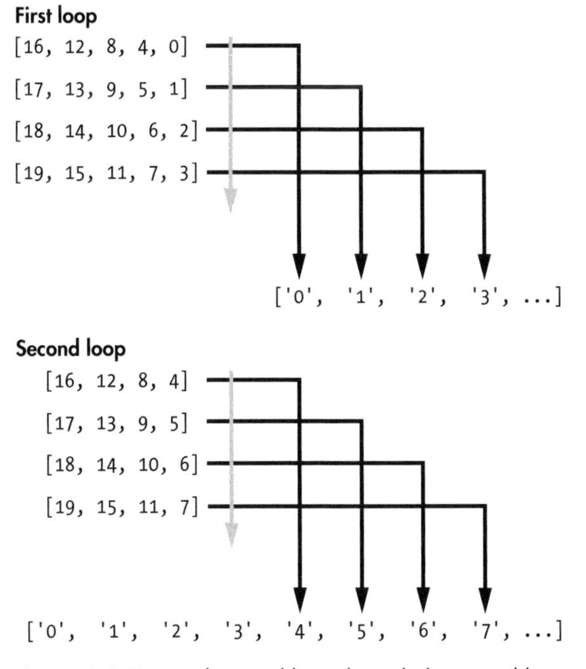

Figure 4-4: First and second loop through the nested lists, removing and appending each end item to the translation string

As soon as you pop off a word, concatenate it to the `plaintext` string and add a space ❾. All that's left to do is display the decrypted ciphertext. The output for the numeric test set looks like this:

```
plaintext = 0 1 2 3 4 5 6 7 8 9 10 11 12 13 14 15 16 17 18 19
```

That looks like success!

Hacking the Route Cipher

The preceding code assumes you know the route through the encryption matrix or have correctly guessed the key. If those assumptions aren't true, your only recourse is to try every possible key and matrix arrangement. You'll get a chance to automate the key selection process—for a given number of columns—in "Route Transposition Cipher: Brute-Force Attack" on page 88. But, as you'll see, the Union route cipher is well fortified against brute-force attacks. You can crack it, but you'll end up with so much data, you'll feel like the dog that chased a car and caught it.

As messages get longer, the number of possible encryption paths in a transposition cipher becomes too large for a brute-force solution, even using modern computers. For example, if there are eight columns, and you allow the route to skip to any column, the number of ways to combine the columns is the factorial of eight: $8 \times 7 \times 6 \times 5 \times 4 \times 3 \times 2 \times 1 = 40{,}320$. That's 40,320 paths *before* you start choosing alternative routes through the columns. If the route can change direction up or down a column, the number of combinations increases to 10,321,920. And if you consider starting *anywhere* in a column—instead of at the very top or bottom—and allow *any* route through the matrix (such as spiraling), things will really start to get out of hand!

For this reason, even short transposition ciphers can have thousands to millions of possible paths. Even if the number of paths is manageable for a computer and a brute-force attack may prevail, you'll still need a way to sift through the myriad outcomes and either choose a winner computationally or select a small subset of candidates to visually examine.

For the more common *letter*-transposition ciphers, it's easy to write a function that detects English by comparing each decryption attempt to a dictionary file. If the number of decrypted words belonging to a dictionary is greater than a certain threshold percentage, you've probably cracked the cipher. Likewise, if there's a high frequency of common letter pairs (*digrams*)—like *er*, *th*, *on*, or *an*—you may have found the solution. Unfortunately, this approach won't work for a *word*-transposition cipher like the one you're using here.

Dictionaries can't help you figure out whether words have been arranged correctly. For word arrangement, you could try using approaches like grammatical rules and probabilistic language models, such as *n*-grams, combing through thousands of decryptions and picking candidate outcomes programmatically, but Stager's wise use of code names and dummy words in his route cipher will greatly complicate the process.

Cryptanalysts consider short, straight-up transposition ciphers to be fairly easy to crack without a computer, despite the issues just described. They look for common word or letter pairs that make sense, and use those to guess the number of rows in the transposition matrix.

To illustrate, let's use our control message composed of numbers. In Figure 4-5, you can see the ciphertext outcomes for a 4×5 matrix, each produced by starting at one of the four corners of the grid, and following an alternating, sequential route. All cases include repetition of adjacent numbers (shaded in Figure 4-5). These indicate where you're moving laterally through the grid, and they provide clues to the design of the matrix and the route taken through it. You can immediately see that there were five rows, because the first of each common pair is a fifth word. Moreover, knowing there are 20 words in the message, you learn the number of columns was four (20 / 5 = 4). Using the reasonable assumption that the plaintext message was written left to right, you can even guess the route. For example, if you start in the lower right, you go up to 3, then left to 2, then down to 18, then left to 17, then up to 1 and left to 0. Of course, this would be more difficult with words, since the connection between words isn't as explicit, but using numbers really makes the point.

5 digits = 5 rows!

Lower right = 19 15 11 7 3 2 6 10 14 18 17 13 9 5 1 0 4 8 12 16

Lower left = 16 12 8 4 0 1 5 9 13 17 18 14 10 6 2 3 7 11 15 19

Upper right = 3 7 11 15 19 18 14 10 6 2 1 5 9 13 17 16 12 8 4 0

Upper left = 0 4 8 12 16 17 13 9 5 1 2 6 10 14 18 19 15 11 7 3

Figure 4-5: Characters or words in logical order (shaded) can be used to guess an encryption route.

Look at Figure 4-6, based on the message in Figure 4-2. End words and possible linked words, like "is just" or "heading to," are shaded.

```
REST TRANSPORT YOU GODWIN VILLAGE ROANOKE WITH ARE YOUR
IS JUST SUPPLIES FREE SNOW HEADING TO GONE TO SOUTH FILLER
```

Figure 4-6: Human hacking of the route cipher in Figure 4-2. A five-row matrix is indicated.

There are 20 total words, for which there could be 4, 5, or 10 rows. It's doubtful that a two-column matrix would be used, so we are realistically dealing with a 4×5 or a 5×4 arrangement. If the route cipher path is like that in Figure 4-5, then we'd expect to see two nonshaded words between shaded words for a four-row matrix and three nonshaded words for a five-row matrix. It's harder to come up with sensical word pairs that honor the four-column pattern, regardless of which direction you read the ciphertext. So, we're probably dealing with a five-column solution that starts on the left side of the matrix—since the linked words make sense read left to right.

Note how the shaded words in Figure 4-6 fill out the top and bottom rows in the transposition matrix in Figure 4-7. This is what we would expect, as the path is "turning around" at the top and bottom of every column. Graphical solutions: God's gift to the innumerate!

VILLAGE	ROANOKE	heading	to
GODWIN	With	SNOW	gone
you	are	free	to
transport	your	supplies	south
REST	IS	JUST	FILLER

Figure 4-7: Shaded words in Figure 4-6 placed in the transposition matrix

This seemed easy, but then again, we know how a route cipher works. Confederate code breakers eventually discovered it too, but the use of code words denied them full entry into the system. To hack the codes, they needed a captured codebook or a large organization capable of acquiring and analyzing big data, which was beyond the reach of the Confederacy in the 19th century.

Adding a User Interface

The second goal of this project is to write the code in such a way as to reduce human error, especially from those with less experience (including technicians, interns, peers, and telegraph clerks in 1864). Of course, the best way to make a program user-friendly is to include a *graphical user interface (GUI)*, but at times, this isn't practical or possible. For example, code-cracking programs automatically loop through thousands of possible keys, and autogenerating these keys is easier than getting them directly from a user.

In this example, you'll proceed with the assumption that the user will crack open the program file and enter some input or even make minor code changes. Here are some guidelines to follow:

1. Start with a useful docstring (see Chapter 1).
2. Place all required user input at the top.
3. Use comments to clarify input requirements.
4. Clearly separate user input from the remaining code.
5. Encapsulate most processes in functions.
6. Include functions to catch predictable user errors.

The nice thing about this approach is that no one's intelligence gets insulted. If a user *wants* to scroll down and look at the code, or even change it, there's nothing stopping them. If all they want to do is enter some values and get a black box solution, then they're happy, too. And we've honored the spirit of Anson Stager by making things simple and reducing the chance for error.

Instructing the User and Getting Input

Listing 4-2 shows the prototype code repackaged for sharing with others. You can find this code at *https://www.nostarch.com/impracticalpython/*.

route_cipher_decrypt.py, part 1

```
❶ """Decrypt a path through a Union Route Cipher.

❷ Designed for whole-word transposition ciphers with variable rows & columns.
  Assumes encryption began at either top or bottom of a column.
  Key indicates the order to read columns and the direction to traverse.
  Negative column numbers mean start at bottom and read up.
  Positive column numbers mean start at top & read down.

  Example below is for 4x4 matrix with key -1 2 -3 4.
  Note "0" is not allowed.
  Arrows show encryption route; for negative key values read UP.

    1   2   3   4
   ___ ___ ___ ___
  | ^ | | | ^ | | | MESSAGE IS WRITTEN
  |_|_|_v_|_|_|_v_|
  | ^ | | | ^ | | | ACROSS EACH ROW
  |_|_|_v_|_|_|_v_|
  | ^ | | | ^ | | | IN THIS MANNER
  |_|_|_v_|_|_|_v_|
  | ^ | | | ^ | | | LAST ROW IS FILLED WITH DUMMY WORDS
  |_|_|_v_|_|_|_v_|
  START        END

  Required inputs - a text message, # of columns, # of rows, key string

  Prints translated plaintext
  """
❸ import sys

  #==============================================================================
❹ # USER INPUT:

❺ # the string to be decrypted (type or paste between triple-quotes):
  ciphertext = """16 12 8 4 0 1 5 9 13 17 18 14 10 6 2 3 7 11 15 19
  """

❻ # number of columns in the transposition matrix:
  COLS = 4

  # number of rows in the transposition matrix:
  ROWS = 5

❼ # key with spaces between numbers; negative to read UP column (ex = -1 2 -3 4):
  key = """ -1 2 -3 4 """
```

```
❽ # END OF USER INPUT - DO NOT EDIT BELOW THIS LINE!
#==============================================================================

❾
```

Listing 4-2: Docstring, imports, and user input for route_cipher_decrypt.py

Start with a multiline docstring in triple quotes ❶. The docstring informs the user that the program only decrypts a typical route cipher—one that starts at either the top or bottom of a column—and how to enter the key information ❷. A diagram is included to help make the point.

Next, import sys for access to system fonts and functions ❸. You're going to check the user's input for acceptance criteria, so you need to display messages in the shell in eye-catching red. Putting this `import` statement here is a catch-22. Since the strategic goal is to hide the working code from the user, you really should apply this later in the program. But the Python convention of putting all `import` statements at the top is too strong to ignore.

Now for the input section. How often have you seen or dealt with code where inputs or changes have to be made *throughout* the program? This can be confusing for the author and even worse for another user. So, move all these important variables to the top for convenience, common courtesy, and error prevention.

First, separate the input section with a line and then let the user know that they're on deck with an all-caps comment ❹. The required inputs are clearly defined with comments. You can use triple quotes for the text input to better accommodate long snippets of text. Note that I've entered the string of numbers from Figure 4-3 ❺. Next, the user needs to add the number of columns and rows for the transposition matrix ❻, followed by the proposed (or known) key ❼.

End the user input section with a declaration comment to that effect and a caution to not edit anything below the following line ❽. Then add some extra spaces to more clearly separate the input section from the rest of the program ❾.

Defining the main() Function

Listing 4-3 defines the `main()` function, which runs the program and prints out the plaintext after the cipher is decoded. The `main()` function can be defined before or after the functions it calls, as long as it is the last function called.

route_cipher_decrypt.py, part 2

```
def main():
    """Run program and print decrypted plaintext."""
 ❶ print("\nCiphertext = {}".format(ciphertext))
    print("Trying {} columns".format(COLS))
    print("Trying {} rows".format(ROWS))
    print("Trying key = {}".format(key))

    # split elements into words, not letters
 ❷ cipherlist = list(ciphertext.split())
```

```
❸ validate_col_row(cipherlist)
❹ key_int = key_to_int(key)
❺ translation_matrix = build_matrix(key_int, cipherlist)
❻ plaintext = decrypt(translation_matrix)

❼ print("Plaintext = {}".format(plaintext))
```

Listing 4-3: Defines the `main()` *function*

Start the `main()` function by printing the user input to the shell ❶. Then turn the ciphertext into a list by splitting on whitespace, as you did in the prototype code ❷.

The next series of statements call functions you will define shortly. The first checks whether the input rows and columns are valid for the message length ❸. The second converts the `key` variable from a string to a list of integers ❹. The third builds the translation matrix ❺, and the fourth runs the decryption algorithm on the matrix and returns a plaintext string ❻. Finish `main()` by printing the plaintext ❼.

Verifying Data

As you continue to package *route_cipher_decrypt.py* for the end user, you need to verify that the input is valid. Listing 4-4 anticipates common user errors and provides the user with helpful feedback and guidance.

route_cipher_decrypt.py, part 3

```
❶ def validate_col_row(cipherlist):
      """Check that input columns & rows are valid vs. message length."""
      factors = []
      len_cipher = len(cipherlist)
    ❷ for i in range(2, len_cipher):  # range excludes 1-column ciphers
          if len_cipher % i == 0:
              factors.append(i)
    ❸ print("\nLength of cipher = {}".format(len_cipher))
      print("Acceptable column/row values include: {}".format(factors))
      print()
    ❹ if ROWS * COLS != len_cipher:
          print("\nError - Input columns & rows not factors of length "
                "of cipher. Terminating program.", file=sys.stderr)
          sys.exit(1)

❺ def key_to_int(key):
      """Turn key into list of integers & check validity."""
    ❻ key_int = [int(i) for i in key.split()]
      key_int_lo = min(key_int)
      key_int_hi = max(key_int)
    ❼ if len(key_int) != COLS or key_int_lo < -COLS or key_int_hi > COLS \
          or 0 in key_int:
        ❽ print("\nError - Problem with key. Terminating.", file=sys.stderr)
          sys.exit(1)
      else:
        ❾ return key_int
```

Listing 4-4: Defines functions for checking and prepping user input

The validate_col_row() function checks that the input column and row numbers are appropriate for the length of the cipherlist, which you pass as an argument ❶. The transposition matrix is always the same size as the number of words in the message, so the number of columns and the number of rows have to be a factor of the message size. To determine all the permissible factors, first make an empty list to hold the factors and then get the length of the cipherlist. Use the *cipherlist*, rather than the input *ciphertext*, as the elements in the ciphertext are *letters*, not words.

Normally, to get the factors of a number, you would use a range of (1, *number* + 1), but you don't want these endpoints in the factors list, because a translation matrix with these dimensions would just be the plaintext. So exclude these values from the range ❷. Since a factor of a number divides evenly into that number, use the modulo operator (%) to find the factors and then append them to the factors list.

Next, display some useful information for the user: the length of the cipherlist and the acceptable choices for rows and columns ❸. Finally, multiply the user's two choices together and compare the product to the length of the cipherlist. If they don't match, print a red warning message in the shell (using our old file=sys.stderr trick) and terminate the program ❹. Use sys.exit(1), as the 1 indicates an abnormal exit.

Now define a function to check the key and convert it from a string to a list ❺. Pass it the key variable as an argument. Split out each item in key and convert it to an integer; name the list key_int to distinguish it from the user-entered key variable ❻. Next, determine the minimum and maximum values in the key_int list. Then use an if statement to make sure the list contains the same number of items as there are columns and none of the items in key is too large, too small, or equal to 0 ❼. Terminate the program with an error message if any of those criteria fail to pass ❽. Otherwise, return the key_int list ❾.

Building and Decoding the Translation Matrix

Listing 4-5 defines two functions, one to build the translation matrix and one to decode it, and calls the main() function as a module or in stand-alone mode.

route_cipher_decrypt.py, part 4

```
❶ def build_matrix(key_int, cipherlist):
      """Turn every n items in a list into a new item in a list of lists."""
      translation_matrix = [None] * COLS
      start = 0
      stop = ROWS
      for k in key_int:
          if k < 0:  # read bottom-to-top of column
              col_items = cipherlist[start:stop]
          elif k > 0:  # read top-to-bottom of columnn
              col_items = list((reversed(cipherlist[start:stop])))
          translation_matrix[abs(k) - 1] = col_items
          start += ROWS
          stop += ROWS
      return translation_matrix
```

```
❷ def decrypt(translation_matrix):
      """Loop through nested lists popping off last item to a string."""
      plaintext = ''
      for i in range(ROWS):
          for matrix_col in translation_matrix:
              word = str(matrix_col.pop())
              plaintext += word + ' '
      return plaintext

❸ if __name__ == '__main__':
      main()
```

Listing 4-5: Defines the functions for building and decoding the translation matrix

These two functions represent encapsulation of code in the *route_cipher_decrypt_prototype.py* program. See Listing 4-1 for a detailed description.

First, define a function to build the translation matrix; pass it the `key_int` and `cipherlist` variables as arguments ❶. Have the function return the list of lists.

Next, bundle the decryption code, where you pop off the end of each nested list, as a function that uses the `translation_matrix` list as an argument ❷. Return the plaintext, which will be printed by the `main()` function.

End with the conditional statement that lets the program run as a module or in stand-alone mode ❸.

If you're an occasional or one-time user of this code, you'll appreciate how straightforward and approachable it is. If you plan to alter the code for your own purposes, you'll also appreciate that the key variables are accessible and the major tasks are modularized. You won't have to dig through the program to tease out what matters or understand the difference between arcane variables like `list1` and `list2`.

Here's the output of the program, using the ciphertext from Figure 4-2:

```
Ciphertext = 16 12 8 4 0 1 5 9 13 17 18 14 10 6 2 3 7 11 15 19

Trying 4 columns
Trying 5 rows
Trying key = -1 2 -3 4

Length of cipher = 20
Acceptable column/row values include: [2, 4, 5, 10]

Plaintext = 0 1 2 3 4 5 6 7 8 9 10 11 12 13 14 15 16 17 18 19
```

You should now be able to easily decrypt a route transposition cipher with a known key or test suspected routes by using the script's clear and accessible interface to adjust the key. You'll get a chance to truly crack one of these ciphers, by automatically trying every possible key, in "Route Transposition Cipher: Brute-Force Attack" on page 88.

Project #9: The Rail Fence Cipher

Confederate officers and spies were pretty much on their own when it came to cryptography. This led to unsophisticated solutions, one of the favorites being the rail fence cipher, so named due to its resemblance to the zigzag pattern of a split-rail fence (shown in Figure 4-8).

Figure 4-8: A rail fence

The rail fence is a simple-to-use transposition cipher, like the Union's route cipher, but differs from the route cipher in that it transposes letters rather than words, making it more error-prone. And since the number of possible keys is much more restrictive than the number of paths through a route cipher, the rail fence cipher is much easier to "tear down."

Both the Union and Confederates used the rail fence as a field cipher, and the spies probably didn't use code words very often. Codebooks needed to be tightly controlled, for obvious reasons, and were more likely to be secured in a military telegraph office than carried around by easily compromised undercover agents.

Sometimes the Confederates used the more complex Vigenère cipher (see "Project #12: Hiding a Vigenère Cipher" on page 106) for important messages—and some unimportant ones to mislead enemies—but it was tedious work to decipher and equally laborious to encrypt and not suitable for fast field communications.

Despite their lack of training in the mechanics of cryptography, the Confederacy, and Southerners in general, were clever and innovative. Among their more impressive accomplishments in the art of secret messages was the use of microphotography, 100 years before it was widely adopted during the Cold War.

THE OBJECTIVE

Write Python programs that will help a spy encrypt and decrypt a "two-rail" (two-row) rail fence cipher. You should write the programs in a way that will reduce potential errors by inexperienced users.

The Strategy

To encrypt a message with the rail fence cipher, follow the steps in Figure 4-9.

`Buy more Maine potatoes`	1) Write plaintext
`BUYMOREMAINEPOTATOES`	2) Remove spaces and capitalize
`B Y O E A N P T T E` ` U M R M I E O A O S`	3) Stack and stagger letters in zigzag pattern
`BYOEANPTTEUMRMIEOAOS`	4) Merge the upper and lower rows
`BYOEA NPTTE UMRMI EOAOS`	5) Split into groups of five

Figure 4-9: Encryption process for a "two-rail" rail fence cipher

After the plaintext is written, the spaces are removed, and all the letters are converted to uppercase (Step 2). Using uppercase is common convention in cryptography, as it obfuscates the presence of proper names and the beginning of sentences, giving a cryptanalyst fewer clues for deciphering the message.

The message is then written in stacked fashion, with every other letter below the previous letter and shifted over one space (Step 3). This is where the "rail fence" analogy becomes apparent.

The first row is then written, followed immediately by the second row on the same line (Step 4), and then the letters are broken into groups of five to create the illusion of distinct words and to further confuse the cryptanalyst (Step 5).

To decrypt a rail fence cipher, reverse the process. Just remove the spaces, divide the message in half, stack the second half below the first, offset by one letter, and read the message using the zigzag pattern. If the ciphertext has an odd number of letters, put the extra letter in the first (upper) half.

To make things easy for people who want to use a rail fence cipher, follow the preceding steps to write two programs, one to encrypt and another to decrypt. Figure 4-9 is essentially your pseudocode, so let's get to it. And since you now know how to package the code for inexperienced users, take that approach from the start.

The Rail Fence Cipher Encryption Code

The code in this section allows a user to enter a plaintext message and have the encrypted results print in the interpreter window. This code is available for download with the book's resources at *https://www.nostarch.com/impracticalpython/*.

Instructing the User and Getting Input

Listing 4-6, at the top of *rail_fence_cipher_encrypt.py*, provides the program's instructions and assigns the plaintext to a variable.

rail_fence_cipher_encrypt.py, part 1

```
❶ r"""Encrypt a Civil War 'rail fence' type cipher.

  This is for a "2-rail" fence cipher for short messages.

  Example text to encrypt:  'Buy more Maine potatoes'

  Rail fence style:  B Y O E A N P T T E
                      U M R M I E O A O S

  Read zigzag:       \/\/\/\/\/\/\/\/\/\/

  Encrypted:  BYOEA NPTTE UMRMI EOSOS

  """
  #------------------------------------------------------------------------------
❷ # USER INPUT:

  # the string to be encrypted (paste between quotes):
❸ plaintext = """Let us cross over the river and rest under the shade of the trees
  """

❹ # END OF USER INPUT - DO NOT EDIT BELOW THIS LINE!
  #------------------------------------------------------------------------------
```

Listing 4-6: Docstring and user input section for rail_fence_cipher_encrypt.py

Start with a multiline docstring, placing an `r` (which stands for "raw") prefix before the first set of triple quotes ❶. Without this prefix, Pylint will complain bitterly about the \/\ slashes used further down. Fortunately, pydocstyle points this out so you can fix it (read Chapter 1 to learn all about Pylint and pydocstyle). If you want to know more about *raw strings*, see Section 2.4.1 in the Python docs (*https://docs.python.org/3.6/reference/lexical_analysis.html#string-and-bytes-literals*).

Next, separate the program's docstring and `import` statements from the input section with a line and let the user know they're on deck with an all-caps comment ❷. Clearly define the input requirement with comments and place the plaintext inside triple quotes to better accommodate long text strings ❸.

Finally, end the user input section with a declaration to that effect and caution to not edit anything below the following line ❹.

Encrypting a Message

Add Listing 4-7 to *rail_fence_cipher_encrypt.py* in order to handle the encryption processes.

rail_fence_cipher_encrypt.py, part 2

```
❶ def main():
      """Run program to encrypt message using 2-rail rail fence cipher."""
      message = prep_plaintext(plaintext)
      rails = build_rails(message)
      encrypt(rails)

❷ def prep_plaintext(plaintext):
      """Remove spaces & leading/trailing whitespace."""
    ❸ message = "".join(plaintext.split())
    ❹ message = message.upper()  # convention for ciphertext is uppercase
      print("\nplaintext = {}".format(plaintext))
      return message

❺ def build_rails(message):
      """Build strings with every other letter in a message."""
      evens = message[::2]
      odds = message[1::2]
    ❻ rails = evens + odds
      return rails

❼ def encrypt(rails):
      """Split letters in ciphertext into chunks of 5 & join to make string."""
    ❽ ciphertext = ' '.join([rails[i:i+5] for i in range(0, len(rails), 5)])
      print("ciphertext = {}".format(ciphertext))

❾ if __name__ == '__main__':
      main()
```

Listing 4-7: Defines functions to encrypt the plaintext message

To start, define a `main()` function to run the program ❶. Having a `main()` function gives you the flexibility to use this program as a module in another program later, should the need arise. This function calls three other functions: one to prepare the input plaintext, one to build the "rails" used by the cipher, and one to break the encrypted text into five-letter chunks.

Next, define a function to take the input string and prepare it for encryption ❷. This involves removing spaces ❸ and converting letters to uppercase (as in Step 2 in Figure 4-9) ❹. Then, after a newline, print the plaintext to the screen and return it.

Now, define a function to build two strings, as in Step 3 of Figure 4-9, by slicing `message` for evens (starting at 0 and stepping by 2) and for odds (starting at 1 and stepping by 2) ❺. The two strings are then concatenated in a new string, named `rails` ❻, and returned.

Define an encryption function that takes the `rails` string as an argument ❼. Use list comprehension to split the ciphertext into chunks of five (as in Step 5 of Figure 4-9) ❽. The encrypted text is then printed to the screen. Finish with the code to run the program as a module or in standalone mode ❾.

Here is the output from this program:

```
plaintext = Let us cross over the river and rest under the shade of the trees
ciphertext = LTSRS OETEI EADET NETEH DOTER EEUCO SVRHR VRNRS UDRHS AEFHT ES
```

The Rail Fence Cipher Decryption Code

The code in this section allows a user to enter a message encrypted with the rail fence cipher and have the plaintext printed in the interpreter window. This code is available for download along with the rest of the book's resources at *https://www.nostarch.com/impracticalpython/*.

Importing Modules, Instructing the User, and Getting Input

Listing 4-8 starts with instructions similar to those in the *rail_fence_cipher_encrypt.py* program (Listing 4-6), imports two modules, and gets the user input.

rail_fence_cipher_decrypt.py, part 1

```
r"""Decrypt a Civil War 'rail fence' type cipher.

This is for a 2-rail fence cipher for short messages.

Example plaintext:  'Buy more Maine potatoes'

Rail fence style:  B Y O E A N P T T E
                    U M R M I E O A O S

Read zigzag:       \/\/\/\/\/\/\/\/\/\/

Ciphertext:  BYOEA NPTTE UMRMI EOSOS

"""
❶ import math
import itertools

#--------------------------------------------------------------------------------
# USER INPUT:

# the string to be decrypted (paste between quotes):
❷ ciphertext = """LTSRS OETEI EADET NETEH DOTER EEUCO SVRHR VRNRS UDRHS AEFHT ES

"""

# END OF USER INPUT - DO NOT EDIT BELOW THIS LINE!
#--------------------------------------------------------------------------------
```

Listing 4-8: Imports modules, instructs the user, and gets user input

One difference here is that you need to import the `math` and `itertools` modules ❶. You'll use `math` for rounding. The `itertools` module is a group of functions in the Python Standard Library that create iterators for efficient looping. You'll use itertool's `zip_longest()` function during the decryption process.

The only other change is that the user should enter ciphertext, rather than plaintext ❷.

Decrypting a Message

Listing 4-9 defines the functions for preparing and decoding the ciphertext and finishes off *rail_fence_cipher_decrypt.py*.

rail_fence_cipher_decrypt.py, part 2

```
❶ def main():
      """Run program to decrypt 2-rail rail fence cipher."""
      message = prep_ciphertext(ciphertext)
      row1, row2 = split_rails(message)
      decrypt(row1, row2)

❷ def prep_ciphertext(ciphertext):
      """Remove whitespace."""
      message = "".join(ciphertext.split())
      print("\nciphertext = {}".format(ciphertext))
      return message

❸ def split_rails(message):
      """Split message in two, always rounding UP for 1st row."""
    ❹ row_1_len = math.ceil(len(message)/2)
    ❺ row1 = (message[:row_1_len])
      row2 = (message[row_1_len:])
      return row1, row2

❻ def decrypt(row1, row2):
      """Build list with every other letter in 2 strings & print."""
    ❼ plaintext = []
    ❽ for r1, r2 in itertools.zip_longest(row1, row2):
          plaintext.append(r1.lower())
          plaintext.append(r2.lower())
    ❾ if None in plaintext:
          plaintext.pop()
      print("rail 1 = {}".format(row1))
      print("rail 2 = {}".format(row2))
      print("\nplaintext = {}".format(''.join(plaintext)))

❿ if __name__ == '__main__':
      main()
```

Listing 4-9: Prepares, decodes, and prints the message

The `main()` function here ❶ is similar to the one used in the encryption program in Listing 4-7. Three functions are called: one to prepare the input string, one to "split the rails" in the rail fence cipher, and one to stitch the two rails back together into readable plaintext.

Start with a function that repeats the preprocessing steps used during encryption ❷. Remove the spaces between the five-letter chunks, as well as any other whitespace created during the pasting of the ciphertext, and print and return the ciphertext.

Next, you need to split the message back into two halves to reverse the encryption process ❸. As I mentioned in "The Strategy" on page 81, the extra letter in a message with an odd number of characters is assigned to the top row. To address the odd-numbered case, use the `math.ceil()` method ❹. "Ceil" stands for "ceiling," so when you divide by 2, the answer is always rounded up to the nearest integer. Assign this number to the `row_1_len` variable. Once you know the length of the first row, use that value and slicing to divide the `message` variable into two strings representing the rows ❺. End the function by returning the row variables.

Now it's just a matter of choosing and joining every other letter from the rows to stitch the plaintext back together. Define a `decrypt()` function and pass it the strings for `row1` and `row2` ❻. Start the translation process by making an empty list to hold the results ❼. Next, you need an easy way to deal with cases where the ciphertext has an odd number of letters—resulting in two rows of different lengths—because Python prevents you from looping through two uneven sequences by raising an index-out-of-range error. This is why we've imported the `itertools` module—its functions help with looping to circumvent this problem.

The `itertools.zip_longest()` function accepts two strings as arguments and loops through them without complaint, appending a null value (`None`) to the `plaintext` list when it gets to the end of the shorter string ❽. You don't want to print this null value, so if it's there, remove it using the `pop()` method you applied in the route cipher code ❾. Complete the decryption process by printing the two rows (rails) to the screen, followed by the decrypted ciphertext.

End with the standard code for running the program as a module or in stand-alone mode ❿. The output from the program is as follows:

```
ciphertext = LTSRS OETEI EADET NETEH DOTER EEUCO SVRHR VRNRS UDRHS AEFHT ES

rail 1 = LTSRSOETEIEADETNETEHDOTERE
rail 2 = EUCOSVRHRVRNRSUDRHSAEFHTES

plaintext = letuscrossovertheriverandrestundertheshadeofthetrees
```

Note that there will be no spaces between words, but that's okay—you don't want to leave the cryptanalyst feeling completely useless!

Summary

That completes our foray into Civil War ciphers. You wrote a program that helps a user decrypt a route cipher, and you gained valuable insights into how it works and how to hack it. You can implement an automated attack on the cipher in the following practice projects, but remember, with its many possible paths and use of code words, the Union route cipher is a tough nut to fully crack.

Next, you wrote programs to encrypt and decrypt two-rail fence ciphers. Given how tedious and error-prone the manual encryption and decryption processes are, having an automated way to do most of the work would have been valuable to both sides in the war. And to further address these types of issues, you wrote your code to be user-friendly to the inexperienced cryptanalyst or spy.

Further Reading

More beginner-level Python programs for working with transposition ciphers are available in *Cracking Codes with Python* (No Starch Press, 2018) by Al Sweigart.

Excellent and well-illustrated overviews of cryptography can be found in *Mysterious Messages: A History of Codes and Ciphers* (The Penguin Group, 2009) by Gary Blackwood and *The Code Book: The Science of Secrecy from Ancient Egypt to Quantum Cryptography* (Anchor, 2000) by Simon Singh.

The sites *http://www.civilwarsignals.org/pages/crypto/crypto.html* and *http://www.mathaware.org/mam/06/Sauerberg_route-essay.html* include descriptions of Edward Porter Alexander's attempt to solve a route cipher. Alexander was the father of the Confederate Army Signal Corps and a brilliant military innovator with many impressive accomplishments.

Practice Projects

Hone your cryptography skills with these projects. Solutions are available in the appendix and online.

Hacking Lincoln

In his book, *Mysterious Messages: A History of Codes and Ciphers*, Gary Blackwood reproduces an actual message sent by Abraham Lincoln and encrypted with a route cipher:

THIS OFF DETAINED ASCERTAIN WAYLAND CORRESPONDENTS OF AT WHY AND IF FILLS IT YOU GET THEY NEPTUNE THE TRIBUNE PLEASE ARE THEM CAN UP

Use the *route_cipher_decrypt.py* program to solve this cryptogram. The number of columns and rows must be factors of the message length, and the route starts in one of the corners, doesn't skip columns, and alternates direction with every column change. The code word definitions and plaintext solution can be found in the appendix.

Identifying Cipher Types

The sooner you know what type of cipher you're dealing with, the sooner you can break it. Word-transposition ciphers are easy to spot, but letter-transposition ciphers can look like letter-*substitution* ciphers. Fortunately, you can distinguish between the two by using the frequency of occurrence of letters in the ciphertext. Since the letters are just scrambled and not replaced in transposition ciphers, their frequency distribution will be the same as for the language in which the plaintext was written. An exception, however, is military messages, which use jargon and omit many common words. For these, you need a frequency table built from other military messages.

Write a Python program that takes a string of ciphertext as input and determines whether it is more likely to be a transposition cipher or a substitution cipher. Test it with the files *cipher_a.txt* and *cipher_b.txt*, downloadable from *https://www.nostarch.com/impracticalpython/*. A solution can be found in the appendix and online at the book's website in *identify_cipher_type_practice.py*.

Storing a Key as a Dictionary

Write a short script to break a route cipher key into two parts: one to record the column order and one to record the direction to read through the rows in the column (up or down). Store the column number as a dictionary key and the reading direction as the dictionary value. Have the program interactively request the key value for each column from the user. A solution can be found in the appendix and online in the file *key_dictionary_practice.py*.

Automating Possible Keys

To attempt to decipher a route cipher using any combination of columns in its path, you need to know what those combinations are, so you can enter them as arguments in a decryption function. Write a Python program that accepts an integer (such as the number of columns) and returns a collection of tuples. Each tuple should contain a unique ordering of column numbers, like `(1, 2, 3, 4)`. Include negative values—for example, `(2, -3, 4, -1)`—to capture encryption routes that go up columns versus down. A solution is provided in the appendix, with a downloadable version on the book's website in *permutations_practice.py*.

Route Transposition Cipher: Brute-Force Attack

Copy and modify the *route_cipher_decrypt.py* program to hack the route cipher in Figure 4-2. Rather than inputting a single key, loop through all possible keys—for an assumed number of columns—and print the results (use the earlier permutations code to generate the keys for this four-column cipher). The impact of switching the order of columns and allowing up-and-down paths through the transposition matrix is clearly illustrated in Figure 4-10. The dashed line is the factorial of the number of columns; the solid line captures the effect of reading up columns as well as down (captured by the inclusion of negative values in the key). If you only needed to deal with the factorial of 4, your job as a cryptanalyst would be easy. But as the cipher gets longer, the number of possible keys explodes. And some actual Union route ciphers had 10 or more columns!

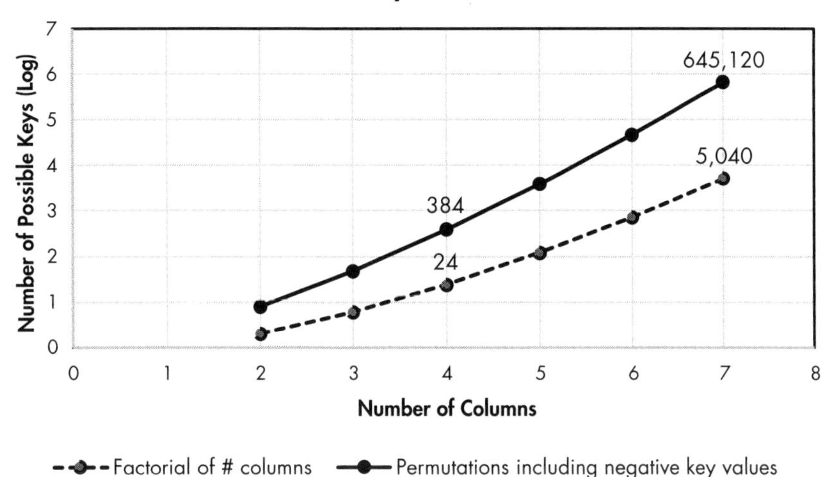

Figure 4-10: Number of possible keys versus number of columns for a route cipher

Here are four translations out of the 384 produced for the ciphertext in Figure 4-2:

```
using key = [-4, -1, -2, -3]
translated = IS HEADING FILLER VILLAGE YOUR SNOW SOUTH GODWIN ARE FREE TO YOU
WITH SUPPLIES GONE TRANSPORT ROANOKE JUST TO REST

using key = [1, 2, -3, 4]
translated = REST ROANOKE HEADING TO TRANSPORT WITH SNOW GONE YOU ARE FREE TO
GODWIN YOUR SUPPLIES SOUTH VILLAGE IS JUST FILLER

using key = [-1, 2, -3, 4]
translated = VILLAGE ROANOKE HEADING TO GODWIN WITH SNOW GONE YOU ARE FREE TO
TRANSPORT YOUR SUPPLIES SOUTH REST IS JUST FILLER

using key = [4, -1, 2, -3]
translated = IS JUST FILLER REST YOUR SUPPLIES SOUTH TRANSPORT ARE FREE TO YOU
WITH SNOW GONE GODWIN ROANOKE HEADING TO VILLAGE
```

The correct answer is present, but you can appreciate how hard it would be to pick it out quickly, given the use of code words and dummy words. Still, you did your job. Go have that mint julep or some sweet tea.

A solution to this project is provided in the appendix and at *https://www.nostarch.com/impracticalpython/* in *route_cipher_hacker.py*. You will also need the *perms.py* program, which is based on the previous practice project.

Challenge Projects

No solutions are provided for challenge projects.

Route Cipher Encoder

A greenhorn Union telegraph clerk needs to encrypt the following message, complete with code words (Table 4-1). Help them out by writing a program that takes the message as input and automatically substitutes the code words, fills the bottom row with dummy words, and transposes the words using the key `[-1, 3, -2, 6, 5, -4]`. Use a 6×7 matrix and make up your own dummy words.

> We will run the batteries at Vicksburg the night of April 16 and proceed to Grand Gulf where we will reduce the forts. Be prepared to cross the river on April 25 or 29. Admiral Porter.

Table 4-1: Code Words

Batteries	HOUNDS
Vicksburg	ODOR
April	CLAYTON
16	SWEET
Grand	TREE
Gulf	OWL
Forts	BAILEY
River	HICKORY
25	MULTIPLY
29	ADD
Admiral	HERMES
Porter	LANGFORD

Consider using a Python dictionary for the lexicon of code words in this table.

Three-Rail Fence Cipher

Write a version of the rail fence cipher that uses three rails (rows) instead of two. You can find a hint at *https://en.wikipedia.org/wiki/Rail_fence_cipher.*

5

ENCODING ENGLISH CIVIL WAR CIPHERS

In 1587, Mary, Queen of Scots, lost her head due to a scrap of paper. Fifty-five years later, Sir John Trevanion, a supporter of another beheaded monarch, Charles the First, had his head saved by a scrap of paper. What made the difference? Steganography.

Steganography is the time-tested practice of concealing messages so well that their existence isn't even suspected. The name is based on the Greek words for "covered writing," and a very literal Grecian example was to take wax-covered wooden tablets used for writing, scrape off the wax, write on the wood, and then cover the board with a new coating of smooth wax. A modern-day example is to embed a message in an image by subtly altering its color components. Even a simple 8-bit JPEG image contains more colors than the human eye can detect, so without digital processing or filtering, the message is essentially invisible.

In this chapter, you'll work with the *null cipher*, which isn't a cipher at all but a steganographic technique for concealing plaintext within other strings of noncipher material. *Null* means "none," so with a null cipher, you have chosen not to encrypt the message. The following is an example of a null cipher using the first letter in every word:

> **N**ice **u**ncles **l**ive **l**onger. **C**ruel, **i**nsensitive **p**eople **h**ave **e**ternal **r**egrets.

First, you'll write code that finds the hidden message that saved Sir John, and then you'll accomplish the much more difficult task of writing a null cipher. Finally, you'll get the opportunity to write a program that might have saved Mary's head, had she used the output.

Project #10: The Trevanion Cipher

Queen Mary relied on both steganography and encryption to protect her messages. The strategy was sound, but her application was flawed. Unknowingly, she relied on a double agent named Gilbert Gifford to smuggle her messages. Gifford first delivered them to Queen Elizabeth's spymaster, who cracked the cipher and replaced it with a forged message that enticed Mary to incriminate herself. The rest, as they say, is history.

For John Trevanion, the outcome was rosier. Sir John, a distinguished cavalier who aided Charles I against Oliver Cromwell in the English Civil War, was captured and imprisoned in Colchester Castle. The day before his execution, he received a letter from one of his friends. The letter was not smuggled in but delivered straight into the hands of his jailors, who examined it but didn't notice any deception. After reading it, Sir John asked for some time alone to pray in the chapel. When his jailors came back to fetch him, he had vanished.

Here is the message Sir John received:

> Worthie Sir John: Hope, that is the beste comfort of the afflicted, cannot much, I fear me, help you now. That I would saye to you, is this only: if ever I may be able to requite that I do owe you, stand not upon asking me. 'Tis not much I can do: but what I can do, bee you verie sure I wille. I knowe that, if deathe comes, if ordinary men fear it, it frights not you, accounting for it for a high honour, to have such a rewarde of your loyalty. Pray yet that you may be spared this soe bitter, cup. I fear not that you will grudge any sufferings; onlie if bie submission you can turn them away, 'tis the part of a wise man. Tell me, an if you can, to do for you anythinge that you wolde have done. The general goes back on Wednesday. Restinge your servant to command. R.T.

As you have probably guessed, this seemingly innocent letter contains a hidden message, revealed below in bold:

> Worthie Sir John: Ho**p**e, th**a**t is the beste comfort of the afflicted, ca**n**not much, I f**e**ar me, he**l**p you now. Th**a**t I would saye to you, is **t**his only: if **e**ver I may be able to requite that I do owe you, st**a**nd not upon asking me. 'Ti**s** not much I can do: bu**t** what I can do, be**e** you verie sure I wille. I k**n**owe that, if **d**eathe comes,

> if **o**rdinary men fear it, it **f**rights not you, ac**c**ounting for it for a high honour, to **h**ave such a rewarde of your loyalty. Pr**a**y yet that you may be spared this soe bitter, cu**p**. I f**e**ar not that you will grudge any sufferings; onl**i**e if bie submission you can turn them away, 'ti**s** the part of a wise man. Te**l**l me, an **i**f you can, to **d**o for you anythinge that you wolde have done. Th**e** general goes back on Wednesday. Re**s**tinge your servant to command. R.T.

This null cipher uses every third letter after a punctuation mark to let Sir John know that a "panel at east end of chapel slides." It's rumored that the remains of a narrow stairway were later discovered in a recess in a wall in the castle. The passage was blocked at the time of discovery, but it may have been Sir John's escape route around 1642.

This last-minute escape would not have been possible with a traditional cipher. Only by expertly concealing the message with steganography was its author able to get it so quickly into Sir John's hands. And the beauty of a null cipher is that, even if Sir John didn't know the pattern but suspected a message was present, he could have found it fairly quickly.

If Sir John's friend had been more careful, concealing encrypted ciphertext instead of plaintext, Sir John probably wouldn't have deciphered the message in the short time he had remaining—unless he'd been informed beforehand of the cipher type and key.

THE OBJECTIVE

Write code that finds the letters hidden after punctuation marks in a null cipher and lets the user choose the number of letters after a punctuation mark to search for a solution.

Strategy and Pseudocode

Null ciphers rely on a repeating pattern known to both the sender and receiver. For example, every third word may be part of the real message or, better, the last letter of every third word. In the Trevanion cipher, it's the third letter after a punctuation mark.

To find the Trevanion cipher, assume punctuation marks are the signal to begin counting, and then write code that locates every *n*th letter after the mark and saves those letters to a string or list. Once you've worked out how to do this, you can easily edit the code to work with any starting point, such as every capitalized word, every second letter per word, or the starting letter of every third word.

The only real point of contention involves punctuation marks. For instance, did the null cipher's writer *want* punctuation marks to be included in the plaintext? How do you handle a second punctuation mark within the desired count range? What happens if two punctuation marks occur in succession?

If you take a close look at the Trevanion cipher, you should see that there are double punctuations caused by the repeated use of the word *'tis.*

There is also a jumble of punctuation marks at the end of the message, where the writer provides his initials. To deal with this, Sir John and his friend may have established some rules before Sir John's incarceration, or Sir John just used trial and error to work them out.

Based on the end of the message, punctuation marks aren't included in the letter count. If Sir John's friend had intended them to be, then the hidden message would end with a capital *T*, because the *T* is three *characters* after a punctuation mark, and crucially not three *letters* after. This means that, if the reader encounters a punctuation mark within the count limit, they have to restart their count.

So these are the rules:

- Initiate a letter count with every punctuation mark.
- Reset the count if a punctuation mark is encountered.
- Punctuation marks cannot be part of the plaintext message.

Since you may not know what the letter count should be, write the code so that it checks all counts up through a limit the user provides. The pseudocode is fairly straightforward:

```
Load a text file and strip it of whitespace
Get user input on how many letters after punctuation to look ahead and examine
Loop through number of letters from 1 to this lookahead value
    Start an empty string to hold the translation
    Start a counter
    Start a ❶first-found marker and set to False
    Loop through characters in the text
        If character is punctuation
            Counter = 0
            First-found = True
        Otherwise, if ❷first-found is True
            Counter + 1
        If counter = lookahead value
            Add character to translation string
    Display translation for this lookahead value
```

Note that the first-found variable ❶ will remain `False` until a punctuation mark is encountered, after which it will be set to `True` ❷. This prevents the program from counting until the first punctuation mark is found.

Now you're ready to write the code!

The Trevanion Cipher Code

The code in this section will find a Trevanion-type null cipher encoded with a specific number of letters after each punctuation mark. You will also need the text file containing the Trevanion cipher. You can download both the script and the text file from *https://www.nostarch.com/impracticalpython/* as *null_cipher_finder.py* and *trevanion.txt*, respectively. Keep these files in the same folder.

Loading the Text

Listing 5-1 imports some useful modules and loads the text file containing the null cipher.

null_cipher_finder.py, part 1

```
❶ import sys
  import string

❷ def load_text(file):
      """Load a text file as a string."""
    ❸ with open(file) as f:
        ❹ return f.read().strip()
```

Listing 5-1: Imports modules and loads the null cipher text

First, import the now-familiar sys module so you can handle exceptions that may occur during user input ❶. Also import the `string` module to gain access to useful collections of constants, like letters and punctuation marks.

Next, define a function to load the text file containing the null cipher ❷. This function is similar to the one you used to load a dictionary file in Chapter 2. It will be called by the `main()`function later to actually load the file.

Start the `load_text()` function by using `with` to open the file ❸. By using `with`, you know the file will be automatically closed after it is loaded. Use `read()` to load the contents and `strip()` to remove leading and trailing whitespace. Note that you can do this on the same line with the `return` statement ❹.

Finding the Hidden Message

Listing 5-2 defines the function that finds the hidden message. It takes two arguments. The first is the message, which is the original text file as a string stripped of whitespace, and the second is the number of letters to check after a punctuation mark. This check value is obtained from the user as part of the `main()` function.

null_cipher_finder.py, part 2

```
def solve_null_cipher(message, lookahead):
    """Solve a null cipher based on number of letters after punctuation mark.

    message = null cipher text as string stripped of whitespace
    lookahead = endpoint of range of letters after punctuation mark to examine
    """
  ❶ for i in range(1, lookahead + 1):
      ❷ plaintext = ''
        count = 0
        found_first = False
      ❸ for char in message:
          ❹ if char in string.punctuation:
                count = 0
                found_first = True
          ❺ elif found_first is True:
                count += 1
          ❻ if count == i:
                plaintext += char
```

```
❼ print("Using offset of {} after punctuation = {}".
          format(i, plaintext))
  print()
```

Listing 5-2: Searches for hidden letters

Treat the lookahead value as the endpoint of a range in a for loop so that you can check all the intervening letters in the message for the presence of a hidden message. Set the range as (1, lookahead + 1) ❶; that way, you start with the first letter after a punctuation mark and include the user's choice in the evaluation.

Now, assign a few variables ❷. First, initialize an empty string to hold the translated plaintext. Then set a counter to 0. Finally, set a found_first variable to False. Remember that the program uses this variable to defer counting until the first punctuation mark is encountered.

Next, begin looping through the characters in the message ❸. If you encounter a punctuation mark, reset the counter to 0 and set found_first to True ❹. If you've found a punctuation mark already and the current character isn't punctuation, advance the counter by 1 ❺. If you've found the letter you're looking for—meaning the count has reached the current lookahead value (i)—add the letter to the plaintext string ❻.

When you've examined all the characters in the message for the current lookahead value, display the current key and the translation ❼.

Defining the main() Function

Listing 5-3 defines the main() function. You may remember from Chapter 3 that the main() function is like your program's project manager: it takes input, keeps track of progress, and tells the other functions when to work.

null_cipher_finder.py, part 3

```
def main():
    """Load text, solve null cipher."""
    # load & process message:
 ❶ filename = input("\nEnter full filename for message to translate: ")
 ❷ try:
        loaded_message = load_text(filename)
    except IOError as e:
        print("{}. Terminating program.".format(e), file=sys.stderr)
        sys.exit(1)
 ❸ print("\nORIGINAL MESSAGE =")
    print("{}".format(loaded_message), "\n")
    print("\nList of punctuation marks to check = {}".
          format(string.punctuation), "\n")

    # remove whitespace:
 ❹ message = ''.join(loaded_message.split())

    # get range of possible cipher keys from user:
 ❺ while True:
     ❻ lookahead = input("\nNumber of letters to check after " \
                          "punctuation mark: ")
     ❼ if lookahead.isdigit():
```

```
            lookahead = int(lookahead)
            break
        else:
          ❽ print("Please input a number.", file=sys.stderr)
    print()

    # run function to decode cipher
  ❾ solve_null_cipher(message, lookahead)
```

Listing 5-3: Defines the `main()` function

Start by asking the user for the name of the file (name + extension) ❶, and then use `try` to call the `load_text()` function ❷. If the file can't be found, print the error in red—for those using the IDLE window—and exit the program using `sys.exit(1)`, where the `1` indicates termination with an error.

Print the message followed by the list of punctuation marks in the `string` module ❸. Only the characters in this list will be recognized by the program as punctuation.

Next, take the loaded message and remove all spaces ❹. You're going to count only letters and punctuation marks, so spaces would just get in the way. Start a `while` loop that keeps asking the user for input in the event they enter a bad value ❺. Ask the user for the number of letters to check after a punctuation mark ❻. This will be treated as a range, starting with 1 and ending with the user's choice plus 1. If the input value is a digit ❼, turn it into an integer, since `input` returns a string. Then, use `break` to exit the loop.

If the user enters an invalid value, like "Bob," use a `print` statement to request a number and, for shell users, make the font red using `sys.stderr` ❽. The `while` loop will then repeat the request for input.

Pass the `lookahead` variable, along with the `message`, to the `solve_null_cipher` function ❾. Now all that's left is to call the `main()` function.

Running the main() Function

Back in the global space, complete the code by calling `main()`—but only if the program is run in stand-alone mode versus being imported into another program (Listing 5-4).

null_cipher_finder.py, part 4

```
if __name__ == '__main__':
    main()
```

Listing 5-4: Calls the `main()` function

The following is example output from the completed program, using the Trevanion cipher as input:

```
Enter full filename for message to translate: trevanion.txt

ORIGINAL MESSAGE =
Worthie Sir John: Hope, that is the beste comfort of the afflicted, cannot
much, I fear me, help you now. That I would saye to you, is this only: if ever
I may be able to requite that I do owe you, stand not upon asking me. 'Tis not
much I can do: but what I can do, bee you verie sure I wille. I knowe that,
```

```
if deathe comes, if ordinary men fear it, it frights not you, accounting for
it for a high honour, to have such a rewarde of your loyalty. Pray yet that
you may be spared this soe bitter, cup. I fear not that you will grudge any
sufferings; onlie if bie submission you can turn them away, 'tis the part of a
wise man. Tell me, an if you can, to do for you anythinge that you wolde have
done. The general goes back on Wednesday. Restinge your servant to command.
R.T.


List of punctuation marks to check = !"#$%&'()*+,-./:;<=>?@[\]^_`{|}~


Number of letters to check after punctuation mark: 4

Using offset of 1 after punctuation = HtcIhTiisTbbIiiiatPcIotTatTRRT

Using offset of 2 after punctuation = ohafehsftiuekfftcorufnienohe

Using offset of 3 after punctuation = panelateastendofchapelslides

Using offset of 4 after punctuation = etnapthvnnwyoerroayaitlfogt
```

In this output, the program has checked up to the fourth letter after a punctuation mark, but as you can see, it finds the solution using three letters after a punctuation mark.

Project #11: Writing a Null Cipher

Here is an unfinished example of a very weak null cipher based on the start of each word. Take a minute and try to complete the sentence:

H_________ e__________ l__________ p__________ m__________ e__________.

You probably found it difficult, because whether you use letters or even whole words, it takes hard work and time to produce a null cipher that doesn't read awkwardly and arouse suspicion. The heart of the problem is context. If the cipher is encapsulated within correspondence, that correspondence has to be coherent to avoid suspicion. That means it has to address a relevant topic and stay true to that topic for a reasonable number of sentences. As you probably saw, drafting even one sentence on any topic is no easy task!

The key is to credibly avoid context, and a good way to do this is with a list. No one expects a shopping list to be rigidly organized or make sense. Lists can also be tailored to the receiver. For example, correspondents might get into a discussion of books or movies and exchange lists of their favorites. A prisoner might start studying a foreign language and receive regular vocabulary lists from their tutor. A businessperson might get monthly inventories from one of their warehouses. With lists, context is honored even while words are shuffled so the correct letter is found in the correct place.

THE OBJECTIVE

Write code that hides a null cipher within a list of words.

The List Cipher Code

The *list_cipher.py* code, in Listing 5-5, embeds a null cipher within a list of dictionary words under the deception of vocabulary training. You'll also need the *load_dictionary.py* program you used in Chapters 2 and 3. You can download this file, along with the following script, from *https://www.nostarch.com/impracticalpython/*. Finally, you'll need one of the dictionary files you used in Chapters 2 and 3. You can find a list of suitable online dictionaries in Table 2-1 on page 20. All of the aforementioned files should be kept in the same folder.

list_cipher.py

```
❶ from random import randint
import string
import load_dictionary

# write a short message that doesn't contain punctuation or numbers!
input_message = "Panel at east end of chapel slides"

message = ''
for char in input_message:
  ❷ if char in string.ascii_letters:
        message += char
print(message, "\n")
❸ message = "".join(message.split())

❹ # open dictionary file
word_list = load_dictionary.load('2of4brif.txt')

# build vocabulary word list with hidden message
❺ vocab_list = []
❻ for letter in message:
    size = randint(6, 10)
  ❼ for word in word_list:
        if len(word) == size and word[2].lower() == letter.lower()\
        and word not in vocab_list:
            vocab_list.append(word)
            break

❽ if len(vocab_list) < len(message):
    print("Word List is too small. Try larger dictionary or shorter message!")
else:
    print("Vocabulary words for Unit 1: \n", *vocab_list, sep="\n")
```

Listing 5-5: Hides null cipher in a list

Start by importing the random module's randint() function ❶. This permits the (pseudo)random selection of an integer value. Then load the string module, for access to ASCII letters. Finish by importing your load_dictionary module.

Next, write a short secret message. Note that the associated comment forbids punctuation marks or numbers. Trying to use these with a dictionary file's contents would be problematic. So, filter out everything but letters by checking for membership in string.ascii_letters, which contains both uppercase and lowercase letters ❷:

```
'abcdefghijklmnopqrstuvwxyzABCDEFGHIJKLMNOPQRSTUVWXYZ'
```

Display the message and then remove the whitespace ❸. Load your dictionary file ❹ and start an empty list to hold the vocabulary words ❺.

Use a for loop to go through each letter in the message ❻. Name a size variable and assign it a random value between 6 and 10 using the randint() function. This variable will ensure the words are long enough to be credible as vocabulary words. You can set the maximum value higher if you wish.

Nest another for loop and use it to go through the dictionary words ❼, checking their length against the size variable and comparing the (lowercase) letter at index 2—the word's third letter—to the current (lowercase) letter in the message loop. You can change the index value on the word, but make sure it doesn't exceed the lowest possible size variable minus 1! A final comparison prevents the same word from being used twice. If the word passes the tests, append it to vocab_list and move on to the next letter in the message.

A typical dictionary file should contain enough words to encrypt a short message. But, to be safe, use a conditional to check that the length of vocab_list is not shorter than the length of the message ❽. If it's shorter, then you ran out of words before reaching the end of the message, and you need to print a warning for the user. Otherwise, print the list of words.

The List Cipher Output

Here is the output from the code (I've highlighted every third letter for readability, though the message is pretty easy to spot without any aid):

```
Panel at east end of chapel slides

Vocabulary words for Unit 1:

alphabets
abandoning
annals
aberration
ablaze
abandoned
```

```
acting
abetted
abasement
abseil
activated
adequately
abnormal
abdomen
abolish
affecting
acceding
abhors
abalone
ampersands
acetylene
allegation
absconds
aileron
acidifying
abdicating
adepts
absent
```

Using a font with a consistent character width and stacking the words really compromises the cipher. We'll look at ways to deal with this in "Saving Mary" on page 102.

Summary

In this chapter, you wrote a program that reveals the hidden message in a Trevanion-type null cipher. Then, you wrote a second program that generates a null cipher and conceals it within a language learner's vocabulary list. In the following practice projects, you can explore ways to make this list cipher more secure.

Further Reading

More details on Mary, Queen of Scots, and Sir John Trevanion can be found in *Mysterious Messages: A History of Codes and Ciphers* (The Penguin Group, 2009) by Gary Blackwood and *The Code Book: The Science of Secrecy from Ancient Egypt to Quantum Cryptography* (Anchor, 2000) by Simon Singh.

Practice Projects

Now that you're an expert on the null cipher, see if you can change the fate of Mary, Queen of Scots, and then sneak a look at Sir John's most secret correspondence.

Saving Mary

The best part of coding is thinking about problems and how to solve them. Let's revisit the sad case of Mary, Queen of Scots. Here's what we know:

- Mary was not allowed correspondence, so letters had to be smuggled in. This means that the traitorous Gilbert Gifford cannot be removed from the equation. Gifford was the only person Mary knew with the means to deliver her mail.
- Mary and her correspondents put too much faith in an insecure cipher and thus spoke too freely. With less confidence, they might have shown more forbearance.
- Mary's jailors, having an obvious cipher in their possession, assumed it contained incriminating material and kept working until they found it.

Gifford, the double agent, wasn't privy to the details of the ciphers Mary used. Now, assume Mary used a null cipher. If the correspondence was somewhat seditious—though not treasonously so—the message might have been overlooked by her captors. In the event a cursory examination was made, the use of a variable pattern might have sufficed to stymie the cryptanalysts.

As you have seen, it's easier to hide a null cipher in a list than in a letter. A list of families supporting Mary could serve the purpose. These could be known supporters or, in a Machiavellian twist, a mix of friends *and* enemies! This message wouldn't be openly seditious, but would be close enough so that a lack of encryption would suggest no form of encryption was being used at all.

For this practice project, write a program that embeds the message "Give your word and we rise" in a list of surnames. To hide the letters in the message, start at the second letter in the second name, move to the third letter in the third name, and then keep alternating between second and third letters for the remaining words.

In addition to the unused first name, include "Stuart" and "Jacob" as null words early in the list to help hide the presence of the cipher. Don't embed letters from the cipher in these null names and completely ignore them when choosing the letter position for the cipher in the following word; if the second letter was used in the word *before* the null name, use the third letter in the word *after* the null name. The null cipher would occupy the following bolded letters (the location of the null words is up to you, but don't let them affect the pattern):

```
First Second Third STUART Fourth Fifth JACOB Sixth Seventh Eighth
```

The program can print the list either vertically or horizontally. The name list should be credibly introduced with a short message, but that message shouldn't be part of the cipher.

The list of names can be downloaded from *https://www.nostarch.com/impracticalpython/* as *supporters.txt* and loaded as a standard dictionary file. You can find a solution in the appendix and online as *save_Mary_practice.py*.

The Colchester Catch

Instead of some ale-sotted dimwit, *you* are left in charge of the prisoner John Trevanion when the following letter arrives at Colchester Castle:

> Sir John: Odd and too hard, your lot. Still, we will band together and, like you, persevere. Who else could love their enemies, stand firm when all others fail, hate and despair? While we all can, let us feel hope. -R.T.

It seems clumsily phrased, even for the 17th century, and you decide to examine it more closely before passing it to your inmate.

Write a Python program that takes an input, *n*, and checks for and displays a null cipher based on the *n*th letter after the start of every *n*th word. For example, an input of `2` would find the bolded letters in this message:

T**h**e cold t**e**a didn't p**l**ease the o**l**d finicky w**o**man.

You can download the text file of the message from *https://nostarch.com/impracticalpython/* as *colchester_message.txt*. A solution can be found in the appendix and online as *colchester_practice.py*. Keep the text and Python files together in the same folder.

6

WRITING IN INVISIBLE INK

In the fall of 2012, the crime drama *Elementary* debuted on the CBS television network. A reimagining of the Sherlock Holmes mythos set in 21st-century New York, it starred Jonny Lee Miller as Holmes and Lucy Liu as his sidekick, Dr. Joan Watson. In a 2016 episode ("You've Got Me, Who's Got You?"), Morland Holmes, Sherlock's estranged father, hires Joan to find a mole in his organization. She quickly solves the case by discovering a Vigenère cipher in an email. But some fans of the show were dissatisfied: the Vigenère cipher is hardly subtle, so how could a man as intelligent as Morland Holmes miss finding it on his own?

In this project, you'll reconcile this dilemma using steganography, but not with a null cipher as in Chapter 5. To hide this message, you'll use a third-party module called `python-docx` that will allow you to conceal text by directly manipulating Microsoft Word documents using Python.

Project #12: Hiding a Vigenère Cipher

In the *Elementary* episode, Chinese investors hire Morland Holmes's consulting company to negotiate with the Colombian government for petroleum licenses and drilling rights. A year has passed, and at the last moment a competitor swoops in and clinches the deal, leaving the Chinese investors high and dry. Morland suspects betrayal by a member of his staff and asks Joan Watson to investigate alone. Joan identifies the mole by finding a Vigenère cipher in one of his emails.

SPOILER ALERT *The decrypted contents of the cipher are never mentioned, and the mole is murdered in a subsequent episode.*

The *Vigenère cipher,* also known as the unbreakable cipher, is arguably the most famous cipher of all time. Invented in the 16th century by the French scholar Blaise de Vigenère, it is a polyalphabetic substitution cipher that, in the most commonly used version, employs a single keyword. This keyword, such as *BAGGINS*, is printed repeatedly over the plaintext, as in the message shown in Figure 6-1.

B	A	G	G	I	N	S	B	A	G	G	I	N	S	B	A	G	G	I
s	**p**	**e**	**a**	**k**	**f**	**r**	**i**	**e**	**n**	**d**	**a**	**n**	**d**	**e**	**n**	**t**	**e**	**r**

Figure 6-1: A plaintext message with the Vigenère cipher keyword BAGGINS *printed above*

A table, or *tableau,* of the alphabet is then used to encrypt the message. Figure 6-2 is an example of the first five rows of a Vigenère tableau. Notice how the alphabet shifts to the left by one letter with each row.

	a	b	c	d	e	f	g	h	i	j	k	l	m	n	o	p	q	r	s	t	u	v	w	x	y	z
A	**A**	**B**	**C**	**D**	**E**	**F**	**G**	**H**	**I**	**J**	**K**	**L**	**M**	**N**	**O**	**P**	**Q**	**R**	**S**	**T**	**U**	**V**	**W**	**X**	**Y**	**Z**
B	**B**	**C**	**D**	**E**	**F**	**G**	**H**	**I**	**J**	**K**	**L**	**M**	**N**	**O**	**P**	**Q**	**R**	**S**	**T**	**U**	**V**	**W**	**X**	**Y**	**Z**	**A**
C	**C**	**D**	**E**	**F**	**G**	**H**	**I**	**J**	**K**	**L**	**M**	**N**	**O**	**P**	**Q**	**R**	**S**	**T**	**U**	**V**	**W**	**X**	**Y**	**Z**	**A**	**B**
D	**D**	**E**	**F**	**G**	**H**	**I**	**J**	**K**	**L**	**M**	**N**	**O**	**P**	**Q**	**R**	**S**	**T**	**U**	**V**	**W**	**X**	**Y**	**Z**	**A**	**B**	**C**
E	**E**	**F**	**G**	**H**	**I**	**J**	**K**	**L**	**M**	**N**	**O**	**P**	**Q**	**R**	**S**	**T**	**U**	**V**	**W**	**X**	**Y**	**Z**	**A**	**B**	**C**	**D**

Figure 6-2: Portion of a Vigenère tableau

The keyword letter above the plaintext letter determines which row to use for the encryption. For example, to encrypt the *s* in *speak,* note that the keyword letter above it is *B*. Go down to the B row and read across to where the plaintext *s* is at the top of the column. Use the *T* at the intersection for the ciphertext letter.

Figure 6-3 shows an example of the full message encrypted with the Vigenère cipher. This kind of text would surely draw attention and become an object of scrutiny if it were visible in a document!

```
TPKGS SJJETJ IAV FNZKZ
```

Figure 6-3: A message encrypted with the Vigenère cipher

The Vigenère cipher remained unbroken until the mid-19th century, when Charles Babbage, inventor of the precursor to the computer, realized that a short keyword used with a long message would result in repeating patterns that could reveal the length of the keyword and, ultimately, the key itself. The breaking of the cipher was a tremendous blow to professional cryptography, and no significant advancements were made in the field during the Victorian era of the original Holmes and Watson.

The presence of this cipher is what causes "suspension of disbelief" issues with the *Elementary* episode. Why would an outside consultant be needed to find such a clearly suspicious email? Let's see if we can come up with a plausible explanation using Python.

THE OBJECTIVE

Assume you are the corporate mole in the episode and use Python to hide a secret message summarizing bid details within an official-looking text document. Start with an unencrypted message and finish with an encrypted version.

The Platform

Your program should work with ubiquitous word-processing software, as the output needs to be sharable between different corporations. This implies use of the Microsoft Office Suite for Windows or compatible versions for macOS or Linux. And restricting the output to a standard Word document makes hardware issues Microsoft's responsibility!

Accordingly, this project was developed with Word 2016 for Windows, and the results checked with Word for Mac v16.16.2. If you don't have a license for Word, you can use the free Microsoft Office Online app, available at *https://products.office.com/en-us/office-online.*

If you currently use alternatives to Word, like LibreOffice Writer or OpenOffice Writer, you can open and view the Word (*.docx*) files used and produced in this project; however, the hidden message will most likely be compromised, as discussed in "Detecting the Hidden Message" on page 119.

The Strategy

You're an accountant with a beginner's knowledge of Python, and you work for a very intelligent and suspicious man. The project you work on is highly proprietary, with controls—such as email filters—to maintain confidentiality. And if you manage to sneak out a message, a thorough investigation will surely follow. So, you need to hide a clearly suspicious message in an email, either directly or as an attachment, yet evade initial detection and later internal audits.

Here are some constraints:

- You can't send the message directly to the competing corporation, only to an intermediary.
- You need to scramble the message to evade the email filters that will search for keywords.
- You need to hide the encrypted message from sight so as not to arouse suspicion.

The intermediary would be easy to set up, and free encryption sites are easy to find on the internet—but the last item is more problematic.

Steganography is the answer, but as you saw in the previous chapter, hiding even a short message in a null cipher is no easy task. Alternative techniques involve shifting lines of text vertically or words horizontally by small amounts, changing the length of letters, or using the file's metadata—but you're an accountant with limited knowledge of Python and even less time. If only there were an easy way, like invisible ink in the old days.

Creating Invisible Ink

Invisible ink, in this age of electronic ink, might be just crazy enough to work! An invisible font would easily foil a visual perusal of online documents and won't even exist in paper printouts. Since the contents would be encrypted, digital filters looking for keywords like *bid* or the Spanish names of the producing oil basins would find nothing. And best of all, invisible ink is easy to use—just set the foreground text to the background color.

Formatting text and changing its color requires a word processor like Microsoft Word. To make invisible electronic ink in Word, you just need to select a character, word, or line and set the font color to white. The recipient of the message would then need to select the whole document and use the Highlighter tool (see Figure 6-4) to paint the selected text black, thus concealing the standard black letters and bringing the hidden white letters into view.

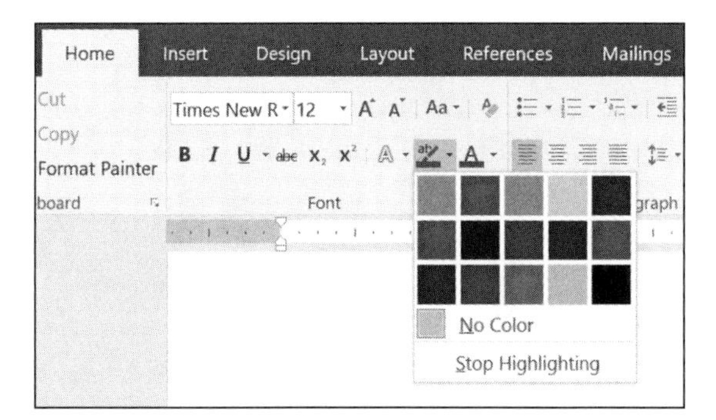

Figure 6-4: The Text Highlight Color tool in Word 2016

Just selecting the document in Word won't reveal the white text (Figure 6-5), so someone would have to be very suspicious indeed to find these hidden messages.

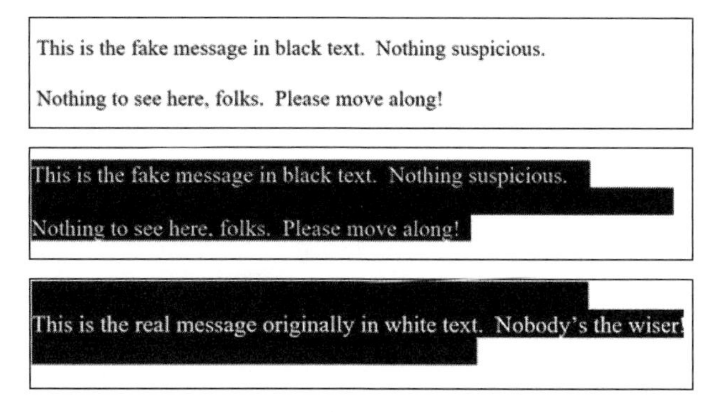

Figure 6-5: Top: a portion of a Word document with the fake message visible; middle: the document selected with CTRL*-A; bottom: the real message revealed using the Highlighter tool with the highlight color set to black*

Of course, you can accomplish all this in a word processor alone, but there are two cases where a Pythonic approach is preferable: 1) when you have to encrypt a long message and don't want to manually insert and hide all the lines and 2) when you need to send more than a few messages. As you'll see, a short Python program will greatly simplify the process!

Considering Font Types, Kerning, and Tracking

Placing the invisible text is a key design decision. One option is to use the spaces between the visible words of the fake message, but this could trigger spacing-related issues that would make the final product look suspicious.

Proportional fonts use variable character widths to improve readability. Example fonts are Arial and Times New Roman. *Monospace fonts* use a constant character width to support the alignment of text and the recognition of individual characters, especially thin ones such as the (or { characters. As a result, monospace fonts are popular in programming interfaces. Example fonts are Consolas and Courier New.

Kerning is a typographical process for adjusting the spacing and overlap between individual character glyphs in order to improve their visual appeal. A process called *tracking* is used to adjust the character spacing across entire lines or blocks of text for the same purpose. These adjustments aid legibility and readability, ensuring that letters aren't so close together that they're indistinguishable or so far apart that words aren't recognizable. Note that we read words, not letters. If you doubt it, read this: peopl raed wrds nt lttrs. Of corase, contxt hlps.

Kerning between pairs of letters is performed first, followed by tracking, during which the relative kerning of the letter pairs is preserved. As mentioned earlier, these variable widths and automatic corrections can cause problems when you're trying to hide characters between words that use proportional fonts:

To a great mind nothing is little.	*Proportional font with no hidden letters*
To a great mind nothing is little.	*Proportional font with hidden letters between words*
To$a3great.mind2nothingKis little.	*Hidden letters revealed ($3.2K)*
`To a great mind nothing is little.`	*Monospace font with no hidden letters*
`To a great mind nothing is little.`	*Monospace font with hidden letters between words.*
`To$a3great.mind2nothingKis little.`	*Hidden letters revealed ($3.2K)*

If you use a monospace font, the consistent spacing provides a convenient hiding place. But since professional correspondence is more likely to use proportional fonts, the invisible ink technique should focus on the more easily controlled spaces between lines.

Using empty lines between paragraphs is the easiest method to program and to read, and it shouldn't require a long fake message because you can summarize the salient points of a bid succinctly. This is important since you don't want empty pages appended to your visible fake message. Consequently, the footprint for your hidden message should be smaller than for your fake one.

Avoiding Issues

When you're developing software, a good question to ask repeatedly is "How can the user screw this up?" One thing that can go wrong here is that the encryption process will change the letters in your hidden message so that kerning and tracking adjustments may push a word past the line break, causing an automatic line wrap. This will result in uneven and suspicious-looking spaces between paragraphs in the fake message. One way to avoid this is to press ENTER a little early as you're typing in each line of the real message. This will leave some space at the end of the line to accommodate changes due to encryption. Of course, you'll still need to verify the results. Assuming code works is as risky as assuming James Bond is dead!

Manipulating Word Documents with python-docx

A free third-party module called `python-docx` allows Python to manipulate Microsoft Word (*.docx*) files. To download and install the third-party modules mentioned in this book, you'll use the Preferred Installer Program (pip), a package management system that makes it easy to install Python-based software. For Python 3 on Windows and macOS, versions 3.4 and later come with pip preinstalled; for Python 2, pip preinstallation starts with version 2.7.9. Linux users may have to install pip separately. If you find you need to install or upgrade pip, see the instructions at *https://pip.pypa.io/en/stable/installing/* or do an online search on installing pip on your particular operating system.

With the pip tool, you can install `python-docx` by simply running **`pip install python-docx`** in a command, PowerShell, or terminal window, depending on your operating system. Online instructions for `python-docx` are available at *https://python-docx.readthedocs.io/en/latest/*.

For this project, you need to understand the `paragraph` and `run` objects. The `python-docx` module organizes data types using three objects in the following hierarchy:

- `document`: The whole document with a list of `paragraph` objects
- `paragraph`: A block of text separated by the use of the ENTER key in Word; contains a list of `run` object(s)
- `run`: A connected string of text with the same *style*

A `paragraph` is considered a *block-level* object, which `python-docx` defines as follows: "a block-level item flows the text it contains between its left and right edges, adding an additional line each time the text extends beyond its right boundary. For a `paragraph` object, the boundaries are generally the page margins, but they can also be column boundaries if the page is laid out in columns, or cell boundaries if the `paragraph` occurs inside a table cell. A table is also a block-level object."

A `paragraph` object has a variety of properties that specify its placement within a container—typically a page—and the way it divides its contents into separate lines. You can access the formatting properties of a `paragraph` with the `ParagraphFormat` object available through the `ParagraphFormat` property of the `paragraph`, and you can set all the `paragraph` properties using a *paragraph style grouping* or apply them directly to a `paragraph`.

A `run` is an *inline-level* object that occurs within paragraphs or other block-level objects. A `run` object has a read-only `font` property providing access to a `font` object. A `font` object provides properties for getting and setting the character formatting for that `run`. You'll need this feature for setting your hidden message's text color to white.

Style refers to a collection of attributes in Word for paragraphs and characters (`run` objects) or a combination of both. Style includes familiar attributes such as font, color, indention, line spacing, and so on. You may have noticed groupings of these displayed in the Styles pane on Word's Home ribbon (see Figure 6-6). Any change in style—to even a single letter—requires the creation of a new `run` object. Currently, only styles that are in the opened *.docx* file are available. This may change in future versions of `python-docx`.

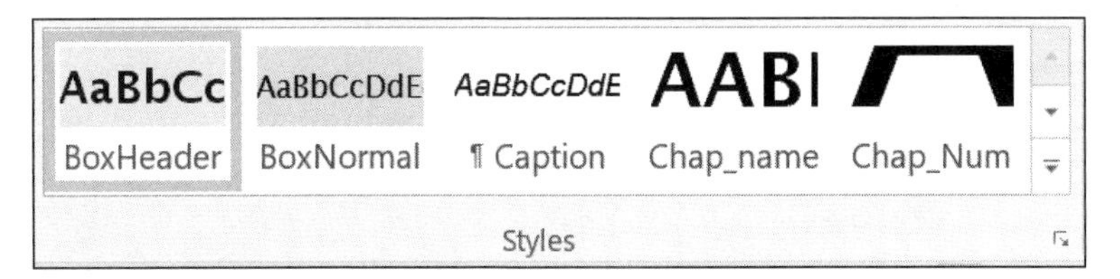

Figure 6-6: The Styles pane in Microsoft Word 2016

You can find full documentation on the use of styles in `python-docx` at *http://python-docx.readthedocs.io/en/latest/user/styles-using.html.*

Here's an example of paragraphs and runs as `python-docx` sees them:

I am a single paragraph of one run because all my text is the same style.

I am a single paragraph with two runs. ***I am the second run because my style changed to bold.***

I am a single paragraph with three runs. ***I am the second run because my style changed to bold. The third run is my last*** *word.*

If any of this seems unclear, don't fret. You don't need to know `python-docx` in any detail. As with any piece of code, you mainly need to know *what you want to do.* An online search should yield plenty of useful suggestions and complete samples of code.

NOTE *For this to work smoothly, don't change styles within the real (hidden) message and make sure you end every line in a hard return by manually pressing the* ENTER *key. Unfortunately, Word doesn't have a special character for soft returns caused by automatic word wrapping. So, you can't go into an existing Word document with automatic line breaks and use Find and Replace to change them all to hard returns. Such is the life of a mole.*

Downloading the Assets

The external files you'll need are downloadable from *https://www.nostarch.com/impracticalpython/* and should be saved in the same folder as the code:

template.docx An empty Word doc formatted with official Holmes Corporation styles, fonts, and margins

fakeMessage.docx The fake message, without letterhead and date, in a Word document

realMessage.docx The real message in plaintext, without letterhead and date, in a Word document

realMessage_Vig.docx The real message encrypted with the Vigenère cipher

example_template_prep.docx An example of the fake message used to create the template document (the program doesn't require this file to run)

NOTE *If you're using Word 2016, an easy way to make a blank template file is to write the fake message (including letterhead) and save the file. Then delete all the text and save the file again with a different name. When you assign this blank file to a variable with* `python-docx`*, all the existing styles will be retained. Of course, you could use a template file with the letterhead already included, but for the purpose of learning more about* `python-docx`*, we'll build the letterhead here using Python.*

Take a moment to view these first four documents in Word. These files comprise the inputs to the *elementary_ink.py* program. The fake and real messages—the second and third items listed—are also shown in Figures 6-7 and 6-8.

Dear Mr. Gerard:

I received your CV on Monday. It is very impressive, but I am sorry to inform you that Mr. Holmes is not looking for additional staff at this time.

While we do not normally accept unsolicited applications, I will keep your CV on file for future consideration. If it is convenient, please send me a list of references, especially those pertaining to skills in negotiation, accounting, and data mining (preferably using the Python programming language). A recent photograph is also recommended.

Best of luck to you. Feel free to check back at this time next year in the event a position becomes available. Use this email address, and include your name and the word "check-back" in the subject line.

Sincerely yours,

Emil Kurtz
Associate Director
International Affairs

Figure 6-7: The "fake" text in the fakeMessage.docx *file*

The Colombian deal will be for 2 new venture wildcat wells, one each in the Llanos & Magdalena Basins. These wells include a carry of thirty percent for the national oil company and will test at least 3 K meters of vertical section. In return, the client will be permitted to drill ten wells in the productive Putumayo province, earning a sixty % interest with a fifty percent royalty rate, increasing to the standard eighty five percent royalty five years after start of production in each well.

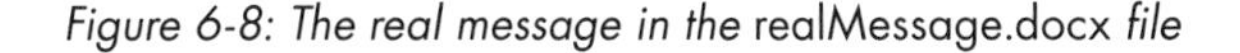

Figure 6-8: The real message in the realMessage.docx *file*

Note that the real message contains some numbers and special characters. These won't be encrypted with the Vigenère tableau we'll use, and I've included them to make that point. Ideally, they would be spelled out (for example, "three" for "3" and "percent" for "%") for maximum secrecy when we add the Vigenère cipher later.

The Pseudocode

The following pseudocode describes how to load the two messages and the template document, interleave and hide the real message in blank lines using a white font, and then save the hybrid message.

```
Build assets:
In Word, create an empty doc with desired formatting/styles (template)
In Word, create an innocuous fake message that will be visible & have enough
blank lines to hold the real message
In Word, create the real message that will be hidden
```

```
Import docx to allow manipulation of Word docs with Python
Use docx module to load the fake & real messages as lists
Use docx to assign the empty doc to a variable
Use docx to add letterhead banner to empty doc
Make counter variable for lines in real message
Define function to format paragraph spacing with docx
For line in fake message:
    If line is blank and there are still lines in the real message:
        Use docx & counter to fill blank with line from real message
        Use docx to set real message font color to white
        Advance counter for real message
    Otherwise:
        Use docx to write fake line
    Run paragraph spacing function
Use docx to save final Word document
```

The Code

The *elementary_ink.py* program in Listing 6-1 loads the real message, the fake message, and the empty template document. It hides the real message in the blank lines of the fake message using a white font, and then saves the hybrid message as an innocuous and professional-looking piece of correspondence that can be attached to an email. You can download the code from *https://www.nostarch.com/impracticalpython/*.

Importing python-docx, Creating Lists, and Adding a Letterhead

Listing 6-1 imports python-docx, turns the lines of text in the fake and real messages into list items, loads the template document that sets the styles, and adds a letterhead.

elementary_ink.py, part 1

```
  import docx
❶ from docx.shared import RGBColor, Pt

❷ # get text from fake message & make each line a list item
  fake_text = docx.Document('fakeMessage.docx')
  fake_list = []
  for paragraph in fake_text.paragraphs:
      fake_list.append(paragraph.text)

❸ # get text from real message & make each line a list item
  real_text = docx.Document('realMessage.docx')
  real_list = []
  for paragraph in real_text.paragraphs:
    ❹ if len(paragraph.text) != 0:  # remove blank lines
          real_list.append(paragraph.text)

❺ # load template that sets style, font, margins, etc.
  doc = docx.Document('template.docx')

❻ # add letterhead
```

```
    doc.add_heading('Morland Holmes', 0)
    subtitle = doc.add_heading('Global Consulting & Negotiations', 1)
    subtitle.alignment = 1
    doc.add_heading('', 1)
❼ doc.add_paragraph('December 17, 2015')
    doc.add_paragraph('')
```

Listing 6-1: Imports python-docx, loads important .docx files, and adds a letterhead

After importing the docx module—not as "python-docx"—use docx.shared to gain access to the color (RGBColor) and length (Pt) objects in the docx module ❶. These will allow you to change the font color and set the spacing between lines. The next two code blocks load the fake ❷ and real ❸ message Word documents as lists. Where the ENTER key was pressed in each Word document determines what items will be in these lists. For the real message to be hidden, remove any blank lines so that your message will be as short as possible ❹. Now you can use list indexes to merge the two messages and keep track of which is which.

Next, load the template document that contains the preestablished styles, fonts, and margins ❺. The docx module will write to this variable and ultimately save it as the final document.

With the inputs loaded and prepped, format the letterhead of the final document to match that of the Holmes Corporation ❻. The add_heading() function adds a heading style paragraph with text and integer arguments. Integer 0 designates the highest-level heading, or Title style, inherited from the template document. The subtitle is formatted with 1, the next heading style available, and is center aligned, again with the integer 1 (0 = left justified, 2 = right justified). Note that, when you add the date, you don't need to supply an integer ❼. When you don't provide an argument, the default is to inherit from the existing style hierarchy, which in the template is left justified. The other statements in this block just add blank lines.

Formatting and Interleaving the Messages

Listing 6-2 does the real work, formatting the spacing between lines and interleaving the messages.

elementary_ink.py, part 2

```
❶ def set_spacing(paragraph):
        """Use docx to set line spacing between paragraphs."""
        paragraph_format = paragraph.paragraph_format
        paragraph_format.space_before = Pt(0)
        paragraph_format.space_after = Pt(0)

❷ length_real = len(real_list)
   count_real = 0  # index of current line in real (hidden) message

   # interleave real and fake message lines
   for line in fake_list:
     ❸ if count_real < length_real and line == "":
         ❹ paragraph = doc.add_paragraph(real_list[count_real])
         ❺ paragraph_index = len(doc.paragraphs) - 1
```

```
        # set real message color to white
        run = doc.paragraphs[paragraph_index].runs[0]
        font = run.font
    ❻ font.color.rgb = RGBColor(255, 255, 255) # make it red to test
    ❼ count_real += 1
    else:
    ❽ paragraph = doc.add_paragraph(line)

  ❾ set_spacing(paragraph)

❿ doc.save('ciphertext_message_letterhead.docx')

print("Done")
```

Listing 6-2: Formats paragraphs and interleaves lines of fake and real messages

Define a function that formats the spacing between paragraphs using `python-docx`'s `paragraph_format` property ❶. Line spacing before and after the hidden line is set to `0` points to ensure that the output doesn't have suspiciously large gaps between paragraphs, like the ones on the left-hand side of Figure 6-9.

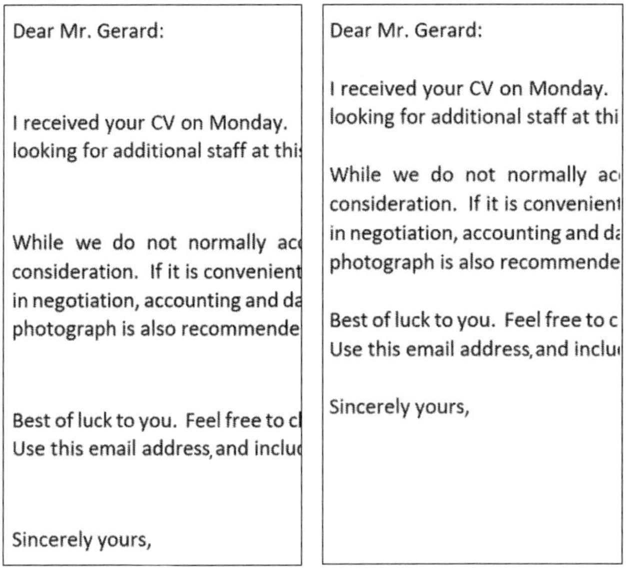

Figure 6-9: Fake message line spacing without `python-docx` paragraph formatting (left) vs. with formatting (right)

Next, define the working space by getting the length of the list that holds the real message ❷. Remember that the hidden real message needs to be shorter than the visible fake message so that there are sufficient blank lines to hold it. Follow this by initiating a counter. The program will use it to keep track of which line (list item) it's currently processing in the real message.

Since the list made from the fake message is the longest and sets the dimensional space for the real message, loop through the fake message using two conditionals: 1) whether you've reached the end of the real message and 2) whether a line in the fake list is blank ❸. If there are still real message lines and the fake message line is blank, use `count_real` as an index for `real_list` and use `python-docx` to add it to the document ❹.

Get the index of the line you just added by taking the length of `doc.paragraphs` and subtracting 1 ❺. Then use this index to set the real message line to a `run` object (it will be the first `run` item `[0]` in the list, as the real message uses a single style) and set its font color to white ❻. Since the program has now added a line from the real list in this block, the `count_real` counter advances by 1 ❼.

The subsequent `else` block addresses the case where the line chosen from the fake list in the `for` loop isn't empty. In this case, the fake message line is added directly to the paragraph ❽. Finish the `for` loop by calling the line spacing function, `set_spacing()` ❾.

Once the length of the real message has been exceeded, the `for` loop will continue to add the remainder of the fake message—in this case, Mr. Kurtz's signature info—and save the document as a Word *.docx* file in the final line ❿. Of course, in real life, you'd want to use a less suspicious filename than *ciphertext_message_letterhead.docx*!

Note that, because you're using a `for` loop based on the fake message, appending any more hidden lines after the `for` loop ends—that is, after you reach the end of the items in the fake list—is impossible. If you want more space, you must enter hard returns at the bottom of the fake message, but be careful not to add so many that you force a page break and create a mysterious empty page!

Run the program, open the saved Word document, use CTRL-A to select all the text, and then set the Highlight color (see Figure 6-4) to dark gray to see both messages. The secret message should be revealed (Figure 6-10).

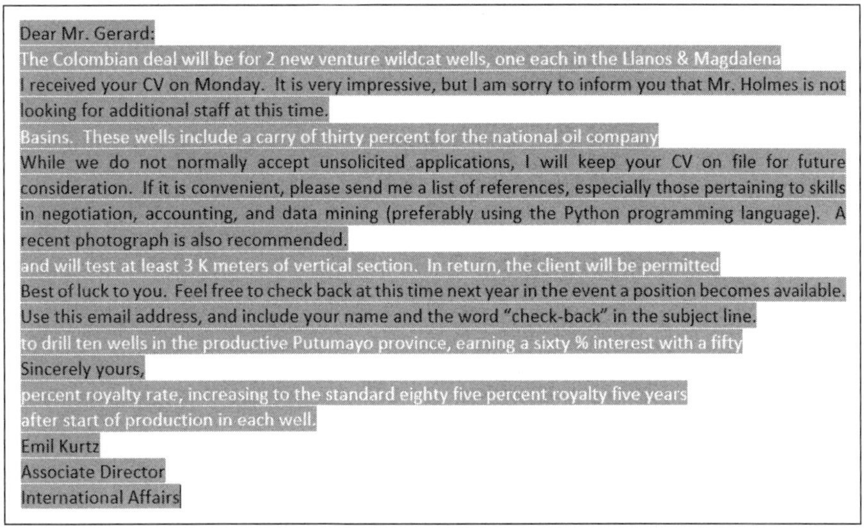

Dear Mr. Gerard:
The Colombian deal will be for 2 new venture wildcat wells, one each in the Llanos & Magdalena
I received your CV on Monday. It is very impressive, but I am sorry to inform you that Mr. Holmes is not looking for additional staff at this time.
Basins. These wells include a carry of thirty percent for the national oil company
While we do not normally accept unsolicited applications, I will keep your CV on file for future consideration. If it is convenient, please send me a list of references, especially those pertaining to skills in negotiation, accounting, and data mining (preferably using the Python programming language). A recent photograph is also recommended.
and will test at least 3 K meters of vertical section. In return, the client will be permitted
Best of luck to you. Feel free to check back at this time next year in the event a position becomes available. Use this email address, and include your name and the word "check-back" in the subject line.
to drill ten wells in the productive Putumayo province, earning a sixty % interest with a fifty
Sincerely yours,
percent royalty rate, increasing to the standard eighty five percent royalty five years
after start of production in each well.
Emil Kurtz
Associate Director
International Affairs

Figure 6-10: Word document highlighted in dark gray to show both the fake message and the unencrypted real message

Adding the Vigenère Cipher

The code so far uses the plaintext version of the real message, so anyone who changes the document's highlight color will be able to read and understand the sensitive information in it. Since you know Mr. Kurtz encrypted this using the Vigenère cipher, go back and alter the code to replace the plaintext with the encrypted text. To do this, find the following line:

```
real_text = docx.Document('realMessage.docx')
```

This line loads the real message as plaintext, so change the filename to the one shown here in bold:

```
real_text = docx.Document('realMessage_Vig.docx')
```

Rerun the program and again reveal the hidden text by selecting the whole document and setting the Highlight color to dark gray (Figure 6-11).

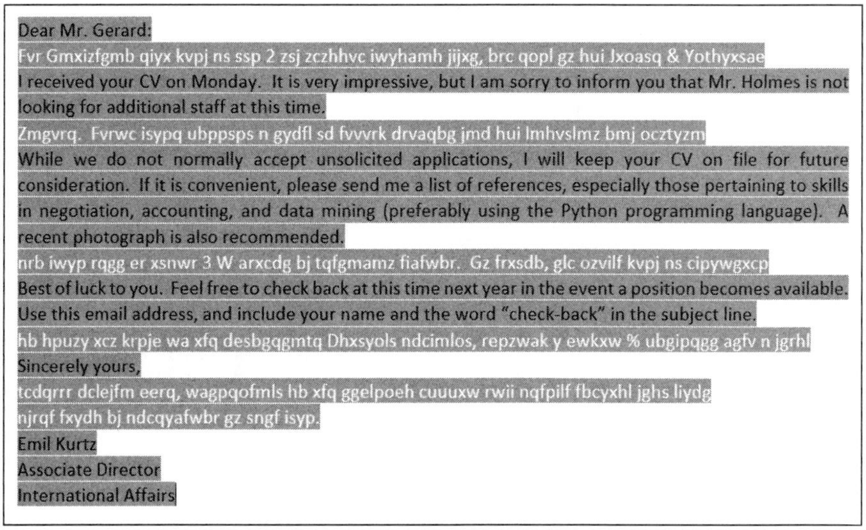

Dear Mr. Gerard:
Fvr Gmxizfgmb qiyx kvpj ns ssp 2 zsj zczhhvc iwyhamh jijxg, brc qopl gz hui Jxoasq & Yothyxsae
I received your CV on Monday. It is very impressive, but I am sorry to inform you that Mr. Holmes is not looking for additional staff at this time.
Zmgvrq. Fvrwc isypq ubppsps n gydfl sd fvvvrk drvaqbg jmd hui lmhvslmz bmj ocztyzm
While we do not normally accept unsolicited applications, I will keep your CV on file for future consideration. If it is convenient, please send me a list of references, especially those pertaining to skills in negotiation, accounting, and data mining (preferably using the Python programming language). A recent photograph is also recommended.
nrb iwyp rqgg er xsnwr 3 W arxcdg bj tqfgmamz fiafwbr. Gz frxsdb, glc ozvilf kvpj ns cipywgxcp
Best of luck to you. Feel free to check back at this time next year in the event a position becomes available. Use this email address, and include your name and the word "check-back" in the subject line.
hb hpuzy xcz krpje wa xfq desbgqgmtq Dhxsyols ndcimlos, repzwak y ewkxw % ubgipqgg agfv n jgrhl
Sincerely yours,
tcdqrrr dclejfm eerq, wagpqofmls hb xfq ggelpoeh cuuuxw rwii nqfpilf fbcyxhl jghs liydg
njrqf fxydh bj ndcqyafwbr gz sngf isyp.
Emil Kurtz
Associate Director
International Affairs

Figure 6-11: Word document highlighted in dark gray to show both the fake message and the encrypted real message

The secret message should be visible but unreadable to anyone who cannot interpret the cipher. Compare the encrypted message in Figure 6-11 to the unencrypted version in Figure 6-10. Note that numbers and the % sign occur in both versions. These were retained to demonstrate the potential pitfalls related to the encryption choice. You would want to augment the Vigenère cipher to include these characters—or just spell them out. That way, even if your message is discovered, you leave as few clues as possible as to the subject matter.

If you want to encode your own message with the Vigenère cipher, do an internet search for "online Vigenère encoder." You'll find multiple sites, such as *http://www.cs.du.edu/~snarayan/crypt/vigenere.html*, that let you type or paste in plaintext. And if you want to write your own Python program for encrypting with the Vigenère cipher, see *Cracking Codes with Python* (No Starch Press, 2018) by Al Sweigart.

If you play around with your own real messages, encrypted or not, make sure you're using the same font as in the fake message. A font is both a typeface, like Helvetica Italic, and a size, such as 12. Remember from "Considering Font Types, Kerning, and Tracking" on page 109 that if you try to mix fonts, especially proportional and monospace fonts, the hidden message lines may wrap, resulting in uneven spacing between paragraphs of the real message.

Detecting the Hidden Message

Could Joan Watson, or any other detective, have found your hidden message quickly? The truth is, probably not. In fact, as I write these words, I am watching an episode of *Elementary* where Joan is busy investigating a company by reading through a box of email printouts! The use of the Vigenère cipher may have been just a bit of lazy writing in an overall intelligently crafted series. Still, we can speculate on what might give you away.

Since the final bid was probably not sent until close to the bid date, the search could be limited to correspondence sent *after* the bid was finalized, thereby eliminating a lot of noise. Of course, a detective won't know exactly what they're looking for—or even if there *is* a mole—which leaves a large search space. And there's always the possibility that the information was passed in a phone conversation or clandestine meeting.

Assuming there was a manageable volume of email and a hidden-message hypothesis was being pursued, an investigator might detect your invisible ink in several ways. For example, the Word spellchecker will not flag the white, nonsensical encrypted words as long as they haven't been made visible. If, as a check, you swiped and reset the font color on some of the hidden words, they will be permanently compromised, even after their color has been restored to white. The spellchecker will underline them with an incriminating red squiggly line (see Figure 6-12).

I received your CV on Monday. It is very impressive, but I am sorry to inform you that Mr. Holmes is not looking for additional staff at this time.

While we do not normally accept unsolicited applications, I will keep your CV on file for future consideration. If it is convenient, please send me a list of references, especially those pertaining to skills in negotiation, accounting, and data mining (preferably using the Python programming language). A recent photograph is also recommended.

Figure 6-12: Previously revealed invisible encrypted words underlined by the Word Spelling and Grammar tool

If the investigating detective uses an alternative to Word to open the document, the product's spellchecker will most likely reveal the hidden words (see Figure 6-13). This risk is mitigated somewhat by the dominance of Microsoft Word in the marketplace.

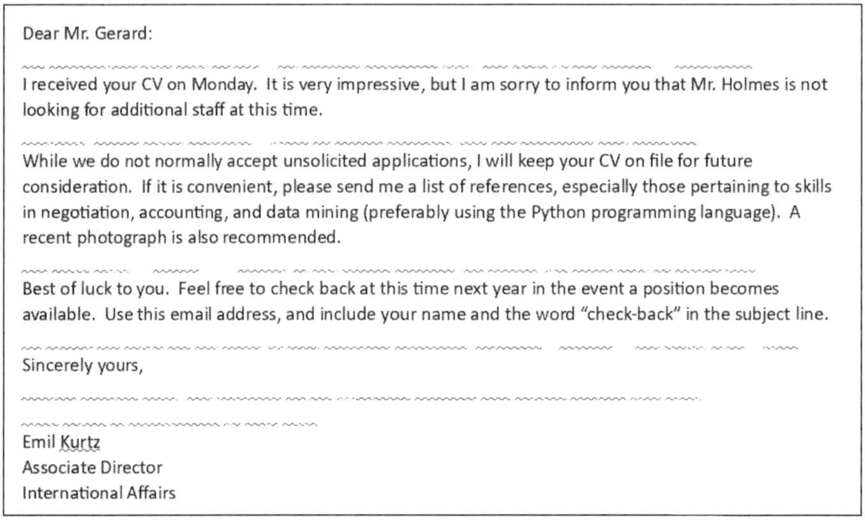

Dear Mr. Gerard:

I received your CV on Monday. It is very impressive, but I am sorry to inform you that Mr. Holmes is not looking for additional staff at this time.

While we do not normally accept unsolicited applications, I will keep your CV on file for future consideration. If it is convenient, please send me a list of references, especially those pertaining to skills in negotiation, accounting, and data mining (preferably using the Python programming language). A recent photograph is also recommended.

Best of luck to you. Feel free to check back at this time next year in the event a position becomes available. Use this email address, and include your name and the word "check-back" in the subject line.

Sincerely yours,

Emil Kurtz
Associate Director
International Affairs

Figure 6-13: The spellchecker in LibreOffice Writer will highlight the invisible words.

Second, using CTRL-A to highlight all the text within Word won't reveal the hidden text, but it would indicate that some blank lines are longer than others (see Figure 6-14), suggesting to the very observant that something is amiss.

Morland Holmes

GLOBAL CONSULTANTING & NEGOTIATIONS

December 17, 2015

Dear Mr. Gerard:

I received your CV on Monday. It is very impressive, but I am sorry to inform you that Mr. Holmes is not looking for additional staff at this time.

While we do not normally accept unsolicited applications, I will keep your CV on file for future consideration. If it is convenient, please send me a list of references, especially those pertaining to skills in negotiation, accounting, and data mining (preferably using the Python programming language). A recent photograph is also recommended.

Best of luck to you. Feel free to check back at this time next year in the event a position becomes available. Use this email address, and include your name and the word "check-back" in the subject line.

Sincerely yours,

Emil Kurtz
Associate Director
International Affairs

Figure 6-14: Selecting the whole Word document reveals differences in the length of blank lines.

Third, opening the Word document using the preview functionality in some email software may reveal the hidden text when the contents are selected through swiping or using CTRL-A (Figure 6-15).

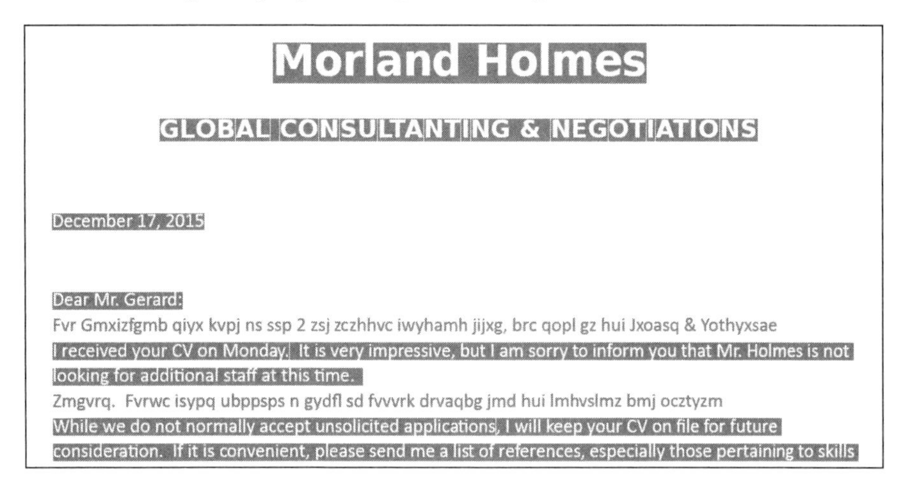
Morland Holmes

GLOBAL CONSULTANTING & NEGOTIATIONS

December 17, 2015

Dear Mr. Gerard:
Fvr Gmxizfgmb qiyx kvpj ns ssp 2 zsj zczhhvc iwyhamh jijxg, brc qopl gz hui Jxoasq & Yothyxsae
I received your CV on Monday. It is very impressive, but I am sorry to inform you that Mr. Holmes is not looking for additional staff at this time.
Zmgvrq. Fvrwc isypq ubppsps n gydfl sd fvvvrk drvaqbg jmd hui lmhvslmz bmj ocztyzm
While we do not normally accept unsolicited applications, I will keep your CV on file for future consideration. If it is convenient, please send me a list of references, especially those pertaining to skills

Figure 6-15: Selecting the whole document in the Yahoo! Mail Preview panel reveals the hidden text.

But while selecting hidden text in the Yahoo! Mail Preview panel reveals the text, the same is not true in the Microsoft Outlook Preview panel in Figure 6-16.

Morland Holmes

GLOBAL CONSULTANTING & NEGOTIATIONS

December 17, 2015

Dear Mr. Gerard:

I received your CV on Monday. It is very impressive, but I am sorry to inform you that Mr. Holmes is not looking for additional staff at this time.

While we do not normally accept unsolicited applications, I will keep your CV on file for future consideration. If it is convenient, please send me a list of references, especially those pertaining to skills

Figure 6-16: Selecting the whole document in the Microsoft Outlook Preview panel does not reveal the hidden text.

Finally, saving the Word document as a plain text (**.txt*) file would remove all formatting and leave the hidden text exposed (Figure 6-17).

```
Dear Mr. Gerard:
Fvr Gmxizfgmb qiyx kvpj ns ssp 2 zsj zczhhvc iwyhamh jijxg, brc qopl gz hui Jxoasq & Yothyxsae
I received your CV on Monday.  It is very impressive, but I am sorry to inform you that Mr. Holmes
is not looking for additional staff at this time.
Zmgvrq.  Fvrwc isypq ubppsps n gydfl sd fvvvrk drvaqbg jmd hui lmhvslmz bmj ocztyzm
While we do not normally accept unsolicited applications, I will keep your CV on file for future consideration.
If it is convenient, please send me a list of references, especially those pertaining to skills in negotiation,
```

Figure 6-17: Saving the Word document as a plain text (.txt) file reveals the hidden text.*

To conceal a secret message with steganography, you have to conceal not only the *contents* of the message but also the fact that a message even *exists*. Our electronic invisible ink can't always guarantee this, but from a mole's point of view, the weaknesses just listed involve either them making a mistake, which could theoretically be controlled, or an investigator taking a dedicated and unlikely action, such as swiping text, saving files in a different format, or using a less-common word processor. Assuming the mole in *Elementary* considered these acceptable risks, electronic invisible ink provides a plausible explanation for why the internal company investigation failed.

Summary

In this chapter, you used steganography to hide an encrypted message within a Microsoft Word document. You used a third-party module, called `python-docx`, to directly access and manipulate the document using Python. Similar third-party modules are available for working with other popular document types, like Excel spreadsheets.

Further Reading

You can find online documentation for `python-docx` at *https://python-docx.readthedocs.io/en/latest/* and *https://pypi.python.org/pypi/python-docx.*

Automate the Boring Stuff with Python (No Starch Press, 2015) by Al Sweigart, covers modules that allow Python to manipulate PDFs, Word files, Excel spreadsheets, and more. Chapter 13 contains a useful tutorial on `python-docx`, and the appendix covers installing third-party modules with pip.

You can find beginner-level Python programs for working with ciphers in *Cracking Codes with Python* (No Starch Press, 2018) by Al Sweigart.

Mysterious Messages (The Penguin Group, 2009) by Gary Blackwood is an interesting and well-illustrated history of steganography and cryptography.

Practice Project: Checking the Number of Blank Lines

Improve the hidden message program by writing a function that compares the number of blank lines in the fake message to the number of lines in the real message. If there is insufficient space to hide the real message, have the function warn the user and tell them how many blank lines to add to the fake message. Insert and call the function in a copy of the *elementary_ink.py* code, just before loading the template document. You can find a solution in the appendix and online at *https://www.nostarch.com/impracticalpython/* in *elementary_ink_practice.py*. For testing, download *realMessageChallenge.docx* from the same site and use it for the real message.

Challenge Project: Using Monospace Font

Rewrite the *elementary_ink.py* code for monospace fonts and hide your own short message in the spaces between words. See "Considering Font Types, Kerning, and Tracking" on page 109 for a description of monospace fonts. As always with challenge projects, no solution is provided.

7

BREEDING GIANT RATS WITH GENETIC ALGORITHMS

Genetic algorithms are general-purpose optimization programs designed to solve complex problems. Invented in the 1970s, they belong to the class of *evolutionary algorithms*, so named because they mimic the Darwinian process of natural selection. They are especially useful when little is known about a problem, when you're dealing with a nonlinear problem, or when searching for brute-force-type solutions in a large search space. Best of all, they are easy algorithms to grasp and implement.

In this chapter, you'll use genetic algorithms to breed a race of super-rats that can terrorize the world. After that, you'll switch sides and help James Bond crack a high-tech safe in a matter of seconds. These two projects should give you a good appreciation for the mechanics and power of genetic algorithms.

Finding the Best of All Possible Solutions

Genetic algorithms *optimize*, which means that they select the best solution (with regard to some criteria) from a set of available alternatives. For example, if you're looking for the fastest route to drive from New York to Los Angeles, a genetic algorithm will never suggest you fly. It can choose only from within an allowed set of conditions that *you* provide. As optimizers, these algorithms are faster than traditional methods and can avoid premature convergence to a suboptimal answer. In other words, they efficiently search the solution space yet do so thoroughly enough to avoid picking a good answer when a better one is available.

Unlike *exhaustive* search engines, which use pure brute force, genetic algorithms don't try every possible solution. Instead, they continuously grade solutions and then use them to make "informed guesses" going forward. A simple example is the "warmer-colder" game, where you search for a hidden item as someone tells you whether you are getting warmer or colder based on your proximity or search direction. Genetic algorithms use a fitness function, analogous to natural selection, to discard "colder" solutions and build on the "warmer" ones. The basic process is as follows:

1. Randomly generate a population of solutions.
2. Measure the fitness of each solution.
3. Select the best (warmest) solutions and discard the rest.
4. Cross over (recombine) elements in the best solutions to make new solutions.
5. Mutate a small number of elements in the solutions by changing their value.
6. Return to step 2 and repeat.

The select–cross over–mutate loop continues until it reaches a *stop condition*, like finding a known answer, finding a "good enough" answer (based on a minimum threshold), completing a set number of iterations, or reaching a time deadline. Because these steps closely resemble the process of evolution, complete with survival of the fittest, the terminology used with genetic algorithms is often more biological than computational.

Project #13: Breeding an Army of Super-Rats

Here's your chance to be a mad scientist with a secret lab full of boiling beakers, bubbling test tubes, and machines that go "BZZZTTT." So pull on some black rubber gloves and get busy turning 100 nimble trash-eating scavengers into massive man-eating monsters.

THE OBJECTIVE

Use a genetic algorithm to simulate breeding rats to an average weight of 110 pounds.

Strategy

Your dream is to breed a race of rats the size of bullmastiffs (we've already established that you're mad). You'll start with *Rattus norvegicus*, the brown rat, then add some artificial sweeteners, some atomic radiation from the 1950s, a lot of patience, and a pinch of Python, but no genetic engineering—you're old-school, baby! The rats will grow from less than a pound to a terrifying 110 pounds, about the size of a female bullmastiff (see Figure 7-1).

Figure 7-1: Size comparison of a brown rat, a female bullmastiff, and a human

Before you embark on such a huge undertaking, it's prudent to simulate the results in Python. And you've drawn up something better than a plan—you've drawn some graphical pseudocode (see Figure 7-2).

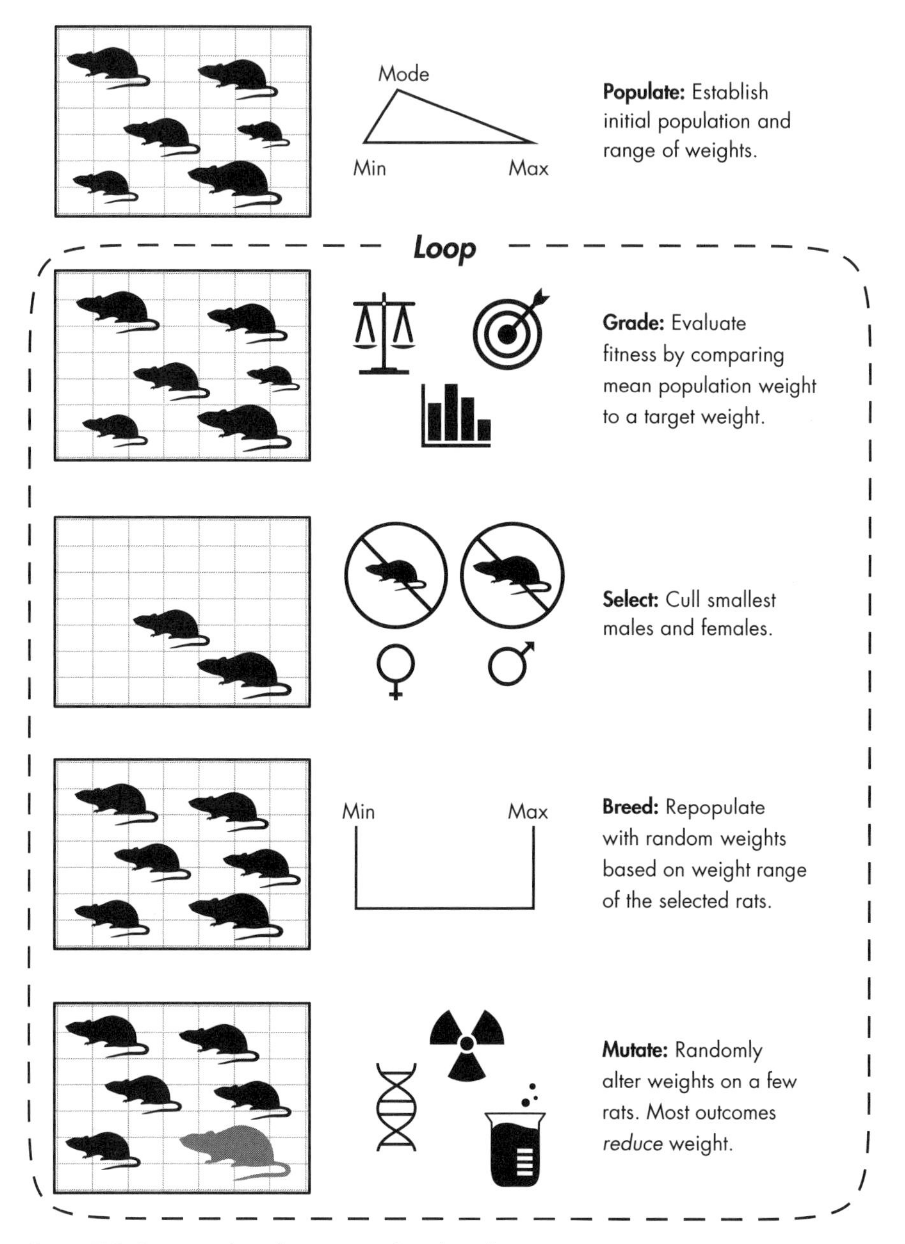

Figure 7-2: Genetic algorithm approach to breeding super-rats

The process shown in Figure 7-2 outlines how a genetic algorithm works. Your goal is to produce a population of rats with an average weight of 110 pounds from an initial population weighing much less than that. Going forward, each population (or *generation*) of rats represents a candidate solution to the problem. Like any animal breeder, you cull undesirable males and females, which you humanely send to—for you *Austin Powers* fans—an evil petting zoo. You then mate and breed the remaining rats, a process known as *crossover* in genetic programming.

The offspring of the remaining rats will be essentially the same size as their parents, so you need to mutate a few. While mutation is rare and usually results in a neutral-to-nonbeneficial trait (low weight, in this case), sometimes you'll successfully produce a bigger rat.

The whole process then becomes a big repeating loop, whether done organically or programmatically, making me wonder whether we really *are* just virtual beings in an alien simulation. At any rate, the end of the loop—the stop condition—is when the rats reach the desired size or you just can't stand dealing with rats anymore.

For input to your simulation, you'll need some statistics. Use the metric system since you're a scientist, mad or not. You already know that the average weight of a female bullmastiff is 50,000 grams, and you can find useful rat statistics in Table 7-1.

Table 7-1: Brown Rat Weight and Breeding Statistics

Parameter	Published values
Minimum weight	200 grams
Average weight (female)	250 grams
Average weight (male)	300–350 grams
Maximum weight	600 grams*
Number of pups per litter	8–12
Litters per year	4–13
Life span (wild, captivity)	1–3 years, 4–6 years

*Exceptional individuals may reach 1,000 grams in captivity.

Because both domestic and wild brown rats exist, there may be wide variation in some of the stats. Rats in captivity tend to be better cared for than wild rats, so they weigh more, breed more, and have more pups. So you can choose from the higher end when a range is available. For this project, start with the assumptions in Table 7-2.

Table 7-2: Input Assumptions for the Super-Rats Genetic Algorithm

Variable and value	Comments
`GOAL = 50000`	Target weight in grams (female bullmastiff)
`NUM_RATS = 20`	Total number of *adult* rats your lab can support
`INITIAL_MIN_WT = 200`	Minimum weight of adult rat, in grams, in initial population
`INITIAL_MAX_WT = 600`	Maximum weight of adult rat, in grams, in initial population
`INITIAL_MODE_WT = 300`	Most common adult rat weight, in grams, in initial population
`MUTATE_ODDS = 0.01`	Probability of a mutation occurring in a rat
`MUTATE_MIN = 0.5`	Scalar on rat weight of least beneficial mutation
`MUTATE_MAX = 1.2`	Scalar on rat weight of most beneficial mutation
`LITTER_SIZE = 8`	Number of pups per pair of mating rats
`LITTERS_PER_YEAR = 10`	Number of litters per year per pair of mating rats
`GENERATION_LIMIT = 500`	Generational cutoff to stop breeding program

Since rats breed so frequently, you shouldn't have to factor in life span. Even though you will retain some of the parents from a previous generation, they will be culled out quickly as their offspring increase in weight from generation to generation.

The Super-Rats Code

The *super_rats.py* code follows the general workflow in Figure 7-2. You can also download the code from *https://www.nostarch.com/impracticalpython/*.

Entering the Data and Assumptions

Listing 7-1, in the global space at the start of the program, imports modules and assigns the statistics, scalars, and assumptions in Table 7-2 as constants. Once the program is complete and working, feel free to experiment with the values in that table and see how they affect your results.

super_rats.py, part 1

```
❶ import time
  import random
  import statistics

❷ # CONSTANTS (weights in grams)
❸ GOAL = 50000
  NUM_RATS = 20
  INITIAL_MIN_WT = 200
  INITIAL_MAX_WT = 600
  INITIAL_MODE_WT = 300
  MUTATE_ODDS = 0.01
  MUTATE_MIN = 0.5
  MUTATE_MAX = 1.2
  LITTER_SIZE = 8
  LITTERS_PER_YEAR = 10
  GENERATION_LIMIT = 500

  # ensure even-number of rats for breeding pairs:
❹ if NUM_RATS % 2 != 0:
      NUM_RATS += 1
```

Listing 7-1: Imports modules and assigns constants

Start by importing the `time`, `random`, and `statistics` modules ❶. You'll use the `time` module to record the runtime of your genetic algorithm. It's interesting to time genetic algorithms, if only to be awed by how quickly they can find a solution.

The `random` module will satisfy the stochastic needs of the algorithm, and you'll use the `statistics` module to get mean values. This is a weak use for `statistics`, but I want you to be aware of the module, since it can be quite handy.

Next, assign the input variables described in Table 7-2 and be sure to note that the units are grams ❷. Use uppercase letters for the names, as these represent constants ❸.

Right now, we're going to assume the use of breeding *pairs*, so check that the user input an even number of rats and, if not, add a rat ❹. Later, in "Challenge Projects" on page 144, you'll get to experiment with alternative gender distributions.

Initializing the Population

Listing 7-2 is the program's shopping representative. It goes to a pet shop and picks out the rats for an initial breeding population. Since you want mating pairs, it should choose an even number of rats. And since you can't afford one of those fancy volcano lairs with unlimited space, you'll need to maintain a constant number of adult rats through each generation—though the number can swell temporarily to accommodate litters. Remember, the rats will need more and more space as they grow to the size of big dogs!

super_rats.py, part 2

```
❶ def populate(num_rats, min_wt, max_wt, mode_wt):
      """Initialize a population with a triangular distribution of weights."""
    ❷ return [int(random.triangular(min_wt, max_wt, mode_wt))\
              for i in range(num_rats)]
```

Listing 7-2: Defines the function that creates the initial rat population

The `populate()` function needs to know the amount of adult rats you want, the minimum and maximum weights for the rats, and the most commonly occurring weight ❶. Note that all of these arguments will use constants found in the global space. You don't have to pass these as arguments for the function to access them. But I do so here and in the functions that follow, for clarity and because local variables are accessed more efficiently.

You'll use the four arguments above with the `random` module, which includes different types of distributions. You'll use a triangular distribution here, because it gives you firm control of the minimum and maximum sizes and lets you model skewness in the statistics.

Because brown rats exist both in the wild and in captivity—in zoos, labs, and as pets—their weights are skewed to the high side. Wild rats tend to be smaller as their lives are nasty, brutish, and short, though lab rats may contest that point! Use list comprehension to loop through the number of rats and assign each one a weight. Bundle it all together with the `return` statement ❷.

Measuring the Fitness of the Population

Measuring the fitness of the rats is a two-step process. First, grade the whole population by comparing the average weight of all the rats to the bullmastiff target. Then, grade each individual rat. Only rats whose weight ranks in the upper *n* percent, as determined by the `NUM_RATS` variable, get to breed again. Although the average weight of the population is a valid fitness measurement, its primary role here is to determine whether it's time to stop looping and declare success.

Listing 7-3 defines the fitness() and select() functions, which together form the measurement portion of your genetic algorithm.

super_rats.py, part 3

```
❶ def fitness(population, goal):
      """Measure population fitness based on an attribute mean vs target."""
      ave = statistics.mean(population)
      return ave / goal

❷ def select(population, to_retain):
      """Cull a population to retain only a specified number of members."""
    ❸ sorted_population = sorted(population)
    ❹ to_retain_by_sex = to_retain//2
    ❺ members_per_sex = len(sorted_population)//2
    ❻ females = sorted_population[:members_per_sex]
      males = sorted_population[members_per_sex:]
    ❼ selected_females = females[-to_retain_by_sex:]
      selected_males = males[-to_retain_by_sex:]
    ❽ return selected_males, selected_females
```

Listing 7-3: Defines the measurement step of the genetic algorithm

Define a function to grade the fitness of the current generation ❶. Use the statistics module to get the mean of the population and return this value divided by the target weight. When this value is equal to or greater than 1, you'll know it's time to stop breeding.

Next, define a function that culls a population of rats, based on weight, down to the NUM_RATS value, represented here by the to_retain parameter ❷. It will also take a population argument, which will be the parents of each generation.

Now, sort the population so you can distinguish large from small ❸. Take the number of rats you want to retain and divide it by 2 using floor division so that the result is an integer ❹. Do this step so you can keep the biggest male and female rats. If you choose only the largest rats in the population, you will theoretically be choosing only males. You obtain the total members of the current population, by sex, by dividing the sorted_population by 2, again using floor division ❺.

Male rats tend to be larger than females, so make two simplifying assumptions: first, assume that exactly half of the population is female and, second, that the largest female rat is no heavier than the smallest male rat. This means that the first half of the sorted population list represents females and the last half represents males. Then create two new lists by splitting sorted_population in half, taking the bottom half for females ❻ and the upper half for males. Now all that's left to do is take the biggest rats from the end of each of these lists ❼—using negative slicing—and return them ❽. These two lists contain the parents of the next generation.

The first time you run this function, all it will do is sort the rats by sex, as the initial number of rats already equals the NUM_RATS constant. After that, the incoming population argument will include both parents and children, and its value will exceed NUM_RATS.

Breeding a New Generation

Listing 7-4 defines the program's "crossover" step, which means it breeds the next generation. A key assumption is that the weight of every child will be greater than or equal to the weight of the mother and less than or equal to the weight of the father. Exceptions to that rule will be handled in the "mutation" function.

super_rats.py, part 4

```
❶ def breed(males, females, litter_size):
      """Crossover genes among members (weights) of a population."""
    ❷ random.shuffle(males)
      random.shuffle(females)
    ❸ children = []
    ❹ for male, female in zip(males, females):
        ❺ for child in range(litter_size):
            ❻ child = random.randint(female, male)
            ❼ children.append(child)
    ❽ return children
```

Listing 7-4: Defines the function that breeds a new generation of rats

The `breed()` function takes as arguments the lists of weights of selected males and females returned from the `select()` function along with the size of a litter ❶. Next, randomly shuffle the two lists ❷, because you sorted them in the `select()` function and iterating over them without shuffling would result in the smallest male being paired with the smallest female, and so on. You need to allow for love and romance; the largest male may be drawn to the most petite female!

Start an empty list to hold their children ❸. Now for the hanky-panky. Go through the shuffled lists using `zip()` to pair a male and female from each list ❹. Each pair of rats can have multiple children, so start another loop that uses the litter size as a range ❺. The litter size is a constant, called `LITTER_SIZE`, that you provided in the input parameters, so if the value is `8`, you'll get eight children.

For each child, choose a weight at random between the mother's and father's weights ❻. Note that you don't need to use `male` + 1, because `randint()` uses *all* the numbers in the supplied range. Note also that the two values can be the same, but the first value (the mother's weight) can never be larger than the second (the father's weight). This is another reason for the simplifying assumption that females must be no larger than the smallest male. End the loop by appending each child to the list of children ❼, then return `children` ❽.

Mutating the Population

A small percentage of the children should experience mutations, and most of these should result in traits that are nonbeneficial. That means lower-than-expected weights, including "runts" that would not survive. But every so often, a beneficial mutation will result in a heavier rat.

Listing 7-5 defines the mutate() function, which applies the mutation assumptions you supplied in the list of constants. After mutate() is called, it will be time to check the fitness of the new population and start the loop over if the target weight hasn't been reached.

super_rats.py, part 5

```
❶ def mutate(children, mutate_odds, mutate_min, mutate_max):
      """Randomly alter rat weights using input odds & fractional changes."""
    ❷ for index, rat in enumerate(children):
          if mutate_odds >= random.random():
            ❸ children[index] = round(rat * random.uniform(mutate_min,
                                                             mutate_max))
      return children
```

Listing 7-5: Defines the function that mutates a small portion of the population

The function needs the list of children, the odds of a mutation occurring, and the minimum and maximum impacts of a mutation ❶. The impacts are scalars that you'll apply to the weight of a rat. In your list of constants at the start of the program (and in Table 7-2), they are skewed to the minimum side, as most mutations do not result in beneficial traits.

Loop through the list of children and use enumerate()—a handy built-in function that acts as an automatic counter—to get an index ❷. Then use the random() method to generate a random number between 0 and 1 and compare it to the odds of a mutation occurring.

If the mutate_odds variable is greater than or equal to the randomly generated number, the rat (weight) at that index is mutated. Choose a mutation value from a uniform distribution defined by the minimum and maximum mutation values; this basically selects a value at random from the min-max range. As these values are skewed to the minimum, the outcome is more likely to be a loss in weight than a gain. Multiply the current weight by this mutation scalar and round it to an integer ❸. Finish by returning the mutated children list.

NOTE *With regard to the validity of mutation statistics, you can find studies that suggest beneficial mutations are very rare and others that suggest they are more common than we realize. The breeding of dogs has shown that achieving drastic variations in size (for example, Chihuahuas vs. Great Danes) doesn't require millions of years of evolution. In a famous 20th-century study, Russian geneticist Dmitry Belyayev started with 130 silver foxes and, over a 40-year period, succeeded in achieving dramatic physiological changes by simply selecting the tamest foxes in each generation.*

Defining the main() Function

Listing 7-6 defines the main() function, which manages the other functions and determines when you've met the stop condition. It will also display all the important results.

super_rats.py, part 6

```
def main():
    """Initialize population, select, breed, and mutate, display results."""
  ❶ generations = 0
```

```
❷ parents = populate(NUM_RATS, INITIAL_MIN_WT, INITIAL_MAX_WT,
                         INITIAL_MODE_WT)
   print("initial population weights = {}".format(parents))
   popl_fitness = fitness(parents, GOAL)
   print("initial population fitness = {}".format(popl_fitness))
   print("number to retain = {}".format(NUM_RATS))

❸ ave_wt = []

❹ while popl_fitness < 1 and generations < GENERATION_LIMIT:
       selected_males, selected_females = select(parents, NUM_RATS)
       children = breed(selected_males, selected_females, LITTER_SIZE)
       children = mutate(children, MUTATE_ODDS, MUTATE_MIN, MUTATE_MAX)
     ❺ parents = selected_males + selected_females + children
       popl_fitness = fitness(parents, GOAL)
     ❻ print("Generation {} fitness = {:.4f}".format(generations,
                                                      popl_fitness))
     ❼ ave_wt.append(int(statistics.mean(parents)))
       generations += 1
❽ print("average weight per generation = {}".format(ave_wt))
   print("\nnumber of generations = {}".format(generations))
   print("number of years = {}".format(int(generations / LITTERS_PER_YEAR)))
```

Listing 7-6: Defines the `main()` *function*

Start the function by initializing an empty list to hold the number of generations. You'll eventually use this to figure out how many years it took to achieve your goal ❶.

Next, call the `populate()` function ❷ and immediately print the results. Then, get the fitness of your initial population and print this along with the number of rats to retain each generation, which is the `NUM_RATS` constant.

For fun, initialize a list to hold the average weight of each generation so you can view it at the end ❸. If you plot these weights against the number of years, you'll see that the trend is exponential.

Now, start the big genetic loop of select-mate-mutate. This is in the form of a `while` loop, with the stop conditions being either reaching the target weight or reaching a large number of generations without achieving the target weight ❹. Note that after mutating the children, you need to combine them with their parents to make a new `parents` list ❺. It takes the pups about five weeks to mature and start breeding, but you can account for this by adjusting the `LITTERS_PER_YEAR` constant down from the maximum possible value (see Table 7-1), as we've done here.

At the end of each loop, display the results of the `fitness()` function to four decimal places so you can monitor the algorithm and ensure it is progressing as expected ❻. Get the average weight of the generation, append it to the `ave_wt` list ❼, and then advance the generation count by 1.

Complete the `main()` function by displaying the list of average weights per generation, the number of generations, and the number of years—calculated using the `LITTERS_PER_YEAR` variable ❽.

Running the main() Function

Finish up with the familiar conditional statement for running the program either stand-alone or as a module. Get the ending time and print how long it took the program to run. The performance information should print only when the module is run in stand-alone mode, so be sure to place it under the `if` clause. See Listing 7-7.

super_rats.py, part 7

```
if __name__ == '__main__':
    start_time = time.time()
    main()
    end_time = time.time()
    duration = end_time - start_time
    print("\nRuntime for this program was {} seconds.".format(duration))
```

Listing 7-7: Runs the `main()` function and `time` module if the program isn't imported

Summary

With the parameters in Table 7-2, the *super_rats.py* program will take about two seconds to run. On average, it will take the rats about 345 generations, or 34.5 years, to reach the target weight of 110 pounds. That's a long time for a mad scientist to stay mad! But armed with your program, you can look for ways to reduce the time to target.

Sensitivity studies work by making multiple changes to a *single* variable and judging the results. You should take care in the event some variables are dependent on one another. And since the results are stochastic (random), you should make multiple runs with each parameter change in order to capture the range of possible outcomes.

Two things you can control in your breeding program are the number of breeding rats (`NUM_RATS`) and the odds of a mutation occurring (`MUTATE_ODDS`). The mutation odds are influenced by factors like diet and exposure to radiation. If you change these variables one at a time and rerun *super_rats.py*, you can judge the impact of each variable on the project timeline.

An immediate observation is that, if you start with small values for each variable and slowly increase them, you get dramatic initial results (see Figure 7-3). After that, both curves decline rapidly and flatten out in a classic example of diminishing returns. The point where each curve flattens is the key to optimally saving money and reducing work.

For example, you get very little benefit from retaining more than about 300 rats. You'd just be feeding and caring for a lot of superfluous rats. Likewise, trying to boost the odds of a mutation above 0.3 gains you little.

With charts like these, it's easy to plan a path forward. The horizontal dotted line marked "Baseline" represents the average result of using the input in Table 7-2. You can potentially reduce this time by over 10 years just by retaining 50 rats rather than 20. You should also focus on increasing the number of beneficial mutations. This will be more rewarding, but riskier and harder to control.

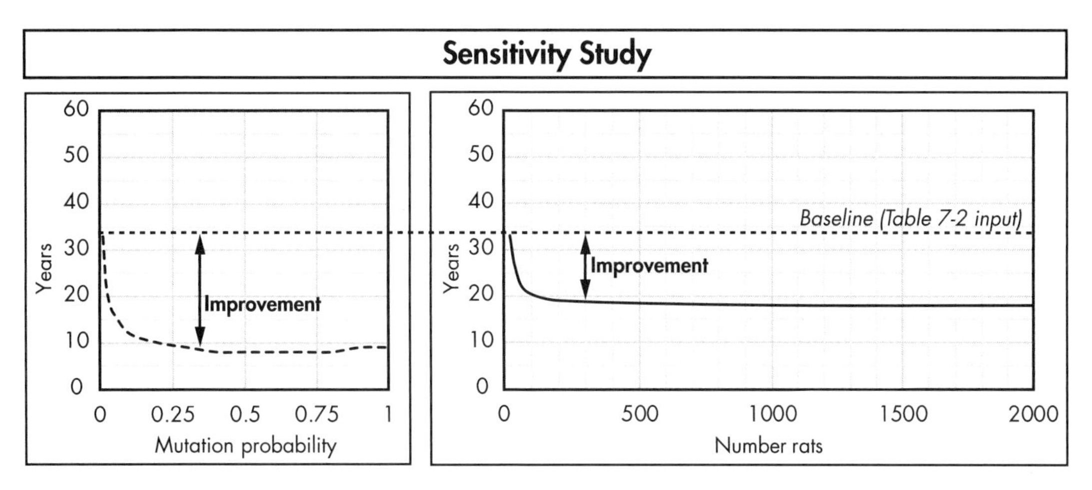

Figure 7-3: Impact of two parameters on the time required to reach the target weight

If you rerun the simulation using 50 rats and bumping the odds of mutation up to 0.05, you can theoretically complete the project in 14 years, an improvement of 246 percent over the initial baseline. Now *that's* optimization!

Breeding super-rats was a fun and simple way to understand the basics of genetic algorithms. But to truly appreciate their power, you need to attempt something harder. You need a brute-force problem that's too big to brute-force, and the next project is that kind of problem.

Project #14: Cracking a High-Tech Safe

You are Q, and James Bond has a problem. He has to attend an elegant dinner party at a villain's mansion, slip away to the man's private office, and crack his wall safe. Child's play for 007, except for one thing: it's a Humperdink BR549 digital safe that takes 10 digits, yielding 10 billion possible combinations. And the lock wheels don't start turning until *after* all the numbers have been entered. There'll be no putting a stethoscope to this safe and slowly turning a dial!

As Q, you already have an autodialer device that can brute-force its way through all possible solutions, but Bond simply won't have time to use it. Here's why.

A combination lock should really be called a *permutation* lock, because it requires *ordered* combinations, which are, by definition, permutations. More specifically, locks rely on *permutations with repetition*. For example, a valid—though insecure—combination could be 999999999.

You used the `itertools` module's `permutations()` iterator when working with anagrams in Chapter 3 and in "Practice Projects" on page 87 in Chapter 4, but that won't help here because `permutations()` returns permutations *without* repetition. To generate the right kind of permutation for a lock, you need to use `itertools`'s `product()` iterator, which calculates the Cartesian product from multiple sets of numbers:

```
>>> from itertools import product
>>> combo = (1, 2)
>>> for perm in product(combo, repeat=2):
    print(perm)
(1, 1)
(1, 2)
(2, 1)
(2, 2)
```

The optional repeat keyword argument lets you take the product of an iterable multiplied by itself, as you need to do in this case. Note that the product() function returns all the possible combinations, whereas the permutations() function would return only (1, 2) and (2, 1). You can read more about product() at *https://docs.python.org/3.6/library/itertools.html#itertools.product.Listing*.

Listing 7-8 is a Python program, called *brute_force_cracker.py*, that uses product() to brute-force its way to the right combination:

brute_force_cracker.py

```
❶ import time
from itertools import product

start_time = time.time()

❷ combo = (9, 9, 7, 6, 5, 4, 3)

# use Cartesian product to generate permutations with repetition
❸ for perm in product([0, 1, 2, 3, 4, 5, 6, 7, 8, 9], repeat=len(combo)):
  ❹ if perm == combo:
        print("Cracked! {} {}".format(combo, perm))

end_time = time.time()
❺ print("\nRuntime for this program was {} seconds.".format
      (end_time - start_time))
```

Listing 7-8: Uses a brute-force method to find a safe's combination

Import time and the product iterator from itertools ❶. Get the start time, and then enter the safe combination as a tuple ❷. Next use product(), which returns tuples of all the permutations with repetition for a given sequence. The sequence contains all the valid single-digit entries (0–9). You should set the repeat argument to the number of digits in the combination ❸. Compare each result to the combination and print "Cracked!" if they match, along with the combination and matching permutation ❹. Finish by displaying the runtime ❺.

This works great for combinations up to eight digits long. After that, the wait becomes increasingly uncomfortable. Table 7-3 is a record of runtimes for the program versus number of digits in the combination.

Table 7-3: Runtimes Versus Digits in Combination (2.3 GHz Processor)

Number of digits	Runtime in seconds
5	0.035
6	0.147
7	1.335
8	12.811
9	133.270
10	1396.955

Notice that adding a number to the combination increases the runtime by an order of magnitude. This is an exponential increase. With 9 digits, you'd wait over 2 minutes for an answer. With 10 digits, over 20 minutes! That's a long time for Bond to take an unnoticed "bathroom break."

Fortunately, you're Q, and you know about genetic algorithms. All you need is some way to judge the fitness of each candidate combination. Options include monitoring fluctuations in power consumption, measuring time delays in operations, and listening for sounds. Let's assume use of a sound-amplifying tool, along with a tool to prevent lockouts after a few incorrect combinations have been entered. Because of the safeguards in the BR549 safe, a sound tool can initially tell you only *how many* digits are correct, not *which* digits, but with very little time, your algorithm can zero in on the solution.

THE OBJECTIVE

Use a genetic algorithm to quickly find a safe's combination in a large search space.

Strategy

The strategy here is straightforward. You'll generate a sequence of 10 numbers at random and compare it to the real combination, grading the result based on matches; in the real world, you'd find the number of matches using the sound detector clamped to the door of the safe. You then change one value in your solution and compare again. If another match is found, you throw away the old sequence and move forward with the new; otherwise, you keep the old sequence and try again.

Since one solution completely replaces the other, this represents 100 percent crossover of genetic material, so you are essentially using just selection and mutation. Selection plus mutation alone generates a robust *hill-climbing* algorithm. Hill climbing is an optimization technique that starts with an arbitrary solution and changes (mutates) a single value in the solution. If the result is an improvement, the new solution is kept and the process repeats.

A problem with hill climbing is that the algorithm can get stuck in *local* minima or maxima and not find the optimal *global* value. Imagine you are looking for the lowest value in the wavelike function in Figure 7-4. The current best guess is marked by the large black dot. If the magnitude of the change you are making (mutation) is too small to "escape" the local trough, the algorithm won't find the true low point. From the algorithm's point of view, because every direction results in a worse answer, it must have found the true answer. So it prematurely converges on a solution.

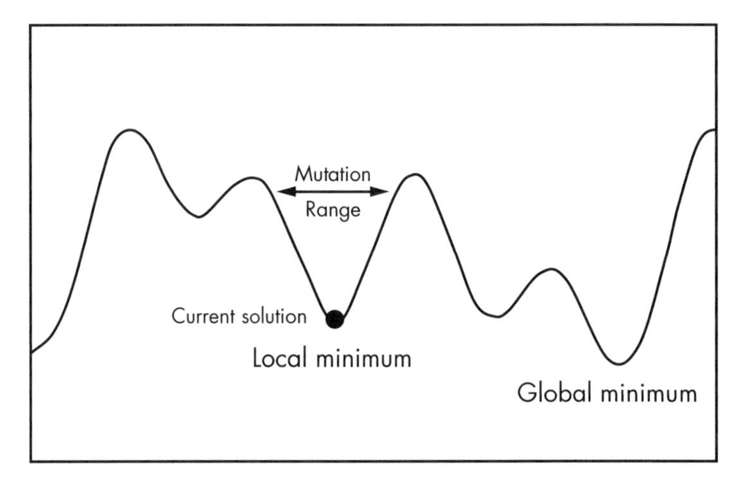

Figure 7-4: Example of a hill-climbing algorithm "stuck" in a local minimum

Using crossover in genetic algorithms helps to avoid premature convergence problems, as does allowing for relatively large mutations. Because you're not worried about honoring biological realism here, the mutation space can encompass every possible value in the combination. That way you can't get stuck, and hill climbing is an acceptable approach.

The Safecracker Code

The *safe_cracker.py* code takes a combination of *n* digits and uses hill climbing to reach the combination from a random starting point. The code can be downloaded from *https://www.nostarch.com/impracticalpython/*.

Setting Up and Defining the fitness() Function

Listing 7-9 imports the necessary modules and defines the `fitness()` function.

safe_cracker.py, part 1

```
❶ import time
  from random import randint, randrange

❷ def fitness(combo, attempt):
      """Compare items in two lists and count number of matches."""
      grade = 0
    ❸ for i, j in zip(combo, attempt):
```

```
        if i == j:
            grade += 1
    return grade
```

Listing 7-9: Imports modules and defines the `fitness()` function

After importing some familiar modules ❶, define a `fitness()` function that takes the true combination and an attempted solution as arguments ❷. Name a variable `grade` and set it to `0`. Then use `zip()` to iterate through each element in the combination and your attempt ❸. If they're the same, add 1 to `grade` and return it. Note that you aren't recording the index that matches, just that the function has found a match. This emulates output from the sound detection device. All it can tell you initially is how many lock wheels turned, not their locations.

Defining and Running the main() Function

Since this is a short and simple program, most of the algorithm is run in the `main()` function, Listing 7-10, rather than in multiple functions.

safe_cracker.py, part 2

```
def main():
    """Use hill-climbing algorithm to solve lock combination."""
❶   combination = '6822858902'
    print("Combination = {}".format(combination))
    # convert combination to list:
❷   combo = [int(i) for i in combination]

    # generate guess & grade fitness:
❸   best_attempt = [0] * len(combo)
    best_attempt_grade = fitness(combo, best_attempt)

❹   count = 0

    # evolve guess
❺   while best_attempt != combo:
        # crossover
❻       next_try = best_attempt[:]

        # mutate
        lock_wheel = int(randrange(0, len(combo)))
❼       next_try[lock_wheel] = randint(0, len(combo)-1)

        # grade & select
❽       next_try_grade = fitness(combo, next_try)
        if next_try_grade > best_attempt_grade:
            best_attempt = next_try[:]
            best_attempt_grade = next_try_grade
        print(next_try, best_attempt)
        count += 1

    print()
❾   print("Cracked! {}".format(best_attempt), end=' ')
    print("in {} tries!".format(count))
```

```
if __name__ == '__main__':
    start_time = time.time()
    main()
    end_time = time.time()
    duration = end_time - start_time
 ❿ print("\nRuntime for this program was {:.5f} seconds.".format(duration))
```

Listing 7-10: Defines the `main()` *function and runs and times the program if it hasn't been imported*

Provide the true combination as a variable ❶ and use list comprehension to convert it into a list for convenience going forward ❷. Generate a list of zeros equal in length to the combination and name it `best_attempt` ❸. At this point, any combination is as good as any other. You should retain this name—`best_attempt`—because you need to preserve only the best solution as you climb the hill. Once you've generated the initial attempt, grade it with the `fitness()` function and then assign the value to a variable, called `best_attempt_grade`.

Start a `count` variable at zero. The program will use this variable to record how many attempts it took to crack the code ❹.

Now, start a `while` loop that continues until you've found the combination ❺. Assign a *copy* of `best_attempt` to a `next_try` variable ❻. You copy it so you don't run into aliasing problems; when you alter an element in `next_try`, you don't want to accidentally change `best_attempt`, because you may continue to use it in the event `next_try` fails the fitness test.

It's now time to mutate the copy. Each digit in the combination turns a lock wheel in the safe, so name a variable `lock_wheel` and randomly set it equal to an index location in the combination. This represents the location of the single element to change in this iteration. Next, randomly choose a digit and use it to replace the value at the location indexed by `lock_wheel` ❼.

Grade `next_try`, and if it's fitter than the previous attempt, reset both `best_attempt` and `best_attempt_grade` to the new values ❽. Otherwise, `best_attempt` will remain unchanged for the next iteration. Print both `next_try` and `best_attempt`, side by side, so you can scroll through the attempts when the program ends and see how they evolved. Finish the loop by advancing the counter.

When the program finds the combination, display the `best_attempt` value and the number of tries it took to find it ❾. Remember, the `end=' '` argument prevents a carriage return at the end of the printed line and places a space between the end of the current line and the beginning of the next line.

Complete the program with the conditional statement for running `main()` stand-alone and display the runtime to five decimal places ❿. Note that the timing code comes after the conditional, and thus will not run if the program is imported as a module.

Summary

The last few lines of output from the *safe_cracker.py* program are shown here. I've omitted most of the evolving comparisons for brevity. The run was for a 10-digit combination.

```
[6, 8, 6, 2, 0, 5, 8, 9, 0, 0] [6, 8, 2, 2, 0, 5, 8, 9, 0, 0]
[6, 8, 2, 2, 0, 9, 8, 9, 0, 0] [6, 8, 2, 2, 0, 5, 8, 9, 0, 0]
[6, 8, 2, 2, 8, 5, 8, 9, 0, 0] [6, 8, 2, 2, 8, 5, 8, 9, 0, 0]
[6, 8, 2, 2, 8, 5, 8, 9, 0, 2] [6, 8, 2, 2, 8, 5, 8, 9, 0, 2]

Cracked! [6, 8, 2, 2, 8, 5, 8, 9, 0, 2] in 78 tries!

Runtime for this program was 0.69172 seconds.
```

Ten billion possible combinations, and the program found a solution in only 78 tries and in less than a second. Even James Bond would be impressed with that.

That does it for genetic algorithms. You've used an example workflow to breed gigantic rodents, then trimmed it to hill climb through a brute-force problem in no time flat. If you want to continue to play digital Darwin and experiment with genetic algorithms, a long list of example applications can be found on Wikipedia (*https://en.wikipedia.org/wiki/List_of_genetic_algorithm_applications*). Examples include:

- Modeling global temperature changes
- Container-loading optimization
- Delivery vehicle–routing optimization
- Groundwater-monitoring networks
- Learning robot behavior
- Protein folding
- Rare-event analysis
- Code breaking
- Clustering for fit functions
- Filtering and signal processing

Further Reading

Genetic Algorithms with Python (Amazon Digital Services LLC, 2016) by Clinton Sheppard is a beginner-level introduction to genetic algorithms using Python. It is available in paperback or as an inexpensive ebook from *https://leanpub.com/genetic_algorithms_with_python/*.

Challenge Projects

Continue to breed super-rats and crack super-safes with these suggested projects. As usual with challenge projects, you're on your own; no solutions are provided.

Building a Rat Harem

Since a single male rat can mate with multiple females, there is no need to have an equal number of male and female rats. Rewrite the *super_rats.py* code to accommodate a variable number of male and female individuals. Then rerun the program with the same total number of rats as before, but use 4 males and 16 females. How does this impact the number of years required to reach the target weight of 50,000 grams?

Creating a More Efficient Safecracker

As currently written, when a lock wheel match is found by the *safe_cracker.py* code, that match is not explicitly preserved. As long as the `while` loop is running, there's nothing to stop a correct match from being stochastically overwritten. Alter the code so that the indexes for correct guesses are excluded from future changes. Do timing comparisons between the two versions of the code to judge the impact of the change.

8

COUNTING SYLLABLES FOR HAIKU POETRY

Poetry may be the supreme form of literature. It is, as Coleridge put it, "the best words in the best order." The poet must—with great brevity—tell a story, promote an idea, describe a scene, or evoke intensity of feeling, all while obeying strict rules on rhythm and rhyme, style and structure.

Computers love rules and structure and even have the potential to evoke emotions. In his 1996 book *Virtual Muse: Experiments in Computer Poetry*, author Charles Hartman describes early attempts to write algorithms that could mimic human poetry. To quote Hartman, "The complexity of poetic interaction, the tricky dance among poet and text and reader, causes a game of hesitation. In this game, a properly programmed computer has a chance to slip in some interesting moves."

The early programs Hartman describes could, at best, produce bad beatnik poetry. The goal at the time was to "introduce calculated bits of mechanized anarchy into the language, put the results back into the contingent world where language lives, and see how the dust settles." As we have touched on in several chapters, context is the weak link in programming things like proper-name anagrams and null ciphers. To write computer poems that pass the "supreme" test of literature, you cannot ignore context.

Getting a computer to simulate this most human of human endeavors is an intriguing challenge—and certainly not one we can pass up. In this chapter and the next, you'll teach your computer how to generate a traditional form of Japanese poetry called *haiku*.

Japanese Haiku

Haiku consist of three lines of five, seven, and five syllables, respectively. The poems rarely rhyme, and the subject matter usually addresses the natural world—mainly the seasons—either directly or indirectly. If done properly, a haiku can immerse you in the scene, as if evoking a memory.

I've provided three example haiku here. The first is by the master Buson (1715–1783), the second by the master Issa (1763–1828), and the third by yours truly, based on memories of childhood road trips.

Standing still at dusk
Listen . . . in far distances
The song of froglings!
—*Buson*

Good friend grasshopper
Will you play the caretaker
For my little grave?
—*Issa*

Faraway cloudbanks
That I let myself pretend
Are distant mountains
—*Vaughan*

Because of its evocative nature, every haiku has a built-in "exploitable gap" for the programmer. This is summed up nicely by Peter Beilenson in his 1955 book *Japanese Haiku*: "the haiku is not expected to be always a complete or even a clear statement. The reader is supposed to add to the words his own associations and imagery, and thus to become a co-creator of his own pleasure in the poem." Hartman adds, "The reader's mind works most actively on sparse materials. We draw the clearest constellations from the fewest stars. So, the nonsense factor is low for a tiny collocation of words that can be imbued with imagistic significance." To put it simply, it's harder to mess up a short poem. Readers always assume the poet had a point and will make one up themselves if they can't find it.

Despite this advantage, training your computer to write poetry is no mean feat, and you'll need two whole chapters to get it done. In this chapter, you'll write a program that counts the number of syllables in words and phrases so that you can honor the syllabic structure of the haiku. In Chapter 9, you'll use a technique called *Markov chain analysis* to capture the essence of haiku—the elusive evocative component—and transform existing poems into something new and, occasionally, arguably better.

Project #15: Counting Syllables

Counting syllables in English is difficult. The problem lies in, as Charles Hartman put it, the quirky spelling and tangled linguistic history of English. For example, a word like *aged* may be one syllable or two depending on whether it describes a man or a cheese. How can a program count syllables accurately without degenerating into an endless list of special cases?

The answer is that it can't, at least not without a "cheat sheet." Fortunately, these cheat sheets exist, thanks to a branch of science known as *natural language processing* (*NLP*), which deals with interactions between the precise and structured language of computers and the nuanced, frequently ambiguous "natural" language used by humans. Example uses for NLP include machine translations, spam detection, comprehension of search engine questions, and predictive text recognition for cell phone users. The biggest impact of NLP is yet to come: the mining of vast volumes of previously unusable, poorly structured data and engaging in seamless conversations with our computer overlords.

In this chapter, you'll use an NLP dataset to help count syllables in words or phrases. You'll also write code that finds words that are missing from this dataset and then helps you build a supporting dictionary. Finally, you'll write a program to help you check your syllable-counting code. In Chapter 9, you'll use this syllable-counting algorithm as a module in a program that helps you computationally produce the highest achievement in literature: poetry.

THE OBJECTIVE

Write a Python program that counts the number of syllables in an English word or phrase.

The Strategy

For you and me, counting syllables is easy. Place the back of your hand just below your chin and start talking. Every time your chin hits your hand you've spoken a syllable. Computers don't have hands or chins, but every vowel sound represents a syllable—and computers can count vowel sounds. It's not easy, however, as there isn't a simple rule for doing this. Some vowels in written language are silent, such as the *e* in *like*, and some combine to make a single sound, such as the *oo* in *moo*. Luckily, the number of words in the English language isn't infinite. Fairly exhaustive lists are available that include much of the information you need.

A *corpus* is a fancy name for a body of text. In Chapter 9, you'll use a *training corpus*—composed of haiku—that teaches Python how to write new haiku. In this chapter, you'll use this same corpus to extract syllable counts.

Your syllable counter should evaluate both phrases and individual words, since you will ultimately use it to count the syllables in entire *lines* in a haiku. The program will take some text as an input, count the number of syllables in each word, and return the total syllable count. You'll also have to deal with things like punctuation, whitespace, and missing words.

The primary steps you need to follow are:

1. Download a large corpus with syllable-count information.
2. Compare the syllable-count corpus to the haiku-training corpus and identify all the words missing from the syllable-count corpus.
3. Build a dictionary of the missing words and their syllable counts.
4. Write a program that uses both the syllable-count corpus and the missing-words dictionary to count syllables in the training corpus.
5. Write a program that checks the syllable-counting program against updates of the training corpus.

Using a Corpus

The Natural Language Toolkit (NLTK) is a popular suite of programs and libraries for working with human language data in Python. It was created in 2001 as part of a computational linguistics course in the Department of Computer and Information Science at the University of Pennsylvania. Development and expansion have continued with the help of dozens of contributors. To learn more, check out the official NLTK website at *http://www.nltk.org/*.

For this project, you will use NLTK to access the Carnegie Mellon University Pronouncing Dictionary (CMUdict). This corpus contains almost 125,000 words mapped to their pronunciations. It is machine readable and useful for tasks such as speech recognition.

Installing NLTK

You can find instructions for installing NLTK on Unix, Windows, and macOS at *http://www.nltk.org/install.html*. If you are using Windows, I suggest you start by opening Windows Command Prompt or PowerShell and trying to install with `pip`:

```
python -m pip install nltk
```

You can check the installation by opening the Python interactive shell and typing:

```
>>> import nltk
>>>
```

If you don't get an error, you're good to go. Otherwise, follow the instructions on the website just cited.

Downloading CMUdict

To get access to CMUdict (or any of the other NLTK corpora), you have to download it. You can do this using the handy NLTK Downloader. Once you've installed NLTK, enter the following into the Python shell:

```
>>> import nltk
>>> nltk.download()
```

The NLTK Downloader window (Figure 8-1) should now be open. Click the **Corpora** tab near the top, then click **cmudict** in the Identifier column. Next, scroll to the bottom of the window and set the Download Directory; I used the default, *C:\nltk_data*. Finally, click the **Download** button to load CMUdict.

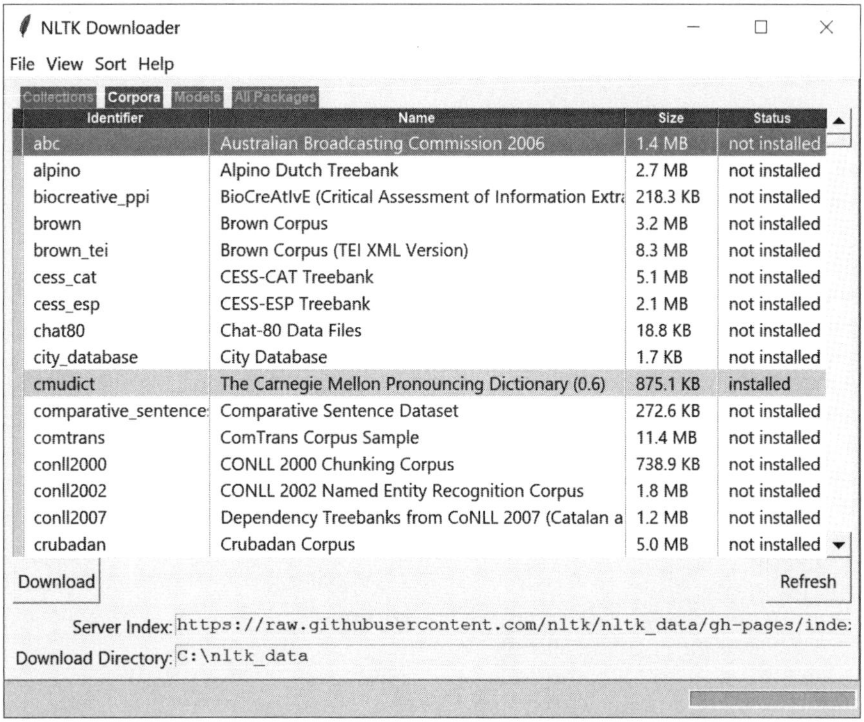

NLTK Downloader

File View Sort Help

Collections Corpora Models All Packages

Identifier	Name	Size	Status
abc	Australian Broadcasting Commission 2006	1.4 MB	not installed
alpino	Alpino Dutch Treebank	2.7 MB	not installed
biocreative_ppi	BioCreAtIvE (Critical Assessment of Information Extra	218.3 KB	not installed
brown	Brown Corpus	3.2 MB	not installed
brown_tei	Brown Corpus (TEI XML Version)	8.3 MB	not installed
cess_cat	CESS-CAT Treebank	5.1 MB	not installed
cess_esp	CESS-ESP Treebank	2.1 MB	not installed
chat80	Chat-80 Data Files	18.8 KB	not installed
city_database	City Database	1.7 KB	not installed
cmudict	The Carnegie Mellon Pronouncing Dictionary (0.6)	875.1 KB	installed
comparative_sentence	Comparative Sentence Dataset	272.6 KB	not installed
comtrans	ComTrans Corpus Sample	11.4 MB	not installed
conll2000	CONLL 2000 Chunking Corpus	738.9 KB	not installed
conll2002	CONLL 2002 Named Entity Recognition Corpus	1.8 MB	not installed
conll2007	Dependency Treebanks from CoNLL 2007 (Catalan a	1.2 MB	not installed
crubadan	Crubadan Corpus	5.0 MB	not installed

Download Refresh

Server Index: https://raw.githubusercontent.com/nltk/nltk_data/gh-pages/inde:

Download Directory: C:\nltk_data

Figure 8-1: The NLTK Downloader window with cmudict selected for download

When CMUdict has finished downloading, exit the Downloader and enter the following into the Python interactive shell:

```
>>> from nltk.corpus import cmudict
>>>
```

If you don't encounter an error, then the corpus has been successfully downloaded.

Counting Sounds Instead of Syllables

The CMUdict corpus breaks words into sets of *phonemes*—perceptually distinct *units* of sound in a specified language—and marks vowels for lexical stress using numbers (0, 1, and 2). The CMUdict corpus marks every vowel with one, and only one, of these numbers, so you can use the numbers to identify the vowels in a word.

Looking at words as a set of phonemes will help you sidestep a few problems. For one, CMUdict will not include vowels in the written word that are unpronounced. For example, here's how CMUdict sees the word *scarecrow*:

```
[['S', 'K', 'AE1', 'R', 'K', 'R', 'OW0']]
```

Each item with a numerical suffix represents a pronounced vowel. Note that the silent *e* at the end of *scare* is correctly omitted.

Second, sometimes multiple and consecutive written vowels are pronounced as just a single phoneme. For example, this is how CMUdict represents *house*:

```
[['HH', 'AW1', 'S']]
```

Note how the corpus treats the written double vowels *ou* as a single vowel, `'AW1'`, for pronunciation purposes.

Handling Words with Multiple Pronunciations

As I mention in the introduction, some words have multiple distinct pronunciations; *aged* and *learned* are just two examples:

```
[['EY1', 'JH', 'D'], ['EY1', 'JH', 'IH0', 'D']]
[['L', 'ER1', 'N', 'D'], ['L', 'ER1', 'N', 'IH0', 'D']]
```

Note the nested lists. The corpus recognizes that both words can be pronounced with one or two syllables. This means it will return more than one syllable count for certain words, something you will have to account for in your code.

Managing Missing Words

CMUdict is very useful, but with a corpus, a word is either there or not. It took only seconds to find more than 50 words—like *dewdrop, bathwater, dusky, ridgeline, storks, dragonfly, beggar,* and *archways*—missing from CMUdict in a 1,500-word test case. So, one of your strategies should be to check CMUdict for missing words and then address any omissions by making a corpus for your corpus!

The Training Corpus

In Chapter 9, you'll use a training corpus of several hundred haiku to "teach" your program how to write new ones. But you can't count on CMUdict to contain all the words in this corpus because some will be Japanese words, like *sake.* And as you already saw, even some common English words are missing from CMUdict.

So the first order of business is to check all the words in the training corpus for membership in CMUdict. To do this, you'll need to download the training corpus, called *train.txt,* from *https://www.nostarch.com/impracticalpython/.* Keep it in the same folder as all the Python programs from this chapter. The file contains slightly under 300 haiku that have been randomly duplicated around 20 times to ensure a robust training set.

Once you find words that aren't in CMUdict, you'll write a script to help you prepare a Python dictionary that uses words as keys and syllable counts as values; then you'll save this dictionary to a file that can support CMUdict in the syllable-counting program.

The Missing Words Code

The code in this section will find words missing from CMUdict, help you prepare a dictionary of the words and their syllable counts, and save the dictionary to a file. You can download the code from *https://nostarch.com/impracticalpython/* as *missing_words_finder.py.*

Importing Modules, Loading CMUdict, and Defining the main() Function

Listing 8-1 imports modules, loads CMUdict, and defines the `main()` function that runs the program.

missing_words_finder.py, part 1

```
  import sys
  from string import punctuation
❶ import pprint
  import json
  from nltk.corpus import cmudict

❷ cmudict = cmudict.dict()  # Carnegie Mellon University Pronouncing Dictionary

❸ def main():
    ❹ haiku = load_haiku('train.txt')
    ❺ exceptions = cmudict_missing(haiku)
```

```
❻ build_dict = input("\nManually build an exceptions dictionary (y/n)? \n")
   if build_dict.lower() == 'n':
       sys.exit()
   else:
     ❼ missing_words_dict = make_exceptions_dict(exceptions)
       save_exceptions(missing_words_dict)
```

Listing 8-1: Imports modules, loads CMUdict, and defines `main()`

You start with some familiar imports and a few new ones. The `pprint` module lets you "pretty print" your dictionary of missing words in an easy-to-read format ❶. You'll write out this same dictionary as persistent data using JavaScript Object Notation (`json`), a text-based way for computers to exchange data that works well with Python data structures; it's part of the standard library, standardized across multiple languages, and the data is secure and human readable. Finish by importing the CMUdict corpus.

Next, call the `cmudict` module's `dict()` method to turn the corpus into a dictionary with the words as keys and their phonemes as values ❷.

Define the `main()` function that will call functions to load the training corpus, find missing words in CMUdict, build a dictionary with the words and their syllable counts, and save the results ❸. You'll define these functions after defining `main()`.

Call the function to load the haiku-training corpus and assign the returned set to a variable named `haiku` ❹. Then call the function that will find the missing words and return them as a set ❺. Using sets removes duplicate words that you don't need. The `cmudict_missing()` function will also display the number of missing words and some other statistics.

Now, ask the user if they want to manually build a dictionary to address the missing words and assign their input to the `build_dict` variable ❻. If they want to stop, exit the program; otherwise, call a function to build the dictionary ❼ and then another one to save the dictionary. Note that the user isn't restricted to pressing y if they want to continue, though that's the prompt.

Loading the Training Corpus and Finding Missing Words

Listing 8-2 loads and prepares the training corpus, compares its contents to CMUdict, and keeps track of the differences. These tasks are divided between two functions.

missing_words_finder.py, part 2

```
❶ def load_haiku(filename):
      """Open and return training corpus of haiku as a set."""
      with open(filename) as in_file:
        ❷ haiku = set(in_file.read().replace('-', ' ').split())
        ❸ return haiku

  def cmudict_missing(word_set):
      """Find and return words in word set missing from cmudict."""
    ❹ exceptions = set()
      for word in word_set:
          word = word.lower().strip(punctuation)
          if word.endswith("'s") or word.endswith("’s"):
```

```
            word = word[:-2]
      ❺ if word not in cmudict:
            exceptions.add(word)
    print("\nexceptions:")
    print(*exceptions, sep='\n')
 ❻ print("\nNumber of unique words in haiku corpus = {}"
          .format(len(word_set)))
    print("Number of words in corpus not in cmudict = {}"
          .format(len(exceptions)))
    membership = (1 - (len(exceptions) / len(word_set))) * 100
 ❼ print("cmudict membership = {:.1f}{}".format(membership, '%'))
    return exceptions
```

Listing 8-2: Defines functions to load the corpus and finds words missing from CMUdict

Define a function to read in the words from the haiku-training corpus ❶. The haiku in *train.txt* have been duplicated many times, plus the original haiku contain duplicate words, like *moon*, *mountain*, and *the*. There's no point in evaluating a word more than once, so load the words as a set to remove repeats ❷. You also need to replace hyphens with spaces. Hyphens are popular in haiku, but you need to separate the words on either side in order to check for them in CMUdict. End the function by returning the haiku set ❸.

It's now time to find missing words. Define a function, `cmudict_missing()`, that takes as an argument a sequence—in this case, the set of words returned by the `load_haiku()` function. Start an empty set called `exceptions` to hold any missing words ❹. Loop through each word in the haiku set, converting it to lowercase and stripping any leading or trailing punctuation. Note that you don't want to remove interior punctuation other than hyphens because CMUdict recognizes words like *wouldn't*. Possessive words typically aren't in a corpus, so remove the trailing *'s*, since this won't affect the syllable count.

NOTE *Be careful of curly apostrophes (') produced by word-processing software. These are different from the straight apostrophes (') used in simple text editors and shells and may not be recognized by CMUdict. If you add new words to either the training or JSON files, be sure to use a straight apostrophe for contractions or possessive nouns.*

If the word isn't found in CMUdict, add it to `exceptions` ❺. Print these words as a check, along with some basic information ❻, like how many unique words, how many missing words, and what percentage of the training corpus are members of CMUdict. Set the percent value precision to one decimal place ❼. End the function by returning the set of exceptions.

Building a Dictionary of Missing Words

Listing 8-3 continues the *missing_words_finder.py* code, now supplementing CMUdict by assigning syllable counts to the missing words as values in a Python dictionary. Since the number of missing words should be relatively small, the user can assign the counts manually, so write the code to help them interact with the program.

missing_words_finder.py, part 3

```
❶ def make_exceptions_dict(exceptions_set):
      """Return dictionary of words & syllable counts from a set of words."""
    ❷ missing_words = {}
      print("Input # syllables in word. Mistakes can be corrected at end. \n")
      for word in exceptions_set:
          while True:
            ❸ num_sylls = input("Enter number syllables in {}: ".format(word))
            ❹ if num_sylls.isdigit():
                  break
              else:
                  print("                 Not a valid answer!", file=sys.stderr)
        ❺ missing_words[word] = int(num_sylls)
      print()
    ❻ pprint.pprint(missing_words, width=1)

    ❼ print("\nMake Changes to Dictionary Before Saving?")
      print("""
      0 - Exit & Save
      1 - Add a Word or Change a Syllable Count
      2 - Remove a Word
      """)

    ❽ while True:
          choice = input("\nEnter choice: ")
          if choice == '0':
              break
          elif choice == '1':
              word = input("\nWord to add or change: ")
              missing_words[word] = int(input("Enter number syllables in {}: "
                                              .format(word)))
          elif choice == '2':
              word = input("\nEnter word to delete: ")
            ❾ missing_words.pop(word, None)

      print("\nNew words or syllable changes:")
    ❿ pprint.pprint(missing_words, width=1)

      return missing_words
```

Listing 8-3: Allows the user to manually count syllables and builds a dictionary

Start by defining a function that takes the set of exceptions returned by the `cmudict_missing()` function as an argument ❶. Immediately assign an empty dictionary to a variable named `missing_words` ❷. Let the user know that if they make a mistake, they'll have a chance to fix it later; then, use a `for` and `while` loop to go through the set of missing words and present each word to the user, asking for the number of syllables as input. The word will be the dictionary key, and the `num_sylls` variable will become its value ❸. If the input is a digit ❹, break out of the loop. Otherwise, warn the user and let the `while` loop request input again. If the input passes, add the value to the dictionary as an integer ❺.

Use pprint to display each key/value pair on a separate line, as a check. The width parameter acts as a newline argument ❻.

Give the user the opportunity to make last-minute changes to the missing_words dictionary before saving it as a file ❼. Use triple quotes to present the options menu, followed by a while loop to keep the options active until the user is ready to save ❽. The three options are exiting, which invokes the break command; adding a new word or changing the syllable count for an existing word, which requires the word and syllable count as input; and removing an entry, which uses the dictionary pop() function ❾. Adding the None argument to pop() means the program won't raise a KeyError if the user enters a word that's not in the dictionary.

Finish by giving the user a last look at the dictionary, in the event changes were made ❿, and then return it.

Saving the Missing Words Dictionary

Persistent data is data that is preserved after a program terminates. To make the missing_words dictionary available for use in the *count_syllables.py* program you'll write later in this chapter, you need to save it to a file. Listing 8-4 does just that.

missing_words_finder.py, part 4

```
❶ def save_exceptions(missing_words):
      """Save exceptions dictionary as json file."""
    ❷ json_string = json.dumps(missing_words)
    ❸ f = open('missing_words.json', 'w')
      f.write(json_string)
      f.close()
    ❹ print("\nFile saved as missing_words.json")

❺ if __name__ == '__main__':
      main()
```

Listing 8-4: Saves missing-words dictionary to a file and calls main()

Use json to save the dictionary. Define a new function that takes the set of missing words as an argument ❶. Assign the missing_words dictionary to a new variable named json_string ❷; then, open a file with a *.json* extension ❸, write the json variable, and close the file. Display the name of the file as a reminder to the user ❹. End with the code that lets the program be run as a module or in stand-alone mode ❺.

The json.dumps() method serializes the missing_words dictionary into a string. *Serialization* is the process of converting data into a more transmittable or storable format. For example:

```
>>> import json
>>> d = {'scarecrow': 2, 'moon': 1, 'sake': 2}
>>> json.dumps(d)
'{"sake": 2, "scarecrow": 2, "moon": 1}'
```

Note that the serialized dictionary is bound by single quotes, making it a string.

I've provided a partial output from *missing_words_finder.py* here. The list of missing words at the top and the manual syllable counts at the bottom have both been shortened for brevity.

```
--snip--
froglings
scatters
paperweights
hibiscus
cumulus
nightingales

Number of unique words in haiku corpus = 1523
Number of words in corpus not in cmudict = 58
cmudict membership = 96.2%

Manually build an exceptions dictionary (y/n)?
y
Enter number syllables in woodcutter: 3
Enter number syllables in morningglory: 4
Enter number syllables in cumulus: 3
--snip--
```

Don't worry—you won't have to assign all the syllable counts. The *missing_words.json* file is complete and ready for download when you need it.

NOTE *For words that have multiple pronunciations, like* jagged *or* our, *you can force the program to use the one you prefer by manually opening the* missing_words.json *file and adding the key/value pair (at any location, since dictionaries are unordered). I did this with the word* sake *so that it uses the two-syllable Japanese pronunciation. Because word membership is checked in this file first, it will override the CMUdict value.*

Now that you've addressed the holes in CMUdict, you're ready to write the code that counts syllables. In Chapter 9, you'll use this code as a module in the *markov_haiku.py* program.

The Count Syllables Code

This section contains the code for the *count_syllables.py* program. You'll also need the *missing_words.json* file you created in the previous section. You can download both from *https://www.nostarch.com/impracticalpython/*. Keep them together in the same folder.

Prepping, Loading, and Counting

Listing 8-5 imports the necessary modules, loads the CMUdict and missing-words dictionaries, and defines a function that will count the syllables in a given word or phrase.

count_syllables.py, part 1

```
import sys
from string import punctuation
import json
from nltk.corpus import cmudict

# load dictionary of words in haiku corpus but not in cmudict
with open('missing_words.json') as f:
    missing_words = json.load(f)

❶ cmudict = cmudict.dict()

❷ def count_syllables(words):
    """Use corpora to count syllables in English word or phrase."""
    # prep words for cmudict corpus
    words = words.replace('-', ' ')
    words = words.lower().split()
  ❸ num_sylls = 0
  ❹ for word in words:
        word = word.strip(punctuation)
        if word.endswith("'s") or word.endswith("’s"):
            word = word[:-2]
      ❺ if word in missing_words:
            num_sylls += missing_words[word]
        else:
          ❻ for phonemes in cmudict[word][0]:
                for phoneme in phonemes:
                  ❼ if phoneme[-1].isdigit():
                        num_sylls += 1
  ❽ return num_sylls
```

Listing 8-5: Imports modules, loads dictionaries, and counts syllables

After some familiar imports, load the *missing_words.json* file that contains all the words and syllable counts missing from CMUdict. Using `json.load()` restores the dictionary that was stored as a string. Next, turn the CMUdict corpus into a dictionary using the `dict()` method ❶.

Define a function called `count_syllables()` to count syllables. It should take both words *and* phrases, because you'll ultimately want to pass it lines from a haiku. Prep the words as you did previously in the *missing_words_finder.py* program ❷.

Assign a `num_sylls` variable to hold the syllable count and set it to `0` ❸. Now start looping through the input words, stripping punctuation and *'s* from the ends. Note that you can get tripped up by the format of the apostrophe, so two versions are supplied: one with a straight apostrophe and one with a curly apostrophe ❹. Next, check whether the word is a member of the small dictionary of missing words. If the word is found, add the dictionary value for the word to `num_sylls` ❺. Otherwise, start looking through the phonemes, which represent a value in CMUdict; for each phoneme, look through the strings that make it up ❻. If you find a digit at the end of the string, then you know that phoneme is a vowel. To illustrate using the word *aged*, only the first string (highlighted in gray here) ends with a digit, so the word contains one vowel:

```
[['EY1', 'JH', 'D'], ['EY1', 'JH', 'IH0', 'D']]
```

Note that you use the first value ([0]) in case there are multiple pronunciations; remember that CMUdict represents each pronunciation in a nested list. This may result in the occasional error, as the proper choice will depend on context.

Check whether the end of the phoneme has a digit, and if it does, add 1 to num_sylls ❼. Finally, return the total syllable count for the word or phrase ❽.

Defining the main() Function

Completing the program, Listing 8-6 defines and runs the main() function. The program will call this function when the program is run in stand-alone mode—for example, to spot-check a word or phrase—but it won't be called if you import syllable_counter as a module.

count_syllables.py, part 2

```
def main():
❶ while True:
        print("Syllable Counter")
      ❷ word = input("Enter word or phrase; else press Enter to Exit: ")
      ❸ if word == '':
            sys.exit()
      ❹ try:
            num_syllables = count_syllables(word)
            print("number of syllables in {} is: {}"
                  .format(word, num_syllables))
            print()
        except KeyError:
            print("Word not found.  Try again.\n", file=sys.stderr)
❺ if __name__ == '__main__':
    main()
```

Listing 8-6: Defines and calls the main() function

Define the main() function and then start a while loop ❶. Ask the user to input a word or phrase ❷. If the user presses ENTER with no input, the program exits ❸. Otherwise, start a try-except block so the program won't crash if a user enters a word not found in either dictionary ❹. An exception should be raised only in stand-alone mode, as you have already prepared the program to run on the haiku-training corpus with no exceptions. Within this block, the count_syllables() function is called and passed the input, and then the results are displayed in the interactive shell. End with the standard code that lets the program run stand-alone or as a module in another program ❺.

A Program to Check Your Program

You have carefully tailored the syllable-counting program to ensure it will work with the training corpus. As you continue with the haiku program, you may want to add a poem or two to this corpus, but adding new haiku might introduce a new word that isn't in either the CMUdict or your exceptions dictionary. Before you go back and rebuild the exceptions dictionary, check whether you really need to do so.

Listing 8-7 will automatically count the syllables in each word in your training corpus and display any word(s) on which it failed. You can download this program from *https://www.nostarch.com/impracticalpython/* as *test_count_syllables_w_full_corpus.py*. Keep it in the same folder as *count_syllables.py*, *train.txt*, and *missing_words.json*.

test_count_syllables_w_full_corpus.py

```
import sys
import count_syllables

with open('train.txt.') as in_file:
 ❶ words = set(in_file.read().split())

❷ missing = []

❸ for word in words:
    try:
        num_syllables = count_syllables.count_syllables(word)
        ##print(word, num_syllables, end='\n') # uncomment to see word counts
 ❹ except KeyError:
        missing.append(word)

❺ print("Missing words:", missing, file=sys.stderr)
```

Listing 8-7: Attempts to count syllables in words in a training corpus and lists all failures

Open your updated *train.txt* training corpus and load it as a set to remove duplicates ❶. Start an empty list, called `missing`, to hold any new words for which syllables can't be counted ❷. Words in `missing` won't be in CMUdict or in your `missing_words` dictionary.

Loop through the words in the new training corpus ❸ and use a `try-except` block to handle the `KeyError` that will be raised if *count_syllables.py* can't find the word ❹. Append this word to the `missing` list and then display the list ❺.

If the program displays an empty list, then all the words in the new haiku are already present in either CMUdict or *missing_words.json*, so you don't need to make any adjustments. Otherwise, you have the choice of manually adding the words to the *missing_words.json* file or rerunning *missing_words_finder.py* to rebuild *missing_words.json.*

Summary

In this chapter, you've learned how to download NLTK and use one of its datasets, the Carnegie Mellon Pronouncing Dictionary (CMUdict). You checked the CMUdict dataset against a training corpus of haiku and built a supporting Python dictionary for any missing words. You saved this Python dictionary as persistent data using JavaScript Object Notation (JSON). Finally, you wrote a program that can count syllables. In Chapter 9, you'll use your syllable-counting program to help you generate novel haiku.

Further Reading

Virtual Muse: Experiments in Computer Poetry (Wesleyan University Press, 1996) by Charles O. Hartman is an engaging look at the early collaboration between humans and computers to write poetry.

Natural Language Processing with Python: Analyzing Text with the Natural Language Toolkit (O'Reilly, 2009) by Steven Bird, Ewan Klein, and Edward Loper is an accessible introduction to NLP using Python, with lots of exercises and useful integration with the NLTK website. A new version of the book, updated for Python 3 and NLTK 3, is available online at *http://www.nltk.org/book/*.

"The Growing Importance of Natural Language Processing" by Stephen F. DeAngelis is a *Wired* magazine article on the expanding role of NLP in big data. An online version is available at *https://www.wired.com/insights/2014/02/growing-importance-natural-language-processing/*.

Practice Project: Syllable Counter vs. Dictionary File

Write a Python program that lets you test *count_syllables.py* (or any other syllable-counting Python code) against a dictionary file. After allowing the user to specify how many words to check, choose the words at random and display a listing of each word and its syllable count on separate lines. The output should look similar to this printout:

```
ululation 4
intimated 4
sand 1
worms 1
leatherneck 3
contenting 3
scandals 2
livelihoods 3
intertwining 4
beaming 2
untruthful 3
advice 2
accompanying 5
deathly 2
hallos 2
```

Downloadable dictionary files are listed in Table 2-1 on page 20. You can find a solution in the appendix that can be downloaded from *https://www.nostarch.com/impracticalpython/* as *test_count_syllables_w_dict.py*.

9

WRITING HAIKU WITH MARKOV CHAIN ANALYSIS

Computers can write poetry by rearranging existing poems. This is basically what humans do. You and I didn't invent the language we speak—we learned it. To talk or write, we just recombine existing words—and rarely in a truly original manner. As Sting once said about writing music, "I don't think there's such a thing as composition in pop music. I think what we do in pop music is collate . . . I'm a good collator."

In this chapter, you're going to write a program that puts the "best words in the best order" in the form of haiku. But to do this, Python needs good examples, so you'll need to provide a training corpus of haiku by the Japanese masters.

To rearrange these words in a meaningful manner, you will use *Markov chains*, named after Russian mathematician Andrey Markov. *Markov chain analysis*, an important part of probability theory, is a process that attempts to predict the subsequent state based on the properties of the current state. Modern-day applications include speech and handwriting recognition, computer performance evaluation, spam filtering, and Google's PageRank algorithm for searching the web.

With Markov chain analysis, a training corpus, and the syllable-counting program from Chapter 8, you'll be able to produce new haiku that follow the syllabic rules of the genre and stay "on subject" to a large degree. You'll also learn how to use Python's `logging` module to help monitor the behavior of your program with easy on-and-off feedback. And in "Challenge Projects" on page 184, you can enlist your friends on social media to see if they can distinguish your simulated haiku from the real thing.

Project #16: Markov Chain Analysis

Like the genetic algorithms in Chapter 7, Markov chain analysis sounds impressive but is easy to implement. You do it every day. If you hear some one say, "Elementary, my dear . . . ," you automatically think, "Watson." Every time your brain has heard this phrase, it has taken a sample. Based on the number of samples, it can predict the answer. On the other hand, if you heard someone say, "I want to go to . . . ," you might think "the bathroom" or "the movies" but probably not "Houma, Louisiana." There are many possible solutions, but some are more likely than others.

Back in the 1940s, Claude Shannon pioneered the use of Markov chains to statistically model the sequences of letters in a body of text. For example, for every occurrence of the digram *th* in an English-language book, the next most likely letter is *e*.

But you don't just want to know what the most likely letter is; you want to know the actual probability of getting that letter, as well as the odds of getting every other letter, which is a problem tailor-made for a computer. To solve this problem, you need to map each two-letter digram in a piece of text to the letter that immediately follows it. This is a classic dictionary application, with the digrams as the keys and the letters as the values.

When applied to letters in words, a *Markov model* is a mathematical model that calculates a letter's probability of occurrence based on the previous k consecutive letters, where k is an integer. A *model of order 2* means that the probability of a letter occurring depends on the two letters that precede it. A *model of order 0* means that each letter is independent. And this same logic applies to words. Consider these two haiku examples:

A break in the clouds
The moon a bright mountaintop
Distant and aloof

Glorious the moon
Therefore our thanks dark clouds come
To rest our tired necks

A Python dictionary that maps each haiku word to each subsequent word looks like this:

```
'a': ['break', 'bright'],
'aloof': ['glorious'],
```

```
'and': ['aloof'],
'break': ['in'],
'bright': ['mountaintop'],
'clouds': ['the', 'come'],
'come': ['to'],
'dark': ['clouds'],
'distant': ['and'],
'glorious': ['the'],
'in': ['the'],
'moon': ['a', 'therefore'],
'mountaintop': ['distant'],
'our': ['thanks', 'tired'],
'rest': ['our'],
'thanks': ['dark'],
'the': ['clouds', 'moon', 'moon'],
'therefore': ['our'],
'tired': ['necks'],
'to': ['rest']
```

Since there are only two haiku, most of the dictionary keys have only one value. But look at *the* near the bottom of the list: *moon* occurs twice. This is because the Markov model stores every occurrence of a word as a separate, duplicate value. So, for the key *the*, if you choose a value at random, the odds of selecting *moon* versus *clouds* are 2:1. Conversely, the model will automatically screen out extremely rare or impossible combinations. For example, many words can potentially follow *the*, but not another *the*!

The following dictionary maps every *pair* of words to the word immediately after; that means it's a model of order 2.

```
'a break': ['in'],
'a bright': ['mountaintop'],
'aloof glorious': ['the'],
'and aloof': ['glorious'],
'break in': ['the'],
'bright mountaintop': ['distant'],
'clouds come': ['to'],
'clouds the': ['moon'],
'come to': ['rest'],
'dark clouds': ['come'],
'distant and': ['aloof'],
'glorious the': ['moon'],
'in the': ['clouds'],
'moon a': ['bright'],
'moon therefore': ['our'],
'mountaintop distant': ['and'],
'our thanks': ['dark'],
'our tired': ['necks'],
'rest our': ['tired'],
'thanks dark': ['clouds'],
'the clouds': ['the'],
'the moon': ['a', 'therefore'],
'therefore our': ['thanks'],
'to rest': ['our']
```

Note that the mapping continues from the first haiku to the second so the dictionary contains the items `'and aloof': ['glorious']` and `'aloof glorious': ['the']`. This behavior means your program can jump from one haiku to another and is not restricted to just the word pairs within a single haiku. It is free to form new word pairs that the masters may never have conceived.

Because of the very short training corpus, *the moon* is the only word pair with multiple keys. For all the others, you are "locked in" to a single outcome. In this example, the size of the training corpus greatly determines the number of values per key, but with a larger corpus, the value of *k* in the Markov model will have a larger influence.

The size of *k* determines whether you produce poppycock, commit plagiarism, or produce a perspicuous piece of originality. If *k* equals 0, then you'll be choosing words at random based on that word's overall frequency in the corpus, and you'll likely produce a lot of gibberish. If *k* is large, the results will be tightly constrained, and you'll begin to reproduce the training text verbatim. So small values of *k* promote creativity, and large values promote duplication. The challenge is finding the proper balance between the two.

To illustrate, if you use a Markov model of order 3 on the previous haiku, all the resulting keys will have one value. The two values associated with the word pair *the moon* are lost because the former word pair becomes two keys, each with a unique value:

```
'the moon a': ['bright'],
'the moon therefore': ['our']
```

Since haiku are short—only 17 syllables long—and available training corpora are relatively small, using a *k* of 2 should be sufficient to enforce *some* order while still allowing for creative word substitutions in your program.

THE OBJECTIVE

Write a program that generates haiku using Markov chain analysis. Allow the user to modify the haiku by independently regenerating lines two and three.

The Strategy

Your general strategy for simulating haiku will be to build Markov models of orders 1 and 2 with a training corpus of haiku written by humans. You'll then use those models and the *count_syllables.py* program from Chapter 8 to generate novel haiku that meet the required syllabic structure of 5-7-5 for the three lines of the haiku.

The program should build the haiku one word at a time, initiating (or *seeding*) the haiku with a random word drawn from the corpus; selecting the haiku's second word using a Markov model of order 1; and then selecting each subsequent word with the order 2 model.

Each word is derived from a *prefix*—a word or word pair that determines which word will be picked to go in the haiku; the key in the word-mapping dictionaries represents the prefix. As a consequence, the word that the prefix determines is the *suffix*.

Choosing and Discarding Words

When the program selects a word, it first counts the word's syllables, and if the word doesn't fit, it chooses a new word. If there are no possible words based on the prefix in the poem, then the program resorts to what I call a *ghost prefix*, which is a prefix that doesn't occur in the haiku. For example, if a word pair in a haiku is *temple gong*, and all the words that follow in the Markov model have too many syllables to complete the line, the program selects a new word pair at random and uses it to pick the next word in the haiku. The new word-pair prefix *should not be included in the line*—that is, *temple gong* will not be replaced. Although you could choose a suitable new word in a number of ways, I prefer this technique because it allows you to simplify by maintaining a consistent process throughout the program.

You can accomplish these steps with the functions in Figures 9-1 and 9-2. Assuming you're working on a five-syllable line, Figure 9-1 is an example of what will happen, at a high level, if all the chosen words match the syllable target.

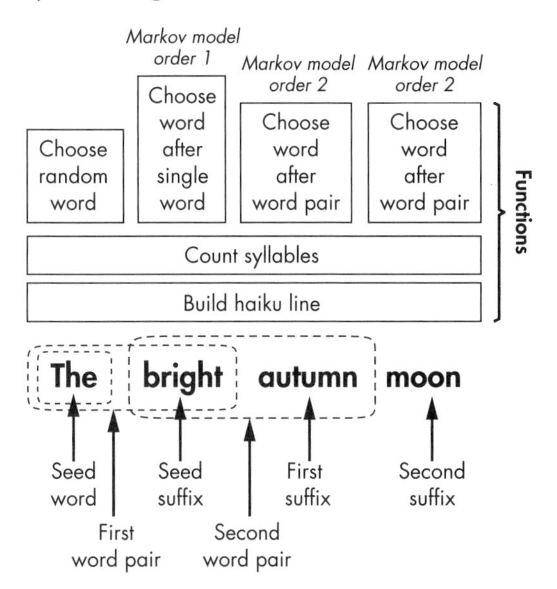

Figure 9-1: High-level graphical pseudocode for a five-syllable haiku line

The program randomly selects the seed word *the* from the corpus, and then counts its syllables. Next, it chooses *bright* from the model of order 1, based on the prefix *the*. Then it counts the number of syllables in *bright* and adds that number to the number of syllables in the line. Since the sum of syllables doesn't exceed five, the program adds *bright* to the line, moves on to select *autumn* from the model of order 2 based on the prefix *The bright*, and then repeats the syllable-counting process. Finally, the program selects *moon* based on the prefix *bright autumn*, counts the syllables, and—since the line's total number of syllables is equal to five—adds moon to the line, completing it.

Figure 9-2 demonstrates a case where the program needs to utilize a ghost prefix to successfully complete a five-syllable line.

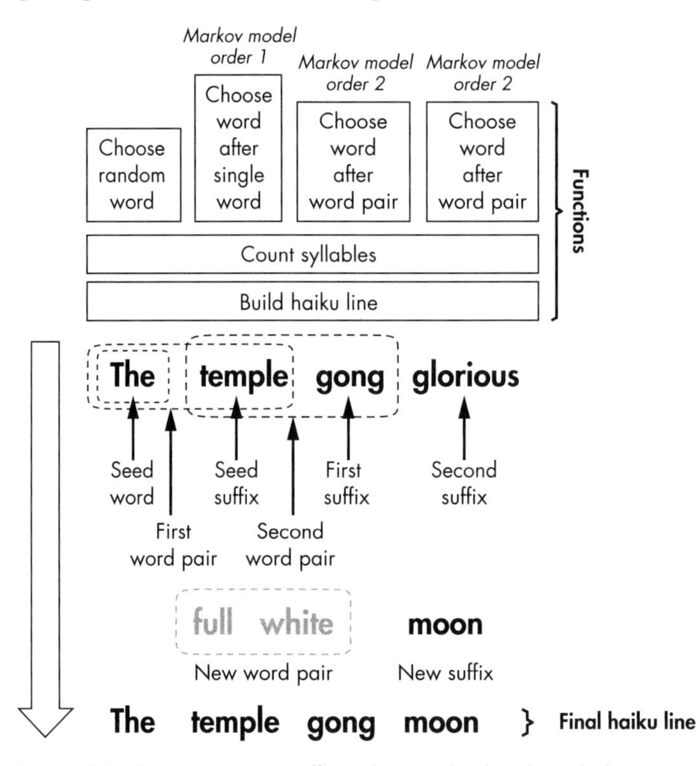

*Figure 9-2: Choosing a new suffix with a randomly selected ghost prefix (*full white*)*

Let's assume that the only word that follows the prefix *temple gong* in the Markov model is *glorious*. This word has too many syllables for the line, so the program selects a ghost prefix, *full white*, at random. The word *moon* follows the ghost prefix and satisfies the remaining syllable count in the line, so the program adds it to the line. The program then discards the *full white* prefix, and the line is complete. With this ghost prefix technique, you can't guarantee that the new suffix will make sense contextually, but at the same time, this is one way to incorporate creativity into the process.

Continuing from One Line to Another

The Markov model is the "special sauce" that allows you to imbue the haiku with context and meaning that continue from one line to another. The Japanese masters *generally* wrote haiku in which each line is a stand-alone phrase but the contextual thread continues across lines, as in this haiku from Bon Cho:

> In silent midnight
> Our old scarecrow topples down
> Weird hollow echo
>
> —*Bon Cho*

Even though the masters preferred that each line of a haiku represent a complete thought, they didn't strictly follow the rule. Here's an example in Buson's haiku:

> My two plum trees are
> So gracious see, they flower
> One now, one later
>
> —*Buson*

The first line of Buson's haiku is not grammatical on its own, so the reader must continue to the next line without a break. When a phrase in poetry moves from one line to the next without a pause or syntactic break, it is said to be *enjambed*. According to Charles Hartman, author of *Virtual Muse*, enjambment is what gives metrical lines much of their supple liveliness. That's a good thing, since it's very hard to get an algorithm to write a coherent poem without some grammatical spillover from line to line. To get your program to continue a "thought" through multiple lines, you need to use the word pair from the end of the previous line as the starting prefix for the current line.

Finally, you should give the user the opportunity to not only build the poem but also to edit it interactively by regenerating lines two and three. Most of writing is rewriting, and it would be unconscionable to leave the user hanging with two perfect lines and no way to throw the dice again on an uncooperative line.

The Pseudocode

If you follow the strategy I've just laid out, your high-level pseudocode should look like this:

```
Import count_syllables module
Load a training-corpus text file
Process the training corpus for spaces, newline breaks, and so on
Map each word in corpus to the word after (Markov model order 1)
Map each word pair in corpus to the word after (Markov model order 2)
Give user choice of generating full haiku, redoing lines 2 or 3, or exiting
```

```
If first line:
    Target syllables = 5
    Get random word from corpus <= 4 syllables (no 1-word lines)
    Add word to line
    Set random word = prefix variable
    Get mapped words after prefix
    If mapped words have too many syllables
        Choose new prefix word at random & repeat
    Choose new word at random from mapped words
    Add the new word to the line
    Count syllables in word and calculate total in line
    If syllables in line equal target syllables
        Return line and last word pair in line
Else if second or third line:
    Target = 7 or 5
    Line equals last word pair in previous line
    While syllable target not reached:
        Prefix = last word pair in line
        Get mapped words after word-pair prefix
        If mapped words have too many syllables
            Choose new word-pair prefix at random and repeat
        Choose new word at random from mapped words
        Add the new word to the line
        Count syllables in word and calculate total in line
        If total is greater than target
            Discard word, reset total, and repeat
        Else if total is less than target
            Add word to line, keep total, and repeat
        Else if total is equal to target
            Add word to line
    Return line and last word pair in line
Display results and choice menu
```

The Training Corpus

Markov models are built from a corpus, so they are unique to that corpus. A model built from the complete works of Edgar Rice Burroughs will be different and distinguishable from one built from the works of Anne Rice. We all have a signature style, or *voice*, and given a large enough sample, a Markov approach can produce a statistical model of your style. Like fingerprints, this model can link you to a document or manuscript.

To build the Markov models, the corpus you'll use is a text file consisting of almost 300 ancient and modern haiku, more than 200 of which were written by the masters. Ideally, your training corpus would consist of thousands of haiku, all by the same author (for a consistent voice), but these are difficult to find, particularly since many of the old Japanese haiku don't obey the syllabic rules, either intentionally or as a result of translation into English.

To increase the number of values per key in the Markov model, the haiku in the initial corpus were duplicated 18 times and randomly distributed throughout the file. This has no impact on word associations *within* haiku but increases the interactions *between* haiku.

To illustrate, assume the word pair at the end of the following haiku is unique, mapping only to the starting word of the second haiku; this results in the fairly useless key/value pair of `'hollow frog': ['mirror-pond']`:

Open mouth reveals
Your whole wet interior
Silly **hollow frog**!

Mirror-pond of stars
Suddenly a summer shower
Dimples the water

If you duplicate and shuffle the haiku, you may introduce a preposition into the mix, greatly increasing the odds of linking the odd *hollow frog* to something sensible:

Open mouth reveals
Your whole wet interior
Silly **hollow frog**!

In the city fields
Contemplating cherry trees
Strangers are like friends

The Markov model now assigns two values to `'hollow frog'`: `'mirror-pond'` and `'in'`. And each time you duplicate the haiku, you'll see an increase in the number of values per key for haiku-ending words or word pairs. But this is helpful only to a point; after a while, diminishing returns set in, and you start adding the same values over and over again, gaining nothing.

Debugging

Debugging is the process of finding and fixing errors (bugs) in computer hardware and software. When you're trying to code a solution to a complex problem, you need to keep a tight rein on your program in order to find the source of an issue when something unexpected arises. For example, if you end up with seven syllables rather than five in the first line of your haiku, you'll want to know if the syllable-counting function failed, if there was a problem mapping words to words, or if the program thought it was on line two. To find out what went wrong, you need to monitor what your program is returning at each key step, and this calls for either *scaffolding* or *logging*. I'll discuss each of these techniques in the following two sections.

Building the Scaffolding

Scaffolding, as defined here, is temporary code you write to help develop your programs, then delete when you're done. The name is an allusion to the scaffolding used in construction—necessary, but nobody wants it around forever.

One common piece of scaffolding is a `print()` statement that checks what a function or calculation returns. The user doesn't need to see the output, so you delete it after you confirm the program is working properly.

Useful scaffolding output includes things like the type of a value or variable, the length of a dataset, and the results of incremental calculations. To quote Allen Downey in *Think Python*, "Time you spend building scaffolding can reduce the time you spend debugging."

The downside to using `print()` statements for debugging is that you have to go back and delete (or comment out) all these statements later, and you risk accidentally removing a `print()` statement that's useful to the end user. Fortunately, there's an alternative to scaffolding that lets you avoid these problems. It's called the `logging` module.

Using the logging Module

The `logging` module is part of the Python Standard Library (*https://docs.python.org/3/library/logging.html*). With `logging`, you can get a customized report on what your program is doing at any location you choose. You can even write the reports to a permanent logfile. The following interactive shell example uses `logging` to check that a vowel-counting program is working correctly:

```
❶ >>> import logging
❷ >>> logging.basicConfig(level=logging.DEBUG,
                          format='%(levelname)s - %(message)s')
  >>> word = 'scarecrow'
  >>> VOWELS = 'aeiouy'
  >>> num_vowels = 0
  >>> for letter in word:
          if letter in VOWELS:
              num_vowels += 1
        ❸ logging.debug('letter & count = %s-%s', letter, num_vowels)

  DEBUG - letter & count = s-0
  DEBUG - letter & count = c-0
  DEBUG - letter & count = a-1
  DEBUG - letter & count = r-1
  DEBUG - letter & count = e-2
  DEBUG - letter & count = c-2
  DEBUG - letter & count = r-2
  DEBUG - letter & count = o-3
  DEBUG - letter & count = w-3
```

To use the `logging` module, first import it ❶. Then set up what debugging information you want to see and in what format ❷. The `DEBUG` level is the lowest level of information and is used for diagnosing the details.

Note that the output uses string formatting with `%s`. You can include more information—for example, the date and time are shown using `format='%(asctime)s'`—but for this snippet of code, all you really need to check is whether the program is counting vowels correctly.

For each letter evaluated, enter the custom text message to display along with the variable values. Note that you have to convert nonstring objects, such as integers and lists, to strings ❸. The `logging` output follows. You can see the cumulative count, along with which letters actually change the count.

Like scaffolding, `logging` is for the developer, not the user. And like the `print()` function, `logging` can slow down your program. To disable the `logging` messages, simply insert the `logging.disable(logging.CRITICAL)` call after you import the module, as follows:

```
>>> import logging
>>> logging.disable(logging.CRITICAL)
```

Placing the disable call near the top of the program will allow you to find it easily and toggle messages on and off. The `logging.disable()` function will suppress all messages at the designated level or lower. Since `CRITICAL` is the highest level, passing it to the `logging.disable()` function turns all messages off. This is a far better solution than manually finding and commenting out `print()` statements!

The Code

The *markov_haiku.py* code in this section will take a training corpus called *train.txt*, prepare Markov models as dictionaries, and generate a haiku one word at a time. The *count_syllables.py* program and *missing_words.json* file from Chapter 8 will ensure *markov_haiku.py* uses the correct number of syllables for each line. You can download all these files from *https://www.nostarch.com/impracticalpython/* (Chapter 9 folder). Be sure to keep them together in the same directory.

Setting Up

Listing 9-1 imports the necessary modules, then loads and prepares external files.

markov_haiku.py, part 1

```
❶ import sys
  import logging
  import random
  from collections import defaultdict
  from count_syllables import count_syllables

❷ logging.disable(logging.CRITICAL)  # comment out to enable debugging messages
  logging.basicConfig(level=logging.DEBUG, format='%(message)s')

❸ def load_training_file(file):
      """Return text file as a string."""
      with open(file) as f:
```

```
    ❹ raw_haiku = f.read()
      return raw_haiku

❺ def prep_training(raw_haiku):
    """Load string, remove newline, split words on spaces, and return list."""
    corpus = raw_haiku.replace('\n', ' ').split()
    return corpus
```

Listing 9-1: Imports, loads, and prepares the training corpus

Start with the imports listed on separate lines ❶. You'll need logging in order to receive debugging messages, and defaultdict will help you build a dictionary from a list by creating a new key automatically, rather than throwing an error. You also import the count_syllables function from the *count_syllables.py* program you wrote in Chapter 8. You should be familiar with the rest of these imports.

Put the statement to disable logging right after the imports so you can find it easily. To see logging messages, you need to comment out this statement ❷. The following statement configures what you will see, as described in the previous section. I chose to omit the level designation from the display.

Next, define a function to load the training-corpus text file ❸. Use the built-in read() function to read the data as a string that the program can prepare before converting it to a list ❹. Return this string for use in the next function.

The prep_training() function ❺ takes the output from the load_training_file() function as an argument. It then replaces newline characters with spaces and splits the words into list items based on spaces. Finally, the function returns the corpus as a list.

Building Markov Models

The Markov models are simply Python dictionaries that use a word or word pair as a key and the word that immediately follows them as a value. The statistical frequency of trailing words is captured by repetition of the trailing word in the list of values—similar to sets, dictionaries can't have duplicate *keys*, but they can have duplicate *values*.

Listing 9-2 defines two functions. Both functions take the corpus as an argument and return a Markov model.

markov_haiku.py, part 2

```
❶ def map_word_to_word(corpus):
    """Load list & use dictionary to map word to word that follows."""
  ❷ limit = len(corpus) - 1
  ❸ dict1_to_1 = defaultdict(list)
  ❹ for index, word in enumerate(corpus):
        if index < limit:
          ❺ suffix = corpus[index + 1]
            dict1_to_1[word].append(suffix)
  ❻ logging.debug("map_word_to_word results for \"sake\" = %s\n",
                  dict1_to_1['sake'])
  ❼ return dict1_to_1
```

```
❽ def map_2_words_to_word(corpus):
       """Load list & use dictionary to map word-pair to trailing word."""
    ❾ limit = len(corpus) - 2
       dict2_to_1 = defaultdict(list)
       for index, word in enumerate(corpus):
           if index < limit:
             ❿ key = word + ' ' + corpus[index + 1]
               suffix = corpus[index + 2]
               dict2_to_1[key].append(suffix)
       logging.debug("map_2_words_to_word results for \"sake jug\" = %s\n",
                     dict2_to_1['sake jug'])
       return dict2_to_1
```

Listing 9-2: Defines functions that build Markov models of order 1 and 2

First, define a function to map every single word to its trailing word ❶. The program will use this function only to select the haiku's second word from the seed word. Its only parameter is the corpus list that the `prep_training()` function returns.

Set a limit so you can't pick the last word in the corpus ❷, because doing so would result in an index error. Now initialize a dictionary using `defaultdict` ❸. You want the dictionary values to be lists that hold all the suffixes you find, so use `list` as the argument.

Start looping through every word in the corpus, using `enumerate` to turn each word's index into an object ❹. Use a conditional and the `limit` variable to prevent choosing the last word as a key. Assign a variable named `suffix` that will represent the trailing word ❺. The value will be the index location of the current word plus 1—the next word in the list. Append this variable to the dictionary as a value of the current word.

To check that everything is working as planned, use `logging` to show the results *for a single key* ❻. There are thousands of words in the corpus, so you're not going to want to print them all. Choose a word that you know is in the corpus, like *sake*. Note that you are using the old string formatting with `%`, as it fits the current design of the logger. Finish by returning the dictionary ❼.

The next function, `map_2_words_to_word()`, is basically the same function, except it uses two consecutive words as the key and maps to trailing single words ❽. Important changes are to set the limit two words back from the end of the corpus ❾, make the key consist of two words with a space between them ❿, and add 2 to the index for the `suffix`.

Choosing a Random Word

The program won't be able to utilize a Markov model without a key, so either the user or the program must supply the first word in a simulated haiku. Listing 9-3 defines a function that picks a first word at random, facilitating automated seeding.

markov_haiku.py, part 3

```
❶ def random_word(corpus):
       """Return random word and syllable count from training corpus."""
    ❷ word = random.choice(corpus)
    ❸ num_syls = count_syllables(word)
```

```
❹ if num_syls > 4:
      random_word(corpus)
  else:
    ❺ logging.debug("random word & syllables = %s %s\n", word, num_syls)
      return (word, num_syls)
```

Listing 9-3: Randomly chooses a seed word to initiate the haiku

Define the function and pass it the corpus list ❶. Then assign a word variable and use the random choice() method to pick a word from the corpus ❷.

Use the count_syllables() function from the count_syllables module to count the syllables in the word; store the count in the num_syls variable ❸. I'm not a fan of single-word lines in haiku, so don't allow the function to choose a word with more than four syllables (recall that the shortest haiku lines have five syllables). If this occurs, call the random_word() function recursively until you get an acceptable word ❹. Note that Python has a default maximum recursion depth of 1,000, but as long as you're using a proper haiku-training corpus, there's little chance you'll exceed that prior to finding a suitable word. If that were not the case, you could address this condition later by calling the function using a while loop.

If the word has fewer than five syllables, use logging to display the word and its syllable count ❺; then return the word and syllable count as a tuple.

Applying the Markov Models

To choose the single word that follows the seed word, use the Markov model of order 1. After that, the program should select all subsequent words using the order 2 model, which uses word pairs as keys. Listing 9-4 defines a separate function for each of these actions.

markov_haiku.py, part 4

```
❶ def word_after_single(prefix, suffix_map_1, current_syls, target_syls):
      """Return all acceptable words in a corpus that follow a single word."""
    ❷ accepted_words = []
    ❸ suffixes = suffix_map_1.get(prefix)
    ❹ if suffixes != None:
        ❺ for candidate in suffixes:
              num_syls = count_syllables(candidate)
              if current_syls + num_syls <= target_syls:
                ❻ accepted_words.append(candidate)
    ❼ logging.debug("accepted words after \"%s\" = %s\n",
                     prefix, set(accepted_words))
      return accepted_words

❽ def word_after_double(prefix, suffix_map_2, current_syls, target_syls):
      """Return all acceptable words in a corpus that follow a word pair."""
      accepted_words = []
    ❾ suffixes = suffix_map_2.get(prefix)
      if suffixes != None:
          for candidate in suffixes:
              num_syls = count_syllables(candidate)
              if current_syls + num_syls <= target_syls:
                  accepted_words.append(candidate)
```

```
    logging.debug("accepted words after \"%s\" = %s\n",
                  prefix, set(accepted_words))
❿ return accepted_words
```

Listing 9-4: Two functions that select a word given a prefix, Markov model, and syllable count

Define a function named `word_after_single()` to select the next word in the haiku based on the preceding single seed word. For arguments, this function takes the preceding word, the Markov order 1 model, the current syllable count, and the target syllable count ❶.

Start an empty list to hold the acceptable words, which are the words that both follow the prefix and whose syllable count doesn't exceed the syllable target ❷. Call these trailing words `suffixes` and use the dictionary `get()` method, which returns a dictionary value given a key, to assign them to the variable ❸. Rather than raising a `KeyError`, the `get()` method will return `None` if you request a key that isn't in the dictionary.

There is the extremely rare chance that the prefix will be the last word in a corpus and that it will be unique. In that case, there will be no suffixes. Use an `if` statement to anticipate this ❹. If there are no suffixes, the function that calls `word_after_single()`, which you'll define in the next section, chooses a new prefix.

Each of the suffixes represents a *candidate* word for the haiku, but the program hasn't yet determined whether a candidate will "fit." So use a `for` loop, the `count_syllables` module, and an `if` statement to determine whether adding the word to the line violates the target number of syllables per line ❺. If the target isn't exceeded, append the word to the list of accepted words ❻. Display the acceptable words in a `logging` message and then return it ❼.

The next function, `word_after_double()`, is like the previous function except that you pass it word pairs and the Markov order 2 model (`suffix_map_2`) ❽ and get the suffixes from this dictionary ❾. But just like the `word_after_single()` function, `word_after_double()` returns a list of acceptable words ❿.

Generating the Haiku Lines

With all the helper functions ready, you can define the function that actually writes the lines of the haiku. The function can build either the whole haiku or just update lines two or three. There are two paths to take: one to use when the program has at most a one-word suffix to work with and another for every other situation.

Building the First Line

Listing 9-5 defines the function that writes haiku lines and initiates the haiku's first line.

markov_haiku.py, part 5

```
❶ def haiku_line(suffix_map_1, suffix_map_2, corpus, end_prev_line, target_syls):
      """Build a haiku line from a training corpus and return it."""
  ❷ line = '2/3'
      line_syls = 0
      current_line = []
```

```
❸ if len(end_prev_line) == 0:  # build first line
    ❹ line = '1'
    ❺ word, num_syls = random_word(corpus)
      current_line.append(word)
      line_syls += num_syls
    ❻ word_choices = word_after_single(word, suffix_map_1,
                                         line_syls, target_syls)
    ❼ while len(word_choices) == 0:
          prefix = random.choice(corpus)
          logging.debug("new random prefix = %s", prefix)
          word_choices = word_after_single(prefix, suffix_map_1,
                                             line_syls, target_syls)
    ❽ word = random.choice(word_choices)
      num_syls = count_syllables(word)
      logging.debug("word & syllables = %s %s", word, num_syls)
    ❾ line_syls += num_syls
      current_line.append(word)
    ❿ if line_syls == target_syls:
          end_prev_line.extend(current_line[-2:])
          return current_line, end_prev_line
```

Listing 9-5: Defines the function that writes haiku lines and initiates the first line

Define a function that takes as arguments both Markov models, the training corpus, the last word pair from the end of the preceding line, and the target number of syllables for the current line ❶. Immediately use a variable to specify which haiku lines are being simulated ❷. Most of the processing will be for lines two and three (and possibly the last part of line one), where you will be working with an existing word-pair prefix, so let these represent the base case. After this, start a counter for the running total of syllables in the line and start an empty list to hold the words in the current line.

Use an `if` statement that's `True` under the condition that the `end_prev_line` parameter's length—the number of syllables in the previous line's last two words—is 0, meaning there was no preceding line and you are on line one ❸. The first statement in that `if` block changes the `line` variable to 1 ❹.

Choose the initial seed word and get its syllable count by calling the `random_word()` function ❺. By assigning the `word` and `num_syls` variables together, you are "unpacking" the `(word, num_sylls)` tuple that the `random_word()` function returns. Functions end at `return` statements, so returning tuples is a great way to return multiple variables. In a more advanced version of this program, you could use generator functions with the `yield` keyword, as `yield` returns a value without relinquishing control of execution.

Next, append the `word` to `current_line` and add the `num_syls` to the running total. Now that you have a seed, collect all the seed's possible suffixes with the `word_after_single()` function ❻.

If there are no acceptable words, start a `while` loop to handle this situation. This loop will continue until a non-empty list of acceptable word choices has been returned ❼. The program will choose a new prefix—a ghost prefix—using the `random` module's `choice` method. (Remember that this prefix will not become part of the haiku but is used only to reaccess the Markov model.) Inside the while loop, a logging message will let you know which ghost prefix has been chosen. Then the program will call word_after_single() function once more.

Once the list of acceptable words is built, use choice again to select a word from the word_choices list ❽. Because the list may include duplicate words, this is where you see the statistical impact of the Markov model. Follow by counting the syllables in the word and logging the results.

Add the syllable count to the line's running total and append the word to the current_line list ❾.

If the number of syllables in the first two words equals 5 ❿, name a variable end_prev_line and assign it the last two words of the previous line; this variable is the prefix for line two. Finally, return the whole line and the end_prev_line variable.

If the target number of syllables for the first line hasn't been reached, the program will jump to the while loop in the next section to complete the line.

Building the Remaining Lines

In Listing 9-6, the last part of the haiku_line() function addresses the case where the haiku already contains a word-pair prefix that the program can use in the Markov order 2 model. The program uses it to complete line one—assuming the first two words didn't already total five syllables—and to build lines two and three. The user will also be able to regenerate lines two or three, after a complete haiku has been written.

markov_haiku.py, part 6

```
❶ else: # build lines 2 and 3
    ❷ current_line.extend(end_prev_line)

❸ while True:
        logging.debug("line = %s\n", line)
    ❹ prefix = current_line[-2] + ' ' + current_line[-1]
    ❺ word_choices = word_after_double(prefix, suffix_map_2,
                                          line_syls, target_syls)
    ❻ while len(word_choices) == 0:
            index = random.randint(0, len(corpus) - 2)
            prefix = corpus[index] + ' ' + corpus[index + 1]
            logging.debug("new random prefix = %s", prefix)
            word_choices = word_after_double(prefix, suffix_map_2,
                                              line_syls, target_syls)
        word = random.choice(word_choices)
        num_syls = count_syllables(word)
        logging.debug("word & syllables = %s %s", word, num_syls)

    ❼ if line_syls + num_syls > target_syls:
            continue
        elif line_syls + num_syls < target_syls:
            current_line.append(word)
            line_syls += num_syls
        elif line_syls + num_syls == target_syls:
            current_line.append(word)
            break
```

```
❽ end_prev_line = []
  end_prev_line.extend(current_line[-2:])

❾ if line == '1':
      final_line = current_line[:]
  else:
      final_line = current_line[2:]

  return final_line, end_prev_line
```

Listing 9-6: Uses a Markov order 2 model to complete the function that writes haiku lines

Start with an else statement that's executed if there is a suffix ❶. Since the last part of the haiku_line() function has to handle line one as well as lines two and three, use a trick where you add the end_prev_line list (built outside the conditional at step ❽) to the current_line list ❷. Later, when you add the finalized line to the haiku, you'll discard this leading word pair.

Start a while loop that continues until the target syllable count for the line has been reached ❸. The start of each iteration begins with a debugging message that informs you of the path the loop is evaluating: '1' or '2/3'.

With the last two words of the previous line added to the start of the current line, the last two words of the current line will always be the prefix ❹.

Using the Markov order 2 model, create a list of acceptable words ❺. In the event the list is empty, the program uses the ghost prefix process ❻.

Evaluate what to do next using the syllable count ❼. If there are too many syllables, use a continue statement to restart the while loop. If there aren't enough syllables, append the word and add its syllable count to the line's syllable count. Otherwise, append the word and end the loop.

Assign the last two words in the line to the end_prev_line variable so the program can use it as a prefix for the next line ❽. If the current path is line '1', copy the current line to a variable called final_line; if the path is line '2/3', use index slicing to exclude the first two words before assigning to final_line ❾. This is how you remove the initial end_prev_line word pair from lines two or three.

Writing the User Interface

Listing 9-7 defines the *markov_haiku.py* program's main() function, which runs the setup functions and the user interface. The interface presents the user with a menu of choices and displays the resulting haiku.

markov_haiku.py, part 7

```
def main():
    """Give user choice of building a haiku or modifying an existing haiku."""
    intro = """\n
    A thousand monkeys at a thousand typewriters...
    or one computer...can sometimes produce a haiku.\n"""
    print("{}".format(intro))

  ❶ raw_haiku = load_training_file("train.txt")
    corpus = prep_training(raw_haiku)
    suffix_map_1 = map_word_to_word(corpus)
```

```
    suffix_map_2 = map_2_words_to_word(corpus)
    final = []

    choice = None
❷ while choice != "0":

    ❸ print(
            """
            Japanese Haiku Generator

            0 - Quit
            1 - Generate a Haiku
            2 - Regenerate Line 2
            3 - Regenerate Line 3
            """
            )

    ❹ choice = input("Choice: ")
        print()

        # exit
    ❺ if choice == "0":
            print("Sayonara.")
            sys.exit()

        # generate a full haiku
    ❻ elif choice == "1":
            final = []
            end_prev_line = []
            first_line, end_prev_line1 = haiku_line(suffix_map_1, suffix_map_2,
                                                    corpus, end_prev_line, 5)
            final.append(first_line)
            line, end_prev_line2 = haiku_line(suffix_map_1, suffix_map_2,
                                              corpus, end_prev_line1, 7)
            final.append(line)
            line, end_prev_line3 = haiku_line(suffix_map_1, suffix_map_2,
                                              corpus, end_prev_line2, 5)
            final.append(line)

        # regenerate line 2
    ❼ elif choice == "2":
            if not final:
                print("Please generate a full haiku first (Option 1).")
                continue
            else:
                line, end_prev_line2 = haiku_line(suffix_map_1, suffix_map_2,
                                                  corpus, end_prev_line1, 7)
                final[1] = line

        # regenerate line 3
    ❽ elif choice == "3":
            if not final:
                print("Please generate a full haiku first (Option 1).")
                continue
```

```
            else:
                line, end_prev_line3 = haiku_line(suffix_map_1, suffix_map_2,
                                                  corpus, end_prev_line2, 5)
                final[2] = line

        # some unknown choice
    ❾ else:
            print("\nSorry, but that isn't a valid choice.", file=sys.stderr)
            continue

    ❿ # display results
        print()
        print("First line = ", end="")
        print(' '.join(final[0]), file=sys.stderr)
        print("Second line = ", end="")
        print(" ".join(final[1]), file=sys.stderr)
        print("Third line = ", end="")
        print(" ".join(final[2]), file=sys.stderr)
        print()

    input("\n\nPress the Enter key to exit.")

if __name__ == '__main__':
    main()
```

Listing 9-7: Starts the program and presents a user interface

After the introduction message, load and prep the training corpus and build the two Markov models. Then create an empty list to hold the final haiku ❶. Next, name a `choice` variable and set it to `None`. Start a `while` loop that continues until the user chooses choice 0 ❷. By entering `0`, the user has decided to quit the program.

Use a `print()` statement with triple quotes to display a menu ❸, and then get the user's choice ❹. If the user chooses 0, exit and say goodbye ❺. If the user chooses 1, they want the program to generate a new haiku, so reinitialize the `final` list and the `end_prev_line` variable ❻. Then call the `haiku_line()` function for all three lines and pass it the correct arguments—including the target syllable count for each line. Note that the `end_prev_line` variable name changes with each line; for example, `end_prev_line2` holds the final two words of line two. The last variable, `end_prev_line3`, is just a placeholder so you can reuse the function; in other words, it is never put to use. Each time the `haiku_line()` function is called, it returns a line that you need to append to the `final` list.

If the user chooses 2, the program regenerates the second line ❼. There needs to be a full haiku before the program can rebuild a line, so use an `if` statement to handle the user jumping the gun. Then call the `haiku_line()` function, making sure to pass it the `end_prev_line1` variable to link it to the preceding line, and set the syllable target to seven syllables. Insert the rebuilt line in the `final` list at index 1.

Repeat the process if the user chooses 3, only make the syllable target `5` and pass `end_prev_line2` to the `haiku_line()` function ❽. Insert the line at index 2 in `final`.

If the user enters anything not on the menu, let them know and then continue the loop ❾. Finish by displaying the haiku. Use the `join()` method and `file=sys.stderr` for an attractive printout in the shell ❿.

End the program with the standard code for running the program as a module or in stand-alone mode.

The Results

To evaluate a poetry-writing program, you need a way to measure something subjective—whether or not poems are "good"—using objective criteria. For the *markov_haiku.py* program, I propose the following categories based on two criteria, originality and humanness:

Duplicate Verbatim duplication of a haiku in the training corpus.

Good A haiku that is—at least to some people—indistinguishable from a haiku written by a human poet. It should represent the initial result or the result of regenerating line two or three a few times.

Seed A haiku that has merit but that many would suspect was written by a computer, or a haiku that you could transform into a good haiku by changing or repositioning no more than two words (described in more detail later). It may require multiple regenerations of lines two or three.

Rubbish A haiku that is clearly a random amalgam of words and has no merit as a poem.

If you use the program to generate a large number of haiku and place the results in these categories, you'll probably end up with the distribution in Figure 9-3. About 5 percent of the time, you'll duplicate an existing haiku in the training corpus; 10 percent of the time, you'll produce a good haiku; around 25 percent will be passable or fixable haiku; and the rest will be rubbish.

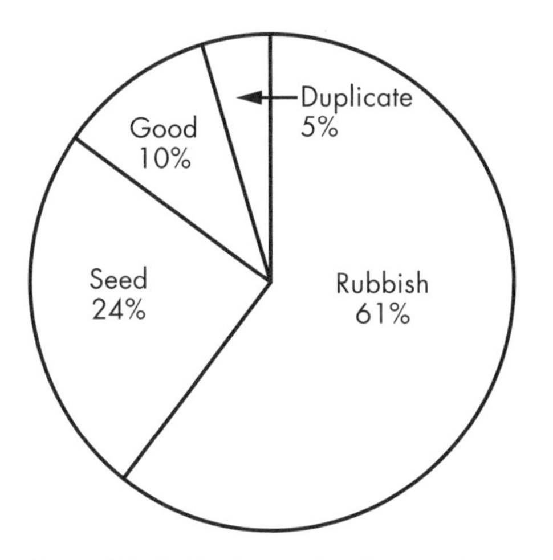

Figure 9-3: Subjective results of generating 500 haiku using markov_haiku.py

Considering how simple the Markov process is, the results in Figure 9-3 are impressive. To quote Charles Hartman once again, "Here is language creating itself out of nothing, out of mere statistical noise. . . . We can watch sense evolve and meaning stagger up onto its own miraculous feet."

Good Haiku

The following are some examples of simulated haiku classified as "good." In the first example, the program has subtly—you might say "skillfully," if you didn't know an algorithm was responsible—altered my haiku from Chapter 8 to produce a new haiku with the same meaning.

Cloudbanks that I let
Myself pretend are distant
Mountains faraway

In the next example, the program has managed to duplicate a common theme in traditional haiku: the juxtaposition of images or ideas.

The mirror I stare
Into shows my father's face
An old silent pond

In this case, you find out that the mirror is really the surface of a still pond, though you may interpret the face itself as the pond.

Running the program is a little like panning for gold: sometimes you find a nugget. The haiku on the left was written by Ringai over 300 years ago. In the haiku on the right, the program has made subtle changes so that the poem now evokes images of a late spring freeze—a setback for the progress of the season.

In these dark waters
Drawn up from my frozen well
Glittering of Spring
—*Ringai*

Waters drawn up from
My frozen well glittering
Of Spring standing still
—*Python*

The following are examples of a few more "good" haiku. The first one is remarkable since it was built from three separate haiku in the training corpus, yet maintains a clear contextual thread throughout.

As I walk the path
Eleven brave knights canter
Through the stormy woods

Cool stars enter the
Window this hot evening all
Heaven and earth ache

Such a thing alive
Rusted gate screeches open
Even things feel pain

The stone bridge! Sitting
Quietly doing nothing
Yet Spring comes grass grows

Dark sky oh! Autumn
Snowflakes! A rotting pumpkin
Collapsed and covered

Desolate moors fray
Black cloudbank, broken, scatters
In the pines, the graves

Seed Haiku

The concept of computers helping humans write poetry has been around for some time. Poets often "prime the pump" by imitating earlier poems, and there's no reason a computer can't provide first drafts as part of a cyber-partnership. Even a fairly poor computer creation has the potential to "seed" the creative process and help a human overcome writer's block.

The following are three examples of seed haiku from the *markov_haiku.py* program. On the left is the not-quite-right computer-generated haiku. On the right is the version that I adjusted. I changed only a single word, highlighted in bold, in each.

My life must end like Another flower what a Hungry wind **it** is	My life must end like Another flower what a Hungry wind is **death**
The dock floating in The hot caressing night just Before the dawn **old**	The dock floating in The hot caressing night just Before the dawn **rain**
Moonrise on the grave And my old sadness a sharp Shovel thrust **the** stars	Moonrise on the grave And my old sadness a sharp Shovel thrust **of** stars

The last has cryptic meaning but seems to work, as it is filled with natural associations (moon and stars, grave and shovel, grave and sadness). At any rate, you shouldn't fret too much over meaning. To paraphrase T.S. Eliot: meaning is like the meat the burglar throws the dog, to keep the mind diverted while the poem does its work!

Summary

It took two chapters, but you now have a program that can simulate Japanese haiku written by the masters—or at least provide a useful starting point for a human poet. In addition, you applied the `logging` module to monitor what the program was doing at key steps.

Further Reading

Virtual Muse: Experiments in Computer Poetry (Wesleyan University Press, 1996) by Charles O. Hartman is an engaging look at the early collaboration between humans and computers to write poetry.

If you want to know more about Claude Shannon, check out *A Mind at Play: How Claude Shannon Invented the Information Age* (Simon & Schuster, 2017) by Jimmy Soni and Rod Goodman.

You can find a digital version of *Japanese Haiku: Two Hundred Twenty Examples of Seventeen-Syllable Poems* (The Peter Pauper Press, 1955), translated by Peter Beilenson, online at Global Grey (*https://www.globalgreyebooks.com/*).

In the paper "Gaiku: Generating Haiku with Word Association Norms" (Association for Computational Linguistics, 2009), Yael Netzer and coauthors explore the use of word association norms (WANs) to generate haiku. You can build WAN corpora by submitting trigger words to people and recording their immediate responses (for example, *house* to *fly*, *arrest*, *keeper*, and so on). This results in the kind of tightly linked, intuitive relationships characteristic of human-generated haiku. You can find the paper online at *http://www.cs.brandeis.edu/~marc/misc/proceedings/naacl-hlt-2009/CALC-09/pdf/CALC-0905.pdf*.

Automate the Boring Stuff with Python (No Starch Press, 2015) by Al Sweigart has a useful overview chapter on debugging techniques, including `logging`.

Challenge Projects

I've described some suggestions for spin-off projects in this section. As with all challenge projects, you're on your own—no solutions are provided.

New Word Generator

In his award-winning 1961 sci-fi novel, *Stranger in a Strange Land*, author Robert A. Heinlein invented the word *grok* to represent deep, intuitive understanding. This word moved into the popular culture—especially the culture of computer programming—and is now in the *Oxford English Dictionary*.

Coming up with a new word that sounds legitimate is not easy, in part because humans are so anchored to the words we already know. But computers don't suffer from this affliction. In *Virtual Muse*, Charles Hartman observed that his poetry-writing program would sometimes create intriguing letter combinations, such as *runkin* or *avatheformitor*, that could easily represent new words.

Write a program that recombines letters using Markov order 2, 3, and 4 models and use the program to generate interesting new words. Give them a definition and start applying them. Who knows—you may coin the next *frickin*, *frabjous*, *chortle*, or *trill*!

Turing Test

According to Alan Turing, "A computer would deserve to be called intelligent if it could deceive a human into believing that it was human." Use your friends to test haiku generated by the *markov_haiku.py* program. Mix the computer haiku with a few haiku written by the masters or yourself. Since computer haiku are often enjambed, be careful to choose human haiku that are also enjambed in order to deny your cleverer friends a free ride. Using lowercase letters and minimal punctuation for all the haiku also helps. I've provided an example, using Facebook, in Figure 9-4.

Lee Vaughan
Just now

Two computer-generated and two Japanese master-generated haiku. Pick the two human-generated ones (no Googling!):

1.
over the dark fields,
catching the fireflies, all
heaven and earth one
2.
reciting scriptures
strange the wondrous blue I find
in morning glories
3.
butterflies only,
fluttering in this gusty
wind, blossoming white
4.
in the farther field,
scarecrow kept me company,
walking as I walked

Like Comment Share

Figure 9-4: Example Turing test experiment post on Facebook

Unbelievable! This Is Unbelievable! Unbelievable!

President Trump is famous for speaking in short, simple sentences that use "the best words," and short, simple sentences are great for haiku. In fact, the *Washington Post* published some inadvertent haiku found in some of his campaign speeches. Among these were:

He's a great, great guy.
I saw him the other day.
On television.

They want to go out.
They want to lead a good life.
They want to work hard.

We have to do it.
And we need the right people.
So Ford will come back.

Use online transcripts of Donald Trump's speeches to build a new training corpus for the *markov_haiku.py* program. Remember that you'll need to revisit Chapter 8 and build a new "missing words" dictionary for any words not in the *Carnegie Mellon University Pronouncing Dictionary*. Then rerun the program and generate haiku that capture this moment in history. Save the best ones and revisit the Turing test challenge to see if your friends can separate your haiku from true Trump quotes.

To Haiku, or Not to Haiku

William Shakespeare wrote many famous phrases that fit the syllabic structure of haiku, such as "all our yesterdays," "dagger of the mind," and "parting is such sweet sorrow." Use one or more of the Bard's plays as a training corpus for the *markov_haiku.py* program. The big challenge here will be counting the syllables for all that olde English.

Markov Music

If you're musically inclined, perform an online search for "composing music with Markov chains." You should find a wealth of material on using Markov chain analysis to compose music, using the notes from existing songs as a training corpus. The resulting "Markov music" is used like our seed haiku—as inspiration for human songwriters.

10

ARE WE ALONE? EXPLORING THE FERMI PARADOX

Scientists use the *Drake equation* to estimate the possible number of civilizations in the galaxy currently producing electromagnetic emissions, such as radio waves. In 2017, the equation was updated to account for new exoplanet discoveries by NASA's Kepler satellite. The result, published in the scientific journal *Astrobiology*, was astonishing. For humanity to be the first and only technologically advanced species, the probability of an advanced civilization developing on a habitable alien planet would have to be less than 1 in 10 billion trillion! And yet, as Nobel Prize–winning physicist Enrico Fermi famously observed, "Where is everybody?"

Fermi was more skeptical about interstellar travel than the existence of extraterrestrials, but his question became known as *Fermi's paradox,* and it morphed into the conjecture "If they were out there, they'd be here." According to the SETI Institute, even with modest rocket technology, an eager civilization could explore the entire galaxy, if not colonize it, within 10 million years. That may sound like a long time, but it's only 1/1,000 the age of the Milky Way! As a result, some have come to accept Fermi's paradox as proof we are alone in the cosmos. Others find holes in the argument.

In this chapter, you'll investigate the absence of alien radio transmissions by calculating the probability of one civilization detecting another based on the volume of their transmissions and output from the Drake equation. You'll also use Python's de facto standard GUI package, `tkinter`, to quickly and easily create a graphical model of the Milky Way.

Project #17: Modeling the Milky Way

Our galaxy, the Milky Way, is a fairly common spiral galaxy, like the one shown in Figure 10-1.

Figure 10-1: Spiral galaxy NGC 6744, "Big Brother" to the Milky Way

In cross-sectional view, the Milky Way is a flattened disc with a central bulge that most likely contains a supermassive black hole at its core. Four "spiral arms"—comprising relatively densely packed gas, dust, and stars—radiate from this central mass. The dimensions of the Milky Way are shown in Figure 10-2.

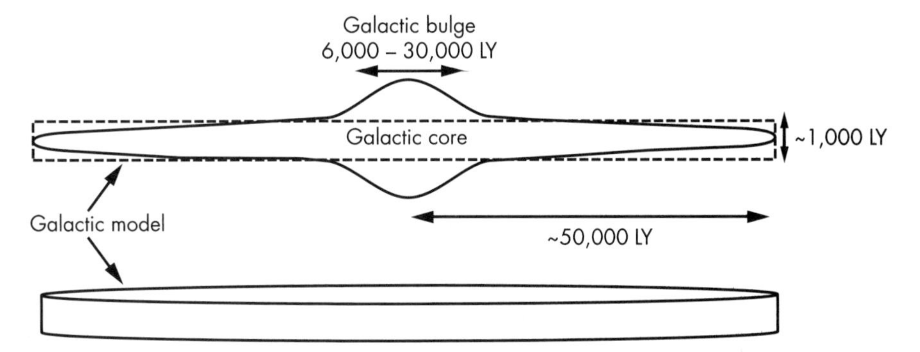

Figure 10-2: Schematic profile (edge view) of the Milky Way galaxy (LY = Light-Years) and a simplified model

The center of the galaxy is considered fairly inhospitable to life due to high levels of radiation associated with the more closely packed stars. So, for this project, you can treat the galaxy as a simple disc to discount some of the volume associated with the bulge but still leave room for some advanced civilizations near the core (see the Galactic Model in Figure 10-2).

THE OBJECTIVE

For a given number of advanced galactic civilizations and an average radio bubble size, estimate the probability of *any* civilization detecting the radio transmissions of *any other* civilization. For perspective, post the size of Earth's current radio bubble on a 2D graphical representation of the Milky Way.

The Strategy

Here are the steps needed to complete this project:

1. Estimate the number of transmitting civilizations using the Drake equation.
2. Choose a size range for their radio bubbles.
3. Generate a formula for estimating the probability of one civilization detecting another.
4. Build a graphical model of the galaxy and post Earth's radio emissions bubble.

In order to keep the description close to the code, each of these tasks will be described in detail in its own section. Note that the first two steps don't require the use of Python.

Estimating the Number of Civilizations

You can manually estimate the number of advanced civilizations using the Drake equation:

$$N = R^{*} \cdot f_{\mathrm{p}} \cdot n_{\mathrm{e}} \cdot f_{\mathrm{l}} \cdot f_{\mathrm{i}} \cdot f_{\mathrm{c}} \cdot L$$

where:

N = The number of civilizations in our galaxy whose electromagnetic emissions are detectable

R^* = The average rate of star formation in the galaxy (new stars per year)

f_p = The fraction of stars with planets

n_e = For stars with planets, the average number of planets with an environment suitable for life

f_l = The fraction of planets that develop life

f_i = The fraction of life-bearing planets with intelligent, civilized life

f_c = The fraction of civilizations that release detectable signs of their existence into space

L = The length of time—in years—over which the civilizations release the detectable signals

Thanks to recent advances in the detection of exoplanets, the first three components (R^*, f_p, n_e) are becoming increasingly constrained. For n_e, recent studies suggest that 10 to 40 percent of all planets may be suitable for *some form* of life.

For the remaining components, Earth is the only example. In the Earth's 4.5-billion-year history, *Homo sapiens* has existed for only 200,000 years, civilization for only 6,000 years, and radio transmissions for only 112 years. With respect to L, wars, plagues, ice ages, asteroid impacts, super-volcanoes, supernovas, and coronal mass ejections can disrupt a civilization's ability to transmit radio signals. And the shorter the time of transmission, the less likely it is for civilizations to coexist.

According to the Wikipedia article on the Drake equation (*https://en.wikipedia.org/wiki/Drake_equation*), in 1961, Drake and his colleagues estimated the number of communicating civilizations in the galaxy to be between 1,000 and 100,000,000. More recent updates have set the range from 1 (just us) to 15,600,000 (Table 10-1).

Table 10-1: Some Drake Equation Inputs and Results

Parameter	Drake 1961**	Drake 2017	Your choices
$R*$	1	3	
f_p	0.35	1	
n_e	3	0.2	
f_l	1	0.13	
f_i	1	1	
f_c	0.15	0.2	
L	50×10^6	1×10^9	
N	7.9×10^6	15.6×10^6	

**midpoint of ranges shown

For input to your program, you can use the estimates in the table, those you find online, or those you calculate yourself (in the final column of the table).

Selecting Radio Bubble Dimensions

Radio waves that aren't focused into a beam for targeted transmission are incidental. Think of these as "planet leakage." Because we choose not to broadcast our presence to aliens who might come and eat us, almost all of our transmissions are incidental. These transmissions currently form an expanding sphere around Earth with a diameter of around 225 light-years (LY).

A 225 LY bubble sounds impressive, but it is the *detectable* size that really matters. A radio wave front is subject to the *inverse square law*, which means it continuously loses power density as it expands. Additional power loss can result from absorption or scattering. At some point, the signal becomes too weak to separate from background noise. Even with our best technology—the radio telescopes of the *Breakthrough Listen* program—we could detect our own radio bubble only out to about 16 LY.

Since we're really investigating why *we* haven't detected aliens, you should assume, for this project, that other civilizations have technology similar to our own. Another assumption should be that, like us, all aliens have a paranoid planetary consciousness and aren't broadcasting "here we are" signals that would announce their presence. Investigating incidental bubble sizes ranging from a little smaller than those currently detectable to those a little larger than our own transmissions should be a reasonable place to start. This would suggest a diameter range of 30 to 250 LY. Although we can't detect a 250 LY bubble, it will be interesting to see what the odds would be if we could.

Generating a Formula for the Probability of Detection

As the number of advanced civilizations in the galaxy increases, the probability that one will detect another also increases. This is intuitive, but how do you assign the actual probabilities?

The nice thing about computers is that they allow us to brute-force our way to solutions that may or may not be intuitive. One approach here would be to make a 3D model of the Milky Way disc, randomly distribute civilizations throughout, and measure the distances between them using one of Python's many tools for calculating Euclidian distance. But with potentially hundreds of millions of civilizations to analyze, this method would be computationally expensive.

Since we're dealing with huge unknowns, there's no need to be super-accurate or precise. We just want to be in the ballpark, so an easy simplification is to compartmentalize the galaxy into a series of radio bubble "equivalent volumes" by dividing the volume of the galactic disc by the volume of a radio bubble (see Figure 10-3).

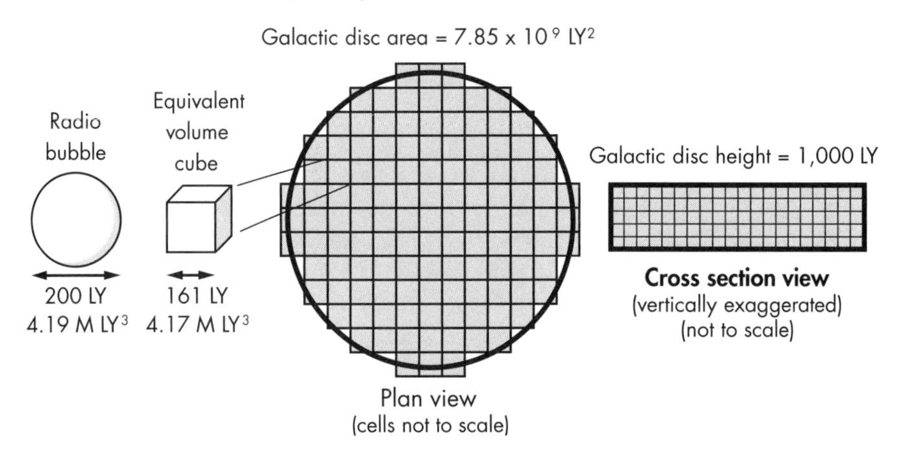

Figure 10-3: Modeling the galaxy using cubes with volumes equivalent to a 200 LY radio bubble

You can find the volumes using the following equations, where R is the radius of the galactic disc and r is the radius of a radio bubble:

$$\text{disc volume} = \pi \times R^2 \times \text{disc height}$$
$$\text{radio bubble volume} = 4/3 \times \pi \times r^3$$
$$\text{scaled disc volume} = \text{disc volume} / \text{radio bubble volume}$$

The scaled disc volume is the number of equivalent volumes that "fit" in the galaxy. Think of these as boxes numbered from 1 to the maximum number of volumes.

To place civilizations, you simply choose a box number at random. Duplicate picks indicate multiple civilizations within the same box. Assume civilizations in the same box can detect each other. This isn't strictly true (see Figure 10-4), but because you'll be using large numbers of civilizations, the discrepancies will tend to cancel each other out, just as when you sum a lot of rounded numbers.

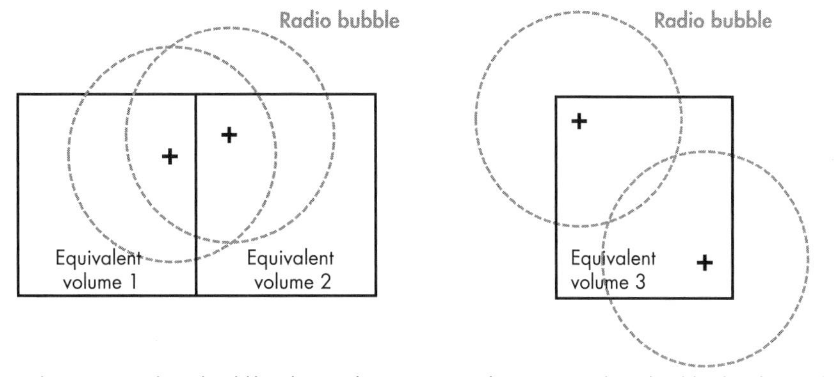

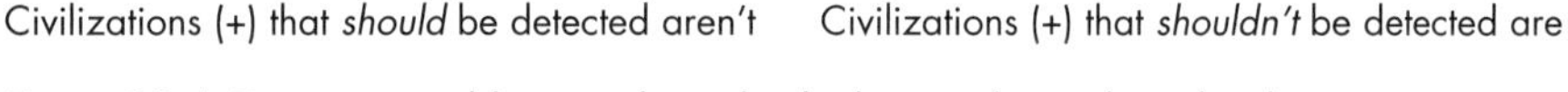

Civilizations (+) that *should* be detected aren't
Civilizations (+) that *shouldn't* be detected are

Figure 10-4: Detection problems at the individual equivalent volume level

To avoid having to repeat this exercise every time you change the number of civilizations and/or radio bubble dimensions, you can capture the results as a formula—a *polynomial equation*—that can be used to generate all future probability estimates. A *polynomial* is the sum or difference of a collection of algebraic terms. The famous *quadratic equation* we all learned in school is a polynomial equation of the second degree (meaning that the exponents of the variables are no greater than 2):

$$ax^2 + bx + c = 0$$

Polynomials make nice curves, so they're tailor-made for this problem. But for the formula to work with variable numbers of civilizations and bubble sizes, you'll need to use the *ratio* of the number of civilizations to the total volume. The total volume is represented by the scaled disc volume, which is the same as the total number of equivalent volumes.

In Figure 10-5, each dot represents the probability of detection for the ratio below it. The equation shown in the figure is the polynomial expression, which generates the line connecting the dots. With this formula, you can predict the probability for any ratio of civilizations per volume, up to a value of 5 (above this, we'll just assume the probability is 1.0).

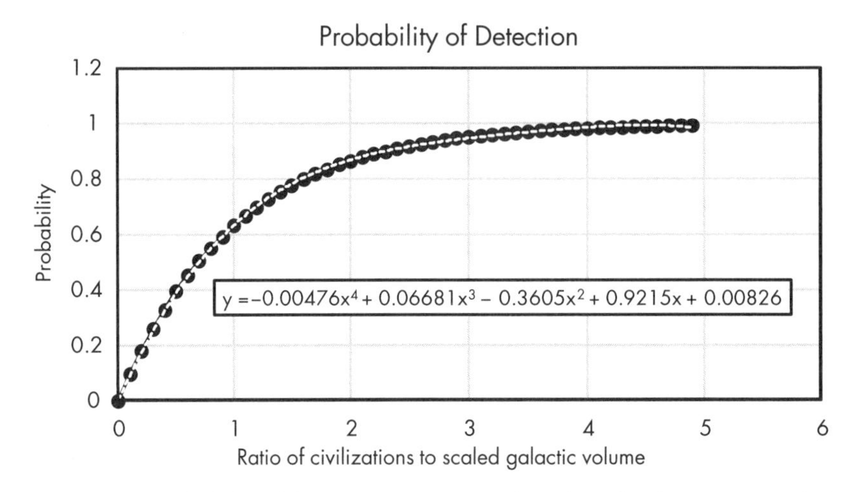

Figure 10-5: Probability of detection versus ratio of number of civilizations to scaled galactic volume

In Figure 10-5, the civilizations-to-volume ratios are posted on the x-axis. A ratio of 0.5, for example, means that there are half as many civilizations as available radio bubble equivalent volumes, a ratio of 2 means there are twice as many civilizations as volumes, and so on. The y-axis is the probability that an equivalent volume contains more than one civilization.

Another thing to note from Figure 10-5 is that it takes a lot of civilizations to ensure that they all have a roommate. Imagine that 999,999 out of 1,000,000 equivalent volumes contain at least two civilizations and you use your God-like powers to randomly place one new civilization. The odds are one in a million that this new civilization will end up in the remaining volume with a single occupant. That last equivalent volume is the proverbial needle in the haystack!

NOTE *An axiom of computer modeling is to start simple and add complexity. The simplest "base case" assumption is that advanced civilizations are randomly distributed throughout the galaxy. In "Challenge Projects" on page 214, you'll get a chance to challenge this assumption using the concept of galactic habitable zones.*

The Probability-of-Detection Code

The probability-of-detection code randomly chooses locations (radio bubble equivalent volumes) for a set number of locations and civilizations, counts how many locations occur only once (that is, contain only one civilization), and repeats the experiment multiple times to converge on a probability estimate. The process is then repeated for a new number of civilizations. The output is presented as probability versus the *ratio* of civilizations per volume, rather than the actual number of civilizations, and turned into a polynomial expression so that the results are easily portable. This means this program only needs to be run once.

To generate the polynomial equation and check that it fits the data, you'll use `NumPy` and `matplotlib`. The `NumPy` library adds support for large, multidimensional arrays and matrices, and it includes many mathematical functions that operate on them. The `matplotlib` library supports 2D plotting and rudimentary 3D plotting, and `NumPy` represents its numerical mathematics extension.

There are several ways to install these scientific Python distributions. One way is to use `SciPy`, an open source Python library used for scientific and technical computing (see *https://scipy.org/index.html*). If you're going to do a lot of data analysis and plotting, you may want to download and use a free package like Anaconda or Enthought Canopy, which works with Windows, Linux, and macOS. These packages spare you the task of finding and installing all the required data science libraries in the correct version. A listing of these types of packages, along with links to their websites, can be found at *https://scipy.org/install.html.*

Alternatively, you may want to download the products directly, using pip. I did this using the instructions at *https://scipy.org/install.html.* Because `matplotlib` requires a large number of dependencies, these need to be installed at the same time. For Windows, I ran the following Python 3–specific command from the PowerShell, launched from within my *Python35* folder (you can leave off the *3* in *python3* unless you have multiple versions installed):

```
$ python3 -m pip install --user numpy scipy matplotlib ipython jupyter pandas sympy nose
```

All the other modules you'll need come bundled with Python. As for the code in Listings 10-1 and 10-2, you can type it in or download a copy from *https://www.nostarch.com/impracticalpython/.*

Calculating Probability of Detection for a Range of Civilizations

Listing 10-1 imports modules and does all the work just described except for fitting the polynomial and displaying the `matplotlib` quality check.

probability_of_detection.py, part 1

```
❶ from random import randint
  from collections import Counter
  import numpy as np
  import matplotlib.pyplot as plt

❷ NUM_EQUIV_VOLUMES = 1000  # number of locations in which to place civilizations
  MAX_CIVS = 5000  # maximum number of advanced civilizations
  TRIALS = 1000  # number of times to model a given number of civilizations
  CIV_STEP_SIZE = 100  # civilizations count step size
```

```
❸ x = []  # x values for polynomial fit
  y = []  # y values for polynomial fit

❹ for num_civs in range(2, MAX_CIVS + 2, CIV_STEP_SIZE):
      civs_per_vol = num_civs / NUM_EQUIV_VOLUMES
      num_single_civs = 0
    ❺ for trial in range(TRIALS):
          locations = []  # equivalent volumes containing a civilization
        ❻ while len(locations) < num_civs:
              location = randint(1, NUM_EQUIV_VOLUMES)
              locations.append(location)
        ❼ overlap_count = Counter(locations)
          overlap_rollup = Counter(overlap_count.values())
          num_single_civs += overlap_rollup[1]

    ❽ prob = 1 - (num_single_civs / (num_civs * TRIALS))

      # print ratio of civs-per-volume vs. probability of 2+ civs per location
    ❾ print("{:.4f}  {:.4f}".format(civs_per_vol, prob))
    ❿ x.append(civs_per_vol)
      y.append(prob)
```

Listing 10-1: Imports modules, randomly chooses radio-bubble-equivalent-volume locations, and calculates the probability of multiple civilizations per location

Import the familiar `random` module and `Counter`, for counting the number of civilizations at each location (designated by how many times a location has been chosen) ❶. How `Counter` works will be explained in a moment. You'll use the `NumPy` and `matplotlib` imports to fit and display the polynomial.

Assign some constants that represent user input for the number of equivalent volumes, the maximum number of civilizations, the number of trials—that is, how many times to repeat the experiment for a given number of civilizations—and a step size for the count ❷. Because the results are predictable, you can use a large step value of 100 without compromising accuracy. Note that you'll get very similar results whether the number of equivalent volumes is 100 or 100,000+.

You'll need a series of paired (*x*, *y*) values for the polynomial expression, so start two lists to hold these ❸. The x-value will be the ratio of civilizations per volume, and the y-value will be the corresponding probability of detection.

Start a series of nested loops, with the highest loop representing the number of civilizations to model ❹. You need at least two civilizations for one to detect the other, and set the maximum to `MAX_CIVS` plus 2, to overshoot when calculating the polynomial. Use the `CIV_STEP_SIZE` constant for the step value.

Next, calculate the overall `civs_per_vol` ratio and start a counter named `num_single_civs` to keep track of the number of locations containing a single civilization.

You've chosen how many civilizations to distribute, so now use a `for` loop to go through the number of trials ❺. For each trial, you distribute the same number of civilizations. Assign an empty list to the variable locations and then, for each civilization ❻, pick a location number at random and append it to the list. Duplicate values in the list will represent locations containing multiple civilizations.

Run Counter on this list ❼ and get the values. End the loop by getting the number of locations that occur only once and add them to the num_single_civs counter. Here's an example of how these three statements work:

```
>>> from collections import Counter
>>> alist = [124, 452, 838, 124, 301]
>>> count = Counter(alist)
>>> count
Counter({124: 2, 452: 1, 301: 1, 838: 1})
>>> value_count = Counter(count.values())
>>> value_count
Counter({1: 3, 2: 1})
>>> value_count[1]
3
```

The alist list contains five numbers, with one (124) duplicated. Running Counter on this list produces a dictionary with the numbers as the keys and the number of times they occur as the values. Passing Counter the values in count—with the values() method—creates another dictionary with the previous values as keys and the number of times they occur as the new values. You want to know how many numbers occur only once, so use the dictionary method value_count[1] to return the number of nonduplicated numbers. These, of course, would represent radio-bubble-equivalent volumes containing a single civilization.

Now use the results from Counter to calculate the probability of multiple civilizations per location for the current number of civilizations being distributed ❽. This is 1 minus the number of single-occupancy locations divided by the number of civilizations in each trial times the number of trials.

Follow this by printing the ratio of civilizations to volume and the probability that multiple civilizations share a location ❾. The first few lines of this output are as follows:

```
0.0020  0.0020
0.1020  0.0970
0.2020  0.1832
0.3020  0.2607
0.4020  0.3305
0.5020  0.3951
0.6020  0.4516
0.7020  0.5041
```

This printout serves as an initial QC step and is optional; comment it out if you want to speed up the runtime. Finish by appending the values to the x and y lists ❿.

Generating a Predictive Formula and Checking the Results

Listing 10-2 uses NumPy to perform polynomial regression on the probability of detection versus the ratio of civilizations per volume calculated in Listing 10-1. You'll use this polynomial equation in the next program to obtain probability estimates. To check that the resulting curve fits the data points, matplotlib displays the actual and predicted values.

probability_of_detection.py, part 2

```
❶ coefficients = np.polyfit(x, y, 4)  # 4th order polynomial fit
❷ p = np.poly1d(coefficients)
  print("\n{}".format(p))
❸ xp = np.linspace(0, 5)
❹ _ = plt.plot(x, y, '.', xp, p(xp), '-')
❺ plt.ylim(-0.5, 1.5)
❻ plt.show()
```

Listing 10-2: Performs polynomial regression and displays a QC plot

Start by assigning a variable, coefficients, to the output from the NumPy polyfit() method ❶. This method takes as arguments the x and y lists and an integer representing the degree of the fitting polynomial. It returns a vector of coefficients, p, that minimizes the squared error.

If you print the coefficients variable, you get the following output:

```
[-0.00475677  0.066811   -0.3605069   0.92146096  0.0082604 ]
```

To get the full expression, pass the coefficients variable to poly1d and assign the results to a new variable ❷. Print this variable, and you'll see a similar equation to that shown in Figure 10-5:

```
           4           3          2
-0.004757 x + 0.06681 x - 0.3605 x + 0.9215 x + 0.00826
```

To check that the polynomial adequately reproduces the input, you'll want to plot the ratio of civilizations to volume on the x-axis, with probability on the y-axis. To get the x-axis values, you can use the NumPy linspace() method, which returns evenly spaced numbers over a specified interval. Use a range of (0, 5), as this will cover almost the full probability range.

To post symbols for the calculated and predicted values, first pass the plot() method the x and y lists, plotting them using a period (dot), which is equivalent to the dots in Figure 10-5 ❹. Then pass the predicted x-axis values (xp) and, to get the predicted y-axis probability, pass p the same variable, plotting the results using a dash.

Finish by limiting the y-axis to values of -0.5 and 1.5 ❺ and use the show() method to actually display the graph (Figure 10-6) ❻. The resultant plot is simple and sparse, as its only purpose is to confirm that the polynomial regression is working as intended. You can alter the polynomial fit by increasing or decreasing the third argument in step ❶.

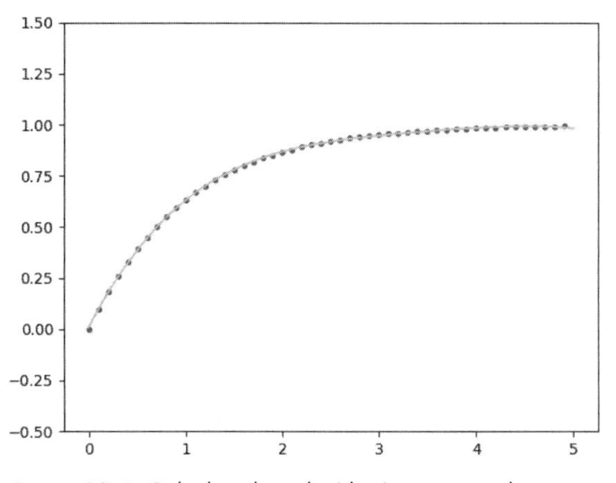

Figure 10-6: Calculated results (dots) versus results predicted by the polynomial (line)

Armed with these results, you can now estimate the probability of detection for any number of civilizations in the blink of an eye. All Python needs to do is solve a polynomial equation.

Building the Graphical Model

The graphical model will be a 2D, top-down view of the galactic disc. Plotting the size of Earth's present emissions bubble on this display will put in perspective both the size of the galaxy and our diminutive place within it.

Modeling the Milky Way is all about modeling the spiral arms. Each spiral arm represents a *logarithmic spiral*, a geometric feature so common in nature it has been dubbed *spira mirabilis*—"miraculous spiral." If you compare Figure 10-7 to Figure 10-1, you can see how closely the structure of a hurricane resembles that of a galaxy. The eye of the hurricane can even be thought of as a supermassive black hole, with the eyewall representing the event horizon!

Figure 10-7: Hurricane Igor

Because spirals radiate out from a central point, or *pole*, you'll more easily graph them with *polar coordinates* (Figure 10-8). With polar coordinates, the (x, y) coordinates used in the more familiar Cartesian coordinate system are replaced by (r, Θ), where r is the distance from the center and Θ is the angle made by r and the x-axis. The coordinates for the pole are (0, 0).

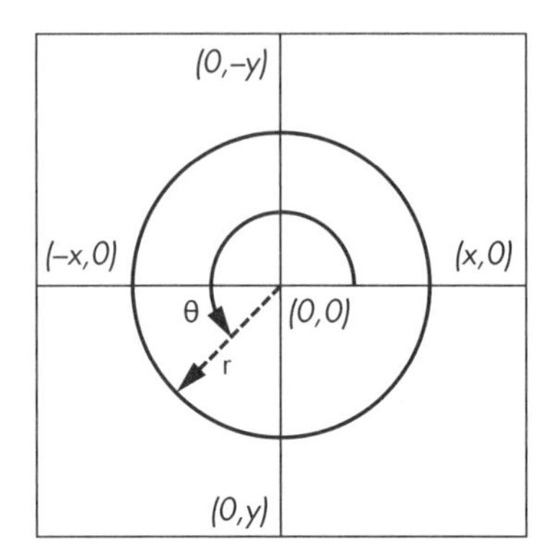

Figure 10-8: Example polar coordinate system

The polar equation for a logarithmic spiral is:

$$r = ae^{b\Theta}$$

where r is the distance from the origin, Θ is the angle from the x-axis, e is the base of natural logarithms, and a and b are arbitrary constants.

You can use this formula to draw a single spiral; then, rotate and redraw the spiral three times to produce the four arms of the Milky Way. You'll build the spirals out of circles of various sizes, which will represent stars. Figure 10-9 is an example of one realization of the graphical model. Because the simulations are stochastic, each will be slightly different, and there are multiple variables you can tweak to change the appearance.

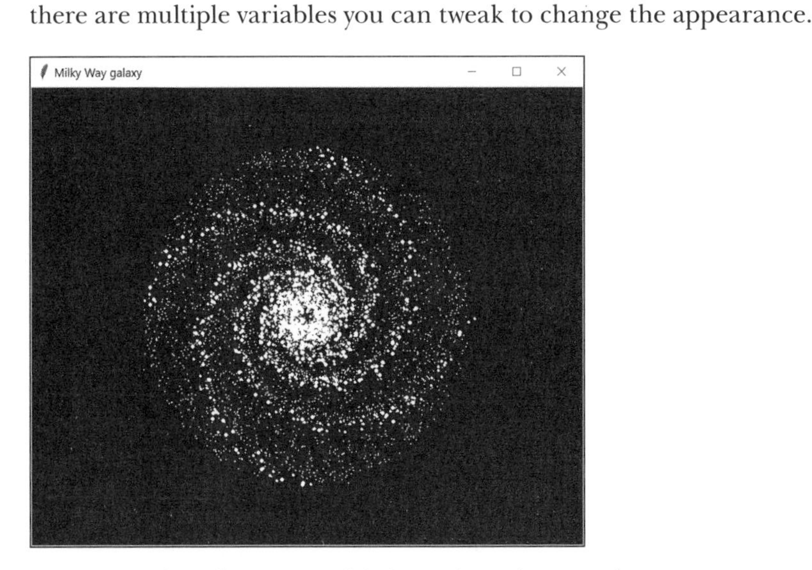

Figure 10-9: The Milky Way, modeled using logarithmic spirals

I generated the image in Figure 10-9 with `tkinter` (pronounced "tee-kay-inter"), the default GUI library for developing desktop applications in Python. Although primarily designed for GUI elements such as windows, buttons, scroll bars, and so on, `tkinter` can also generate graphs, charts, screensavers, simple games, and more. Among its advantages is that, as part of the standard Python distribution, it's portable across all operating systems and there's no need to install external libraries. It's also well documented and easy to use.

Most Windows, macOS, and Linux machines come with `tkinter` already installed. If you don't have it or need the latest version, you can download and install it from *https://www.activestate.com/*. As always, if the module is already installed, you should be able to import it in the interpreter window with no errors:

```
>>> import tkinter
>>>
```

Introductory Python books sometimes include overviews of `tkinter`, and you can find the official online documentation at *https://docs.python.org/3/library/tk.html*. Some other references on `tkinter` are included in "Further Reading" on page 212.

Scaling the Graphical Model

The scale of the graphical model is in light-years per pixel, and the width of each pixel will equate to the diameter of a radio bubble. As a result, when the radio bubble being investigated changes diameter, the scale units will change, and the graphical model will need to be rebuilt. The following equation will scale the model to the bubble:

$$\text{scaled disc radius} = \text{disc radius} \,/\, \text{bubble diameter}$$

where the disc radius is 50,000 and the length unit is light-years.

When the selected radio bubble is small, the graphical model "zooms in," and when it is large, it "zooms out" (Figure 10-10).

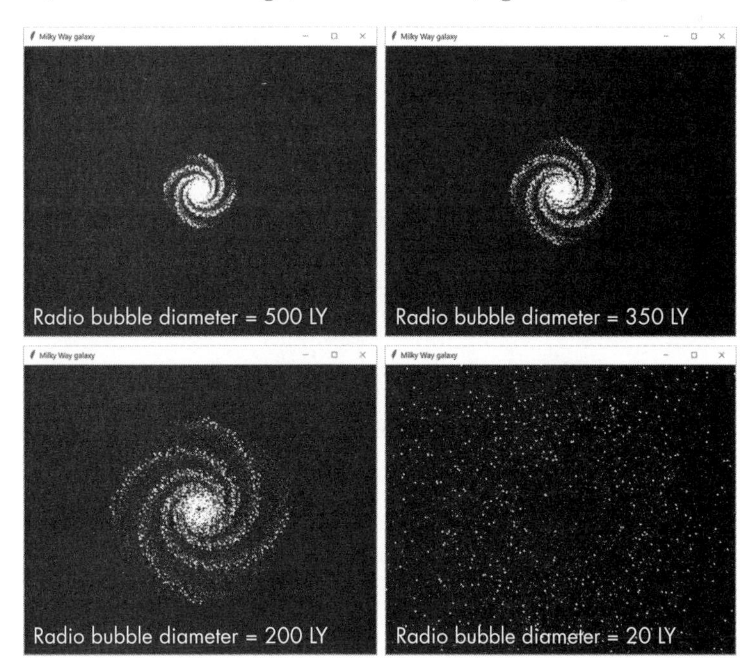

Figure 10-10: Impact of radio bubble diameter on the appearance of the galactic model

The Galaxy Simulator Code

The galaxy simulator code will calculate the probability of detection for any number of civilizations and radio bubble sizes, and then generate a graphical model of the galaxy. When a bubble the size of our current emissions bubble is used, it will post and annotate our bubble in red, in the approximate location of our solar system. You can download the code from *https://www.nostarch.com/impracticalpython/*.

Entering Inputs and Key Parameters

Listing 10-3 starts *galaxy_simulator.py* by importing modules and putting the frequently accessed user input near the top.

galaxy_simulator.py, part 1

```
❶ import tkinter as tk
  from random import randint, uniform, random
  import math

  #=============================================================================
❷ # MAIN INPUT

  # scale (radio bubble diameter) in light-years:
❸ SCALE = 225  # enter 225 to see Earth's radio bubble

  # number of advanced civilizations from the Drake equation:
❹ NUM_CIVS = 15600000
  #=============================================================================
```

Listing 10-3: Imports modules and assigns constants

Import tkinter as tk, so you don't have to type the full name when calling tkinter classes ❶. If you're using Python 2, use Tkinter—with an uppercase *T*. You'll also need the random and math modules.

Use a comment to highlight the main user-input section ❷ and assign the two inputs. Use SCALE for the diameter, in light-years, of the detectable electromagnetic bubble around each civilization ❸; NUM_CIVS is the number of civilizations to model, which you can determine using anything from the Drake equation to a total guess ❹.

Setting Up the tkinter Canvas and Assigning Constants

The code in Listing 10-4 instantiates a tkinter window object with a canvas on which you can draw things. This is where the galaxy map, or graphical model, will appear. It also assigns constants related to the dimensions of the Milky Way.

galaxy_simulator.py, part 2

```
  # set up display canvas
❶ root = tk.Tk()
  root.title("Milky Way galaxy")
❷ c = tk.Canvas(root, width=1000, height=800, bg='black')
```

```
❸ c.grid()
❹ c.configure(scrollregion=(-500, -400, 500, 400))

  # actual Milky Way dimensions (light-years)
❺ DISC_RADIUS = 50000
  DISC_HEIGHT = 1000
❻ DISC_VOL = math.pi * DISC_RADIUS**2 * DISC_HEIGHT
```

Listing 10-4: Sets up `tkinter` window and canvas and assigns constants

Start by creating a window with the conventional name `root` ❶. This is a *top-level* window that will hold everything else. In the next line, give the window a title—"Milky Way galaxy"—which will appear in the upper left of the window frame (see Figure 10-9 for an example).

Next, add a component, known as a *widget*, to the root window. *Widget* stands for "Windows gadget." There are 21 core widgets in `tkinter`, including labels, frames, radio buttons, and scroll bars. Assign a `Canvas` widget to contain all the drawing objects ❷. This is a general-purpose widget intended for graphics and other complex layouts. Specify the parent window, the screen width and height, and the background color. Name the canvas `c`, for *canvas*.

You can divide the `Canvas` widget into rows and columns, like a table or spreadsheet. Each cell in this grid can hold a different widget, and these widgets can span multiple cells. Within a cell, you can align a widget using the `STICKY` option. To manage each widget in a window, you'll need to use the `grid` geometry manager. Since you're using only one widget in this project, you don't need to pass the manager anything ❸.

Finish by configuring the `canvas` to use a `scrollregion` ❹. This sets the origin coordinates `(0, 0)` to the center of the `canvas`. You need this to draw the galaxy's spiral arms with polar coordinates. Without it, the default origin would be the top-left corner of the `canvas`.

The arguments passed to `configure` set the limits of the `canvas`. These should be half of the `canvas` width and height; for example, scroll limits of `600, 500` will require `canvas` dimensions of `1200, 1000`. The values shown here work well on a small laptop, but feel free to alter them later if you find you need a larger window.

Follow the input section with dimensional constants for the galaxy ❺. You could assign some of these variables within functions, but having them in the global space allows for a more logical flow to the code explanation. The first two are the radius and height of the galactic disc from Figure 10-2. The final constant represents the disc volume ❻.

Scaling the Galaxy and Calculating the Probability of Detection

Listing 10-5 defines functions to scale the galaxy dimensions based on the diameter of the radio bubble in use and to calculate the probability of one civilization detecting another. The latter function is where you apply the polynomial equation built with the *probability_of_detection.py* program described previously.

galaxy_simulator.py, part 3

```
❶ def scale_galaxy():
      """Scale galaxy dimensions based on radio bubble size (scale)."""
      disc_radius_scaled = round(DISC_RADIUS / SCALE)
    ❷ bubble_vol = 4/3 * math.pi * (SCALE / 2)**3
    ❸ disc_vol_scaled = DISC_VOL/bubble_vol
    ❹ return disc_radius_scaled, disc_vol_scaled

❺ def detect_prob(disc_vol_scaled):
      """Calculate probability of galactic civilizations detecting each other."""
    ❻ ratio = NUM_CIVS / disc_vol_scaled  # ratio of civs to scaled galaxy volume
    ❼ if ratio < 0.002:  # set very low ratios to probability of 0
          detection_prob = 0
      elif ratio >= 5:  # set high ratios to probability of 1
          detection_prob = 1
    ❽ else:
          detection_prob = -0.004757 * ratio**4 + 0.06681 * ratio**3 - 0.3605 * \
                           ratio**2 + 0.9215 * ratio + 0.00826
    ❾ return round(detection_prob, 3)
```

Listing 10-5: Scales galactic dimensions and calculates detection probability

Define a function called `scale_galaxy()` to scale the galactic dimensions to the radio bubble size ❶. It will use the constants from the global space, so there is no need to pass it any arguments. Calculate the scaled disc radius and then the radio bubble volume, using the equation for the volume of a sphere, and assign the results to `bubble_vol` ❷.

Next, divide the actual disc volume by `bubble_vol` to get the scaled disc volume ❸. This is the number of radio bubble "equivalent volumes" that can fit in the galaxy. Each bubble constitutes a possible location for a civilization.

End the function by returning the `disc_radius_scaled` and `disc_vol_scaled` variables ❹.

Now, define a function called `detect_prob()` to calculate the probability of detection, which takes the scaled disc volume as an argument ❺. For the `x` term in the polynomial, calculate the ratio of the number of civilizations to the scaled disc volume ❻. Since the polynomial regression can have problems at the endpoints, use conditionals to set very small ratios to `0` and large ratios to `1` ❼. Otherwise, apply the polynomial expression generated by the *probability_of_detection.py* code ❽, then return the probability rounded to three decimal places ❾.

Using Polar Coordinates

Listing 10-6 defines a function to select random (x, y) locations using polar coordinates. This function will choose the locations of some of the stars posted in the graphical model. Because the display is 2D, there's no need to choose a z location.

galaxy_simulator.py, part 4

```
❶ def random_polar_coordinates(disc_radius_scaled):
      """Generate uniform random (x, y) point within a disc for 2D display."""
    ❷ r = random()
    ❸ theta = uniform(0, 2 * math.pi)
```

```
❹ x = round(math.sqrt(r) * math.cos(theta) * disc_radius_scaled)
  y = round(math.sqrt(r) * math.sin(theta) * disc_radius_scaled)
❺ return x, y
```

Listing 10-6: Defines a function to randomly pick an (x, y) pair with polar coordinates

The function takes the scaled disc radius as an argument ❶. Use the `random()` function to choose a float value between 0.0 and 1.0 and assign it to the variable `r` ❷. Next, randomly choose `theta` from a uniform distribution between 0 and 360 degrees (2π is the radian equivalent of 360 degrees) ❸.

The transformation to generate points over a *unit* disc is as follows:

$$x = \sqrt{r} * \cos$$
$$y = \sqrt{r} * \sin\theta$$

The equations yield (x, y) values between 0 and 1. To scale the results to the galactic disc, multiply by the scaled disc radius ❹. End the function by returning `x` and `y` ❺.

Building Spiral Arms

Listing 10-7 defines a function that builds the spiral arms using the logarithmic spiral equation. This spiral may be miraculous, but a large part of the magic is tinkering with the initial bare-bones spiral to flesh out the arm. You'll accomplish this by varying the size of stars, randomly altering their positions a tiny amount, and duplicating the spiral for each arm in order to shift it slightly backward and dim its stars.

galaxy_simulator.py, part 5

```
❶ def spirals(b, r, rot_fac, fuz_fac, arm):
      """Build spiral arms for tkinter display using logarithmic spiral formula.

      b = arbitrary constant in logarithmic spiral equation
      r = scaled galactic disc radius
      rot_fac = rotation factor
      fuz_fac = random shift in star position in arm, applied to 'fuzz' variable
      arm = spiral arm (0 = main arm, 1 = trailing stars)
      """
  ❷ spiral_stars = []
  ❸ fuzz = int(0.030 * abs(r)) # randomly shift star locations
      theta_max_degrees = 520
  ❹ for i in range(theta_max_degrees):  # range(0, 600, 2) for no black hole
          theta = math.radians(i)
          x = r * math.exp(b * theta) * math.cos(theta + math.pi * rot_fac)\
              + randint(-fuzz, fuzz) * fuz_fac
          y = r * math.exp(b * theta) * math.sin(theta + math.pi * rot_fac)\
              + randint(-fuzz, fuzz) * fuz_fac
          spiral_stars.append((x, y))
  ❺ for x, y in spiral_stars:
      ❻ if arm == 0 and int(x % 2) == 0:
              c.create_oval(x-2, y-2, x+2, y+2, fill='white', outline='')
          elif arm == 0 and int(x % 2) != 0:
              c.create_oval(x-1, y-1, x+1, y+1, fill='white', outline='')
```

```
❼ elif arm == 1:
      c.create_oval(x, y, x, y, fill='white', outline='')
```

Listing 10-7: Defines the `spirals()` *function*

Define a function called `spirals()` ❶. Its parameters are listed in the function docstring. The first two parameters, `b` and `r`, are from the logarithmic spiral equation. The next, `rot_fac`, is the rotation factor that lets you move the spiral around the center point so you can produce a new spiral arm. The fuzz factor, `fuz_fac`, lets you tweak how far you move stars away from the center of the spiraling line. Finally, the `arm` parameter lets you specify either the leading arm or the trailing arm of faint stars. The trailing arm will be shifted—that is, plotted a little behind the leading arm—and its stars will be smaller.

Initialize an empty list to hold the locations of the stars that will make up the spiral ❷. Assign a `fuzz` variable, where you multiply an arbitrary constant by the absolute value of the scaled disc radius ❸. The spiral equation alone produces stars that are lined up (see the left two panels in Figure 10-11). Fuzzing will move stars in the spiral back and forth a little, to either side of the spiral line. You can see the effect on the bright stars in the rightmost panel in Figure 10-11. I determined these values through trial and error; feel free to play with them if you like.

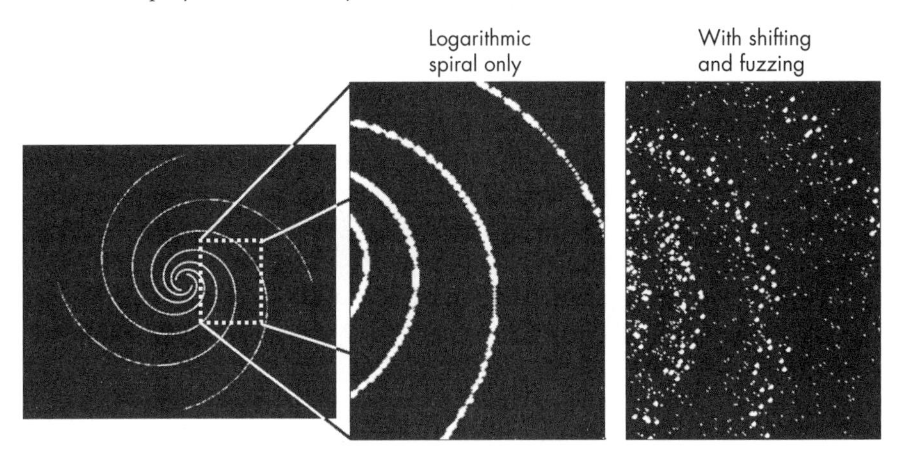

Figure 10-11: Filling out the spiral arms by shifting spirals and randomly changing star positions

Now it's time to build the spiral lines. First, use a range of values to represent θ in the logarithmic spiral equation ❹. A range of about `520` will produce the galaxy in Figure 10-9, which has a central "black hole." Otherwise, use a range of `(0, 600, 2)`—or similar—to produce a bright central core fully packed with stars (Figure 10-12). You can tinker with these values until you get your preferred result. Loop through the values in `theta` and apply the logarithmic spiral equation, using cosine for the x-value and sine for the y-value. Note that you add the `fuzz` value, multiplied by the fuzz factor, to the result. Append each (*x*, *y*) pair to the `spiral_stars` list.

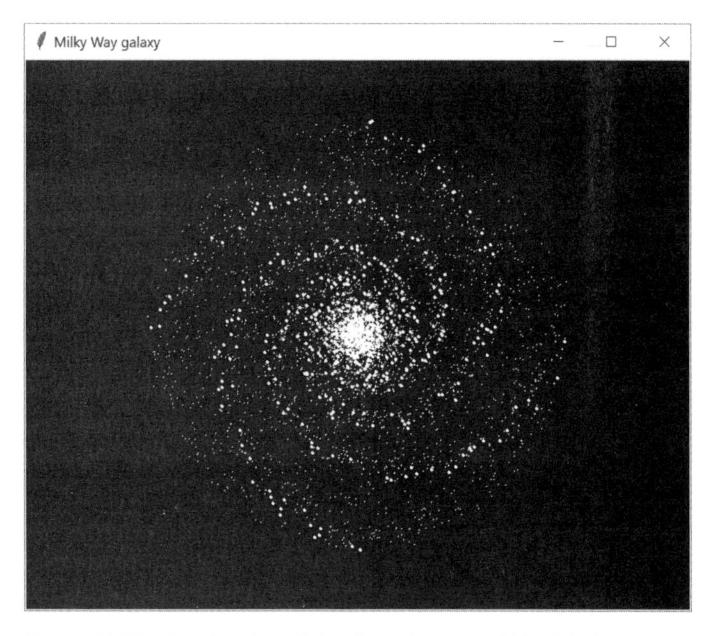

Figure 10-12: Graphical model without the central black hole (compare to Figure 10-9)

Later, in the `main()` function, you'll specify the `rot_fac` variable, which will move the spiral around the center. After the program builds the four main arms, it will use `rot_fac` to build four new arms, slightly offset from the first four, to produce the band of dim, trailing stars seen to the left of each arc of bright stars in Figure 10-11.

Now that you have the list of star locations, start a `for` loop through the (*x*, *y*) coordinates ❺. Then use a conditional statement to choose the main, leading arm and locations for which `x` is even ❻. For these, use the `canvas` widget's `create_oval()` method to create a star object to post. This method's first four arguments define a bounding box into which the oval fits. The larger the number after `x` and `y`, the larger the oval. Make the fill white and don't use an outline; the default outline is a thin black line.

If the x-value is odd, make the star a step smaller. And if the `arm` value is `1`, the star is in the shifted arm, so make it as small as possible ❼.

NOTE *The star objects are for visual impact only. Neither their size nor number is to scale. To be realistic, they would be much, much smaller and much more numerous (over 100 billion!).*

Scattering Star Haze

The space between the spiral arms isn't devoid of stars, so the next function (Listing 10-8) randomly casts points across the galactic model, with no regard for spiral arms. Think of this as the glow you see in photographs of distant galaxies.

galaxy_simulator.py, part 6

```
❶ def star_haze(disc_radius_scaled, density):
      """Randomly distribute faint tkinter stars in galactic disc.

      disc_radius_scaled = galactic disc radius scaled to radio bubble diameter
      density = multiplier to vary number of stars posted
      """
    ❷ for i in range(0, disc_radius_scaled * density):
        ❸ x, y = random_polar_coordinates(disc_radius_scaled)
        ❹ c.create_text(x, y, fill='white', font=('Helvetica', '7'), text='.')
```

Listing 10-8: Defines the `star_haze()` function

Define the `star_haze()` function and pass it two arguments: the scaled disc radius and an integer multiplier that the function will use to increase the base number of random stars ❶. So, if you prefer a thick fog rather than a light haze, increase the value of the density value when you call the function in `main()`.

Start a `for` loop where the maximum range value is equal to the scaled disc radius multiplied by `density` ❷. By using the radius value, you scale the number of stars to the size of the disc being displayed. Then call the `random_polar_coordinates()` function to get an (*x*, *y*) pair ❸.

End by creating a display object for the canvas using the (*x*, *y*) pair ❹. Since you've already used the smallest oval size for the stars along and around the spiral, use the `create_text()` method instead of `create_oval()`. With this method, you can use a period to represent a star. The font size parameter will allow you to scale the haze stars until you find something aesthetically pleasing.

Figure 10-13 is a comparison between the galactic model without the star haze (left) and with the star haze (right).

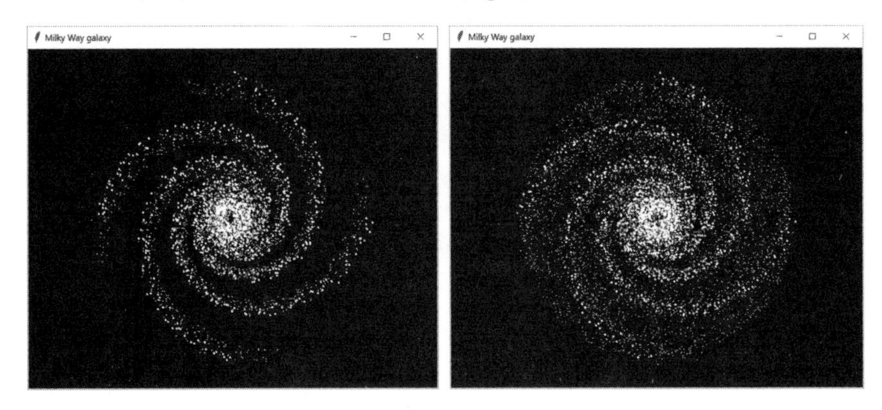

Figure 10-13: Galactic model without star haze (left) versus with star haze (right)

You can be creative with the haze. For example, you can make the stars more numerous and color them gray, or use a loop to vary both their size and color. Don't use green, however, as there are no green stars in the universe!

Defining the main() Function

Listing 10-9 defines the main() function in *galaxy_simulator.py*. It will make the calls to scale the galaxy, calculate the probability of detection, build the galaxy display, and post statistics. It will also run the tkinter main loop.

galaxy_simulator.py, part 8

```
def main():
    """Calculate detection probability & post galaxy display & statistics."""
 ❶ disc_radius_scaled, disc_vol_scaled = scale_galaxy()
    detection_prob = detect_prob(disc_vol_scaled)

    # build 4 main spiral arms & 4 trailing arms
 ❷ spirals(b=-0.3, r=disc_radius_scaled, rot_fac=2, fuz_fac=1.5, arm=0)
    spirals(b=-0.3, r=disc_radius_scaled, rot_fac=1.91, fuz_fac=1.5, arm=1)
    spirals(b=-0.3, r=-disc_radius_scaled, rot_fac=2, fuz_fac=1.5, arm=0)
    spirals(b=-0.3, r=-disc_radius_scaled, rot_fac=-2.09, fuz_fac=1.5, arm=1)
    spirals(b=-0.3, r=-disc_radius_scaled, rot_fac=0.5, fuz_fac=1.5, arm=0)
    spirals(b=-0.3, r=-disc_radius_scaled, rot_fac=0.4, fuz_fac=1.5, arm=1)
    spirals(b=-0.3, r=-disc_radius_scaled, rot_fac=-0.5, fuz_fac=1.5, arm=0)
    spirals(b=-0.3, r=-disc_radius_scaled, rot_fac=-0.6, fuz_fac=1.5, arm=1)
    star_haze(disc_radius_scaled, density=8)

    # display legend
 ❸ c.create_text(-455, -360, fill='white', anchor='w',
                  text='One Pixel = {} LY'.format(SCALE))
    c.create_text(-455, -330, fill='white', anchor='w',
                  text='Radio Bubble Diameter = {} LY'.format(SCALE))
    c.create_text(-455, -300, fill='white', anchor='w',
                  text='Probability of detection for {:,} civilizations = {}'.
                  format(NUM_CIVS, detection_prob))

    # post Earth's 225 LY diameter bubble and annotate
 ❹ if SCALE == 225:
     ❺ c.create_rectangle(115, 75, 116, 76, fill='red', outline='')
        c.create_text(118, 72, fill='red', anchor='w',
                      text="<---------- Earth's Radio Bubble")
    # run tkinter loop
 ❻ root.mainloop()

❼ if __name__ == '__main__':
    main()
```

Listing 10-9: Defines and calls the main() function

Start main() by calling the scale_galaxy() function to get the scaled disc volume and radius ❶. Then call the detect_prob() function and pass it the disc_vol_scaled variable. Assign the results to a variable named detection_prob.

Now build the galaxy display (graphical model) ❷. This calls the spirals() function multiple times, with small changes to each call. The arm parameter designates the bright main arms and the faint trailing arms. The rot_fac (rotation factor) variable determines where the spiral plots. The slight change in rotation factor between arms 0 and 1 (for example, 2 to 1.91) is what causes the faint arm to plot slightly offset from the bright arm. Finish the display by calling the `star_haze()` function. Again, feel free to experiment with any of these parameters.

Next, display a legend and statistics. Start with the scale ❸ and radio bubble diameter followed by the probability of detection for the given number of civilizations. Arguments include the x and y coordinates, a fill (text) color, a justification anchor—with left represented by `w` for "west"—and the text. Note the use of `{:,}` to insert a comma as a thousand separator. This is part of the newer *string format method*. You can read more about it at *https://docs.python.org/3/library/string.html#string-formatting*.

If the user has selected a radio bubble diameter of `225` LY ❹, then the display is at the same scale as our own emissions bubble, so post a red pixel at the approximate location of our solar system and annotate it ❺. There are a number of ways to display a single pixel using `tkinter`. Here, you use the `create_rectangle()` method, but you can also make a line that is one pixel long with the following statement:

```
c.create_line(115, 75, 116, 75, fill='red')
```

With the `create_rectangle()` method, the first two arguments are points (`x0`, `y0`), which correspond to the top-left corner, and (`x1`, `y1`), the location of the pixel just outside of the bottom-right corner. With the `create_line()` method, the arguments are for the starting and ending points. The default line width is one pixel.

End the `main()` function by executing the `tkinter` `mainloop()` function, also known as the *event loop* ❻. This keeps the `root` window open until you close it.

Back in the global space, end the program by allowing it to be run stand-alone or called as a module in another program ❼.

The final display will look like Figure 10-14, shown with the Earth's radio bubble and a central black hole.

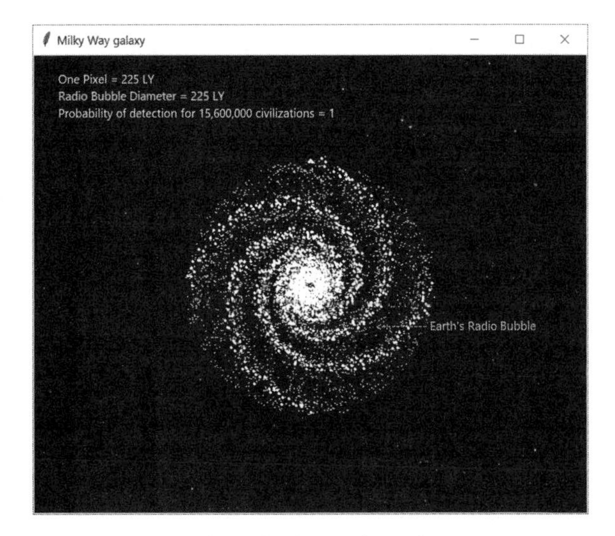

Figure 10-14: The final display, with Earth's 225 LY diameter radio bubble posted on the galactic map

Note that, despite the fact that our radio bubble is no bigger than a pinprick at this scale, if civilizations had a detection range of 112.5 light-years, and if there were as many of these civilizations as predicted by current high-side parameters for the Drake equation, the probability of detection is 1!

Results

Given the enormous uncertainty in the inputs and the use of simplifying assumptions, you're not looking for accuracy here. What you're looking for is *directionality*. Should we (or anyone like us) expect to detect another civilization that isn't actively trying to contact us? Based on Figure 10-15, probably not.

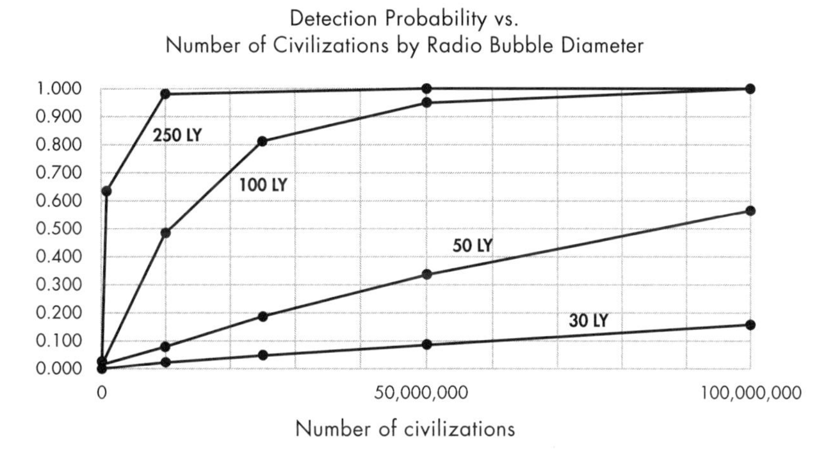

Figure 10-15: Probability of one civilization detecting another for different radio bubble diameters and different numbers of civilizations in the galaxy

With our current technology, we could detect emissions from a civilization as far away as 16 LY, which equates to a 32 LY diameter radio bubble. Even if the galaxy is filled with 15.6 million advanced civilizations, as predicted by the updated Drake equation in the Wikipedia article, the chance of detecting 32 LY radio bubbles is less than 4 percent!

Take another look at Figure 10-14, and you can begin to appreciate the sheer enormity and emptiness of our galaxy. Astronomers even have a word for this: *Laniakea*, Hawaiian for "immeasurable heaven."

Earth is, as Carl Sagan described it, just a "mote of dust, suspended in a sunbeam." And recent studies suggest that the window of opportunity for detecting civilizations with radio waves is much smaller than we thought. If other civilizations follow our lead and switch to digital signals and satellite communications, then their incidental radio leakage will drop by at least a factor of four. We all become unintentionally stealthy, blooming for a hundred years or so, then fading away.

Given these facts, it's not surprising that the government no longer funds the search for extraterrestrial intelligence using radio telescopes.

These days, efforts are shifting to optical methods that look for signature gases in the atmospheres of exoplanets, such as the waste products of life and industrial activity.

Summary

In this chapter, you gained experience using `tkinter`, `matplotlib`, and `NumPy`. You generated a polynomial expression for making reasonable estimates of the likelihood of detecting incidental alien radio transmissions, and you used the always-available `tkinter` module to add a cool visual component to the analysis.

Further Reading

Are We Alone? Philosophical Implications of the Discovery of Extraterrestrial Life (BasicBooks, 1995) by Paul Davies is a thoughtful look at the search for alien life, told by an eminent scientist and award-winning science writer.

"A New Formula Describing the Scaffold Structure of Spiral Galaxies" (*Monthly Notices of the Royal Astronomical Society*, July 21, 2009) by Harry I. Ringermacher and Lawrence R. Mead (*https://arxiv.org/abs/0908.0892v1*) provides formulas for modeling the shapes of spiral galaxies observed by the Hubble telescope.

"Tkinter 8.5 Reference: A GUI for Python" (New Mexico Tech Computer Center, 2013) by John W. Shipman is a useful supplement to the official `tkinter` docs. It can be found at *http://infohost.nmt.edu/tcc/help/pubs/tkinter/tkinter.pdf*.

Another useful online `tkinter` resource is *https://wiki.python.org/moin/TkInter/*.

Tkinter GUI Application Development HOTSHOT (Packt Publishing, 2013) by Bhaskar Chaudhary uses a project-based approach to teach `tkinter`.

Practice Projects

Try these three spin-off projects. You can find them in the appendix or download them from *https://www.nostarch.com/impracticalpython/*.

A Galaxy Far, Far Away

Tired of living in the Milky Way galaxy? Heck, who isn't? Fortunately, there's more in heaven and earth than just logarithmic spirals. Use Python and `tkinter` to build us a new home—but not necessarily a realistic home. For inspiration, visit online articles like Alexandre Devert's post on his Marmakoide's Blog, "Spreading Points on a Disc and on a Sphere" (*http://blog.marmakoide.org/*). The example shown in Figure 10-16 was built with *galaxy_practice.py*.

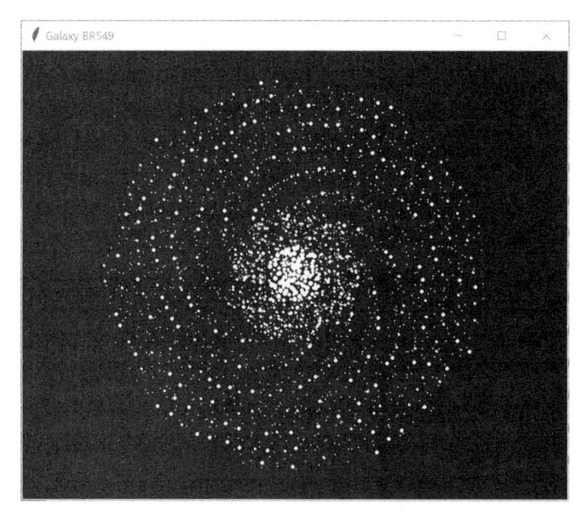

Figure 10-16: Galaxy produced by the galaxy_practice.py *program*

Building a Galactic Empire

Pick a location in the galaxy, an average travel speed of 5 to 10 percent of the speed of light, and a time step of 500,000 years. Then model the expansion of a space-faring empire. At each time step, calculate the size of the expanding *colonization bubble* and update the galaxy map. Check your results by placing the home-world location at the center of the galaxy, setting the speed to `1`, and confirming that it takes 50,000 years to reach the edge of the galaxy.

When you have the program up and running, you can perform interesting experiments. For example, you can test how fast we would need to go to explore the galaxy in 10 million years, as mentioned in the introduction to this chapter (see Figure 10-17).

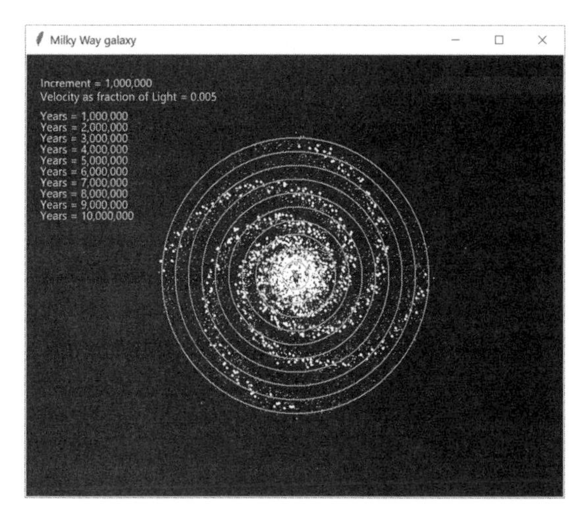

Figure 10-17: A core-located empire's expansion using travel below light speed over 10 million years

You could also estimate how much of the galaxy the *Star Trek* Federation could have explored in its first 100 years, assuming they averaged 100x light speed at warp 4 (Figure 10-18).

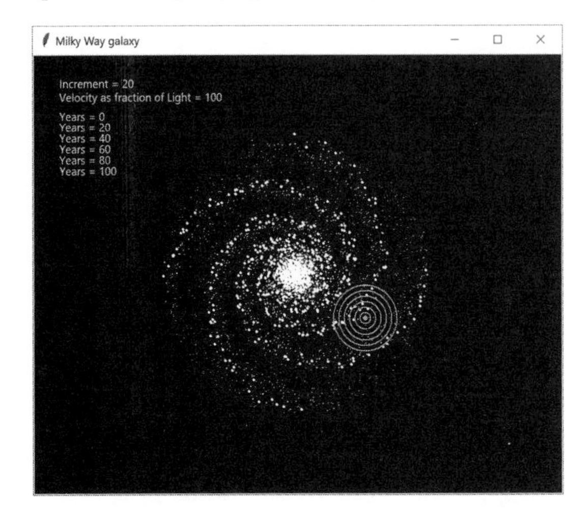

Figure 10-18: Expansion of the Star Trek *Federation in first 100 years under warp factor 4*

These figures were built with the *empire_practice.py* program.

A Roundabout Way to Predict Detectability

Another way to predict the probability of detection is to use polar coordinates to distribute civilizations—as xyz points—in the galactic disc and then round the points to the nearest radio bubble *radius*. Points that share the same location represent civilizations that could detect each other. But be careful—this method rounds using cubes rather than spheres, so you'll need to convert the radius to the side of a cube that produces the same volume.

Write the program so that it predicts the probability of detecting 16 LY *radius* bubbles (the limit of our current technology) given 15,600,000 transmitting civilizations randomly distributed throughout the galaxy (updated Drake equation output from Wikipedia). Use the full 50,000 LY radius and 1,000 LY height of the galactic model when distributing the civilizations.

For a solution, see *rounded_detection_practice.py*. Note that the program will take several minutes to run.

Challenge Projects

Here are a few follow-up projects to try on your own. Remember that I don't provide solutions to challenge projects.

Creating a Barred-Spiral Galaxy

Our understanding of the Milky Way evolves as we obtain and analyze new astronomical data. Scientists now believe that the core of the galaxy is elongated and bar shaped. Use the equations provided in the Ringermacher and Mead paper, cited in "Further Reading" on page 212, to create a new `tkinter` visual model of the galaxy that honors the barred-spiral concept.

Adding Habitable Zones to Your Galaxy

Solar systems have *Goldilocks zones* that are favorable for the development of life. Planets orbiting in these zones stay warm enough for at least some of their water to remain in liquid state.

There is also a theory that galaxies, like solar systems, have *habitable zones* in which life is more likely to develop. One definition of the habitable zone for the Milky Way places its inner boundary about 13,000 LY from the galactic center and its outer boundary about 33,000 LY from the center (Figure 10-19). The core is excluded due to the high levels of radiation, large number of supernovas, and complex orbit-disrupting gravitational fields resulting from all the closely spaced stars. The rim areas are condemned due to low metallicity, which is crucial to the development of planets.

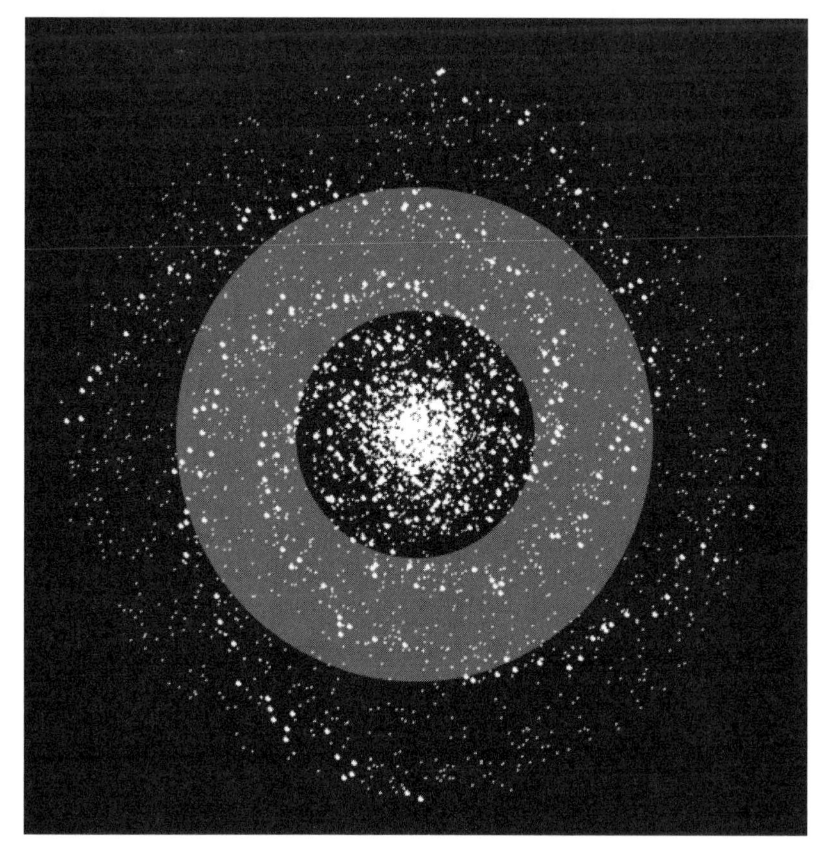

Figure 10-19: Approximate galactic habitable zone (shaded) superimposed on the Milky Way model

A refinement of the habitable zone model excludes spiral arms, for reasons similar to those applied to the core. Our own existence doesn't contradict this. Earth is located in the Orion "spur," a relatively small feature between the Sagittarius and Perseus arms.

Edit the *galaxy_simulation.py* program so that it uses only the volume in the galactic habitable zone, however you define it. You should research what these volumes may be and what effect they'll have on the number of civilizations (*N*) that the Drake equation calculates. Consider using *regions*, such as the core, spirals, outer rim, and so on, within which *N* is different but civilizations are still randomly distributed. Highlight these regions on the galactic map and post their probability-of-detection estimates.

11

THE MONTY HALL PROBLEM

As host of the TV game show *Let's Make a Deal*, Monty Hall would show contestants three closed doors and ask them to choose one. Behind one door was a valuable prize; behind the other two were smelly old goats. As soon as the contestant chose a door, Monty would open one of the remaining doors to reveal a goat. The contestant was then given a final choice: switch doors or stay with their initial pick.

In 1990, Marilyn vos Savant, "the world's smartest woman," stated in her weekly *Parade* magazine column, "Ask Marilyn," that the contestant should choose to switch doors. Though her answer was correct, it ignited a firestorm of hate mail, gender profiling, and academic persecution. Many math professors embarrassed themselves in the process, but there was a bright side to the ugly affair. The heated discussion exposed the public to the science of statistics, and an exercise that vos Savant proposed found its way into thousands of classrooms. These manual tests—later duplicated by computers—all vindicated her derided "female logic."

In this chapter, you'll use *Monte Carlo simulation (MCS)*, a method for modeling the probability of different outcomes from a range of random inputs, to verify that vos Savant was right. After that, you'll use tkinter to build a fun graphical interface that addresses her request for schoolchildren to help with the experiment.

Monte Carlo Simulation

Imagine you want to know the probability of rolling a die six times and getting a different face with each roll. If you're a math whiz, you'd probably just compute this using the deterministic equation $6! / 6^6$ or

$$\frac{6}{6} \times \frac{5}{6} \times \frac{4}{6} \times \frac{3}{6} \times \frac{2}{6} \times \frac{1}{6}$$

yielding 0.015. If you're not so mathematically inclined, you could get the same answer with Python and a lot of rolls:

```
>>> from random import randint
>>> trials = 100000
>>> success = 0
>>> for trial in range(trials):
    faces = set()
    for rolls in range(6):
        roll = randint(1, 6)
        faces.add(roll)
    if len(faces) == 6:
        success += 1
>>> print("probability of success = {}".format(success/trials))
probability of success = 0.01528
```

This example uses a for loop and randint to randomly pick a number between 1 and 6, representing one of the faces on the die, six times in a row. It adds each result to a set named faces, which doesn't permit duplicates. The only way for the length of the set to reach 6 is if each roll yields a unique number, which equals a success case. An outer for loop performs the six-roll trial 100,000 times. Dividing the number of successes by the number of trials yields the same probability, 0.015, as the deterministic equation.

Monte Carlo simulation uses *repeated random sampling*—in this case, each roll of the die is a random sample—to predict different outcomes under a specified range of conditions. For this example, the range of conditions was one six-faced die, six rolls with no repeats per trial, and 100,000 trials.

Of course, MCS is usually applied to more complex problems—those with lots of variables and wide ranges of uncertainty, where the results cannot be easily predicted.

There are multiple types of MCS, but most applications follow these basic steps:

- List the input variables.
- Provide a probability distribution for each variable.
- Start a loop:
    - Randomly select a value from the distributions for each input.
    - Use the values in a deterministic calculation, which is a calculation that will always produce the same output from the same input.
    - Repeat a specified number of times.
- Aggregate the results and generate statistics, such as the average outcome for the calculation.

For the die-roll example, these steps were:

- Input variables = the results of six die rolls.
- Probability distribution for roll = uniform (1/6 for each face).
- Loop:
    - Randomly selected value = die roll (draw from distribution).
    - Calculation = add the six values to a set and, if set length equals 6, add 1 to `success` variable.
    - Repeat = 100,000 times.
- Aggregate: divide `success` variable by 100,0000 for probability calculation.

Nassim Taleb, the critically acclaimed author of *The Black Swan* and *Fooled by Randomness*, is a fan of MCS. He posits that our brains are designed to get us out of trouble quickly, rather than handle complicated uncertainty or probability problems. We aren't cut out for highly skewed distributions and nonlinearities, but some people's brains are inherently more capable of understanding risks using MCS than other methods. In real life, we don't observe probability distributions; we just observe events.

Each MCS run represents a single event, such as whether you run out of money in retirement. For many of us, MCS makes risk real. It helps us understand how bad or good things can be—something we can't always glean from mathematical abstractions. With the insight from MCS, we can prepare to both defend against the downside and exploit the upside.

To support the math behind the Monty Hall problem, you'll use an MCS application like the preceding die-roll example. Then, in Chapter 12, you'll use MCS to build a nest-egg simulator to plan your (or your parents') secure retirement.

Project #18: Verify vos Savant

To verify that vos Savant was right, use a Monte Carlo approach and simulate tens of thousands of "games" in order to see how things shake out. This can be a bare-bones program, since the goal is a simple confirmation with no embellishments.

THE OBJECTIVE

Write a simple Python program that uses Monte Carlo simulation to determine the probability of winning the Monty Hall problem by changing the initial pick.

The Strategy

The correct response to the Monty Hall problem is to switch doors after Monty reveals the goat. Statistically, this will double your chances of winning!

Look at Figure 11-1. At the start of the game, all the doors are closed, and the odds of a given door hiding the prize are 1 in 3. The user can choose only one door, which means the odds of the prize being behind one of the other two doors are 2 in 3. After the goat is revealed, the odds remain 2 in 3, but they revert to the remaining door. Remember, Monty knows where the prize is hidden, and he will never reveal *that* door. So the probability of success is 1/3 for staying with your first choice versus 2/3 for switching.

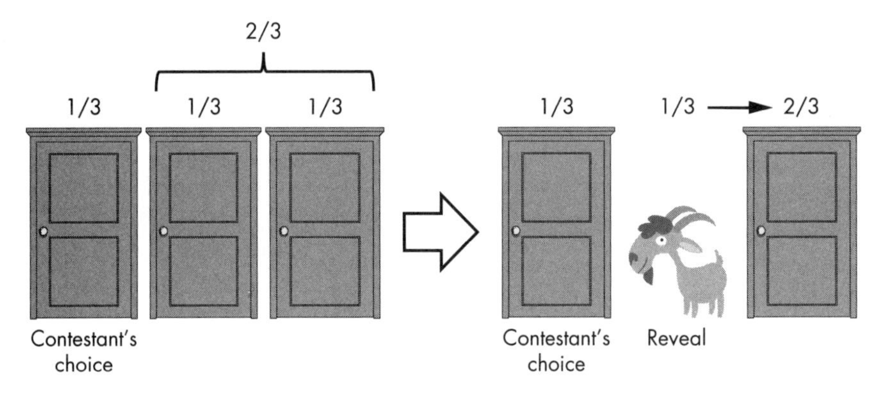

Figure 11-1: Odds of winning the Monty Hall problem before and after a goat is revealed

If you're dubious about the math, you can use MCS to provide corroborating evidence, just as we did with the die-roll example. You simply need to pick a winning door at random, choose a contestant's pick at random, and record how many times the two coincide. Repeat this thousands of times, and you will converge on the deterministic mathematical solution.

The vos Savant Verification Code

The *monty_hall_mcs.py* program described in this section will automate the process of choosing doors and recording the results so that you can run thousands of trials and evaluate them in less than a second. You can download the code from *https://www.nostarch.com/impracticalpython.com/.*

Getting the Number of Runs Input

Listing 11-1 starts the *monty_hall_mcs.py* program by asking the user how many runs—or games—they want to simulate. You'll also provide the user with a default value. This is a great way to guide a user to a reasonable first response, as well as save them a few keystrokes.

monty_hall_mcs.py, part 1

```
❶ import random

❷ def user_prompt(prompt, default=None):
      """Allow use of default values in input."""
    ❸ prompt = '{} [{}]: '.format(prompt, default)
    ❹ response = input(prompt)
    ❺ if not response and default:
          return default
      else:
          return response

  # input number of times to run simulation
❻ num_runs = int(user_prompt("Input number of runs", "20000"))
```

Listing 11-1: Imports modules and defines the user_prompt() function

Start by importing the `random` module to run MCS ❶. Next, define a function, called `user_prompt()`, that asks the user to either input the number of games to run or else accept a default value, if provided ❷. This function takes two arguments; the first is the text prompt that tells the user what to do, and the second is the default value, which will start out as `None`. Immediately redefine the `prompt` variable so that it will display with the default value in brackets, per convention ❸. Assign the user's input to a variable named `response` ❹. If the user presses ENTER without providing any input and a default value exists, the `user_prompt()` function will return the default value ❺. Otherwise, the function returns the user's input. Use the function to determine the number of runs to make by assigning the returned value to the `num_runs` variable ❻. Each run will represent a contestant playing the game once.

Running MCS and Displaying the Results

Listing 11-2 picks the winning door and the user's first choice at random, then aggregates and presents the statistics. Interestingly, the user's second choice—to switch doors or not—isn't required to get the correct answer. If the initial choice is the winning door, the correct answer is to not change doors. Likewise, if the initial choice and the winning door differ, the correct answer is to change doors. There's no reason to model what a contestant might or might not do.

monty_hall_mcs.py, part 2

```
    # assign counters for ways to win
❶ first_choice_wins = 0
   pick_change_wins = 0
❷ doors = ['a', 'b', 'c']

   # run Monte Carlo
❸ for i in range(num_runs):
       winner = random.choice(doors)
       pick = random.choice(doors)

     ❹ if pick == winner:
           first_choice_wins += 1
       else:
           pick_change_wins += 1

❺ print("Wins with original pick = {}".format(first_choice_wins))
   print("Wins with changed pick = {}".format(pick_change_wins))
   print("Probability of winning with initial guess: {:.2f}"
         .format(first_choice_wins / num_runs))
   print("Probability of winning by switching: {:.2f}"
         .format(pick_change_wins / num_runs))

❻ input("\nPress Enter key to exit.")
```

Listing 11-2: Runs the Monte Carlo simulation and displays the results

Assign two variables to keep track of whether switching or staying put is the winning outcome ❶. Then, create a list to represent the three doors ❷.

MCS starts with a `for` loop that goes through the number of runs ❸. Inside that loop, choose the winning door and the user's first choice from the `doors` list, using `random.choice()`, and assign them to variables.

Since this is a binary system—the user switches or doesn't—you'll only need a conditional that adds to the counters based on the relationship of the `pick` variable to the `winning` variable ❹.

Finish the program by presenting the final results. Display the actual counts, plus the calculated probabilities ❺. Then let the user know the program is finished ❻.

Here's an example output for the default 20,000 runs:

```
Input number of runs [20000]:
Wins with original pick = 6628
Wins with changed pick = 13372
Probability of winning with initial guess: 0.33
Probability of winning by switching: 0.67

Press Enter key to exit.
```

Some people aren't impressed with a computer printout. They need something more convincing, so in the next project, you'll repackage your code in a more hands-on format—one that's complete with doors, prizes, and goats. This will also satisfy Marilyn vos Savant's appeal for schoolchildren to join in and help restore her honor.

Project #19: The Monty Hall Game

The three-door game used in the Monty Hall problem is simple enough for you to build with `tkinter`. You began working with `tkinter` graphics in Chapter 10. Now you'll build on this knowledge by adding interactive buttons for the user to click.

THE OBJECTIVE

Simulate the Monty Hall problem using a GUI built with `tkinter`. Keep track of whether switching doors or staying put results in a win. In addition, update and display these statistics as the game is played.

A Brief Introduction to Object-Oriented Programming

The `tkinter` module was written using *object-oriented programming (OOP)*. OOP is a language model built around data structures, known as *objects*, consisting of *data* and *methods* and the interactions between them—as opposed to the *actions* and *logic* used in procedural programming. Objects are built from *classes*, which are like blueprints for the objects.

OOP is an abstract concept and easier to appreciate when you're writing large, complex programs. It reduces code duplication and makes code easier to update, maintain, and reuse. As a result, most commercial software is now built using OOP.

If you implemented OOP in small programs, like the ones we've written so far, most of them would feel overengineered. In fact, one of my all-time favorite quotes, attributed to British computer scientist Joe Armstrong, concerns this aspect of OOP: "The problem with object-oriented languages is they've got all this implicit environment that they carry around with them. You wanted a banana, but what you got was a gorilla holding the banana and the entire jungle!"

Despite this, the objects produced by OOP lend themselves very well to GUIs and gaming, even for some small projects. Let's look at an example using a *Dungeons and Dragons*–type board game in which players can be different characters, such as dwarves, elves, and wizards. These games use character cards to list important information for each character type. If you let your playing piece represent a dwarf, it inherits the characteristics on the card (see Figure 11-2).

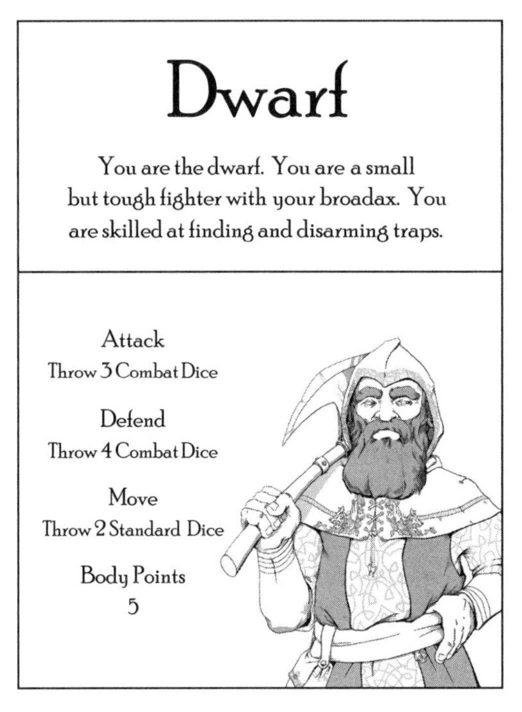

Dwarf
You are the dwarf. You are a small but tough fighter with your broadax. You are skilled at finding and disarming traps.
Attack
Throw 3 Combat Dice
Defend
Throw 4 Combat Dice
Move
Throw 2 Standard Dice
Body Points
5

Figure 11-2: A dwarf character card from a role-playing board game

Listings 11-3 and 11-4 reproduce board game–style play, letting you create virtual cards for a dwarf and an elf, name your pieces, and have them fight. The outcome of the fight will impact one of the character's *body points*, which represent the character's health. Be sure to note how OOP can allow you to easily create many identical objects—in this case, dwarves or elves—by "stamping" them out of the predefined template, called a *class*.

```
❶ >>> import random
❷ >>> class Dwarf(object):
      ❸ def __init__(self, name):
          ❹ self.name = name
             self.attack = 3
             self.defend = 4
             self.body = 5
      ❺ def talk(self):
             print("I'm a blade-man, I'll cut ya!!!")
❻ >>> lenn = Dwarf("Lenn")
   >>> print("Dwarf name = {}".format(lenn.name))
   Dwarf name = Lenn
   >>> print("Lenn's attack strength = {}".format(lenn.attack))
   Lenn's attack strength = 3
   >>>
❼ >>> lenn.talk()
   I'm a blade-man, I'll cut ya!!!
```

Listing 11-3: Imports `random` module, creates a `Dwarf` class, and instantiates a dwarf object

Start by importing random to simulate rolling a die ❶; this is how your character will fight. Now define a class for a dwarf character, capitalizing the first letter of the class name, and pass it an object argument, which will be the name of your dwarf ❷. A class is a template for creating objects of a certain type. For example, when you create a list or dictionary, you are creating them from a class.

The Dwarf class definition is like the card in Figure 11-2; it is basically the genetic blueprint for a dwarf. It will assign *attributes*, like strength and vitality, and *methods*, like how the character moves or talks. Attributes are variables scoped to an *instance* of the class, and methods are attributes that also happen to be functions, which are passed a reference to their instance when they run. A class is a data type, and when you create an object of that data type, it is also known as an instance of that class. The process of setting the initial values and behaviors of the instance is called *instantiation*.

Next, define a *constructor* method, also referred to as the *initialization* method. It sets up the initial attribute values for your object ❸. The __init__() method is a special built-in method that Python automatically invokes as soon as a new object is created. In this case, you'll pass two arguments: self and the name of your object.

The self parameter is a reference to the instance of this class that is being created, or a reference to the instance a method was invoked on, technically referred to as a *context* instance. If you create a new dwarf and name it "Steve," self will become Steve behind the scenes. For example, self.attack becomes "Steve's attack." If you create another dwarf named "Sue," self for that object will become "Sue." This way, the scope of Steve's health attribute is kept separate from Sue's.

Next, list some attributes for a dwarf beneath the constructor definition ❹. You'll want a name so you can tell one dwarf from another, as well as the value of key combat characteristics. Notice how this list resembles the card in Figure 11-2.

Define a talk() method and pass it self ❺. By passing it self, you link the method to the object. In more comprehensive games, methods might include behaviors like movement and the ability to disarm traps.

With the class definition complete, create an instance of the Dwarf class and assign this object to the local variable lenn, the dwarf's name ❻. Now, print the name and attack attributes to demonstrate that you have access to them. Finish by invoking the talk() method ❼. This should display a message.

Listing 11-4 creates an elf character, using the same process you used in Listing 11-3, and has it fight the dwarf. The elf's body attribute is updated to reflect the outcome of the battle.

```
❶ >>> class Elf(object):
          def __init__(self, name):
              self.name = name
              self.attack = 4
              self.defend = 4
              self.body = 4
  >>> esseden = Elf("Esseden")
```

```
>>> print("Elf name = {}".format(esseden.name))
Elf name = Esseden
>>> print("Esseden body value = {}".format(esseden.body))
Esseden body value = 4
>>>
❷ >>> lenn_attack_roll = random.randrange(1, lenn.attack + 1)
>>> print("Lenn attack roll = {}".format(lenn_attack_roll))
Lenn attack roll = 3
❸ >>> esseden_defend_roll = random.randrange(1, esseden.defend + 1)
>>> print("Esseden defend roll = {}".format(esseden_defend_roll))
Esseden defend roll = 1
>>>
❹ >>> damage = lenn_attack_roll - esseden_defend_roll
>>> if damage > 0:
        esseden.body -= damage
❺ >>> print("Esseden body value = {}".format(esseden.body))
Esseden body value = 2
```

Listing 11-4: Creates an `Elf` *class, instantiates an elf object, simulates a battle, and updates an object attribute*

Define an `Elf` class and provide some attributes ❶. Make them slightly different from the dwarf's and well balanced, like an elf. Instantiate an elf named `Esseden` and access his `name` and `body` attributes using `print`.

Have your two characters interact using the roll of a virtual die with a maximum value equal to the character's attack or defend value. Use the `random` module to choose a roll value in a range of 1 to Lenn's `attack` attribute plus 1 ❷, then repeat this process to get Esseden's defense ❸. Calculate the damage to Esseden by subtracting Esseden's roll value from Lenn's roll value ❹, and if the damage is a positive number, subtract it from Esseden's body attribute. Use `print()` to confirm the elf's current health ❺.

As you can imagine, building many similar characters and keeping track of their changing attributes could quickly get complicated with procedural programming. OOP provides a modular structure for your program, makes it easy to hide complexity and ownership of scope with encapsulation, permits problem solving in bite-sized chunks, and produces sharable templates that can be modified and used elsewhere.

The Strategy and Pseudocode

Now back to our three-door game. The rules for the game form the bulk of the pseudocode for the program:

```
Initialize game window and show closed doors and instructions
Choose winning door at random
Get player's door choice
Reveal a door that isn't the winning door or the player's choice
Get player's choice to switch doors or not
If player switches:
    Reveal new door
```

```
    If winner:
        Record as win for switching
    Otherwise:
        Record as win for staying put
Else if player stays with first choice:
    Reveal chosen door
    If winner:
        Record as win for staying put
    Otherwise:
        Record as win for switching
Display number of wins for each strategy in game window
Reset game and close all doors
```

It's useful to start designing a game by sketching out how the game window should look, complete with instructions, messages, and button types. I doubt you want to see my crude scribblings, so instead check out Figure 11-3.

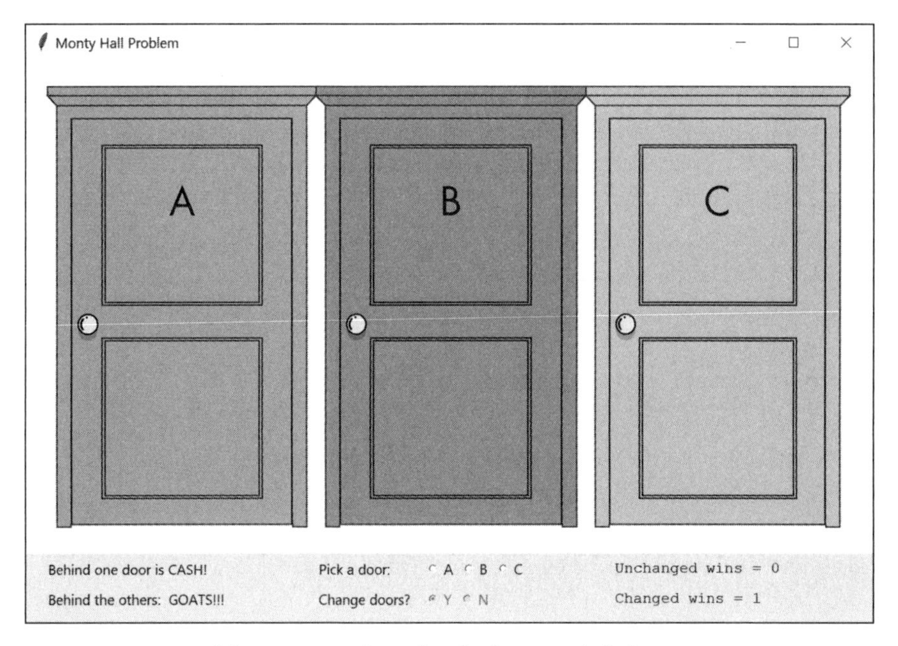

Figure 11-3: View of the game window after the first round of play

This is how the finished game will look after the first round, with the win statistics visible at the far right. Note that the radio buttons for changing doors are grayed out until an initial pick has been made.

Game Assets

Game assets is a fancy term for things that you'll need to build the game. These will consist of a series of images to represent the doors, goats, and prize (Figure 11-4).

Figure 11-4: Building-block images for the monty_hall_gui.py *program*

I used Microsoft PowerPoint to composite the 3 base images into 10 images that represent all the possible states of the game (Figure 11-5). This was a design decision; with extra lines of code, I could have obtained the same results using only the base images.

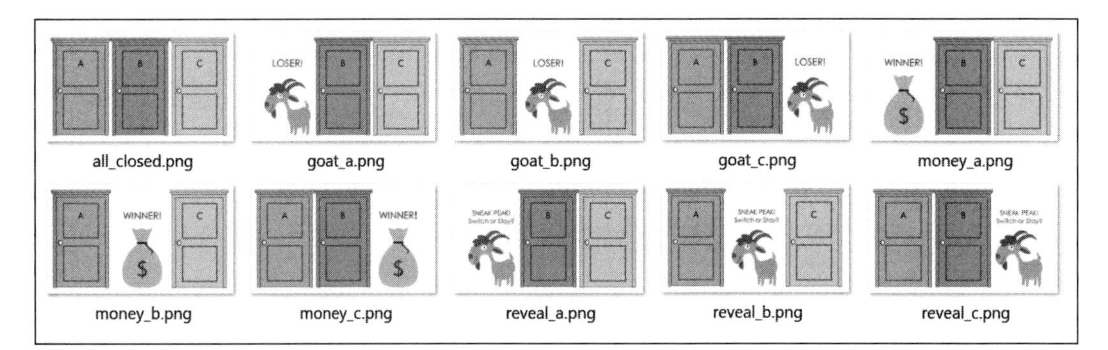

Figure 11-5: Composited images for the monty_hall_gui.py *program*

The Monty Hall Game Code

The *monty_hall_gui.py* program described in this section turns the Monty Hall problem into a fun and educational game. You will also need the 10 game assets shown in Figure 11-5. Download them from *https://www.nostarch.com/impracticalpython/* and keep all the files in the same folder.

Importing Modules and Defining the Game Class

Listing 11-5 imports modules and defines the `Game` class and the initialization method, `__init__()`.

monty_hall _gui.py, part 1

```
❶ import random
  import tkinter as tk

❷ class Game(tk.Frame):
      """GUI application for Monty Hall Problem game."""

    ❸ doors = ('a', 'b', 'c')

    ❹ def __init__(self, parent):
          """Initialize the frame."""
        ❺ super(Game, self).__init__(parent)  # parent will be the root window
        ❻ self.parent = parent
          self.img_file = 'all_closed.png'  # current image of doors
          self.choice = ''  # player's door choice
          self.winner = ''  # winning door
          self.reveal = ''  # revealed goat door
        ❼ self.first_choice_wins = 0  # counter for statistics
          self.pick_change_wins = 0  # counter for statistics
        ❽ self.create_widgets()
```

Listing 11-5: Imports modules and defines the `Game` *class and* `__init__()` *method*

Start by importing the `random` and `tkinter` modules ❶. Next, define a class called `Game` ❷. The *ancestor* for this class, shown in parentheses, will be a `tkinter` `Frame` class. This means that the `Game` class is *derived* from the existing `Frame` "base" class and will conveniently inherit useful methods from it. The `Frame` widget mainly serves as a geometry master for other widgets, helping to group them into complex layouts.

Note that classes have their own docstring conventions, which you can find at *https://www.python.org/dev/peps/pep-0257/*. As stated in Chapter 1, I will mainly show single-line docstrings in this book for brevity.

Every instance of `Game` will use the same three doors, so you can use a *class attribute* for this ❸. Any variable assigned a value outside of a method becomes a class attribute, much as variables assigned outside of functions in procedural programs become global variables. You don't want this attribute to get changed inadvertently, so make it immutable by using a tuple. Later, you'll make lists from this tuple whenever you want to manipulate the doors.

Now, just as with the earlier dwarf and elf examples, define an initializer method for the game object ❹. A `self` parameter is required, but you'll also need a `parent`, which will be the `root` window that will hold the game.

A base class can also be called a *superclass*, and the `super()` function lets you invoke the method of a superclass to gain access to inherited methods—in this case, from a parent class. First, pass `Game` to `super()`, which means you want to invoke a method of the superclass of `Game`, which is `Frame` ❺. Then pass it `self` as an argument to reference the newly instantiated `Game` object. The `__init__(parent)` part of the statement invokes the initializer method of `Frame` with `parent` (the root window) as the argument. Now attributes in the prebuilt `tkinter` `Frame` class can be used by your `Game` object. Note that this statement can be simplified to `super().__init__()`.

Next, assign values to a series of instance attributes ❻. It is best to initialize attributes through the __init__() method, as it is the first method called after an object is created. This way, these attributes will be immediately available to any other methods in the class. Start by assigning the parent, which will be the root window, to the instance. Then name an attribute to hold one of the image files (shown in Figure 11-5) and assign it the image with all the doors closed, which is what the player will see at the start of each game. Next, name attributes for the player's door choice, the winning door, and the door used to reveal the first goat.

Use a counter to keep track of the number of wins achieved if the player sticks with the first door choice and another to record wins achieved when the player switches doors ❼. Finally, call a method that will create the label, button, and text widgets needed to run the game ❽.

Creating Widgets for Images and Instructions

Listing 11-6 defines the first part of the create_widgets() method, used to build the labels, buttons, and text widgets for the game. The first two widgets will be tkinter labels used to display the images in Figure 11-5 and to provide game instructions.

monty_hall_gui.py, part 2

```
❶ def create_widgets(self):
       """Create label, button, and text widgets for game."""
       # create label to hold image of doors
     ❷ img = tk.PhotoImage(file='all_closed.png')
     ❸ self.photo_lbl = tk.Label(self.parent, image=img,
                                  text='', borderwidth=0)
     ❹ self.photo_lbl.grid(row=0, column=0, columnspan=10, sticky='W')
     ❺ self.photo_lbl.image = img

       # create the instruction label
     ❻ instr_input = [
           ('Behind one door is CASH!', 1, 0, 5, 'W'),
           ('Behind the others:  GOATS!!!', 2, 0, 5, 'W'),
           ('Pick a door:', 1, 3, 1, 'E')
           ]
     ❼ for text, row, column, columnspan, sticky in instr_input:
           instr_lbl = tk.Label(self.parent, text=text)
           instr_lbl.grid(row=row, column=column, columnspan=columnspan,
                          sticky=sticky, ❽ipadx=30)
```

Listing 11-6: Defines a method to create widgets

Define a method, called create_widgets(), that takes self as an argument ❶. Then assign an attribute to hold an image of the doors ❷. Note that you don't have to precede this attribute name with self, as it will be used only locally within the method. The PhotoImage class, which takes the image filename as an argument, is used by tkinter to display images in canvas, label, text, or button widgets. After this step, you can use the image in a tkinter label, so assign a photo_lbl variable, pass it the parent and image as arguments, and specify no text and a thin border ❸.

To place the label in the parent window, use the `grid()` method and pass it the first row and first column, let the image span 10 columns, and left-justify it using `W` ❹. This will fill the top part of the window with the image of the closed doors. The `columnspan` option lets the widget span more than one column. The value won't affect the image size but *will* change the number of locations available for placing the instruction text and other widgets below the image. For example, if you set `columnspan=2`, you'll have only two columns available for placing instructions, buttons, and messages.

Finish the photo label by creating a reference to the image object ❺. If you don't do this, the image won't always show up.

According to the `tkinter` documentation, `tkinter` is a layer built over another product (`Tk`), and the interface between the two doesn't handle references to image objects properly. The `Tk` widget holds a reference to the internal object, but `tkinter` doesn't. Python uses a garbage-collector module to automatically reclaim memory from objects no longer needed. When the garbage collector in Python's memory allocator discards the `tkinter` object, `tkinter` tells `Tk` to release the image. But because it's in use, `Tk` can't, so it sets it to transparent instead. Suggestions for solving the problem include using a global variable, using an instance attribute, or as you did here, adding an attribute to the widget instance (`photo_lbl.image = img`). For more information, see *http://effbot.org/tkinterbook/photoimage.htm.*

Finally, add the instruction text as label widgets. The process is to provide a list of parameters and then loop through them to build the widgets. Start with a list of tuples ❻, where each tuple contains the options for making a `Label` object; you can see what each represents in the next statement ❼. As you progress through the `for` loop, create each label in the `parent` window and assign it some text. Then use the `grid()` method to place the text, based on the information in the list of tuples, into the window.

Use the `ipadx` option with `grid()` ❽. This option refers to internal padding in the x-direction within the label, so you can play with it to tweak the appearance of the text in the window. In this case, you add 30 pixels to the label so that the text will align in a visually pleasing way.

Creating Radio Buttons and Text Widgets

Listing 11-7 continues the definition of the `create_widgets()` method by creating radio button widgets for the three doors. The player makes their initial door choice by selecting the A, B, or C radio button. Their choice is then processed by the `win_reveal()` method, which you'll build later. This method will determine the winning door and reveal a goat.

Another set of radio buttons is created to get the player's choice to switch doors or not. The result will be processed by the `show_final()` method, also defined later. Besides revealing what's behind the player's final door choice, this method will update the win statistics, using `Text` widgets defined at the end of this listing.

monty_hall_gui.py, part 3

```
        # create radio buttons for getting initial user choice
❶       self.door_choice = tk.StringVar()
        self.door_choice.set(None)
```

```
❷ a = tk.Radiobutton(self.parent, text='A', variable=self.door_choice,
                      value='a', command=self.win_reveal)
  b = tk.Radiobutton(self.parent, text='B', variable=self.door_choice,
                      value='b', command=self.win_reveal)
  c = tk.Radiobutton(self.parent, text='C', variable=self.door_choice,
                      value='c', command=self.win_reveal)

  # create widgets for changing door choice
❸ self.change_door = tk.StringVar()
  self.change_door.set(None)

❹ instr_lbl = tk.Label(self.parent, text='Change doors?')
  instr_lbl.grid(row=2, column=3, columnspan=1, sticky='E')

❺ self.yes = tk.Radiobutton(self.parent, state='disabled', text='Y',
                             variable=self.change_door, value='y',
                             command=self.show_final)
  self.no = tk.Radiobutton(self.parent, state='disabled', text='N',
                            variable=self.change_door, value='n',
                            command=self.show_final)

  # create text widgets for win statistics
❻ defaultbg = self.parent.cget('bg')
❼ self.unchanged_wins_txt = tk.Text(self.parent, width=20,
                                     height=1, wrap=tk.WORD,
                                     bg=defaultbg, fg='black',
                                     borderwidth=0)
  self.changed_wins_txt = tk.Text(self.parent, width=20,
                                   height=1, wrap=tk.WORD, bg=defaultbg,
                                   fg='black', borderwidth=0)
```

Listing 11-7: Builds radio buttons and text widgets for the `create_widgets()` method

Start by creating radio buttons for doors A, B, and C. When a user interacts with a `tkinter` widget, the result is an *event*. You can use variables to track these events, such as when the player selects a door by pressing a radio button. For widget-specific variables, `tkinter` has a variable class. Use the *string* variable class, `StringVar`, and assign it to a variable named `door_choice` ❶. Immediately use the `set()` method to assign the variable a value of `None`.

Next, set up the button widgets for the three doors ❷. The player will click on one of these for their first door pick. Use the `Radiobutton` class and pass it the parent window, the text to display, the `door_choice` variable you just assigned, a value equal to the door name, and a command. The command calls the `win_reveal()` method, which you'll define shortly. Note that you don't include the parentheses after the method name.

Repeat this process for buttons B and C. This is mainly a cut-and-paste exercise, because all you need to change are the door designations.

Now, build the radio buttons for switching doors. Start by making another string variable, as you did for the initial door choice ❸. This will hold either `y` or `n`, depending on which radio button is selected.

Build an instruction label using the `Label` class ❹. Then build the `self.yes` radio button ❺. Use the `Radiobutton` class, pass it the parent window, and set its state to `disabled`. This way, the window will initialize with the yes/no buttons grayed out, so the player can't jump the gun and try to change a door before first choosing one. The text parameter is the button name; use an abbreviated Y for *yes*. Set the widget's variable argument to the `change_door` variable, set its value to `y`, and call the `show_final()` function. Repeat the process for the no button.

The last widgets you'll need are `Text` widgets to show the counts for switching doors versus staying put. Use the `Text` class to display the statistics and set the text box color to match the parent window. To do this, use `cget()` to get the background (`bg`) color of `parent` and then assign it to a variable ❻. The `cget()` method returns the current value for a `tkinter` option as a string.

Create a text object to display the wins for sticking with the first choice ❼. You need to pass the widget the parent window, a width and height, how to wrap text if it extends beyond a row, a background color, a foreground color—the text color—and a border width for the text box. Note that you don't include any actual text; this will be added later by the `show_final()` method.

Finish with another text widget to display the number of wins attributed to switching doors.

Arranging the Widgets

Listing 11-8 completes the `create_widgets()` method by using the `tkinter` `Grid` geometry manager to position the remaining nongridded widgets in the game window.

monty_hall_gui.py, part 4

```
    # place the widgets in the frame
❶ a.grid(row=1, column=4, sticky='W', padx=20)
    b.grid(row=1, column=4, sticky='N', padx=20)
    c.grid(row=1, column=4, sticky='E', padx=20)
    self.yes.grid(row=2, column=4, sticky='W', padx=20)
    self.no.grid(row=2, column=4, sticky='N', padx=20)
❷ self.unchanged_wins_txt.grid(row=1, column=5, columnspan=5)
    self.changed_wins_txt.grid(row=2, column=5, columnspan=5)
```

Listing 11-8: Calls the `grid()` method on the widgets to position them in the frame

Use `grid()` to position the door buttons in the parent window ❶. Group the three door buttons together in the same row and column and separate them using the `sticky` justification: `W` means left, `N` is center, and `E` is right. Use `padx` to tweak the positions laterally. Repeat this process for the remaining buttons, then position the win statistics text widgets and allow them to span the five columns on the right side of the window ❷.

Updating the Door Image

You'll need to open and close doors throughout the game, so Listing 11-9 defines a helper method to update the door image as appropriate. Note that, with OOP, you don't need to pass a filename to the method as an argument. All the methods for an object have direct access to attributes that begin with `self`.

monty_hall_gui.py, part 5

```
❶ def update_image(self):
      """Update current doors image."""
    ❷ img = tk.PhotoImage(file=self.img_file)
    ❸ self.photo_lbl.configure(image=img)
    ❹ self.photo_lbl.image = img
```

Listing 11-9: Defines a method to update the current door image

Define a function, called `update_image()`, that takes `self` as an argument ❶. Then use the `PhotoImage` class as you did in Listing 11-6 ❷. The filename, *self.img_file*, will be updated in other methods.

Because you've already created the label that holds the door image, use the `configure()` method to change the label—in this case, by loading a new image ❸. You can use either `configure()` or `config()`. Finish by assigning the image to a widget attribute to fend off garbage collection ❹, as described for Listing 11-6.

Selecting the Winning Door and Revealing a Goat

Listing 11-10 defines a method that selects the winning door and the reveal door and then opens and closes the reveal door. It also activates the yes/no buttons, which are grayed out until the player makes their first door choice.

monty_hall_gui.py, part 6

```
❶ def win_reveal(self):
      """Randomly pick winner and reveal unchosen door with goat."""
    ❷ door_list = list(self.doors)
    ❸ self.choice = self.door_choice.get()
      self.winner = random.choice(door_list)

    ❹ door_list.remove(self.winner)

    ❺ if self.choice in door_list:
          door_list.remove(self.choice)
          self.reveal = door_list[0]
      else:
          self.reveal = random.choice(door_list)

    ❻ self.img_file = ('reveal_{}.png'.format(self.reveal))
      self.update_image()

      # turn on and clear yes/no buttons
    ❼ self.yes.config(state='normal')
      self.no.config(state='normal')
      self.change_door.set(None)
```

```
    # close doors 2 seconds after opening
❽ self.img_file = 'all_closed.png'
    self.parent.after(2000, self.update_image)
```

Listing 11-10: Defines a method to randomly select the winning door and reveal door

Define a method, called `win_reveal()`, that takes `self` as an argument ❶. Immediately make a list of the doors from the class attribute `doors` ❷. You'll alter this list based on the player's first door choice and then the winning door, picked at random by the program.

Now, assign a `self.choice` attribute to the `self.door_choice` string variable, accessed with the `get()` method ❸. The value of this attribute was determined by the door radio button that the user clicked as their first choice. Next, choose the winning door, at random, from the door list.

Remove the winning door from the door list ❹. Then use a conditional to see whether the player's choice is still in the door list; if it is, remove it so that it can't be revealed ❺. This will leave only one door in the list, so assign it to the `self.reveal` attribute.

If the player picked the winning door, there are two doors left in the list, so randomly choose one of them and assign it to `self.reveal`. Update the `self.img_file` attribute for this door ❻, then call the method that updates the photo label to show the new image. Figure 11-6 is an example of the reveal image for door B.

Figure 11-6: The reveal image for Door B

Next, set the state of the yes and no buttons to `normal` ❼. After this, they will no longer be grayed out. End the method by changing the image file to *all_closed.png* and calling the `self.update_image()` method on the `parent` window after 2,000 milliseconds have elapsed ❽. This will ensure the doors stay open no longer than 2 seconds.

Revealing the Player's Final Choice

Listing 11-11 defines the first part of a function that takes the player's final door choice and reveals what's behind it. The function will also keep track of the number of wins for switching doors or staying put.

monty_hall _gui.py, part 7

```
❶ def show_final(self):
      """Reveal image behind user's final door choice & count wins."""
    ❷ door_list = list(self.doors)

    ❸ switch_doors = self.change_door.get()

    ❹ if switch_doors == 'y':
          door_list.remove(self.choice)
          door_list.remove(self.reveal)
        ❺ new_pick = door_list[0]
        ❻ if new_pick == self.winner:
              self.img_file = 'money_{}.png'.format(new_pick)
              self.pick_change_wins += 1
          else:
              self.img_file = 'goat_{}.png'.format(new_pick)
              self.first_choice_wins += 1
    ❼ elif switch_doors == 'n':
        ❽ if self.choice == self.winner:
              self.img_file = 'money_{}.png'.format(self.choice)
              self.first_choice_wins += 1
          else:
              self.img_file = 'goat_{}.png'.format(self.choice)
              self.pick_change_wins += 1

      # update door image
    ❾ self.update_image()
```

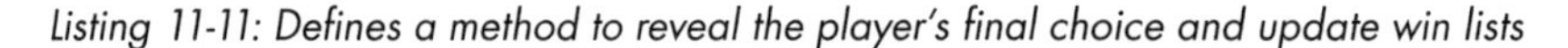

Listing 11-11: Defines a method to reveal the player's final choice and update win lists

Define a method, called `show_final()`, that takes—you guessed it—`self` as an argument ❶. Make a new copy of the door list ❷, then get the `self.change_doors` variable and assign it to an attribute named `switch_doors` ❸. This variable will hold either a `'y'` or an `'n'`, depending on which radio button the player clicked.

If the player chose to switch doors ❹, remove their first choice and the revealed door from the list and assign a `new_pick` attribute to the remaining door ❺. If this new pick is the winning door ❻, reference the proper image and advance the `self.pick_change_wins` counter. Otherwise, set the image to a goat and advance the `self.first_choice_wins` counter.

If the player decides to not change doors ❼ and if their first choice was the winning door ❽, reveal the money bag and advance the `self.first_choice_wins` counter. Otherwise, show a goat and advance the `self.pick_change_wins` counter.

Finish by calling the `update_image()` method to update the image ❾. Again, you don't need to pass it the name of the new image file, as it can access the `self.img_file` attribute that you changed in the preceding code.

Displaying Statistics

Listing 11-12 completes the `show_final()` method by updating the game window for the number of wins statistics, disabling the yes/no buttons, and closing all the doors.

monty_hall_gui.py, part 8

```
        # update displayed statistics
     ❶ self.unchanged_wins_txt.delete(1.0, 'end')
     ❷ self.unchanged_wins_txt.insert(1.0, 'Unchanged wins = {:d}'
                                       .format(self.first_choice_wins))
        self.changed_wins_txt.delete(1.0, 'end')
        self.changed_wins_txt.insert(1.0, 'Changed wins = {:d}'
                                     .format(self.pick_change_wins))

        # turn off yes/no buttons and clear door choice buttons
     ❸ self.yes.config(state='disabled')
        self.no.config(state='disabled')
     ❹ self.door_choice.set(None)

     ❺ # close doors 2 seconds after opening
        self.img_file = 'all_closed.png'
        self.parent.after(2000, self.update_image)
```

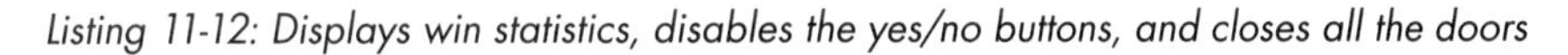

Listing 11-12: Displays win statistics, disables the yes/no buttons, and closes all the doors

Start by deleting any text in the `self.unchanged_wins_txt` text widget ❶. Begin deleting at a text index of `1.0`. The format is `line.column`, so you are specifying the first line and first column of the text widget (line numbering starts at 1, column numbering at 0). Finish with `'end'`, which will ensure that all the text after the starting index is deleted.

Next, use the `insert()` method to add the `self.first_choice_wins` attribute value, along with some descriptive text, to the text widget ❷. Begin inserting at text index `1.0`.

Repeat this process for the `self.changed_wins_txt` text widget, and then disable the yes/no buttons by setting their `config` state to `'disabled'` ❸. Set the `self.door_choice` string variable back to `None`, and you're ready to start a new game ❹.

End the method by closing the doors, as you did in Listing 11-10 ❺.

Setting Up the Root Window and Running the Event Loop

Listing 11-13 completes the *monty_hall_gui.py* program by setting up the `tkinter` root window, instantiating the game object, and running `mainloop()`. Alternatively, this code could be encapsulated in a `main()` function.

monty_hall_gui.py, part 9

```
  # set up root window & run event loop
❶ root = tk.Tk()
❷ root.title('Monty Hall Problem')
❸ root.geometry('1280x820')  # pics are 1280 x 720
❹ game = Game(root)
  root.mainloop()
```

Listing 11-13: Sets up the `root` window, creates a game object, and runs `mainloop()`

The `Tk` class is instantiated without arguments ❶. This creates a top-level `tkinter` widget, which will be the main window of the game application. Assign it to a variable named `root`.

Give the window a title ❷ and a size in pixels ❸. Note that the size of the images influences the geometry so that they fit attractively in the window, with ample room below for instructions and messages.

Now, create the game ❹. Pass it the `root` window, which will be the *master* that will contain the game. This results in a new game being placed inside the `root` window.

Finish by invoking the `mainloop()` method on `root`, which keeps the window open and waiting to handle events.

Summary

In this chapter, you used a simple Monte Carlo simulation to confirm that switching doors is the best strategy for the Monty Hall problem. You then used `tkinter` to build a fun interface to let schoolchildren test this conclusion manually, game by game. Best of all, you learned how to use object-oriented programming to build interactive widgets that respond to user input.

Further Reading

Useful `tkinter` references can be found in "Further Reading" on page 212.

You can find a summary of the 1990 Monty Hall problem controversy online at *http://marilynvossavant.com/game-show-problem/*.

Practice Project: The Birthday Paradox

How many people need to be in a room for there to be a 50/50 chance that two of them share the same birth month and day? According to the *birthday paradox*, not that many! As with the Monty Hall problem, the outcome is counterintuitive.

Use MCS to determine how many people it takes to reach the 50 percent mark. Have the program print out the number of people and the probability for a range of room occupants. If you find yourself looking up how to format dates, stop and simplify! You can find a solution, *birthday_paradox_practice.py*, in the appendix or online at *https://www.nostarch.com/impracticalpython/*.

12

SECURING YOUR NEST EGG

Baby boomers are Americans born between 1946 and 1964. They form a large demographic cohort—about 20 percent of the American population—so they've had a huge influence on all aspects of American culture. The financial industry was quick to cater to their needs, which for decades concerned investment growth. But in 2011, the oldest boomers reached age 65 and began retiring in droves, at the rate of 10,000 *per day*! With an average life span longer than that of preceding generations, a boomer may enjoy a retirement as long as their career. Funding this 30- to 40-year period is a big problem and a big business.

In the years when financial advisers were mainly focused on *growing* boomers' wealth, they relied on the simple "4 Percent Rule" for retirement planning. Simply stated, for every year you're retired, if you spend an amount no larger than 4 percent of the savings you had *in the first year of retirement*, you'll never run out of money. But as Mark Twain observed,

"All generalizations are false, including this one!" The value of our investments and the amount we spend are constantly in flux, often due to forces outside of our control.

As a more sophisticated alternative to the 4 Percent Rule, the financial industry adopted Monte Carlo simulation (see Chapter 11 for an overview of MCS). With MCS, you can test and compare retirement strategies over thousands of lifetimes. The goal is to identify how much money you can spend each year in retirement, given your life expectancy, without exhausting your savings.

The advantage of MCS over other methods increases as the sources of uncertainty increase. In Chapter 11, you applied MCS to a single variable with a simple probability distribution. Here you'll look at uncertainty around life spans, while capturing the true cyclicity and interdependency of the stock and bond markets and inflation. This will allow you to evaluate and compare different strategies for achieving a secure and happy retirement.

Project #20: Simulating Retirement Lifetimes

If you think you're too young to worry about retirement, think again. The baby boomers thought the same thing, and now over half of them have insufficient savings for retirement. For most people, the difference between eating Kobe beef or dog food in retirement is how soon they start saving. Due to the magic of compounding interest, even modest savings can add up over decades. Knowing early the numbers you'll need later enables you to set realistic goals for a painless transition to your golden years.

THE OBJECTIVE

Build a Monte Carlo simulation for estimating the probability of running out of money in retirement. Treat years in retirement as a key uncertainty and use historical stock, bond, and inflation data to capture the observed cyclicity and dependency of these variables.

The Strategy

To plan your project, don't hesitate to check out the competition. Numerous nest-egg calculators are available online for free. If you play with these, you'll see that they display a high level of input-parameter variability.

Calculators with many parameters may seem better (see Figure 12-1), but with each added detail, you start going down rabbit holes, especially when it comes to the US's complex tax code. When you're predicting outcomes 30 to 40 years into the future, details can become noise. So, you're better off keeping it simple, focusing on the most important and controllable issues. You can control when you retire, your investment asset allocation, how much you save, and how much you spend, but you can't control the stock market, interest rates, and inflation.

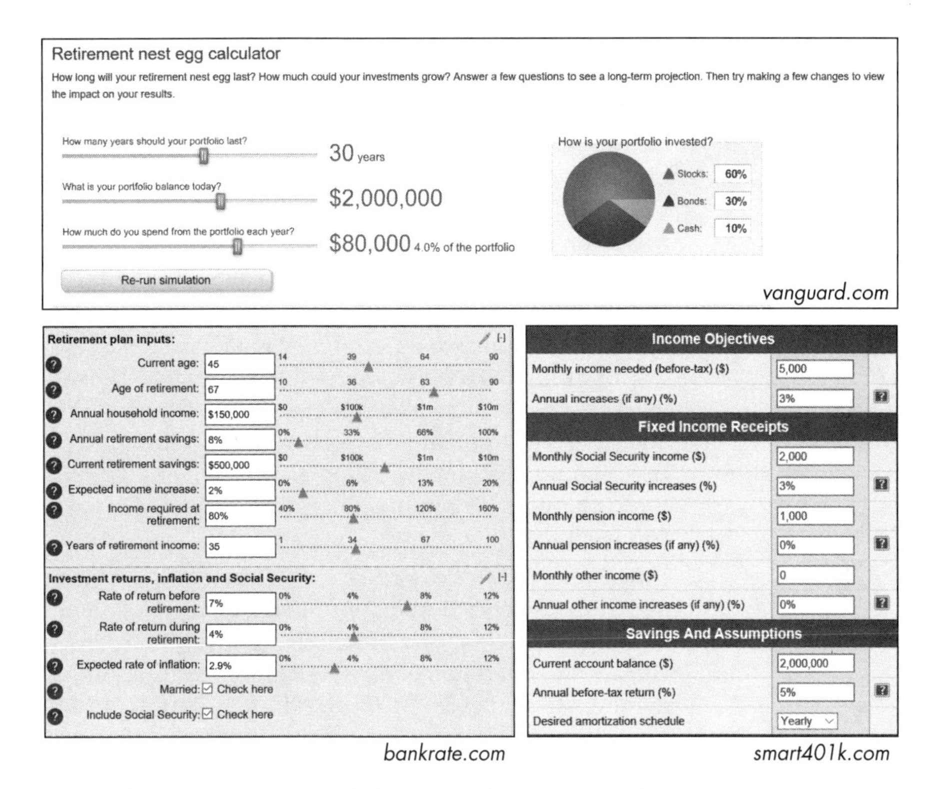

Figure 12-1: Example input panels for three online nest-egg calculators

When you can't know the "correct" answer to a problem, looking at a range of scenarios and making decisions based on probabilities is best. For decisions that involve a "fatal error," like running out of money, desirable solutions are those that lower the likelihood of that event.

Before you get started, you need to speak the language, so I put together a list of the financial terms you'll use in this project:

Bonds A bond is debt investment in which you loan money to an entity—usually a government or corporation—for a set length of time. The borrower pays you an agreed-upon rate of interest (the bond's *yield*) and, at the end of the term, returns the full value of the loan, assuming the issuing entity doesn't go broke and default. The value of bonds can go up and down over time, so you may lose money if you sell a bond early. Bonds are appealing to retirees, as they offer safe, steady, predictable returns. Treasury bonds, issued by the US government, are considered the safest of all. Unfortunately, most bond returns tend to be low, so they are vulnerable to inflation.

Effective tax rate This is the average rate at which an individual or married couple is taxed. It includes local, state, and federal taxes. Taxes can be complicated, with large variances in state and local tax rates, many opportunities for deductions and adjustments, and variable rates for different types of income (such as short- versus long-term capital gains). The tax code is also *progressive*, which means you pay proportionally more as your income increases. According to The Motley Fool, a financial services company, the average American's overall income-based tax rate was 29.8 percent in 2015. And this excludes sales and property taxes! You can also count on Congress to tinker with these rates at least once in a 30-year retirement. Due to these complexities, for this project you should adjust your *withdrawal* (spending) parameter to account for taxes.

Index It is safest to invest in many assets, rather than putting all your (nest) eggs in one basket. An index is a hypothetical portfolio of securities, or group of baskets, designed to represent a broad part of a financial market. The Standard & Poor (S&P) 500, for example, represents the 500 largest US companies, which are mostly dividend-paying companies. Index-based investments—such as an index mutual fund—allow an investor to conveniently buy one thing that contains the stocks of hundreds of companies.

Inflation This is the increase in prices over time due to increasing demand, currency devaluation, rising energy costs, and so on. Inflation is an insidious destroyer of wealth. The inflation rate is variable, but has averaged about 3 percent annually since 1926. At that rate, the value of money is halved every 24 years. A little inflation (1 to 3 percent) generally indicates that the economy is growing and wages are going up. Higher inflation and negative inflation are both undesirable.

Number of cases These are the trials or runs performed during MCS; each case represents a single retirement lifetime and is simulated with a new set of randomly selected values. For the simulations you will be running, somewhere between 50,000 and 100,000 cases should provide a suitably repeatable answer.

Probability of ruin This is the probability of running out of money before the end of retirement. You can calculate it as the number of cases that end with no money divided by the total number of cases.

Start value The starting value is the total value of liquid investments, including checking accounts, brokerage accounts, tax-deferred Individual Retirement Accounts (IRAs), and so on, that are held at the start of retirement. It doesn't equate to *net worth*, which includes assets like houses, cars, and Fabergé eggs.

Stocks A stock is a security that signifies ownership in a corporation and represents a claim on part of the corporation's assets and earnings. Many stocks pay *dividends*, a regular payment similar to the interest paid by a bond or a bank account. For the average person, stocks are the quickest way to grow wealth, but they're not without risk. The price of a stock can go up and down rapidly over a short time—both because of the company's performance and because of speculation arising from investor greed or fear. Retirees tend to invest in the largest dividend-paying US companies because they offer regular income and a less volatile stock price than do smaller companies.

Total returns The sum of capital gains (changes in asset value, like stock price), interest, and dividends is considered the total return of an investment. It is usually quoted on an annual basis.

Withdrawal Also referred to as costs or spending, withdrawal is the pretax, gross income you'll need to cover all expenses in a given year. For the 4 Percent Rule, this would represent 4 percent of the start value in the first year of retirement. This number should be adjusted for inflation in each subsequent year.

Historical Returns Matter

Nest-egg simulators that use constant values for investment returns and inflation (see Figure 12-1) grossly distort reality. Predictive ability is only as good as the underlying assumptions, and returns can be highly volatile, interdependent, and cyclical. This volatility impacts retirees the most when the start of retirement—or a large unexpected expense—coincides with the beginning of a big market downturn.

The chart in Figure 12-2 displays the annual returns for both the S&P 500 index of the largest US companies and the 10-year Treasury bond, which is a reasonably safe, medium-risk, fixed-income investment. It also includes annual inflation rates and significant financial events like the Great Depression.

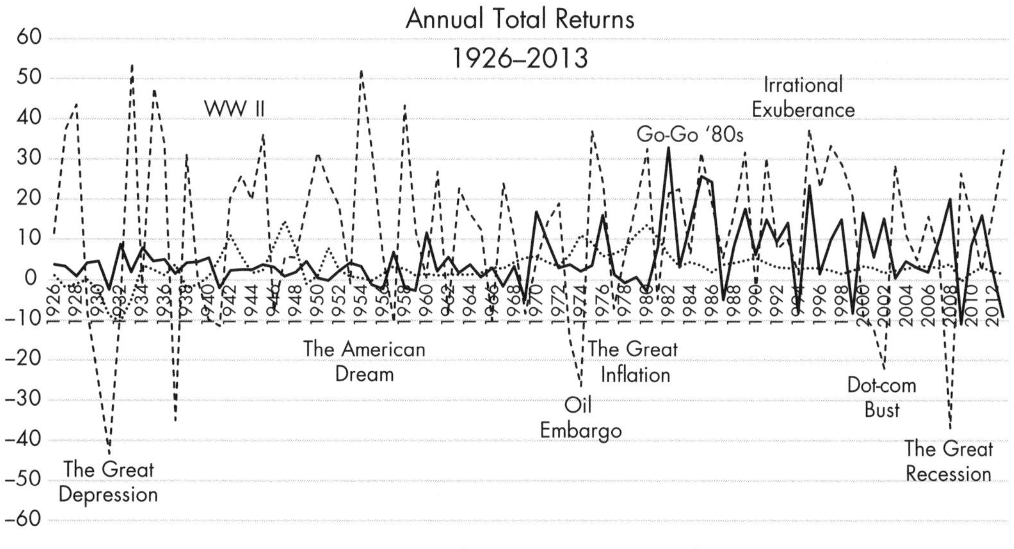

Figure 12-2: Annual rate of inflation plus total returns for stock and bond markets, 1926 to 2013

Financial scholars' long study of the trends in Figure 12-2 have led to some useful observations about US markets:

- Upward-moving (bull) markets tend to last five times as long as downward-moving (bear) markets.

- Harmful high inflation rates can persist for as long as a decade.
- Bonds tend to deliver low returns that struggle to keep up with inflation.
- Stock returns outpace inflation easily, but at the cost of great volatility in prices.
- Stock and bond returns are often inversely correlated; this means that bond returns decrease as stock returns increase, and vice versa.
- Neither the stocks of large companies nor Treasury bonds can guarantee you a smooth ride.

Based on this information, financial advisers recommend that most retirees hold a diversified portfolio that includes multiple investment types. This strategy uses one investment type as a "hedge" against another, dampening the highs but raising the lows, theoretically reducing volatility.

In Figure 12-3, annual investment returns are plotted using both the S&P 500 and a hypothetical 40/50/10 percent blend of, respectively, the S&P 500, the 10-year Treasury bond, and cash. The three-month Treasury bill, which is a very short-term bond with a stable price and low yield (like money stuffed in your mattress), represents cash.

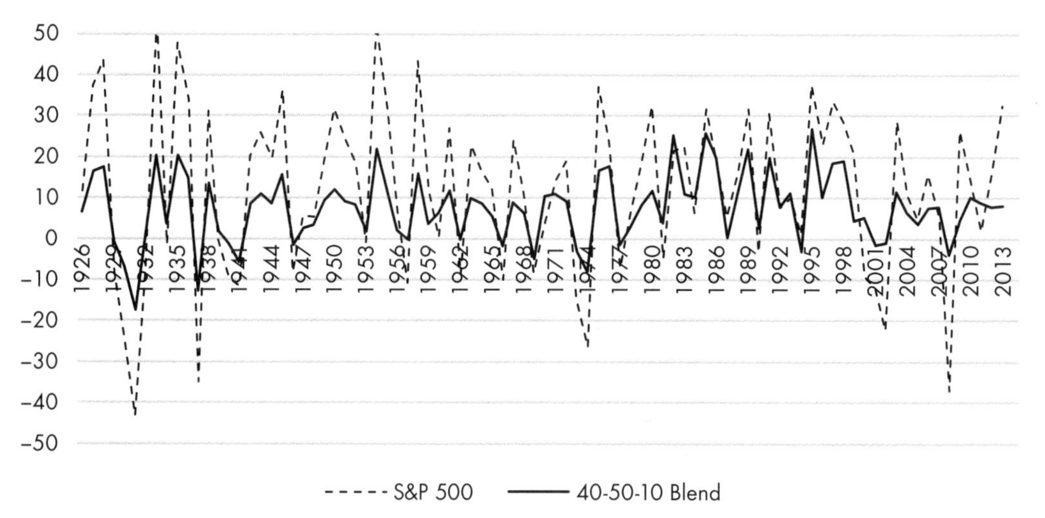

Figure 12-3: Annual returns of the S&P 500 versus a blend of the S&P 500, 10-year Treasury bond, and cash, 1926 to 2013

This diversified portfolio provides a smoother ride than the stock market alone, while still providing protection from inflation. But it will clearly produce different results than online calculators that assume returns are *always* constant and positive in value.

By using historical data, you capture the true *measured* duration of good times and bad, along with the highest highs and the lowest lows. You also account for something completely ignored by the 4 Percent Rule: *the black swan.*

Black swans are consequential, improbable events. These can be good, like meeting your spouse, or bad, like Black Monday, the stock market crash of October 1987. An advantage of MCS is that it can factor in these unexpected events; a disadvantage is that you have to program them, and if they are truly unforeseeable, how can you know what to include?

Black swans that have already occurred, like the Great Depression, are captured in the annual values in lists of historical returns. So, a common approach is to use historical results and assume that nothing worse—or better—will occur in the future. When a simulation uses data from the Great Depression, the modeled portfolio will experience the same stock, bond, and inflation behavior as real portfolios at the time.

If using past data seems too restrictive, you can always edit the past results to reflect lower lows and higher highs. But most people are practical and are happier dealing with events they *know* have occurred—as opposed to zombie apocalypses or alien invasions—so true historical results offer a *credible* way to inject reality into financial planning.

Some economists argue that inflation and returns data before 1980 are of limited use, because the Federal Reserve now takes a more active role in monetary policy and the control of inflation. On the other hand, that is *exactly* the kind of thinking that leaves us exposed to black swans!

The Greatest Uncertainty

The greatest uncertainty in retirement planning is the date you—or your surviving spouse—die, euphemistically referred to as "end of plan" by financial advisers. This uncertainty affects every retirement-related decision, such as when you retire, how much you spend in retirement, when you start taking Social Security, how much you leave your heirs, and so on.

Insurance companies and the government deal with this uncertainty with *actuarial life tables.* Based on the mortality experience of a population, actuarial life tables predict the life expectancy at a given age, expressed as the average remaining number of years expected prior to death. You can find the Social Security table at *https://www.ssa.gov/oact/STATS/table4c6.html.* Based on this table, a 60-year-old woman in 2014 would have a life expectancy of 24.48 years; this means end of plan would occur during her 84th year.

Actuarial tables work fine for large populations, but for individuals, they're just a starting point. You should examine a range of values, tailored to family history and personal health issues, when preparing your own retirement plan.

To handle this uncertainty in your simulation, consider years in retirement a *random variable,* whose values are chosen at random from a frequency distribution. For example, you can enter the most likely, minimum, and maximum number of years you expect to be retired and use these values to build a triangular distribution. The most-likely value can come from an actuarial table, but the endpoints should be based on your personal health outlook and family history.

An example outcome, based on a triangular distribution for years in retirement for a 60-year-old man, is shown in Figure 12-4. The minimum retirement period was set to 20 years, the most likely to 22 years, and the maximum to 40 years. The number of draws from the distribution was 1,000.

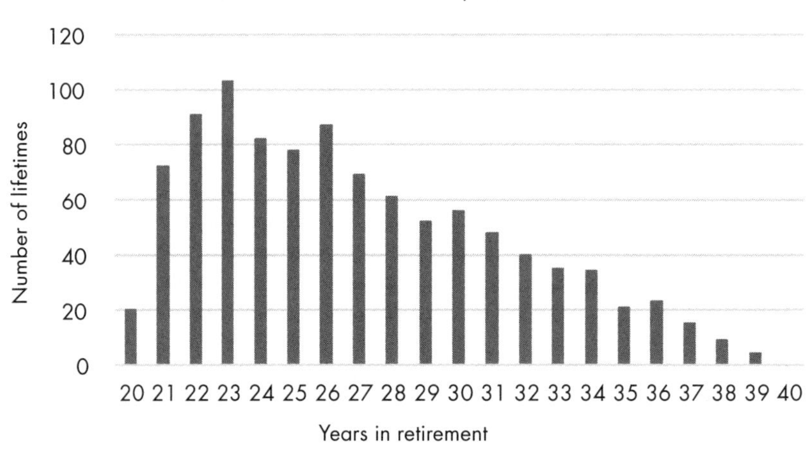

Figure 12-4: Number of lifetimes versus years in retirement based on 1,000 draws from a triangular distribution

As you can see, every possible time interval between the minimum and maximum values is available for simulation, but the intervals taper off in frequency from the most likely value to the maximum value, indicating that living to 100 is possible but unlikely. Note also that the plot is significantly skewed to the high side. This will ensure conservative results, since—from a financial perspective—dying early is an optimistic outcome and living longer than expected represents the greatest financial risk.

A Qualitative Way to Present Results

An issue with MCS is making sense of thousands of runs and presenting the results in an easily digestible manner. Most online calculators present outcomes using a chart like the one in Figure 12-5. In this example, for a 10,000-run simulation, the calculator plots a few selected outcomes with age on the x-axis and investment value on the y-axis. The curves converge on the left at the starting value of the investments at retirement, and they end on the right with their value at end of plan. The overall probability of the money's lasting through retirement may also be presented. Financial advisers consider probabilities below 80 to 90 percent risky.

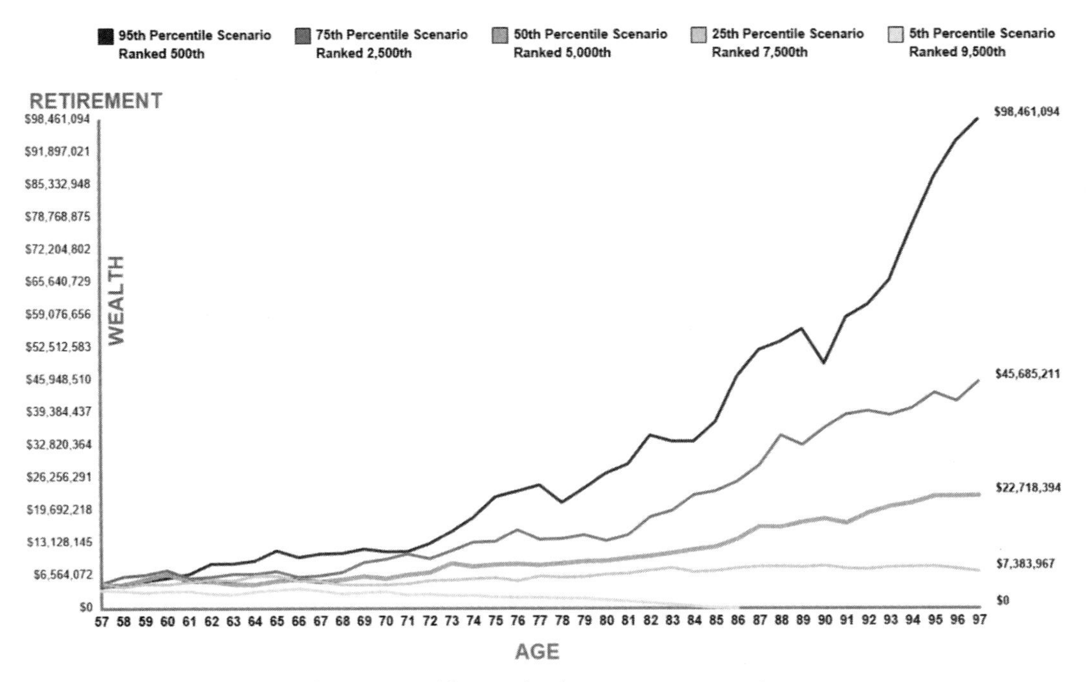

Figure 12-5: Example display from a typical financial industry retirement simulator

The most important piece of information from this type of analysis is the probability of running out of money. It is also interesting to see the endpoint and average outcomes and a summary of the input parameters. In your Python simulator, you can print these in the interpreter window, as shown here:

```
Investment type: bonds
Starting value: $1,000,000
Annual withdrawal: $40,000
Years in retirement (min-ml-max): 17-25-40
Number of runs: 20,000

Odds of running out of money: 36.1%

Average outcome: $883,843
Minimum outcome: $0
Maximum outcome: $7,607,789
```

For a graphical presentation, rather than duplicate what others have done, let's find a new way to present the outcomes. A subset of the results of each case—that is, the money remaining at the end of retirement—can be presented as a vertical line in a bar chart, as in Figure 12-6.

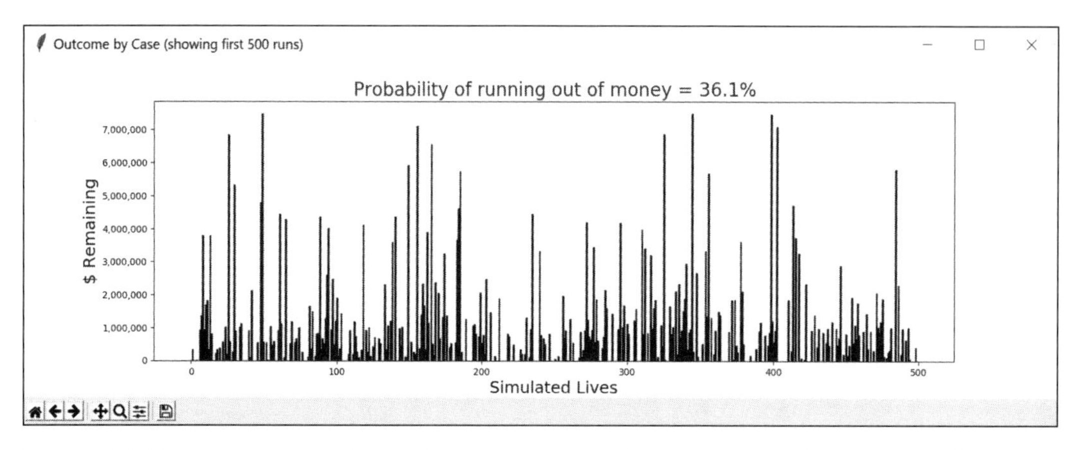

Figure 12-6: The outcomes of simulated retirement periods displayed as vertical columns in a bar chart

In this chart, each bar represents the retirement portion of a single simulated lifetime, and the height of each bar represents the money remaining at the end of that life. Because each bar represents an individual category rather than intervals for continuous measurement, you can arrange the bars in any order without affecting the data. Gaps, representing cases that ran out of money, can be included in the order they occurred in the simulation. With the quantitative statistics recorded in the interpreter window, this diagram provides a qualitative way to present the results.

The peaks and valleys of this chart represent the changing fortunes of many possible futures. In one lifetime, you can die destitute; in the next, you're a multimillionaire. It's evocative of the old saying "There but for the grace of God go I." But, on the other hand, it reinforces General Eisenhower's observation that "plans are useless, but planning is indispensable." Through financial planning, you can "raise the valleys" in the chart and eliminate or greatly reduce your odds of going broke in retirement.

To make this chart, you'll use `matplotlib`, a library that supports 2D plotting and rudimentary 3D plotting. To learn more about `matplotlib` and how to install it, see "The Probability-of-Detection Code" on page 194.

The Pseudocode

Based on the preceding discussion, the program design strategy should be to focus on a few important retirement parameters and simulate outcomes using the historical behavior of the financial markets. Here's the high-level pseudocode:

```
Get user input for investment type (all stocks, all bonds, or a blend)
Map investment type choice to a list of historical returns
Get user input for the starting value of investments
Get user input for the initial yearly withdrawal amount
Get user input for the minimum, most likely, and maximum duration of retirement
Get user input on number of cases to run
Start list to hold outcomes
```

```
Loop through cases:
    For each case:
        Extract random contiguous sample of returns list for duration period
        Extract same interval from inflation list
        For each year in sample:
            If year not equal to year 1:
                Adjust withdrawal for inflation
            Subtract withdrawal from investments
            Adjust investments for returns
            If investments <= 0:
                Investments = 0
                Break
    Append investments value to outcomes list
Display input parameters
Calculate and display the probability of ruin
Calculate and display statistics
Display a subset of outcomes as a bar chart
```

Finding Historical Data

You can find returns and inflation information on numerous websites (see "Further Reading" on page 263 for some examples), but I have already compiled the information you need as a series of downloadable text files. If you choose to compile your own lists, be aware that estimates of both inflation and returns may vary slightly from site to site.

For returns, I used three investment vehicles: the S&P 500 stock index, the 10-year Treasury bond, and the three-month Treasury bill, all for the period 1926 to 2013 (1926–1927 values for the Treasury bill are estimates). I used this data to generate additional blended returns for the same period. The following list describes the filenames and contents:

SP500_returns_1926-2013_pct.txt Total returns for the S&P 500 (1926–2013)

10-yr_TBond_returns_1926-2013_pct.txt Total returns for the 10-year Treasury bond (1926–2013)

3_mo_TBill_rate_1926-2013_pct.txt Rate of three-month Treasury bill (1926–2013)

S-B_blend_1926-2013_pct.txt 50/50 percent mix of S&P 500 and 10-year Treasury bond (1926–2013)

S-B-C_blend_1926-2013_pct.txt 40/50/10 percent mix of S&P 500, 10-year Treasury bond, three-month Treasury bill (1926–2013)

annual_infl_rate_1926-2013_pct.txt Average annual US inflation rate (1926–2013)

Here's an example of the first seven lines of the S&P 500 text file:

```
11.6
37.5
43.8
-8.3
```

```
-25.1
-43.8
-8.6
```

The values are percentages, but you'll change them to decimal values when you load them in the code. Note that years aren't included, as the values are in chronological order. If all the files cover the same time interval, the actual years are irrelevant, though you should include them in the filename for good bookkeeping.

The Code

Name your retirement nest-egg simulator *nest_egg_mcs.py*. You'll need the text files described in "Finding Historical Data" on page 249. Download these files from *https://www.nostarch.com/impracticalpython/* and keep them in the same folder as *nest_egg_mcs.py*.

Importing Modules and Defining Functions to Load Data and Get User Input

Listing 12-1 imports modules and defines a function to read the historical returns and inflation data, as well as another function to get the user's input. Feel free to alter or add to the historical data to conduct experiments after the program is up and running.

nest_egg_mcs.py, part 1

```
   import sys
   import random
❶ import matplotlib.pyplot as plt

❷ def read_to_list(file_name):
       """Open a file of data in percent, convert to decimal & return a list."""
     ❸ with open(file_name) as in_file:
         ❹ lines = [float(line.strip()) for line in in_file]
         ❺ decimal = [round(line / 100, 5) for line in lines]
         ❻ return decimal

❼ def default_input(prompt, default=None):
       """Allow use of default values in input."""
❽ prompt = '{} [{}]: '.format(prompt, default)
❾ response = input(prompt)
❿ if not response and default:
           return default
       else:
           return response
```

Listing 12-1: Imports modules and defines functions to load data and get user input

The import statements should all be familiar. The matplotlib library is needed to build the bar chart of results. You only need the plotting functionality, as specified in the import statement ❶.

Next, define a function called read_to_list() to load a data file and process its contents ❷. You'll pass it the name of the file as an argument.

Open the file using `with`, which will automatically close it ❸, and then use list comprehension to build a list of the contents ❹. Immediately convert the list items, which are in percents, to decimal values rounded to five decimal places ❺. Historical returns are usually presented to two decimal places at most, so rounding to five should be sufficient. You may notice more accuracy in the values of some of the data files used here, but that's just the result of some preprocessing in Excel. End by returning the `decimal` list ❻.

Now, define a function called `default_input()` to get the user's input ❼. The function takes a prompt and a default value as arguments. The prompt and default will be specified when the function is called, and the program will display the default in brackets ❽. Assign a `response` variable to the user's input ❾. If the user enters nothing and a default value exists, the default value is returned; otherwise, the user's response is returned ❿.

Getting the User Input

Listing 12-2 loads the data files, maps the resulting lists to simple names using a dictionary, and gets the user's input. The dictionary will be used to present the user with multiple choices for an investment type. Overall, user input consists of:

- The type of investment to use (stocks, bonds, or a blend of both)
- The starting value of their retirement savings
- A yearly withdrawal, or spending, amount
- The minimum, most likely, and maximum number of years they expect to live in retirement
- The number of cases to run

nest_egg_mcs.py, part 2

```
# load data files with original data in percent form
❶ print("\nNote: Input data should be in percent, not decimal!\n")
try:
    bonds = read_to_list('10-yr_TBond_returns_1926-2013_pct.txt')
    stocks = read_to_list('SP500_returns_1926-2013_pct.txt')
    blend_40_50_10 = read_to_list('S-B-C_blend_1926-2013_pct.txt')
    blend_50_50 = read_to_list('S-B_blend_1926-2013_pct.txt')
    infl_rate = read_to_list('annual_infl_rate_1926-2013_pct.txt')
except IOError as e:
    print("{}. \nTerminating program.".format(e), file=sys.stderr)
    sys.exit(1)

# get user input; use dictionary for investment-type arguments
❷ investment_type_args = {'bonds': bonds, 'stocks': stocks,
                        'sb_blend': blend_50_50, 'sbc_blend': blend_40_50_10}

❸ # print input legend for user
print("   stocks = SP500")
print("    bonds = 10-yr Treasury Bond")
print(" sb_blend = 50% SP500/50% TBond")
print("sbc_blend = 40% SP500/50% TBond/10% Cash\n")
```

```
print("Press ENTER to take default value shown in [brackets]. \n")

# get user input
❹ invest_type = default_input("Enter investment type: (stocks, bonds, sb_blend,"\
                               " sbc_blend): \n", 'bonds').lower()
❺ while invest_type not in investment_type_args:
      invest_type = input("Invalid investment. Enter investment type " \
                          "as listed in prompt: ")

  start_value = default_input("Input starting value of investments: \n", \
                              '2000000')
❻ while not start_value.isdigit():
      start_value = input("Invalid input! Input integer only: ")

❼ withdrawal = default_input("Input annual pre-tax withdrawal" \
                             " (today's $): \n", '80000')
  while not withdrawal.isdigit():
      withdrawal = input("Invalid input! Input integer only: ")

  min_years = default_input("Input minimum years in retirement: \n", '18')
  while not min_years.isdigit():
      min_years = input("Invalid input! Input integer only: ")

  most_likely_years = default_input("Input most-likely years in retirement: \n",
                                    '25')
  while not most_likely_years.isdigit():
      most_likely_years = input("Invalid input! Input integer only: ")

  max_years = default_input("Input maximum years in retirement: \n", '40')
  while not max_years.isdigit():
      max_years = input("Invalid input! Input integer only: ")

  num_cases = default_input("Input number of cases to run: \n", '50000')
  while not num_cases.isdigit():
      num_cases = input("Invalid input! Input integer only: ")
```

Listing 12-2: Loads data, maps choices to lists, and gets user input

After printing a warning that input data should be in percent form, use the `read_to_list()` function to load the six data files ❶. Use `try` when opening the files to catch exceptions related to missing files or incorrect filenames. Then handle the exceptions with an `except` block. If you need a refresher on `try` and `except`, refer to "Handling Exceptions When Opening Files" on page 21.

The user will have a choice of investment vehicles to test. To allow them to type in simple names, use a dictionary to map the names to the lists of data you just loaded ❷. Later, you'll pass a function this dictionary and its key to serve as an argument: `montecarlo(investment_type_args[invest_type])`. Before asking for input, print a legend to aid the user ❸.

Next, get the user's investment choice ❹. Use the `default_input()` function and list the names of the choices, which are mapped back to the data lists. Set the default to `'sbc_blend'`, since this is theoretically the most stable mix of the four choices. Be sure to tack on the .lower() method in case the user accidently includes an uppercase letter or two. For other possible input errors, use a while loop to check the input versus the names in the investment_type_args dictionary; if you don't find the input, prompt the user for a correct answer ❺.

Continue gathering the input and use the default values to guide the user to reasonable inputs. For example, $80,000 is 4 percent of the starting value of $2,000,000; also, 25 years is a good most-likely value for women entering retirement at 60, a maximum value of 40 will allow them to reach 100, and 50,000 cases should quickly yield a good estimate of the probability of ruin.

For numerical inputs, use a while loop to check that the input is a digit, just in case the user includes a dollar sign ($) or commas in the number ❻. And for the withdrawal amount, use the prompt to guide the user by letting them know to input *today's* dollars and not to worry about inflation ❼.

Checking for Other Erroneous Input

Listing 12-3 checks for additional input errors. The order of the minimum, most likely, and maximum years in retirement should be logical, and a maximum length of 99 years is enforced. Allowing for a long time in retirement permits the optimistic user to evaluate cases where medical science makes significant advances in anti-aging treatments!

nest_egg_mcs.py, part 3

```
   # check for other erroneous input
❶ if not int(min_years) < int(most_likely_years) < int(max_years) \
      or int(max_years) > 99:
    ❷ print("\nProblem with input years.", file=sys.stderr)
      print("Requires Min < ML < Max with Max <= 99.", file=sys.stderr)
      sys.exit(1)
```

Listing 12-3: Checks for errors and sets limits in the retirement years input

Use a conditional to ensure that the minimum years input is less than the most likely, the most likely is less than the maximum, and the maximum does not exceed 99 ❶. If a problem is encountered, alert the user ❷, provide some clarifying instructions, and exit the program.

Defining the Monte Carlo Engine

Listing 12-4 defines the first part of the function that will run the Monte Carlo simulation. The program uses a loop to run through each case, and the number of years in retirement inputs will be used to sample the historical data. For both the returns and inflation lists, the program chooses a starting year, or index, at random. The number of years in retirement, assigned to a duration variable, is drawn from a triangular distribution built from the user's input. If 30 is chosen, then 30 is added to this starting index to create the ending index. The random starting year will determine the retiree's financial fortunes for the rest of their life! Timing is everything, as they say.

nest_egg_mcs.py, part 4

```
❶ def montecarlo(returns):
      """Run MCS and return investment value at end-of-plan and bankrupt count."""
    ❷ case_count = 0
      bankrupt_count = 0
      outcome = []

    ❸ while case_count < int(num_cases):
          investments = int(start_value)
        ❹ start_year = random.randrange(0, len(returns))
        ❺ duration = int(random.triangular(int(min_years), int(max_years),
                                            int(most_likely_years)))
        ❻ end_year = start_year + duration
        ❼ lifespan = [i for i in range(start_year, end_year)]
          bankrupt = 'no'

          # build temporary lists for each case
        ❽ lifespan_returns = []
          lifespan_infl = []
          for i in lifespan:
            ❾ lifespan_returns.append(returns[i % len(returns)])
              lifespan_infl.append(infl_rate[i % len(infl_rate)])
```

Listing 12-4: Defines the Monte Carlo function and starts a loop through cases

The `montecarlo()` function takes a `returns` list as an argument ❶. The first step is to start a counter to keep track of which case is being run ❷. Remember that you don't need to use actual dates; the first year in the lists is index 0, rather than 1926. In addition, start a counter for the number of cases that run out of money early. Then start an empty list to hold the outcomes of each run, which will be the amount of money remaining at the end of the run.

Begin the `while` loop that will run through the cases ❸. Assign a new variable, called `investments`, to the starting investment value that the user specified. Since the `investments` variable will change constantly, you need to preserve the original input variable to reinitialize each case. And since all the user input came in as strings, you need to convert the values to integers before using them.

Next, assign a `start_year` variable and pick a value at random from the range of available years ❹. To get the time spent in retirement for this simulated life, use the `random` module's `triangular()` method to draw from a triangular distribution defined by the user's `min_years`, `most_likely_years`, and `max_years` inputs ❺. According to the documentation, `triangular()` returns a random floating-point number *N* such that low <= *N* <= high and with the specified *mode* between those bounds.

Add this `duration` variable to the `start_year` variable and assign the result to an `end_year` variable ❻. Now, make a new list, named `lifespan`, that captures all the indexes between the starting year and the ending year ❼. These indexes will be used to match the retirement period to the historical data. Next, assign a `bankrupt` variable to `'no'`. Bankrupt means you've run out of money, and later this outcome will end the `while` loop early, using a `break` statement.

Use two lists to store the applicable returns and inflation data for the chosen `lifespan` ❽. Populate these lists using a `for` loop that uses each item in `lifespan` as the index for the returns and inflation lists. If the `lifespan` index is out of range compared to the other lists, use the modulo (`%`) operator to wrap the indexes ❾.

Let's cover a little more background on this listing. The randomly selected `start_year` variable and the calculated `end_year` variable determine how the returns and inflation lists are sampled. The sample is a continuous piece of financial history and constitutes a case. Selecting an *interval* at random distinguishes this program from online calculators that select individual *years* at random and may use a *different year* for each asset class and inflation! Market results aren't pure chaos; bull and bear markets are cyclic, as are inflationary trends. The same events that cause stocks to decline also impact the price of bonds and the rate of inflation. Picking years at random ignores this interdependency and disrupts known behaviors, leading to unrealistic results.

In Figure 12-7, the retiree (known as Case 1) has chosen to retire in 1965—at the start of the Great Inflation—and to invest in bonds. Because the end year occurs before the end of the returns list, the retirement span fits nicely in the list. Both returns and inflation are sampled over the same interval.

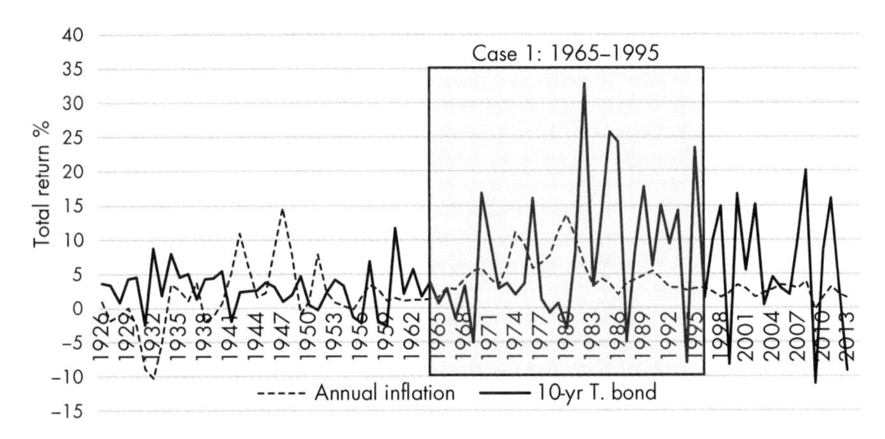

Figure 12-7: Graph of bond and inflation lists, with a retirement starting in 1965 annotated

In Figure 12-8, the retiree, or Case 2, has chosen to retire in 2000. Because the list ends in 2013, the 30-year sample taken by the MCS function must "wrap around" and cover years 1926 through 1941. This forces the retiree to endure two recessions and a depression.

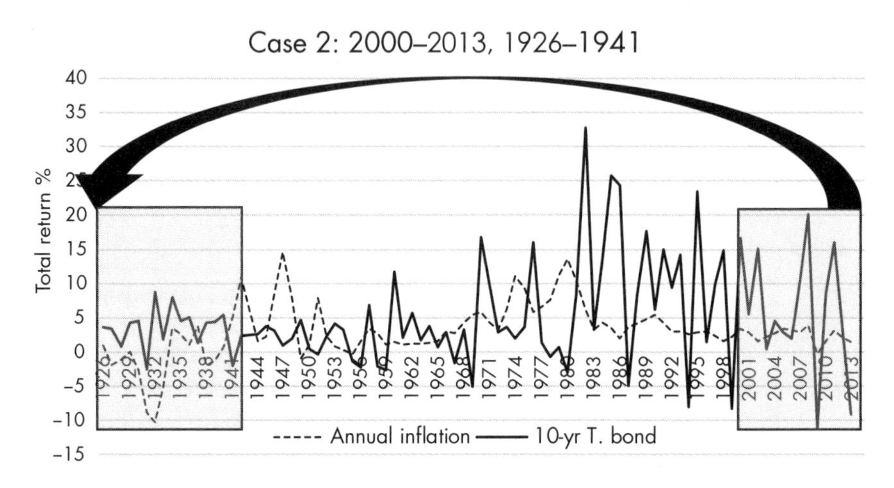

Figure 12-8: Graph of bonds and inflation lists, with segments used in Case 2 annotated

The program will need to simulate the wrap-around segment you see in Case 2—hence the use of the modulo operator, which allows you to treat the lists as endless loops.

Simulating Each Year in a Case

Listing 12-5 continues the `montecarlo()` function and loops through each year of retirement for a given case, increasing or decreasing the investment value based on the returns for that year, subtracting the inflation-adjusted withdrawal amount from the investments, and checking whether the investments are exhausted. The program saves the final investment value—representing the savings remaining at death—to a list so that the overall probability of ruin can be calculated at the end.

nest_egg_mcs.py, part 5

```
        # loop through each year of retirement for each case run
     ❶ for index, i in enumerate(lifespan_returns):
         ❷ infl = lifespan_infl[index]

         ❸ # don't adjust for inflation the first year
            if index == 0:
                withdraw_infl_adj = int(withdrawal)
            else:
                withdraw_infl_adj = int(withdraw_infl_adj * (1 + infl))

         ❹ investments -= withdraw_infl_adj
            investments = int(investments * (1 + i))

         ❺ if investments <= 0:
                bankrupt = 'yes'
                break

     ❻ if bankrupt == 'yes':
            outcome.append(0)
            bankrupt_count += 1
        else:
```

```
            outcome.append(investments)

     ❼ case_count += 1

 ❽ return outcome, bankrupt_count
```

Listing 12-5: Simulates results for each year in retirement (per case)

Start the for loop that will run through all the years in a case ❶. Use enumerate() on the returns list and use the index that enumerate() produced to get the year's average inflation value from the inflation list ❷. Use a conditional to start applying inflation after the first year ❸. This will slowly increase or decrease the withdrawal amount over time, depending on whether you're in inflationary or deflationary times.

Subtract the inflation-adjusted withdrawal value from the investments variable, then adjust investments for the year's returns ❹. Check that the value of investments is greater than 0. If it's not, set the bankrupt variable to 'yes' and end the loop ❺. For a bankrupt case, append 0 to the outcome list ❻. Otherwise, the loop continues until the duration of retirement is reached, so you append the remaining value of investments to outcome.

A human life has just ended: 30 to 40 years' worth of vacations, grandkids, bingo games, and illnesses gone in much less than a second. So, advance the case counter before looping through the next lifetime ❼. End the function by returning the outcome and bankrupt_count variables ❽.

Calculating the Probability of Ruin

Listing 12-6 defines a function that calculates the probability of running out of money, also known as the "probability of ruin." If you're risk averse or want to leave a sizeable sum to your heirs, you probably want this number to be less than 10 percent. Those with a greater appetite for risk may be content with up to 20 percent or more. After all, you can't take it with you!

nest_egg_mcs.py, part 6

```
❶ def bankrupt_prob(outcome, bankrupt_count):
       """Calculate and return chance of running out of money & other stats."""
     ❷ total = len(outcome)
     ❸ odds = round(100 * bankrupt_count / total, 1)

     ❹ print("\nInvestment type: {}".format(invest_type))
       print("Starting value: ${:,}".format(int(start_value)))
       print("Annual withdrawal: ${:,}".format(int(withdrawal)))
       print("Years in retirement (min-ml-max): {}-{}-{}"
             .format(min_years, most_likely_years, max_years))
       print("Number of runs: {:,}\n".format(len(outcome)))
       print("Odds of running out of money: {}%\n".format(odds))
       print("Average outcome: ${:,}".format(int(sum(outcome) / total)))
       print("Minimum outcome: ${:,}".format(min(i for i in outcome)))
       print("Maximum outcome: ${:,}".format(max(i for i in outcome)))

     ❺ return odds
```

Listing 12-6: Calculates and displays the "probability of ruin" and other statistics

Define a function called bankrupt_prob() that takes the outcome list and bankrupt_count variable returned from the montecarlo() function as arguments ❶. Assign the length of the outcome list to a variable named total ❷. Then, calculate the probability of running out of money as a percentage rounded to one decimal place by dividing the number of bankrupt cases by the total number of cases ❸.

Now, display the input parameters and results of the simulation ❹. You saw an example of this text printout in "A Qualitative Way to Present Results" on page 246. Finish by returning the odds variable ❺.

Defining and Calling the main() Function

Listing 12-7 defines the main() function that calls the montecarlo() and bankrupt_count() functions and creates the bar chart display. The outcomes for the various cases can have a large variance—sometimes you go broke, and other times you're a multimillionaire! If the printed statistics don't make this clear, the bar chart certainly will.

nest_egg_mcs.py, part 7

```
❶ def main():
      """Call MCS & bankrupt functions and draw bar chart of results."""
   ❷ outcome, bankrupt_count = montecarlo(investment_type_args[invest_type])
      odds = bankrupt_prob(outcome, bankrupt_count)

   ❸ plotdata = outcome[:3000]  # only plot first 3000 runs

   ❹ plt.figure('Outcome by Case (showing first {} runs)'.format(len(plotdata)),
                 figsize=(16, 5))  # size is width, height in inches
   ❺ index = [i + 1 for i in range(len(plotdata))]
   ❻ plt.bar(index, plotdata, color='black')
      plt.xlabel('Simulated Lives', fontsize=18)
      plt.ylabel('$ Remaining', fontsize=18)
   ❼ plt.ticklabel_format(style='plain', axis='y')
   ❽ ax = plt.gca()
      ax.get_yaxis().set_major_formatter(plt.FuncFormatter(lambda x, loc: "{:,}"
                                                           .format(int(x))))
      plt.title('Probability of running out of money = {}%'.format(odds),
                fontsize=20, color='red')
   ❾ plt.show()

  # run program
❿ if __name__ == '__main__':
      main()
```

Listing 12-7: Defines and calls the main() function

Define a main() function, which requires no arguments ❶, and immediately call the montecarlo() function to get the outcome list and the bankrupt_count() function ❷. Use the dictionary mapping of investment names to returns lists that you made in Listing 12-2. The argument you pass to the montecarlo() function is the dictionary name, investment_type_args, with the user's input, invest_type, as the key. Feed the returned values to the bankrupt_prob() function to get the odds of running out of money.

Assign a new variable, `plotdata`, to the first 3,000 items in the `outcome` list ❸. The bar chart can accommodate many more items, but displaying them will be slow as well as unnecessary. As the results are stochastic, you won't gain a lot of extra information by showing more cases.

Now you'll use `matplotlib` to create and show the bar chart. Start by making a plot figure ❹. The text entry will be the title of the new window. The `figsize` parameter is the width and height of the window, in inches. You can scale this by adding a dots-per-inch argument, such as `dpi=200`.

Next, use list comprehension to build indexes, starting with 1 for year one, based on the length of the `plotdata` list ❺. The x-axis location of each vertical bar will be defined by the index, and the height of each bar will be the corresponding `plotdata` item, which represents the money remaining at the end of each simulated life. Pass these to the `plt.bar()` method and set the bar color to black ❻. Note that there are additional display options for bars, such as changing the color of the bar outline (`edgecolor='black'`) or its thickness (`linewidth=0`).

Provide labels for the x- and y-axes and set the font size to 18. Outcomes can reach into the millions, and by default, `matplotlib` will use scientific notation when it annotates the y-axis. To override this, call the `ticklabel_format()` method and set the y-axis style to `'plain'` ❼. This takes care of scientific notation, but there are no thousand separators, making the numbers hard to read. To fix this, first get the current axes using `plt.gca()` ❽. Then, in the next line, get the y-axis and use the `set_major_formatter()` and `Func_Formatter()` methods and a lambda function to apply Python's string-formatting technique for comma separators.

For the plot's title, display the probability of running out of money—captured in the `odds` variable—with a large font in eye-catching red. Then draw the chart to the screen with `plt.show()` ❾. Back in the global space, finish with the code that allows the program to be imported as a module or run in stand-alone mode ❿.

Using the Simulator

The *nest_egg_mcs.py* program greatly simplifies the complex world of retirement planning, but don't hold that against it. Simple models add value by challenging assumptions, raising awareness, and focusing questions. It's easy to get lost in the details of retirement planning—or any complex issue—so you're better off starting with a lay of the land.

Let's work an example that assumes a starting value of $2,000,000, a "safe and secure" bond portfolio, a 4 percent withdrawal rate (equal to $80,000 per year), a 30-year retirement, and 50,000 cases. If you run this scenario, you should get results similar to those in Figure 12-9. You run out of money almost half the time! Because of relatively low yields, bonds can't keep pace with inflation—remember, you can't blindly apply the 4 Percent Rule, because your asset allocation matters.

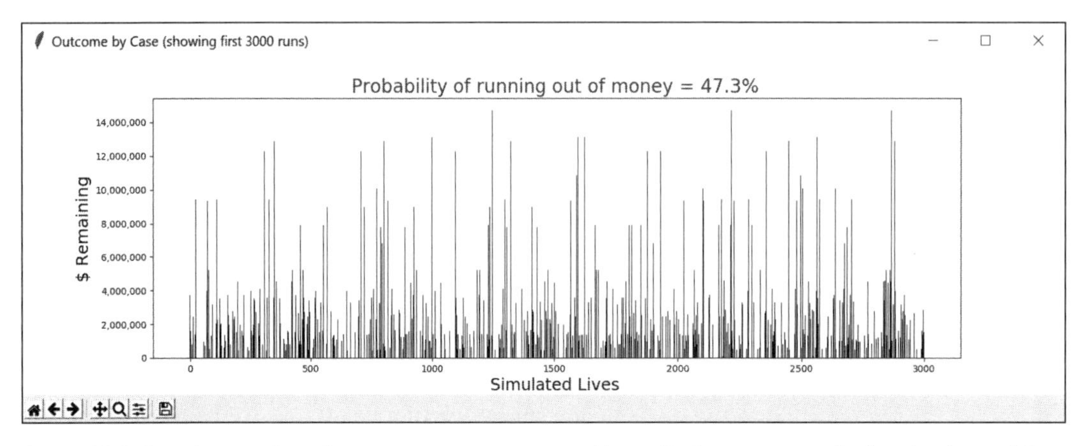

Figure 12-9: Bar chart made with `matplotlib` *to represent a Monte Carlo simulation of a bond-only portfolio*

Note that the $80,000 withdrawal is *pretax*. Assuming a 25 percent effective tax rate, this leaves a net income of only $60,000. According to the Pew Research Center, the median disposable (after-tax) income of the American middle class is currently $60,884, so you're hardly living high on the hog, despite being a millionaire. If you want $80,000 in *disposable* income, you must divide by 1 minus the effective tax rate; in this case, that's $80,000 / (1 – 0.25) = $106,667. This requires withdrawing slightly over 5 percent per year, with a 20 to 70 percent chance of going broke, depending on the investment type!

Table 12-1 records the results of varying the previous scenario for asset type and withdrawal rate. Results that would be widely considered safe are shaded in gray. If you avoid an all-bond portfolio, the 4 Percent Rule holds up well. Above 4 percent, the growth potential of stocks offers the best chance—of the options considered—to reduce the probability of ruin, and with less risk than most people assume. That's why financial advisers recommend including a healthy dose of stocks in your retirement portfolio.

Table 12-1: Probability of Ruin by Asset Type and Withdrawal Rate for 30-Year Retirement

Asset type	**Annual (pretax) withdrawal percentage**			
	3%	**4%**	**5%**	**6%**
10-year Treasury bond	0.135	0.479	0.650	0.876
S&P 500 stocks	0	0.069	0.216	0.365
50/50 blend	0	0.079	0.264	0.466
40/50/10 blend	0	0.089	0.361	0.591

Financial advisers also advise against overdoing it in the early years of retirement. A few cruises for the extended family, a posh new house, or an expensive new hobby can push you over the cliff in your later years. To investigate this, copy *nest_egg_mcs.py* and name the copy *nest_egg_mcs_1st_5yrs.py*; adjust the code as described in Listings 12-8, 12-9, and 12-10:

nest_egg_mcs_1st_5yrs.py, part 1

```
  start_value = default_input("Input starting value of investments: \n", \
                              '2000000')
  while not start_value.isdigit():
      start_value = input("Invalid input! Input integer only: ")

❶ withdrawal_1 = default_input("Input annual pre-tax withdrawal for " \
                               "first 5 yrs(today's $): \n", '100000')
  while not withdrawal_1.isdigit():
      withdrawal_1 = input("Invalid input! Input integer only: ")

❷ withdrawal_2 = default_input("Input annual pre-tax withdrawal for " \
                               "remainder (today's $): \n", '80000')
  while not withdrawal_2.isdigit():
      withdrawal_2 = input("Invalid input! Input integer only: ")

  min_years = default_input("Input minimum years in retirement: \n", '18')
```

Listing 12-8: Breaks the user's withdrawal input into two parts

In the user-input section, replace the original `withdrawal` variable with two withdrawal variables, and edit the prompt to request the first five years in the first ❶ and the remainder of retirement in the second ❷. Set the defaults to indicate that the user should expect higher withdrawals in the first five years. Include the `while` loops that validate user input.

In the `montecarlo()` function, change the code that adjusts the withdrawal amount for inflation.

nest_egg_mcs_1st_5yrs.py, part 2

```
            # don't adjust for inflation the first year
            if index == 0:
              ❶ withdraw_infl_adj_1 = int(withdrawal_1)
              ❷ withdraw_infl_adj_2 = int(withdrawal_2)
            else:
              ❸ withdraw_infl_adj_1 = int(withdraw_infl_adj_1 * (1 + infl))
              ❹ withdraw_infl_adj_2 = int(withdraw_infl_adj_2 * (1 + infl))

          ❺ if index < 5:
              ❻ withdraw_infl_adj = withdraw_infl_adj_1
            else:
                withdraw_infl_adj = withdraw_infl_adj_2

        investments -= withdraw_infl_adj
            investments = int(investments * (1 + i))
```

Listing 12-9: Adjusts the two withdrawal variables for inflation and determines which to use

Set the inflation-adjusted withdrawal equal to the input withdrawal for just the first year ❶❷. Otherwise, adjust both for inflation ❸❹. This way, the second withdrawal amount will be "ready" when you switch to it after five years.

Use a conditional to specify when to apply each inflation-adjusted withdrawal ❺. Assign these to the existing `withdraw_infl_adj` variable so you won't have to alter any more code ❻.

Finally, update the printed statistics in the bankrupt_prob() function to include the new withdrawal values, as shown in Listing 12-10. These should replace the old withdrawal print statement.

nest_egg_mcs_1st_5yrs.py, part 3

```
print("Annual withdrawal first 5 yrs: ${:,}".format(int(withdrawal_1)))
print("Annual withdrawal after 5 yrs: ${:,}".format(int(withdrawal_2)))
```

Listing 12-10: Prints the withdrawal values for the two withdrawal periods

You can now run the new experiment (see Table 12-2).

Table 12-2: Probability of Ruin by Asset Type and Multiple Withdrawal Rates for 30-Year Retirement

Asset allocation	Annual (pretax) withdrawal percentage (first five years / remainder)			
	4% / 4%	5% / 4%	6% / 4%	7% / 4%
10-year Treasury bond	0.479	0.499	0.509	0.571
S&P 500 stocks	0.069	0.091	0.116	0.194
50/50 blend	0.079	0.115	0.146	0.218
40/50/10 blend	0.089	0.159	0.216	0.264

Safe outcomes are shaded in gray in Table 12-2, and the first column repeats the constant 4 percent results, as a control. With enough stocks in your portfolio, you can tolerate some early spending, and for this reason, some advisers replace the 4 Percent Rule with either the 4.5 Percent or 5 Percent Rule. But if you retire early—say, between age 55 and 60—your risk of going broke will be greater, whether you experience any high-spending years or not.

If you run the simulator for the 50/50 blend of stocks and bonds, using different years in retirement, you should get results similar to those in Table 12-3. Only one outcome (shaded gray) has a probability of ruin below 10 percent.

Table 12-3: Probability of Ruin vs. Retirement Duration for 4% Withdrawal Rate (50/50 Stock-Bond Blend)

Years in retirement	4% withdrawal
30	0.079
35	0.103
40	0.194
45	0.216

Running simulations like these forces people to face hard decisions and form realistic plans for a large segment of their lives. While the simulation "sells" assets every year to fund retirement, a better real-life solution is the *guardrail strategy*, where interest and dividends are spent first and a cash reserve is maintained to avoid having to sell assets during market lows. Assuming you can remain disciplined as an investor, this strategy will allow you to stretch your withdrawals a bit beyond what the simulator calculates as safe.

Summary

In this chapter, you wrote a Monte Carlo–based retirement calculator that realistically samples from historical financial data. You also used `matplotlib` to provide an alternative way of viewing the calculator output. While the example used could have been modeled deterministically, if you add more random variables—like future tax rates, Social Security payments, and health care costs—MCS quickly becomes the only practical approach for modeling retirement strategies.

Further Reading

The Intelligent Investor: The Definitive Book on Value Investing, Revised Edition (HarperBusiness, 2006) by Benjamin Graham is considered by many, including billionaire investor Warren Buffet, the greatest book on investing ever written.

Fooled by Randomness: The Hidden Role of Chance in Life and in the Markets, Revised Edition (Random House Trade Paperbacks, 2005) by Nassim Nicholas Taleb is "an engaging look at the history and reasons for our predilection for self-deception when it comes to statistics." It includes discussions on the use of Monte Carlo simulation in financial analysis.

The Black Swan: The Impact of the Highly Improbable, 2nd Edition (Random House Trade Paperbacks, 2010) by Nassim Nicholas Taleb is a "delightful romp through history, economics, and the frailties of human nature" that also includes discussion of the use of Monte Carlo simulation in finance.

You can find an overview of the 4 Percent Rule at *https://www.investopedia.com/terms/f/four-percent-rule.asp*.

Possible exceptions to the 4 Percent Rule are discussed at *https://www.cnbc.com/2015/04/21/the-4-percent-rule-no-longer-applies-for-most-retirees.html*.

You can find historical financial data at the following websites:

- *http://pages.stern.nyu.edu/~adamodar/New_Home_Page/datafile/histretSP.html*
- *http://www.econ.yale.edu/~shiller/data.htm*
- *http://www.moneychimp.com/features/market_cagr.htm*
- *http://www.usinflationcalculator.com/inflation/historical-inflation-rates/*
- *https://inflationdata.com/Inflation/Inflation_Rate/HistoricalInflation.aspx*

Challenge Projects

Become a chartered Certified Financial Analyst (CFA)[1] by completing these challenge projects.

A Picture Is Worth a Thousand Dollars

Imagine you're a CFA and your prospective client, a wealthy Texas oil prospector, doesn't understand your MCS results on his $10 million portfolio. "Tarnation, boy! What kind of durn fool contraption could have me goin' broke in one case and worth 80 million in the next?"

Make it clearer to him by editing the *nest_egg_mcs.py* program so it runs single, 30-year cases using historical intervals that will result in bad and good results, such as starting at the beginning of the Great Depression versus the end of WWII, but only run the extreme cases. For each year in each case, print out the year, the returns rate, the inflation rate, and the outcome. Even better, edit the bar chart display to use each *year's* outcome rather than each *case's* outcome, for a convincing visual explanation.

Mix and Match

Edit *nest_egg_mcs.py* so that the user can generate their own blend of investments. Use the S&P 500, 10-year Treasury bond, and three-month Treasury bill text files that I provided at the start of the chapter and add anything else you like, such as small-cap stocks, international stocks, or even gold. Just remember that the time intervals should be the same in each file or list.

Have the user pick the investment types and percentage of each. Make sure their input adds up to 100 percent. Then create a blended list by weighting and adding the returns for each year. Finish it off by displaying the investment types and percentages at the top of the bar chart display.

Just My Luck!

Edit *nest_egg_mcs.py* to calculate the probability of encountering a Great Depression (1939–1949) or a Great Recession (2007–2009) during a 30-year retirement. You'll need to identify which index numbers in the returns lists correspond to these events, then tally how many times they occur over however many cases are run. Display the results in the shell.

All the Marbles

For a different way to view the results, copy and edit *nest_egg_mcs.py* so that the bar chart displays all the outcomes sorted from smallest to largest.

1. Not really.

13

SIMULATING AN ALIEN VOLCANO

Quick! Name the most volcanically active body in the solar system! If you thought Earth, then you'd be mistaken—it's Io ("EYE-oh"), one of Jupiter's four Galilean moons.

The first evidence of volcanism on Io came in 1979, when *Voyager 1* made its famous fly-by of the Jovian system. But the spectacular photographs it recorded were no real surprise. Astrophysicist Stan Peale and two coauthors had already published this result based on models of Io's interior.

Computer modeling is a powerful tool for understanding nature and making predictions. Here's the general workflow:

1. Gather data.
2. Analyze, interpret, and integrate the data.
3. Generate numerical equations that explain the data.
4. Construct a computer model that best "fits" the data.
5. Use the model to make predictions and investigate error ranges.

Applications of computer modeling are far-reaching and include such areas as wildlife management, weather forecasts, climate predictions, hydrocarbon production, and black-hole simulations.

In this chapter, you'll use a Python package called `pygame`—normally used to create games—to simulate one of Io's volcanoes. You'll also experiment with different types of *ejecta* (erupted particles) and compare their simulated behaviors to a photo of Io's mammoth Tvashtar plume.

Project #21: The Plumes of Io

Tidal heating is responsible for the volcanism on Io. As its elliptical orbit carries it through the gravity fields of Jupiter and its sister moons, Io experiences variations in tidal pull. Its surface flexes up and down by as much as 100 meters, resulting in significant friction-related heating and melting in its interior. Hot magma migrates to the surface and forms great lava lakes from which degassing sulfur (S_2) and sulfur dioxide (SO_2) are sprayed skyward with speeds of 1 km/s. Because of Io's low gravity and lack of atmosphere, these plumes of gas can reach heights of hundreds of kilometers (see the Tvashtar plume in Figure 13-1a).

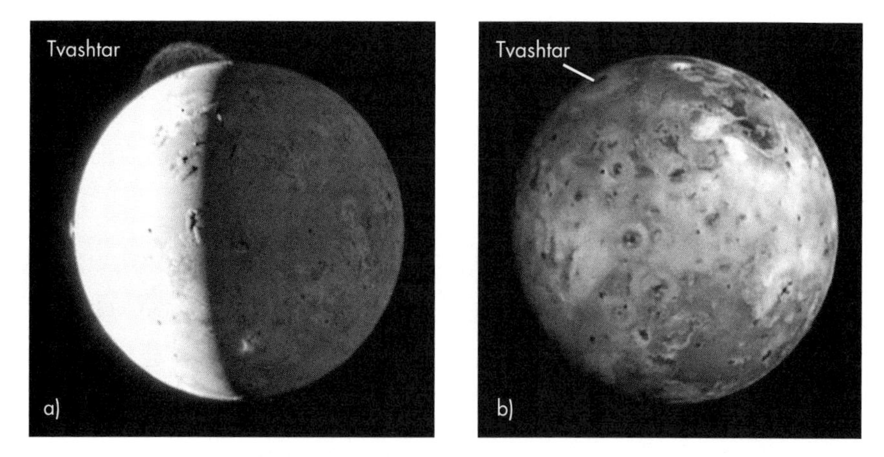

Figure 13-1: a) Io with the 330 km Tvashtar plume at the top and the shorter Prometheus plume at the 9 o'clock position; b) Io with volcanic ring deposits (NASA images)

The plumes' pleasing umbrella shape is produced as gas and dust shoot upward, then fall back in every direction. The resulting surface deposits form concentric rings of red, green, black, and yellow. If Figure 13-1b were in color, it would look a bit like a moldy pepperoni pizza.

A Slice of pygame

The `pygame` package is a cross-platform set of Python modules that are typically used to program 2D arcade-style video games. It supports graphics, animations, sound effects, music, and multiple input devices, such as the keyboard and mouse. Learning `pygame` is more than just a fun way to learn programming. Arcade-style games have seen a resurgence in popularity thanks to the proliferation of smartphones and tablets, and mobile gaming now earns almost as much as console and PC gaming combined.

The `pygame` package uses the *Simple DirectMedia Library (SDL)*, which is an *application programming interface (API)*. APIs are reusable code libraries that make handling graphics fairly easy, allowing you to focus on game design while using a high-level language like Python. The Microsoft *DirectX* API is used for creating games and multimedia apps for the Windows platform. For working across multiple platforms, two open source libraries are SDL, mainly for 2D work, and *OpenGL (Open Graphics Library)* for 3D applications. As mentioned, you'll be working with SDL, which officially supports Windows, macOS, Linux, iOS, and Android.

The `pygame` package also uses object-oriented programming (OOP). If you are unfamiliar with OOP or need a refresher, see "A Brief Introduction to Object-Oriented Programming" on page 223. Additionally, introductory books on Python often include a section on `pygame`, and there are whole books written on the package (see "Further Reading" on page 281 for some examples).

Before you can continue, you'll need to install `pygame` onto your system. Instructions for installing a free copy on your preferred platform are available at *http://pygame.org/wiki/GettingStarted#Pygame%20Installation.*

Video tutorials on how to install `pygame` are also available online. To ensure a video is appropriate to your situation, be sure to check the date of the video, the platform discussed, and the versions of `pygame` and Python in use. You can find additional instructions for Mac users with older Python installs at *http://brysonpayne.com/2015/01/10/setting-up-pygame-on-a-mac/.*

THE OBJECTIVE

Use `pygame` to build a 2D, gravity-based simulation of Io's Tvashtar volcanic plume. Calibrate the plume dimensions using a NASA image. Use multiple particle types in the plume, trace the particles' flight paths and allow the eruption to run automatically until stopped.

The Strategy

Building a comprehensive, full-physics simulation of one of Io's plumes is best accomplished with a supercomputer. Since you probably don't have one of those and since your goal is to make a cool pygame display, you're going to cheat by reverse-engineering the parameters you need to make SO_2 fit the Tvashtar plume. Remember, cheating is the gift humans give ourselves; it's what separates us from the animals—except for the cheetahs!

Since the composition of Io's plumes is already known, you're going to calibrate your gravity field to SO_2 and sulfur (S_2) gas, which conveniently have the same atomic weight. When the flight paths of these particles match the dimensions of the Tvashtar plume in the NASA photograph, you will scale the velocity of other ejected particles, based on the difference in atomic weight between the new particle and SO_2, to see how particle type affects plume dimensions. Lighter particles will be ejected higher and vice versa.

Using a Game Sketch to Plan

I suggest you begin any pygame project with a sketch of how the game should look and how the action should progress. Even the simplest arcade games can become complicated, and a sketch will help you manage the complexity. Among the many things you must consider in a typical game are player actions, scorekeeping, messages and instructions, game entities and their interactions (such as collisions, sound effects, and music), and game-ending conditions.

Sketching the game—or in this case, the simulation—is best done on a whiteboard, either real or digital. My layout for the Io volcano simulator is shown in Figure 13-2.

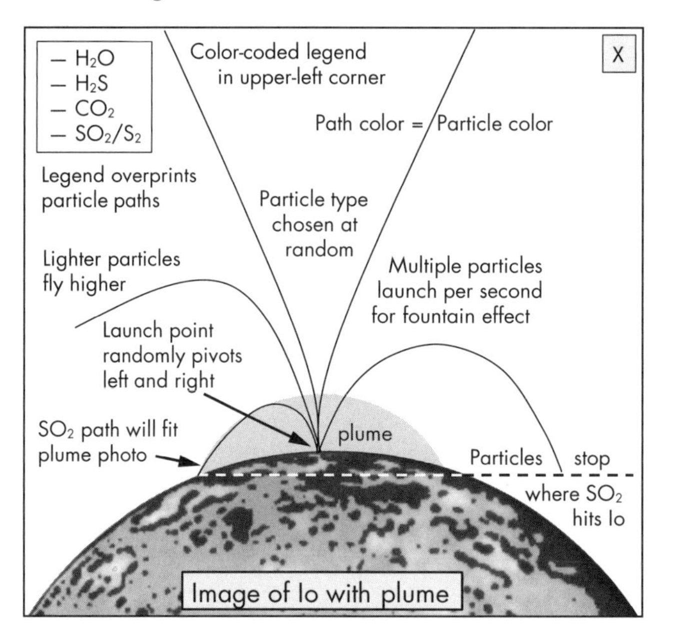

Figure 13-2: Game sketch of Io volcano simulator

The sketch in Figure 13-2 contains guidelines and key behaviors for the volcano simulator:

- **No direct player interactions.** You'll control the simulation by editing the Python code, not through the mouse or keyboard.
- **The background will be a NASA image of a plume.** To calibrate the simulation to SO_2/S_2 particles, you'll need a backdrop of the actual Tvashtar plume.
- **The launch point pivots.** The particles should be ejected from the central base of the plume image and should spray out over a range of angles, rather than just straight up.
- **Particles are chosen at random.** The program will choose the type of particle at random. Each particle will have a unique color that distinguishes it from others.
- **The particle flight path should be visible and persistent.** The flight of each particle should be recorded as a line that remains visible throughout the simulation, and the line color should match the particle color.
- **A color-coded legend lists the particle types.** The program should post a legend with the particle names in the upper-left corner of the screen. The font colors should match the particle colors, and the legend should print on top of particle paths so that it's always visible.
- **Particle motion should stop at the level at which SO_2 particles intersect the surface of Io.** The simulation is tuned to the behavior of SO_2, so falling particles should stop at the appropriate location for an SO_2 plume.
- **There are no sound effects.** In space, no one can hear you scream.

Once you complete your diagram, you can begin picking parts from it and listing them in logical order; this breaks the plan into a series of manageable steps. For example, you'll need to find and prepare an appropriate background image, decide which particles you want to simulate and look up their atomic weights, locate a launch point, calibrate SO_2 behavior to the plume image, and so on. You're still writing pseudocode, but a game sketch makes it a much more enjoyable process!

Planning the Particle Class

Since this simulation is based on *particles*, it makes sense to have an OOP `Particle` class to serve as a blueprint for multiple particle types. The class should support the random generation of particle types, and constants and other attributes common to all particles can be stored as *class attributes*. These are attributes assigned at the same indentation level as methods. The `Particle` class should also contain methods that allow instances of the class to be ejected, affected by gravity, made visible, and destroyed when they move beyond the boundaries of the simulation.

The attributes and methods used in the class are shown in Tables 13-1 and 13-2, respectively. Class attributes—that is, those shared by all instances of the class—are shown in italics; otherwise, instance attributes are shown.

Table 13-1: Attributes of the `Particle` Class (*Italics* = Class Attribute)

Attributes	Attribute description
gases_colors	Dictionary of available particle types and their colors
VENT_LOCATION_XY	x- and y-location of mouth of Tvashtar volcano in image
IO_SURFACE_Y	Io surface y-value at SO_2 plume margin in image
VELOCITY_SO2	Speed (pixels per frame) of SO_2 particle
GRAVITY	Acceleration of gravity in pixels per frame
vel_scalar	Dictionary of ratios of SO_2/particle atomic weights
screen	The game screen
background	A NASA image of the Tvashtar plume
image	A square `pygame` surface representing a particle
rect	A rectangular object used to get surface dimensions
gas	The type of an individual particle (SO_2, CO_2, etc.)
color	Color of an individual particle type
vel	Particle's velocity relative to SO_2 velocity
x	Particle's x-location
y	Particle's y-location
dx	Particle's delta-x
dy	Particle's delta-y

Table 13-2: Methods of the `Particle` Class

Method	Method description
`__init__()`	Initializes and sets up parameters for randomly selected particle type
`vector()`	Randomly selects ejection orientation and calculates motion vector (dx and dy)
`update()`	Adjusts particle trajectory for gravity, draws path behind particle, and destroys particles that move beyond the boundaries of the simulation

I will explain each of these attributes and methods in more detail in the next section.

The Code

The *tvashtar.py* code will generate a pygame-based simulation of Io's Tvashtar plume. You will also need the background image, *tvashtar_plume.gif*. Download both files from *https://www.nostarch.com/impracticalpython/* and keep them in the same folder.

Importing Modules, Initiating pygame, and Defining Colors

Begin with several set-up steps, such as choosing colors, as shown in Listing 13-1.

tvashtar.py, part 1

```
❶ import sys
  import math
  import random
  import pygame as pg

❷ pg.init()  # initialize pygame

❸ # define color table
  BLACK = (0, 0, 0)
  WHITE = (255, 255, 255)
  LT_GRAY = (180, 180, 180)
  GRAY = (120, 120, 120)
  DK_GRAY = (80, 80, 80)
```

Listing 13-1: Imports modules, initiates pygame, and defines a table of colors

Start with some familiar imports and one for pygame ❶. Next, call the pygame.init() function. This initializes the pygame module and starts up all the underlying parts that let it use sounds, check keyboard input, run graphics, and so on ❷. Note that pygame can be initialized from multiple places, such as the first line in a main() function:

```
def main():
    pg.init()
```

or at the end of the program when main() is called in stand-alone mode:

```
if __name__ == "__main__":
    pg.init()
    main()
```

Stop and assign some color variables using the RGB color model ❸. This model mixes red, green, and blue, where each color consists of values from 0 to 255. If you do an online search for "RGB color codes," you can find the numerical codes for millions of colors. But since the NASA image you'll calibrate against is in grayscale, stick with black, white, and shades of gray. Defining this table now will allow you to simply enter a name when pygame needs a color defined later.

Defining the Particle Class

Listing 13-2 defines the Particle class and its initializer method. You'll use these to instantiate a particle object. The particle's key attributes, such as type, velocity, color, and so on, are established with the initializer method.

tvashtar.py, part 2

```
❶ class Particle(pg.sprite.Sprite):
      """Builds ejecta particles for volcano simulation."""

   ❷ gases_colors = {'SO2': LT_GRAY, 'CO2': GRAY, 'H2S': DK_GRAY, 'H2O': WHITE}

   ❸ VENT_LOCATION_XY = (320, 300)
      IO_SURFACE_Y = 308
      GRAVITY = 0.5  # pixels-per-frame; added to dy each game loop
      VELOCITY_SO2 = 8  # pixels-per-frame

      # scalars (SO2 atomic weight/particle atomic weight) used for velocity
   ❹ vel_scalar = {'SO2': 1, 'CO2': 1.45, 'H2S': 1.9, 'H2O': 3.6}

   ❺ def __init__(self, screen, background):
          super().__init__()
          self.screen = screen
          self.background = background
       ❻ self.image = pg.Surface((4, 4))
          self.rect = self.image.get_rect()
       ❼ self.gas = random.choice(list(Particle.gases_colors.keys()))
          self.color = Particle.gases_colors[self.gas]
       ❽ self.vel = Particle.VELOCITY_SO2 * Particle.vel_scalar[self.gas]
       ❾ self.x, self.y = Particle.VENT_LOCATION_XY
       ❿ self.vector()
```

Listing 13-2: Defines the `Particle` *class and the* `Particle` *initializer method*

Define a class called `Particle` to represent *any* molecule of gas that might form the volcanic plume ❶. The *ancestor* for this class, shown in parentheses, will be a `Sprite` class. This means that the `Particle` class is derived from a built-in `pygame` type called `Sprite`. Sprites are just 2D bitmaps that represent discrete game objects, like missiles or asteroids. You *inherit* from the `Sprite` class—that is, add its attributes and methods to your new class—by passing `pg.sprite.Sprite` to your `Particle` class, just as you would pass an argument to a function.

Assign properties common to all particles as class attributes. The first is a dictionary that maps particle types to a color, so that you can differentiate the particles during the simulation ❷. These colors will be used for the particle, its path, and its name in the legend.

Now, assign four constants, `VENT_LOCATION_XY`, `IO_SURFACE_Y`, `GRAVITY`, and `VELOCITY_SO2` ❸. The first constant is the x- and y-coordinates for the mouth of the Tvashtar volcano in the image, which will represent the "launch point" for all the particles (see Figure 13-3). I initially guessed at these values and then fine-tuned them when the simulation was up and running.

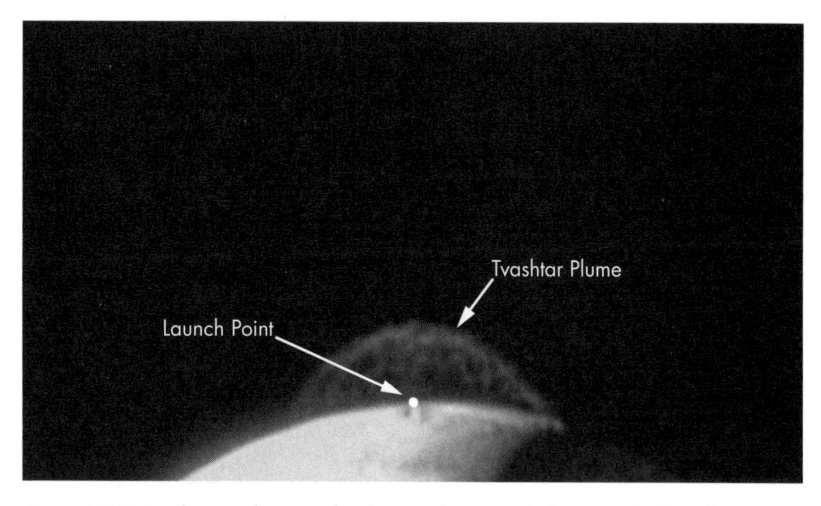

Figure 13-3: Background image for the simulation with the particle launch point annotated

The second constant is the y-value for the highest point on Io's surface (in the image) that intersects with the outer edge of the SO_2 plume (see Figure 13-2). You will stop all the falling particles at this y-value, so the view will be optimized for SO_2.

The third constant represents the acceleration of gravity, which on Earth is 9.86 m/s^2 and on Io is 1.796 m/s^2. But you're dealing with pixels and frames here, not real-world units, so you need to experiment to find a value that looks good at the scale of your game/simulation. My choice of `0.5` was arbitrary, though guided by knowledge of what works well in arcade games.

The fourth constant is the speed, in pixels per frame, of an SO_2 particle when it is ejected. Remember, the plumes are composed primarily of SO_2, so you want to use parameters that will allow the SO_2 particles to "fit" the image of the Tvashtar plume, then adjust the speed of the remaining particles *relative* to SO_2. Neither the `GRAVITY` nor the `VELOCITY_SO2` value is unique. Had I chosen a larger value for `GRAVITY`, I would've needed to increase `VELOCITY_SO2` so that the SO_2 particles still "fill out" the area of the plume in the NASA image.

Next, build a dictionary of scalars for particle velocity ❹. For each particle, dividing the atomic weight of SO_2 (64) by the atomic weight of the particle gives you the scalar. Since SO_2 is the reference particle, its scalar is 1. Later, to get the velocity of non-SO_2 particles, you will multiply the `VELOCITY_SO2` constant by the scalar. As you can see, all of the other particles are lighter than SO_2 and should produce a larger plume.

Define a constructor method for the particle object ❺. You'll need a `self` parameter and `screen` to draw on and check the simulation's boundaries, and you'll need a `background`, which will be an image of the Tvashtar plume. You'll assign `screen` and `background` later in the `main()` function, defined near the end of the program. Note that while I'm using one-line docstrings in this book for brevity, you would want to include these types of parameters in the class docstring. For more guidelines on class docstrings, see *https://www.python.org/dev/peps/pep-0257/.*

Inside the `__init__()` method, immediately invoke the initialization method for the built-in `Sprite` class using `super`. This will initialize the sprite and establish the `rect` and `image` attributes it needs. With `super`, you don't need to refer to the base class (`Sprite`) explicitly. For more on `super`, visit the docs at *https://docs.python.org/3/library/functions.html#super.*

Next, let the particle (`self`) know that it will be using the `screen` and `background` variables by assigning them to attributes.

The images and drawings are placed on a rectangular surface by `pygame`. In fact, the `Surface` object is the heart and soul of `pygame`; even the `screen` attribute represents an instance of `Surface`. Assign the particle image to a `Surface` object and make it a square with 4-pixel-length sides ❻.

Next, you need to get a `rect` object for your image surface. This is basically a rectangle *associated* with the `Surface` object, which `pygame` needs to determine the dimensions and position of your `Surface` object.

Choose a particle (`gas`) type by randomly choosing from the keys in the `gases_colors` dictionary ❼. Note that you turn it into a list to do this. Since it's possible to assign an instance attribute named `gases_colors` from within the `__init__()` method, include the class name—rather than `self`—to ensure the *class* attribute is being referenced.

Once you have a type, you can use it as the key in the dictionaries you built earlier to access things like colors and scalars. Start by getting the correct color for the chosen particle, then get its `vel_scalar` value and use that to determine the particle's velocity ❽.

The particle object will be instantiated in the mouth of the volcano, so get its initial x- and y-location by unpacking the `VENT_LOCATION_XY` tuple ❾. Finish by calling the `vector()` method, which will calculate the particle's motion vector ❿.

Ejecting a Particle

Listing 13-3 defines the `vector()` method, which determines a particle's launch orientation and calculates its initial delta-x and delta-y vector components.

tvashtar.py, part 3

```
❶ def vector(self):
      """Calculate particle vector at launch."""
    ❷ orient = random.uniform(60, 120)  # 90 is vertical
    ❸ radians = math.radians(orient)
    ❹ self.dx = self.vel * math.cos(radians)
      self.dy = -self.vel * math.sin(radians)
```

Listing 13-3: Defines the `vector()` method of the `Particle` class

The `vector()` method ❶ calculates the motion vector for a particle. Start by choosing a launch direction for the particle and assigning it to an `orient` variable ❷. Because explosive volcanic eruptions blast material in multiple directions rather than straight up, choose the direction at random, using a range that is 30 degrees to either side of 90 degrees, where 90 represents a vertical launch.

The range for the `orient` variable was chosen through trial and error. This parameter, along with the `VELOCITY_SO2` and `GRAVITY` constants, represents the "knobs" you can turn to calibrate the behavior of the SO_2 particle to the plume image. After you've adjusted the constants so that the particle's maximum height corresponds to the apex of the plume, you can adjust the range of angles so that the SO_2 particles reach—but don't exceed—the lateral limits of the plume (see Figure 13-4).

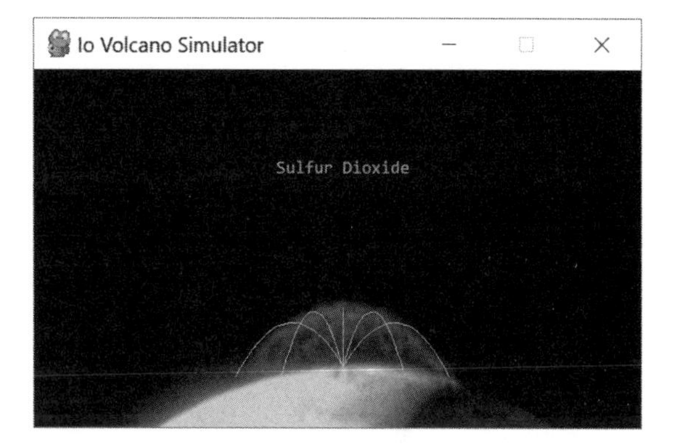

Figure 13-4: Calibrating the `orient` variable to the Tvashtar plume

The `math` module uses *radians* rather than degrees, so convert `orient` to radians ❸. A radian is a standard unit of angular measurement equal to the angle made when the radius is wrapped around a circle (see the left-hand side of Figure 13-5). One radian is slightly less than 57.3 degrees. The right-hand side of Figure 13-5 is a comparison of radians and degrees for some common angles. To convert degrees to radians, you can either multiply the degrees by π and divide by 180—like a chump—or just use the `math` module!

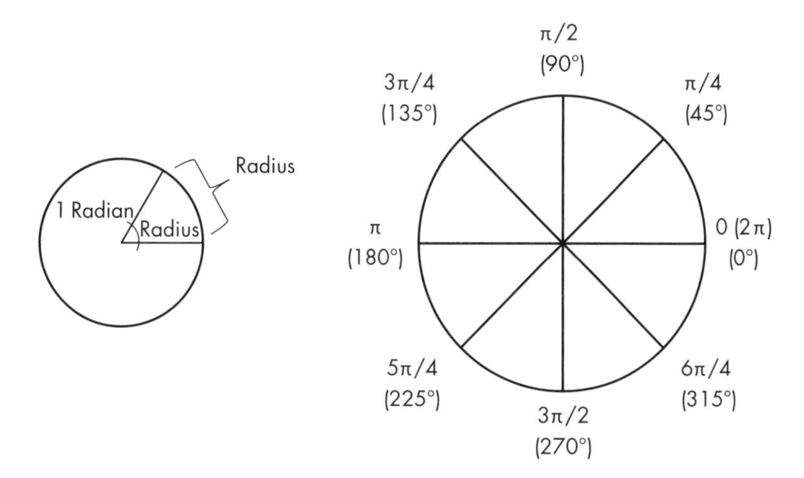

Figure 13-5: Definition of a radian (left) and common angles in radians and degrees (right)

Objects move in pygame by increments of x and y. The direction and speed of a particle are used to get its *delta-x (dx)* and *delta-y (dy)* vector components. These represent the difference between a particle's initial position and its position after completion of a single game loop.

You calculate vector components using trigonometry. Useful trigonometric equations are provided in Figure 13-6.

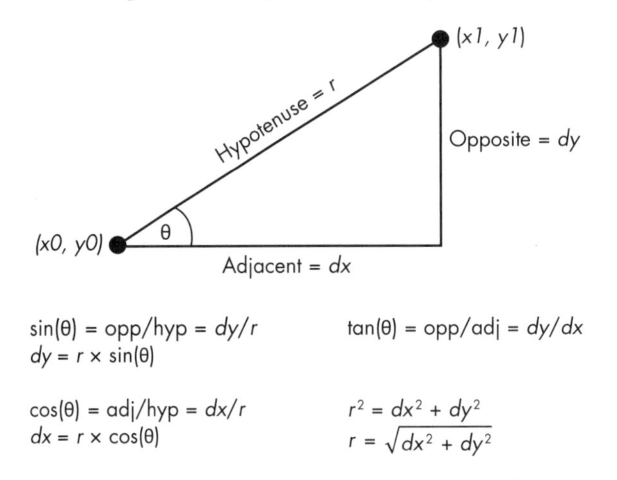

$\sin(\theta) = opp/hyp = dy/r$

$dy = r \times \sin(\theta)$

$\tan(\theta) = opp/adj = dy/dx$

$\cos(\theta) = adj/hyp = dx/r$

$dx = r \times \cos(\theta)$

$r^2 = dx^2 + dy^2$

$r = \sqrt{dx^2 + dy^2}$

Figure 13-6: Common trigonometric equations used in gaming

For the angle θ, you use the `orient` variable. The `self.vel` attribute equates to *r*. Knowing these two components, you can use a trigonometric equation to derive `self.dx` and `self.dy` ❹. To derive `self.dx`, multiply `self.vel` by the cosine of `orient`, and to derive `self.dy`, multiply `self.vel` by the sine of `orient`. Note that you must make `self.dy` negative, as the particles are ejected upward and y-values in pygame increase *downward*.

Updating the Particle and Handling Boundary Conditions

Listing 13-4 completes the `Particle` class by defining a method to update particles as they move across the screen. This includes applying the force of gravity, drawing a line to trace the particle's path, and "killing" the particle when it moves offscreen or below the surface of Io.

tvashtar.py, part 4

```
❶ def update(self):
       """Apply gravity, draw path, and handle boundary conditions."""
     ❷ self.dy += Particle.GRAVITY
     ❸ pg.draw.line(self.background, self.color,(self.x, self.y),
                     (self.x + self.dx, self.y + self.dy))
     ❹ self.x += self.dx
       self.y += self.dy

     ❺ if self.x < 0 or self.x > self.screen.get_width():
         ❻ self.kill()
```

```
    ❼ if self.y < 0 or self.y > Particle.IO_SURFACE_Y:
          self.kill()
```

Listing 13-4: Defines the `update()` method and completes the `Particle` class

Define the `update()` method, which takes `self` as an argument ❶. Apply the force of gravity by adding the `GRAVITY` class attribute to `self.dy` during each game loop ❷. Gravity is a force vector that works only in the vertical direction, so only `self.dy` is affected.

To draw a path behind the particle, use `pygame`'s `draw.line()` method, which takes the background image of Io, the color of the particle, and the coordinates for the previous and current locations of the particle as arguments ❸. To get the current location, you add the `self.dx` and `self.dy` attributes to `self.x` and `self.y`.

Next, update the particle's `self.x` and `self.y` attributes by adding `self.dx` and `self.dy`, just as you did in the `draw.line()` method ❹.

Now, check to see if the particle has passed the left or right boundaries of the screen ❺. Use a `self.x` equal to zero for the left side and get the width of the `screen` attribute for the right side. If the particle has passed off either side of the screen, use the built-in `kill()` method to remove it from all the groups that contain it ❻. As you will see later, `pygame` uses containers—called *groups*—to manage sprites, and removing a sprite from a group takes it out of play.

Repeat this process for the y-direction ❼, but for a maximum value, use the `IO_SURFACE_Y` constant of the `Particle` class, which will stop the particle near the surface of Io, where an SO_2 particle would stop (see Figures 13-2 and 13-4).

Defining the main() Function

Listing 13-5 defines the first part of the `main()` function that sets up the game screen, the window caption, the legend, the sprite group, and the game clock.

tvashtar.py, part 5

```
def main():
    """Set up and run game screen and loop."""
  ❶ screen = pg.display.set_mode((639, 360))
  ❷ pg.display.set_caption('Io Volcano Simulator')
  ❸ background = pg.image.load('tvashtar_plume.gif')

    # Set up color-coded legend
  ❹ legend_font = pg.font.SysFont('None', 24)
  ❺ water_label = legend_font.render('--- H2O', True, WHITE, BLACK)
    h2s_label = legend_font.render('--- H2S', True, DK_GRAY, BLACK)
    co2_label = legend_font.render('--- CO2', True, GRAY, BLACK)
    so2_label = legend_font.render('--- SO2/S2', True, LT_GRAY, BLACK)

  ❻ particles = pg.sprite.Group()

  ❼ clock = pg.time.Clock()
```

Listing 13-5: Defines the first part of the `main()` function

The first step is to assign the `screen` variable using `pygame`'s `display.set_mode()` method ❶. The arguments are pixel dimensions; in this case, you use values slightly smaller than those for the NASA image to ensure a good fit. Note that the dimensions must be provided as a tuple, so you need to include two sets of parentheses.

Next, name your game window using `pygame`'s `display.set_caption()` method ❷, then assign the `background` variable to the NASA photo of the Tvashtar plume ❸. Use `pygame`'s `image.load()` method to create a new `Surface` object from the image. The `pygame` package supports several image formats, including PNG, JPG, and GIF. The returned `Surface` will inherit color and transparency information from the image file. Since you're importing a grayscale image here, your color choices will be limited.

Now, add some code to build the legend that will be displayed in the upper left of the screen.

Name a `legend_font` variable and use `pygame`'s `font.SysFont()` method to choose `None` at size 24 ❹. You will use this when you render the text. The `pygame` package's `font` module lets you render a new set of fonts, called TrueType fonts, onto a new `Surface` object. If you don't want to specify a font, `pygame` comes with a built-in default font, which you can access by passing `None` as the font name.

Post the particle names in order of weight, with the lightest on the top. To make a label, call `render()` on the `legend_font` object you made earlier to generate a new surface object ❺. Pass it some text, then `True` (to turn on anti-aliasing so the text looks smoother), and then the color of the particle being described. The last argument, `BLACK`, is optional and sets the background color of the label to black so the text will be legible above all the particle paths drawn on the screen. Repeat this process for the three remaining particles and add `S2` to the `so2_label`, as both gases share the same atomic weight and will behave the same in the simulation.

Now, start a sprite group named `particles` ❻. Since games typically have multiple sprites moving around the screen, `pygame` uses a container—the sprite group—to manage them. In fact, you *must* put sprites in a group or else they won't do anything.

Finish this section by creating a `Clock` object to track and control the frame rate of the simulation ❼. A `pygame` "clock" controls how fast the game runs, based on the number of *frames per second (fps)* being displayed. You'll set this value in the next section.

Completing the main() Function

Listing 13-6 completes `main()` by setting the speed the simulation will run—in frames per second—and starting the `while` loop that actually runs the simulation. It also handles *events,* which occur when a user exerts control on the program using a mouse, joystick, or keyboard. Since this is a simulation and not a true game, user control is limited to closing the window. The listing ends in the global scope with the standard code for running the program as a module or in stand-alone mode.

tvashtar.py, part 6

```
❶ while True:
    ❷ clock.tick(25)
    ❸ particles.add(Particle(screen, background))
    ❹ for event in pg.event.get():
            if event.type == pg.QUIT:
                pg.quit()
                sys.exit()

    ❺ screen.blit(background, (0, 0))
       screen.blit(water_label, (40, 20))
       screen.blit(h2s_label, (40, 40))
       screen.blit(co2_label, (40, 60))
       screen.blit(so2_label, (40, 80))

    ❻ particles.update()
       particles.draw(screen)

    ❼ pg.display.flip()

❽ if __name__ == "__main__":
    main()
```

Listing 13-6: Starts the game clock and loop and handles events in the `main()` *function*

Start a `while` loop to run the simulation ❶. Then use the `clock.tick()` method to set the speed limit for the simulation ❷. Pass it `25`, which sets the maximum frame rate at 25 frames per second. Feel free to increase this value if you want a more energetic volcano.

It's now time for the star of the show to make its appearance. Instantiate a particle using the `Particle` class, passing it the `screen` and `background` as arguments, and add the new particle to the `particles` sprite group ❸. With each frame, a new particle will be created at random and launched from the volcanic vent, producing a pleasing spray of particles (see Figure 13-7).

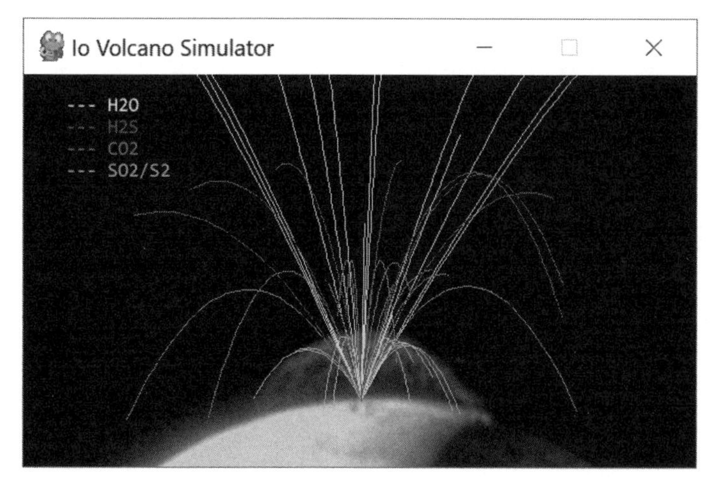

Figure 13-7: Startup of the simulation, with random particles being generated at the rate of 25 frames per second

Start a for loop to handle events ❹. All the events that happened during the current frame are recorded by pygame and kept in an *event buffer*. Its event.get() method creates a list of all these events so that you can evaluate them in turn. If a QUIT event occurs (when a user closes the game window), the pygame quit() and system exit() methods are called to end the simulation.

To render the game objects and update the visual display, pygame uses a process called *blitting*. *Blit* stands for *block transfer*, which is just copying pixels from one rectangular Surface object onto another. By blitting the background onto the screen, you cover the screen with the Io image. With blitting, you can take the same image and draw it multiple times at different places on the screen. It can be a slow process, so game developers use clever techniques to address this deficiency, such as blitting only around areas that are currently being updated, rather than blitting the whole screen in every game loop.

To blit the background onto the screen, call the blit() method on the screen and pass it the required arguments for source and destination ❺. In the first example, the background variable is the source, and the destination is the coordinates for where you want the *upper left-hand corner* of the background. Since the background will cover the whole screen, use the origin point for the screen, which is (0, 0). Repeat this for the legend labels, placing them in the upper-left corner of the screen.

Next, call the update() method on the particles group ❻. This method doesn't update the screen but has the sprites run their own self.update() methods. After this, you use the draw() method to blit the sprites onto the screen based on each sprite's rect attributes. This method needs a drawing surface, so pass it the screen.

The draw() method took care of blitting sprites, so all you need to do now is use the flip() method to update the actual game graphics ❼. *Flipping* is a type of double buffering where you blit everything from the screen object to the actual display. Flipping gets around the inherently slow process of displaying graphics, which can cause the screen to flicker, by doing the work on a behind-the-scenes rectangle and then using a version of the blit() method to copy to the final display

The listing ends outside the main() function with the code that lets the program run as a module or in stand-alone mode ❽.

Running the Simulation

Figure 13-8 shows the result of running the simulator for about a minute. The water vapor plume extends beyond the top of the window. The next highest plume is formed by hydrogen sulfide, followed by carbon dioxide, and then sulfur dioxide/sulfur (S_2) gas, which by design perfectly matches the Tvashtar plume.

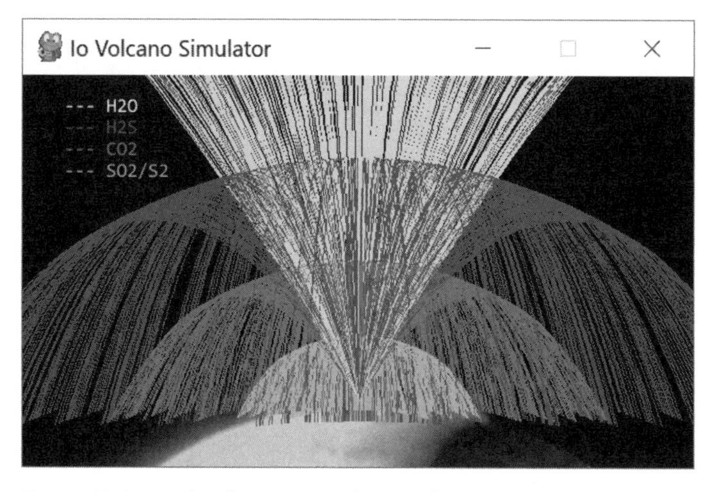

Figure 13-8: Results of running tvashtar.py *for one minute*

To run the simulator with *only* SO_2, go to the `__init__` method of the `Particle` class and change the lines where you select the `gas` and `color` instance attributes:

```
self.gas = 'SO2'
self.color = random.choice(list(Particle.gases_colors.values()))
```

By choosing a color at random, you maintain a sense of movement in the plume after all of the possible `self.orient` angles have been exhausted. And if you want to speed up or slow down the eruption, go to the `main()` function and experiment with the `clock.tick()` method's frames-per-second parameter.

In real life, the composition of plume material was inferred with *spectroscopy*, a measurement technique that analyzes how light interacts with matter. This includes both visible and nonvisible wavelengths that are absorbed, emitted, or scattered. The "spectra of the ejecta," together with the colors painted on the surface, provided the key evidence for sulfur-rich plumes.

Summary

In this chapter, you learned how to use the `pygame` package to simulate gravity and build an animation of an extraterrestrial volcano. In the next chapter, you'll use `pygame` to build a true arcade game with player interactions and win-lose conditions.

Further Reading

Game Programming: The L-Line, The Express Line to Learning (Wiley, 2007) by Andy Harris is a tremendously useful and thorough 570-page introduction to `pygame`.

More Python for the Absolute Beginner (Cengage Learning Course Technology, 2012) by Jonathon Harbour builds on the prequel, *Python for the Absolute Beginner*, using a (py)game-focused approach.

Invent Your Own Computer Games with Python, 4th Edition (No Starch Press, 2016) by Al Sweigart is a good introduction to both Python and game design for beginners.

An online "newbie guide" for `pygame` is available at *https://www.pygame.org/docs/tut/newbieguide.html*, and a "cheat sheet" can be found at *http://www.cogsci.rpi.edu/~destem/gamedev/pygame.pdf*.

Three-Dimensional Simulation of Gas and Dust in Io's Pele Plume, by William J. McDoniel and others, documents the simulation of Io's Pele Plume using direct Monte Carlo simulation and supercomputers at the Texas Advanced Computing Center at the University of Texas. The article is available at *http://cfpl.ae.utexas.edu/wp-content/uploads/2016/01/McDoniel_PeleDust.pdf*.

Practice Project: Going the Distance

You're one of King Henry's archers at the battle of Agincourt. The French are charging, and you want to strike them as far away as possible. At what angle do you hold your longbow?

If you've ever had a physics class, you probably know the answer is 45 degrees. But can you trust that pencil-necked physicist? Better run a quick computer simulation to check it out. Copy and edit the *tvashtar.py* code to randomly fire particles at 25, 35, 45, 55, and 65 degrees. Set `self.color` to `WHITE` for 45 degrees and `GRAY` for all other angles (see Figure 13-9).

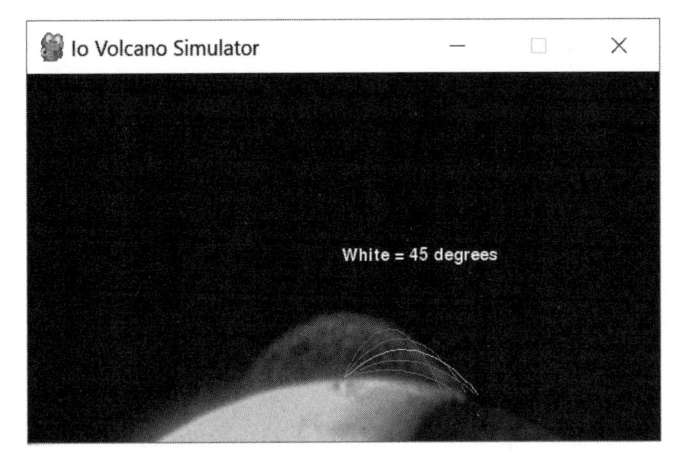

Figure 13-9: Io volcano simulator modified for ejection angles of 25, 35, 45, 55, and 65 degrees

You can find a solution, *practice_45.py*, in the appendix or for download at *https://www.nostarch.com/impracticalpython/*. Keep it in the same folder as the *tvashtar_plume.gif* file.

Challenge Projects

Continue your experiments with these challenge projects. No solutions are provided.

Shock Canopy

The visibility of Io's giant plumes is believed to be enhanced by gas condensing into dust in the *shock canopy*, the point where the gas particles reach their apex and begin falling back to the surface. Use the `self.dy` attribute to edit the path colors in a copy of the *tvashtar.py* program. Paths in the apex of the plume should be brighter than those below (see Figure 13-10). As with all Challenge Projects, no solution is provided.

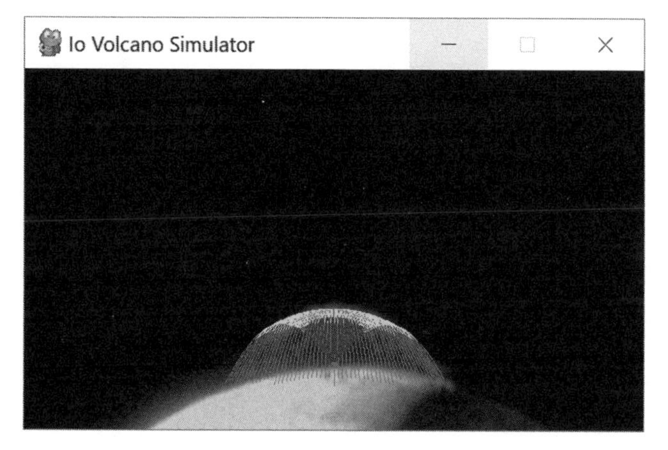

Figure 13-10: Highlighting the shock canopy using lighter path colors

The Fountainhead

Copy and edit *tvashtar.py* so that only SO_2 is simulated and particles are represented by small white circles with no trailing paths (see Figure 13-11).

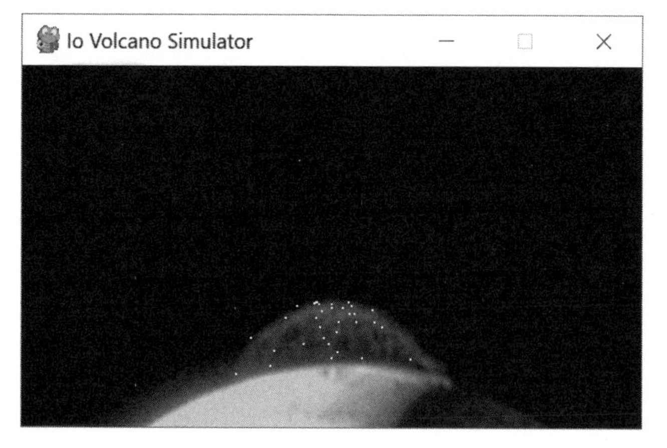

Figure 13-11: Screenshot of SO_2 simulation with circles representing individual particles

With a Bullet

If you fire a gun straight up on a planet with no atmosphere, will the bullet hit the ground with the same velocity as when it left the muzzle? Many people struggle with this question, but you can answer it with Python. Copy and edit the *tvashtar.py* code so that it ejects a single SO_2 particle with an orientation of 90 degrees. Print the particle's `self.y` attribute and the absolute value of `self.dy` at the launch point coordinate (y = 300). Compare the starting and ending velocity values at this point to see whether they are the same or similar.

NOTE *Episode 50 of the TV show* MythBusters *addressed the myth that bullets fired into the air maintain their lethal capability when they eventually fall back down. They found that bullets fired perfectly vertical on Earth would tumble and slow on their way back down due to wind resistance. If fired slightly off-vertical, the bullets would maintain their spin and ballistic trajectory and return to Earth at lethal speed. It was the only myth that ever received all three ratings (Busted, Plausible, and Confirmed)!*

14

MAPPING MARS WITH THE MARS ORBITER

The *Mars Orbiter* space probe has been successfully injected into Martian orbit, but all is not well. The orbit is highly elliptical, and the project's mapping objectives require a low-altitude circular orbit. Fortunately, there's just enough propellant on board to correct things, assuming the eggheads at Mission Control have the patience and skill to pull it off!

In this chapter, you'll design and build a game based on this scenario. You'll use pygame again (for an overview of pygame, see "A Slice of pygame" on page 267), and you'll do your part to advance STEM (science, technology, engineering, and mathematics) education by making the game real enough to teach players the fundamentals of orbital mechanics.

NOTE *Although they share the same name, the* Mars Orbiter *space probe in the game bears no direct relationship to the* Mars Orbiter Mission *launched by the* Indian Space Research Organization (ISRO) *in 2014. The game probe is patterned after the* Mars Global Surveyor, *launched by NASA in 1996.*

Astrodynamics for Gamers

Because you'll want your game to be as realistic as possible, a quick review of some of the basic science underlying spaceflight is in order. This will be short, sweet, and tailored to game development and play.

The Law of Universal Gravity

The theory of gravity states that massive objects—like stars and planets—warp both space and time around them, similar to how a heavy bowling ball placed on a mattress causes a depression that is sudden and sharp near the ball but quickly levels off. This behavior is captured mathematically by Isaac Newton's law of universal gravitation:

$$F = \frac{m_1 * m_2}{d^2} G$$

where F is the force of gravity, m_1 is the mass of object 1, m_2 is the mass of object 2, d is the distance between objects, and G is the gravitational constant ($6.674 \times 10^{-11}\ N \cdot m^2 \cdot \text{kg}^{-2}$).

Two objects pull on each other according to the product of their masses divided by the square of the distance between them. So, gravity is much stronger when objects are close together, like the deep bowing of the mattress just beneath the bowling ball. To illustrate, a 220-pound (100 kg) man would weigh over half a pound less on top of Mt. Everest than he would at sea level, where he would be 8,848 m closer to the center of Earth. (This assumes the mass of the planet is 5.98×10^{24} kg and sea level is 6.37×10^6 m from the center.)

Today, we generally think of gravity as a *field*—like the mattress in the bowling ball analogy—rather than as Newton's point of attraction. This field is still defined with Newton's law and results in *acceleration*, usually expressed in m/sec^2.

According to Newton's second law of motion, force is equal to mass × acceleration. You can calculate the force exerted by object 1 (m_1) on object 2 (m_2) by rewriting the gravitational equation as:

$$a = \frac{-G * m_1}{d^2}$$

where a = acceleration, G is the gravitational constant, m_1 is the mass of one of the objects, and d is the distance between objects. The direction of force is from object 2 toward the center of mass of object 1 (m_1).

The pull of very small objects on large ones is generally ignored. For example, the force exerted by a 1,000 kg satellite on Mars is about 1.6×10^{-21} times smaller than the force exerted by Mars on the satellite! Thus, you can safely ignore the satellite's mass in your simulation.

NOTE *As a simplification in this project, distance is calculated from the center points of objects. In real life, an orbiting satellite would experience subtle changes in gravitational acceleration due to changes in a planet's shape, topography, crustal density, and so on. According to the* Encyclopedia Britannica, *these changes cause gravitational acceleration at Earth's surface to vary by about 0.5 percent.*

Kepler's Laws of Planetary Motion

In 1609, astronomer Johann Kepler discovered that planetary orbits are ellipses, allowing him to explain and predict the motion of the planets. He also found that a line segment drawn between the sun and an orbiting planet sweeps out equal areas in equal time intervals. This idea, known as Kepler's second law of planetary motion, is demonstrated in Figure 14-1, where a planet is shown at different points in its orbit.

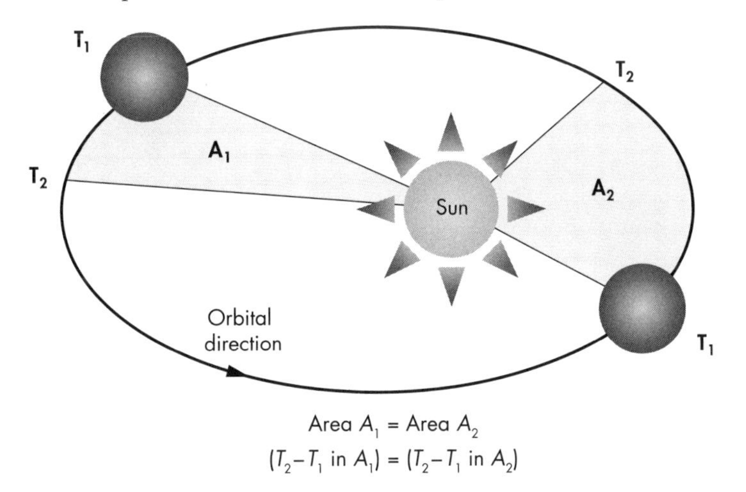

Figure 14-1: Kepler's second law of planetary motion: orbital speed increases as planets near the sun.

This law applies to all celestial bodies, and it means that an orbiting object speeds up as it gets close to the body it is orbiting and slows down as it travels farther away.

Orbital Mechanics

Orbiting is basically free-falling forever. You're falling into the core of a planet's gravity well—located at its literal core—but your tangential velocity is fast enough that you keep missing the planet (see Figure 14-2). As long as you balance your momentum with the force of gravity, the orbit will never end.

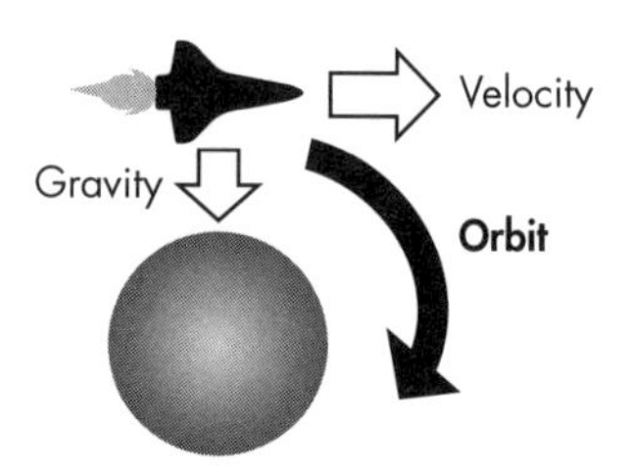

Figure 14-2: Orbit is achieved when a spacecraft's velocity keeps it "free-falling" around a celestial body.

Some counterintuitive things can happen when you orbit a planet in the vacuum of space. With no friction or wind resistance, spacecraft can behave in unexpected ways.

Flying Backward

If you've ever watched an episode of *Star Trek*, you've probably noticed how the orbiting *Enterprise* seems to steer its way around planets, like a car going around a track. This is certainly possible to do—and definitely looks cool—but it requires the expenditure of precious fuel. If there's no need to continuously point a specific part of a spacecraft at a planet, then the nose of the spacecraft will always point in the same direction throughout its orbit. As a result, there will be times in each orbit when it appears to fly backward (see Figure 14-3).

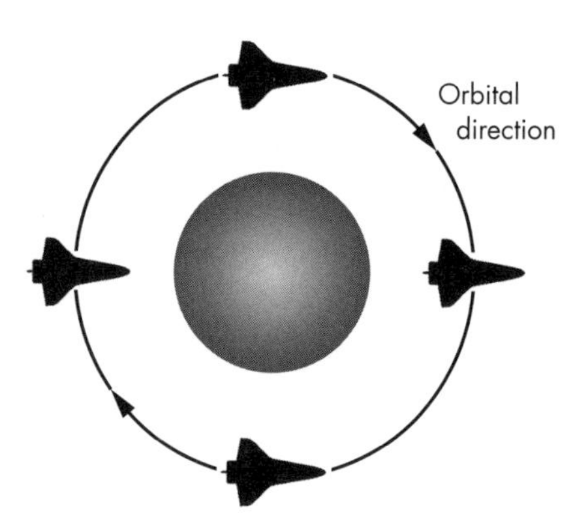

Figure 14-3: Spacecraft retain the same attitude in orbit unless forced to do otherwise.

You can blame this on Newton and his law of inertia, which states that an object at rest stays at rest and an object in motion stays in motion with the same speed and in the same direction unless acted upon by an unbalanced force.

Raising and Lowering Orbits

Brakes don't work in space, there's no friction, and inertia takes itself very seriously. To lower a spacecraft's orbit, you have to fire thrusters to reduce its velocity so that it falls farther into a planet's gravity well. To accomplish this, you have to *retrograde* your spacecraft so that its nose faces away from the present velocity vector—a fancy way of saying you have to fly tail-first. This assumes, of course, that the main thrusters are at the back of the spacecraft. Conversely, if you want to raise the orbit, you have to *prograde* the spacecraft, so that its nose will be pointed in the direction you are traveling. These two concepts are shown in Figure 14-4.

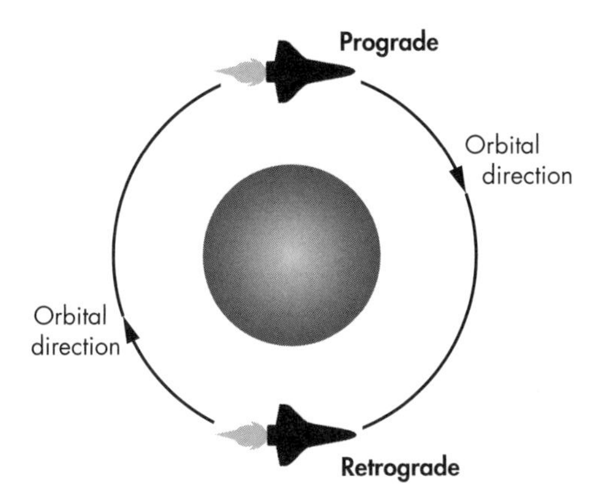

Figure 14-4: Prograde and retrograde are defined by the orientation of a spacecraft's nose with respect to the direction it is traveling around the body it is orbiting.

Taking the Inside Track

If you're chasing another spacecraft in orbit, do you speed up or slow down to catch it? According to Kepler's second law, you slow down. This will lower your orbit, resulting in a faster orbital velocity. Just as in horse racing, you want to take the inside track.

On the left side of Figure 14-5, two space shuttles are side by side in essentially the same orbit, traveling at the same velocity.

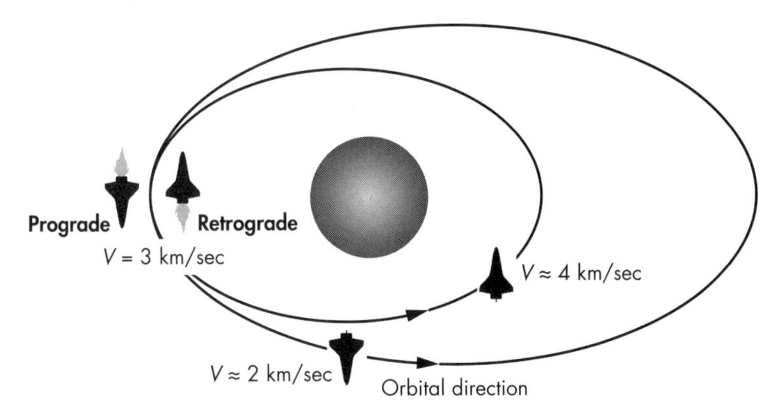

Figure 14-5: The orbital paradox: slow down to speed up!

The shuttle closest to the planet rotates 180 degrees and does a retrograde thrust to slow its immediate velocity. The outer shuttle performs a prograde thrust that increases its immediate velocity. They simultaneously stop thrusting, and the inner shuttle drops to a lower orbit while the outer shuttle transfers to a higher orbit. After an hour or so, the inner shuttle is traveling much faster, due to its closer proximity to the planet, and is well on its way to catch and lap the outer shuttle.

Circularizing an Elliptical Orbit

You can make highly elliptical orbits circular by applying engine impulses at either the *apoapsis* or *periapsis*, depending on the situation. The apoapsis (called the *apogee* if the object is orbiting Earth) is the highest point in an elliptical orbit—the point where the object is the farthest away from the body it is orbiting (Figure 14-6). The periapsis (*perigee* if the object's orbiting Earth) is the point lowest in an orbit.

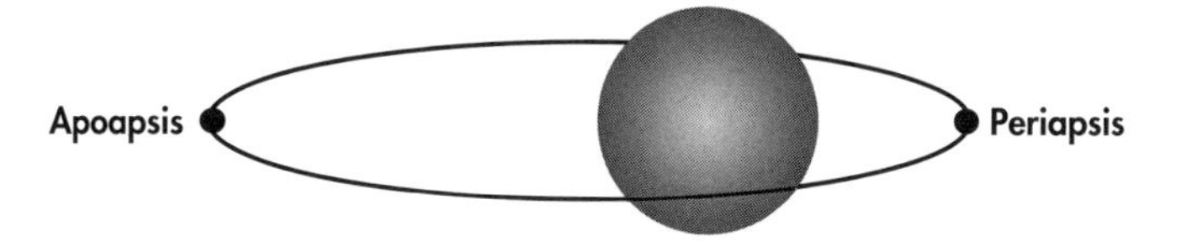

Figure 14-6: Location of the apoapsis and periapsis in an elliptical orbit

To raise the periapsis, the spacecraft performs a prograde thrust at the apoapsis (see the left-hand side of Figure 14-7). To lower the orbit while circularizing, the spacecraft must perform a retrograde thrust at the periapsis (see the right-hand side of Figure 14-7).

A somewhat counterintuitive part of this maneuver is that the initial orbit—that's the orbit that would have been—and the final, or actual, orbit will coincide at the point the engine impulse was applied.

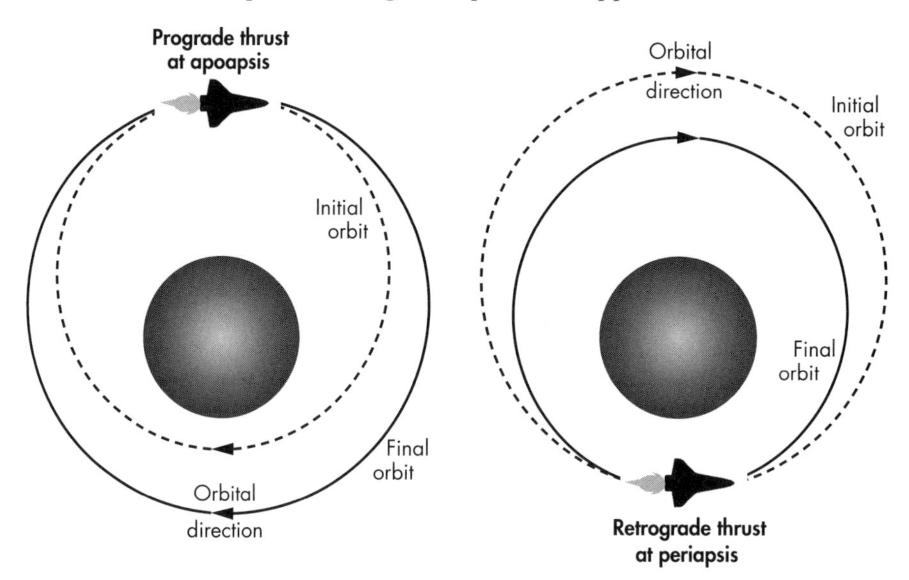

Figure 14-7: Circularizing and raising an orbit at apoapsis (left) and circularizing and lowering an orbit at periapsis (right)

Raising and Lowering Orbits with the Hohmann Transfer

A *Hohmann transfer orbit* uses an elliptical orbit to switch between two circular orbits in the same plane (see Figure 14-8). The orbit can be either raised or lowered. The maneuver is relatively slow, but it consumes the least possible amount of fuel.

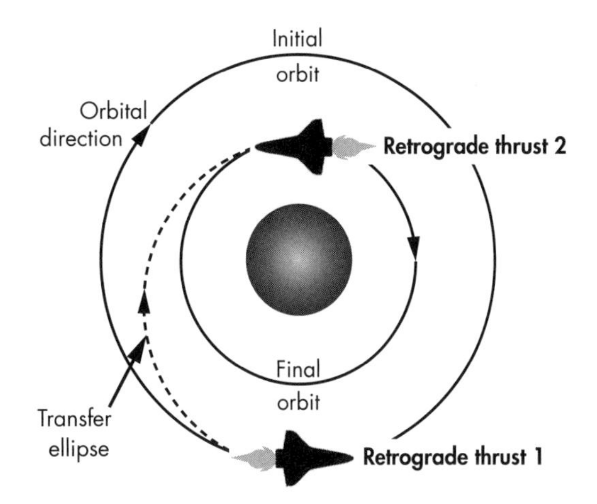

Figure 14-8: Transferring to a lower circular orbit with the Hohmann transfer technique

To change to an orbit with both a different periapsis *and* apoapsis, a spacecraft requires two engine impulses. One impulse moves the spacecraft onto the transfer orbit, and another moves it onto the final, destination orbit. When raising an orbit, the spacecraft applies the change in velocity in the direction of motion, and when lowering an orbit, it applies the change of velocity opposite to the direction of motion. The velocity changes have to occur at opposite sides of the orbit, as shown in Figure 14-8. Without the second thrust, the orbits will still intersect at the point of the first thrust, as shown on the right side of Figure 14-7.

Raising and Lowering Orbits with the One-Tangent Burn

The *One-Tangent Burn* technique transfers a spacecraft between orbits faster but less efficiently than a Hohmann transfer. A *burn* is just another term for thrust or impulse. As with the Hohmann transfer, orbits can be either raised or lowered.

The maneuver requires two engine impulses, the first tangential to the orbit and the second nontangential (see Figure 14-9). If the initial orbit is circular, as in the figure, then all points along it represent both the apoapsis and the periapsis, and the spacecraft can apply its first burn at any time.

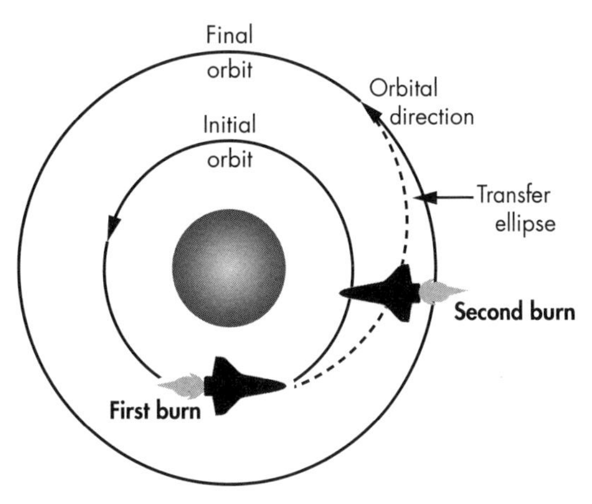

Figure 14-9: Transferring to a higher circular orbit with the One-Tangent Burn

Just as with the Hohmann transfer, a prograde burn raises the orbit, and a retrograde burn lowers it. If the orbit is elliptical, the first burn would be a prograde burn at the apoapsis to raise the orbit, or a retrograde burn at periapsis to lower it.

Executing a Spiral Orbit with the Spiral Transfer

A *spiral transfer* uses a continuous, low-thrust burn to change the size of an orbit. In gameplay, you can simulate this using retrograde or prograde burns that are short and regularly spaced, like those shown in Figure 14-10.

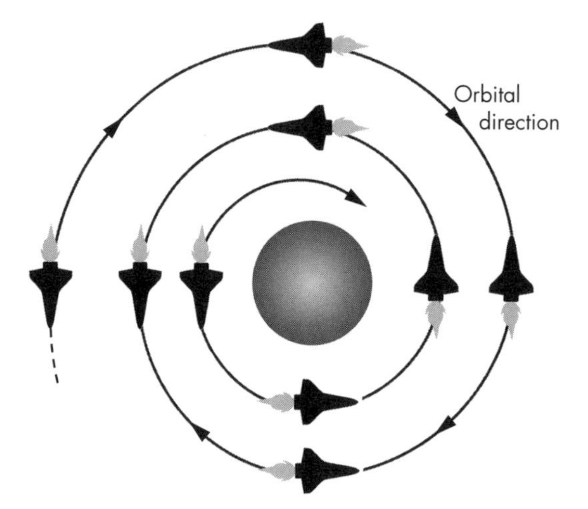

Figure 14-10: Executing a spiral orbit using short retrograde burns at regular intervals

To lower an orbit, all the burns must be retrograde; to raise an orbit, the spacecraft uses prograde burns.

Executing Synchronous Orbits

In a *synchronous orbit*, a spacecraft takes the same amount of time to make one revolution around a planet as it takes the planet to make one rotation around its axis. If a synchronous orbit is parallel to the equator, with no orbital inclination, it is a *stationary* orbit; to an observer on the orbited body, the satellite appears motionless in a fixed position in the sky. Communications satellites commonly use *geostationary* orbits, which have an altitude of 22,236 miles around Earth. A similar orbit would be called *aerostationary* around Mars and *selenostationary* around the moon.

Project #22: The Mars Orbiter Game

In real life, a series of equations is used to precisely execute orbital maneuvers. In gameplay, you'll use your intuition, patience, and reflexes! You'll also need to fly by instruments to a certain extent, using mainly the spacecraft's altitude readout and a measure of the orbit's circularity.

THE OBJECTIVE

Use pygame to build an arcade game that teaches the fundamentals of orbital mechanics. The game's goal is to nudge a satellite into a circular mapping orbit without running out of fuel or burning up in the atmosphere.

The Strategy

Start the design phase with a game sketch, as you did in Chapter 13. This sketch should capture all of the salient points of the game, like how it will look, how it will sound, how things will move, and how the game will communicate with the player (Figure 14-11).

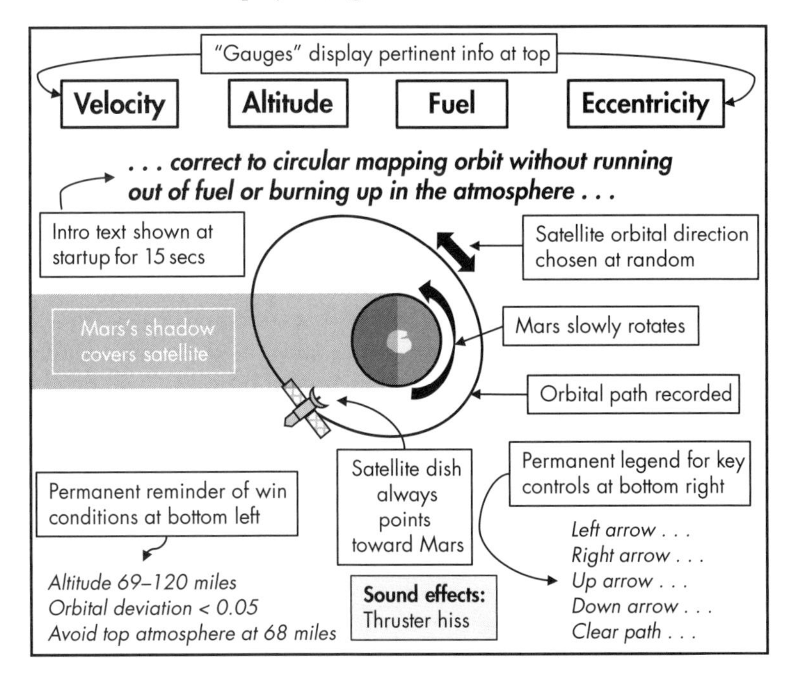

Figure 14-11: Sketch of the main gameplay of the Mars Orbiter game

The sketch in Figure 14-11 describes the main gameplay. You'll need a separate sketch to describe the win-lose conditions. For the main gameplay, the key points are:

- **The viewpoint is Mission Control.** The game screen should resemble a monitor at Mission Control from which the player can operate the errant space probe.
- **Mars is at front and center.** Everybody loves the Red Planet, so it will occupy the center of the jet-black screen.
- **Mars is animated.** The Martian globe will slowly rotate around its axis and cast a shadow. The satellite will dim appreciably when it passes through this shadow.
- **The satellite's initial orbit is chosen at random.** The satellite will appear at startup with a randomized—but constrained—orientation and velocity. On rare occasions, this may result in an instant game loss. That's still better than real missions, which fail 47 percent of the time!
- **There's no need to prograde or retrograde the satellite.** Constantly rotating the space probe before firing its thrusters greatly diminishes gameplay. Assume that attitudinal thrusters are arrayed around the fuselage and use the arrow keys to choose which thrusters to fire.
- **Firing thrusters causes an audible hiss.** Despite the fact that there's no sound in space, give the player the satisfaction of hearing a nice hiss whenever they fire the thrusters.
- **The satellite dish always points toward Mars.** The satellite will slowly and automatically rotate so that its remote-sensing dish is always aimed at Mars.
- **The satellite's orbital path is visible.** A thin white line will trail out from behind the satellite and persist until the player clears it by pressing the space bar.
- **The data readouts are placed at the top of the screen.** You will display information useful for gameplay in boxes at the top of the window. Key data are the space probe's velocity, altitude, fuel, and orbital eccentricity (a measure of the orbit's circularity).
- **A short introduction is shown at startup.** Text introducing the game will appear at the center of the screen when the game starts and stay up for about 15 seconds. The text will not disrupt gameplay, so the player can start manipulating the satellite immediately.
- **Win conditions and key controls are shown in permanent legends.** Critical information, like mission objectives and control keys, will be displayed permanently in the lower-left and -right corners of the screen.

The game sketch in Figure 14-12 describes what happens in success and failure cases. The player needs a reward when they win and an interesting outcome when they lose.

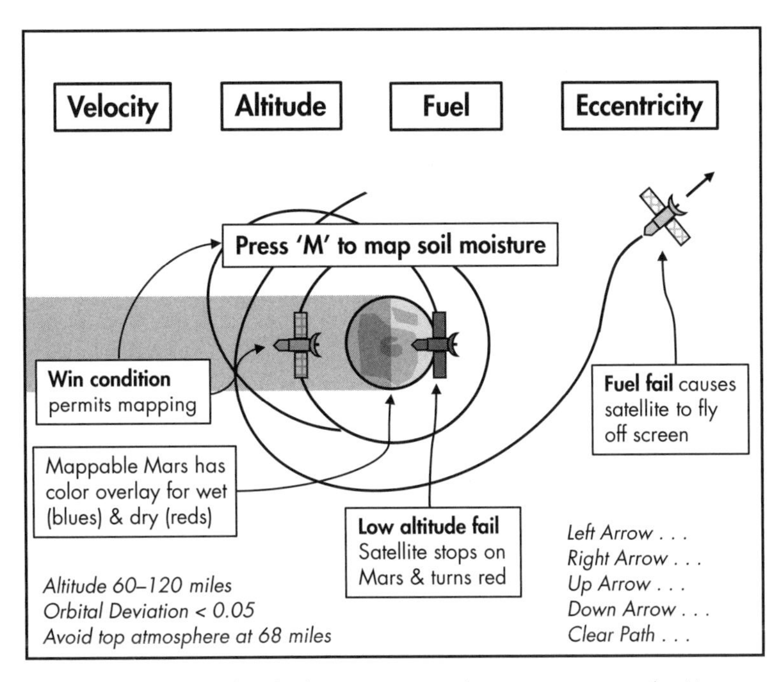

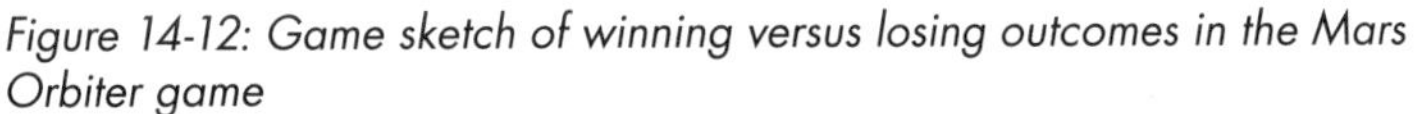

Figure 14-12: Game sketch of winning versus losing outcomes in the Mars Orbiter game

For winning and losing outcomes, the key points are:

- **Change the satellite image for crash and burn.** If the satellite's altitude drops below 68 miles, it burns up in the atmosphere. The moving satellite image will be replaced with a glowing red version that sticks to the side of Mars; this is similar to something you might see on a real Mission Control display.
- **The satellite is lost in space if it runs out of fuel.** Although unrealistic, have the satellite fly off the screen and into the depths of space if it runs out of fuel. This really rubs the player's nose in it!
- **Win conditions unlock a prize.** If the satellite achieves a circular orbit within the target altitude range, new text will urge the player to press the M key.
- **Pressing M changes the Mars image.** When the M key is unlocked, pressing it causes the Mars image to change to a rainbow image where cool colors represent areas of high soil moisture and warm colors represent drier areas.

For gameplay, the size of the satellite and its orbital speed won't be realistic, but the overall behavior will be correct. You should be able to correctly execute all of the orbital maneuvers described in "Astrodynamics for Gamers" on page 286.

Game Assets

The assets you'll need for the Mars Orbiter game are two satellite images, two planet images, and a sound file. You can prepare these together at the start of the process or build them when you need them. The latter approach lets you take episodic breaks from coding, which some people prefer.

Finding good, copyright-free graphics and sound files can be a challenge. You can find suitable assets online—either for free or for a fee—but it's best to make your own whenever possible. This lets you avoid any legal issues down the road.

The sprites (2D icons or images) I used for this project are shown in Figure 14-13. You need a satellite, a red "burned" version of the satellite, a view of Mars with a polar cap centered, and the same view with a colorful overlay that will represent mapped soil-moisture gradations. I found the satellite sprite at the free icon site AHA-SOFT (*http://www.aha-soft.com/*) and then copied and recolored it to make the crashed version. Both of the Mars sprites are NASA images modified for the game.

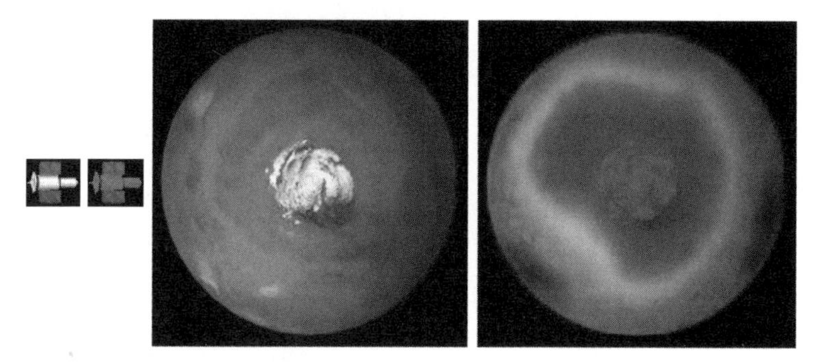

Figure 14-13: The satellite, crashed satellite, Mars, and Mars overlay images used as game sprites

I made a sound file for when the satellite is firing its thrusters using the white noise generator in the open source program Audacity. You can download a free copy of Audacity at *https://www.audacityteam.org/*. I saved the file in *Ogg Vorbis* format, an open source standard audio compression format that is free and works well with Python and `pygame`. You can use other formats, like MP3 and WAV, with `pygame`, but some have documented problems or have proprietary components that can raise legal issues if you try to commercialize your game.

You can download these files from this book's website at *https://www.nostarch.com/impracticalpython/* as *satellite.png*, *satellite_crash_40x33.png*, *mars.png*, *mars_water.png*, and *thrust_audio.ogg*. Download them, preserving the filenames, into the same folder as the code.

The Code

Figure 14-14 is an example of the final game screen you'll be building. You can refer back to this figure to get an idea of what the code is doing.

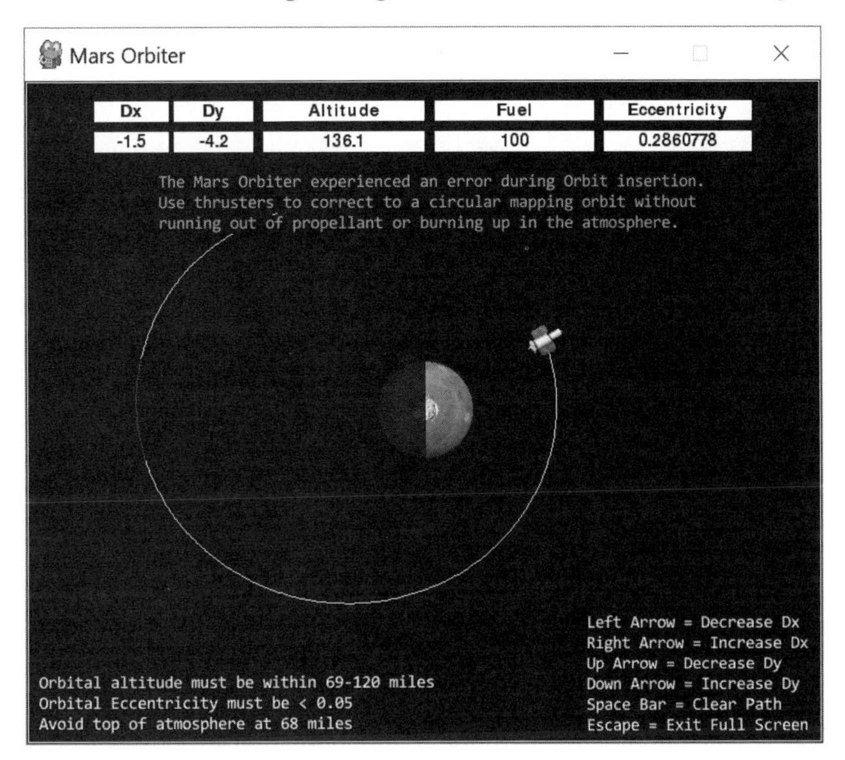
Mars Orbiter
Dx
Dy
Altitude
Fuel
Eccentricity
-1.5
-4.2
136.1
100
0.2860778
The Mars Orbiter experienced an error during Orbit insertion.
Use thrusters to correct to a circular mapping orbit without
running out of propellant or burning up in the atmosphere.
Left Arrow = Decrease Dx
Right Arrow = Increase Dx
Up Arrow = Decrease Dy
Down Arrow = Increase Dy
Space Bar = Clear Path
Escape = Exit Full Screen
Orbital altitude must be within 69-120 miles
Orbital Eccentricity must be < 0.05
Avoid top of atmosphere at 68 miles

Figure 14-14: Example startup game screen for the final version of mars_orbiter.py

You can download the complete program (*mars_orbiter.py*) at *https://www.nostarch.com/impracticalpython/*.

Importing and Building a Color Table

Listing 14-1 imports the required modules and builds a color table.

mars_orbiter.py, part 1

```
❶ import os
  import math
  import random
  import pygame as pg

❷ WHITE = (255, 255, 255)
  BLACK = (0, 0, 0)
  RED = (255, 0, 0)
  GREEN = (0, 255, 0)
  LT_BLUE = (173, 216, 230)
```

Listing 14-1: Imports modules and builds a color table

First, import the operating system, designated by os ❶. The game will launch in full-screen mode, but the player will have the option of escaping out of full screen. This module will let you control the location of the game window after the player presses ESC.

You'll use the math module for gravity and trigonometric calculations and random to start the satellite off with a random position and velocity. Import pygame as you did in Chapter 13, using pg, rather than pygame, to reduce typing.

Finish by building an RGB color table ❷ as you did in Chapter 13. This lets you type in color names, rather than RGB-value tuples, when you need to assign one of these colors.

Defining the Satellite Class Initialization Method

Listing 14-2 defines the Satellite class and its initialization method, which you'll use to instantiate a satellite object in the game. Since this method definition is long, it's split over two listings.

mars_orbiter.py, part 2

```
❶ class Satellite(pg.sprite.Sprite):
      """Satellite object that rotates to face planet & crashes & burns."""

   ❷ def __init__(self, background):
       ❸ super().__init__()
       ❹ self.background = background
       ❺ self.image_sat = pg.image.load("satellite.png").convert()
          self.image_crash = pg.image.load("satellite_crash_40x33.png").convert()
       ❻ self.image = self.image_sat
       ❼ self.rect = self.image.get_rect()
       ❽ self.image.set_colorkey(BLACK)  # sets transparent color
```

Listing 14-2: Defines the first part of the Satellite class initialization method

Define a class for a Satellite object ❶; if you need a refresher on object-oriented programming, read Chapter 11. Pass it the pygame Sprite class, as objects instantiated from the Satellite class will be sprites. As described in Chapter 13, Sprite is a built-in class that serves as a template for making sprites. Your new class will inherit features that your sprites will need from this base class. These include important attributes like rect and image, which you'll deal with shortly.

Next, define the __init__() method for the Satellite object ❷ and pass it self, which—by convention—is a special name within a class definition that refers to the current object. You also need to pass the method a background object. The satellite's path will be drawn on this object.

Inside the __init_() method, immediately invoke the initialization method for the built-in Sprite class using super ❸. This will initialize the sprite and establish the rect and image attributes it needs. With super, you don't need to refer to the base class (Sprite) explicitly. For more on super, see Listing 11-5 on page 229 or visit the docs at *https://docs.python.org/3/library/functions.html?highlight=super#super.*

Next, assign the background to self as an object attribute ❹. Then use pygame's image.load() method to load your two satellite images—one operational and one crashed—and in the same step, run the convert() method on them ❺. This converts the object into a graphic format that pygame can use efficiently once the game loop starts. Without this step, the game may slow noticeably as the png format is converted, on the fly, 30 or more times per second.

You'll use only one of the satellite images at a time, depending on whether or not the player burned up in the atmosphere, so use a generic self.image attribute to hold the loaded and converted image ❻. The unburned satellite image will be the default image; it will be replaced with the red crashed image if the satellite object gets too close to Mars.

Now, get the rectangle information for the image ❼. Remember that pygame places the sprites on rectangular surface objects, and it needs to know the dimensions and location of these rectangles as the game runs.

Finally, make the black parts of the satellite image invisible ❽. The satellite icon is on a field of black (see Figure 14-13), and you want the crashed-and-burned image to plot partially over Mars, so use the BLACK constant with the image object's colorkey() method in order to make the icon's background transparent. Otherwise, you'll see a black box with a red satellite overlapping the Red Planet. Note that if you want to type in the RGB equivalent for black, you need to enter it as a tuple: (0, 0, 0).

Setting the Satellite's Initial Position, Speed, Fuel, and Sound

Listing 14-3 completes the definition of the Satellite class initialization method. The satellite object's initial position and velocity are chosen at random from a limited range of choices; the orientation of the remote-sensing dish is initialized, the fuel tank topped off, and sound effects added.

mars_orbiter.py, part 3

```
❶ self.x = random.randrange(315, 425)
  self.y = random.randrange(70, 180)
❷ self.dx = random.choice([-3, 3])
❸ self.dy = 0
❹ self.heading = 0  # initializes dish orientation
❺ self.fuel = 100
  self.mass = 1
  self.distance = 0  # initializes distance between satellite & planet
❻ self.thrust = pg.mixer.Sound('thrust_audio.ogg')
❼ self.thrust.set_volume(0.07)  # valid values are 0-1
```

Listing 14-3: Completes the Satellite class initialization method by initializing parameters

When the game starts, the satellite will appear at a random point near the top of the screen. You'll choose the exact location from a range of x- and y-values ❶.

You'll also choose the satellite's velocity at random, but it will be slow enough that the satellite can't escape from orbit. Randomly set the velocity to either –3 or 3. Negative values result in a counterclockwise orbit, and vice versa. Use the delta-x (dx) attribute only ❷ and let gravity take care of dy. As discussed in Chapter 13, pygame moves sprites around the screen using incremental changes in the x-location (called delta-x or *dx*) and incremental changes in the y-location (called delta-y or *dy*). These vector components are calculated and added to the sprite's current position (self.x, self.y) with each game loop.

Next, set the dy attribute to 0 ❸. Later, the gravity() method will establish an initial dy value when it accelerates the newly instantiated satellite downscreen toward the planet.

Assign an attribute for the satellite's heading ❹. The remote-sensing dish, which will read soil moisture on the planet's surface, should always point toward Mars, and if you remember from Figure 14-3, this won't occur unless you overcome inertia. You'll use a method to actually rotate the satellite, so for now, just initialize the heading attribute with 0.

Now, top off the fuel tank with 100 units of fuel ❺. If you want to relate this to real life, it would probably represent 100 kilograms of hydrazine, similar to what was used in the *Magellan* probe that mapped Venus.

Next, set the object's mass to 1. This basically means you'll just use the mass of Mars in the gravity equation, because you multiply the masses of two objects together. As stated earlier, the pull of the satellite on Mars is inconsequential, so you don't need to calculate it. The satellite's mass attribute is included for completeness and as a placeholder in case you want to experiment with different values later.

The following distance attribute stores the distance between the satellite and the body it is orbiting. The actual value will be calculated by a method you'll define later.

It's time to add sound effects. You'll initialize pygame's sound mixer in the main() function, but for now, name a thrust attribute for the thrusting sound effect ❻. Pass the mixer's Sound class the short clip of white noise in Ogg Vorbis format (*.ogg*). Finally, set the playback volume, using values between 0 and 1 ❼. You may need to calibrate this to your PC. Ideally, you want a value that every player will be able to at least *hear* and then fine-tune with their own computer's volume control.

Firing Thrusters and Checking for Player Input

Listing 14-4 defines the thruster() and check_keys() methods of the Satellite class. The first determines the actions taken if one of the satellite's thrusters is fired. The second checks whether a player has interacted with the thrusters by pressing an arrow key.

mars_orbiter.py, part 4

```
❶ def thruster(self, dx, dy):
       """Execute actions associated with firing thrusters."""
     ❷ self.dx += dx
       self.dy += dy
     ❸ self.fuel -= 2
     ❹ self.thrust.play()

❺ def check_keys(self):
       """Check if user presses arrow keys & call thruster() method."""
     ❻ keys = pg.key.get_pressed()
```

```
        # fire thrusters
    ❼ if keys[pg.K_RIGHT]:
        ❽ self.thruster(dx=0.05, dy=0)
        elif keys[pg.K_LEFT]:
            self.thruster(dx=-0.05, dy=0)
        elif keys[pg.K_UP]:
            self.thruster(dx=0, dy=-0.05)
        elif keys[pg.K_DOWN]:
            self.thruster(dx=0, dy=0.05)
```

Listing 14-4: Defines the thruster() and check_keys() methods for the Satellite class

The thruster() method takes self, dx, and dy as arguments ❶. The last two arguments, which can be positive or negative, are immediately added to the satellite's self.dx and self.dy velocity components ❷. Next, the fuel level is decreased by two units ❸. Altering this value is one way to make the game either harder or easier. Finish by calling the play() method on the thrust audio attribute to make the hissing sound ❹. Note that, instead of *returning* values, OOP methods *update* existing object attributes.

The check_keys() method takes self as an argument ❺. First you use the pygame key module to determine whether the player has pressed a key ❻. The get_pressed() method returns a tuple of Boolean values—1 for True and 0 for False—that represent the current state of each key on the keyboard. True means a key has been pressed. You can index this tuple by using the key constants. You can find a list of all the keyboard constants at *https://www.pygame.org/docs/ref/key.html.*

For example, the right arrow key is K_RIGHT. If this key has been pressed ❼, call the thruster() method and pass it dx and dy values ❽. In pygame, x-values increase toward the right of the screen, and y-values increase toward the bottom of the screen. So, if the user presses the left arrow key, subtract from dx; likewise, if the up arrow is pressed, decrement the dy value. The right arrow will increase dx, and the down arrow will increase dy. Readouts at the top of the screen will help the player relate the satellite's movements to the underlying dx and dy values (see Figure 14-14).

Locating the Satellite

Still in the Satellite class, Listing 14-5 defines the locate() method. This method calculates the distance of the satellite from the planet and determines the heading for pointing the dish at the planet. You'll use the distance attribute later when calculating the force of gravity and the *eccentricity* of the orbit. Eccentricity is a measurement of the deviation of an orbit from a perfect circle.

mars_orbiter.py, part 5

```
❶ def locate(self, planet):
        """Calculate distance & heading to planet."""
    ❷ px, py = planet.x, planet.y
    ❸ dist_x = self.x - px
        dist_y = self.y - py
        # get direction to planet to point dish
    ❹ planet_dir_radians = math.atan2(dist_x, dist_y)
```

```
❺ self.heading = planet_dir_radians * 180 / math.pi
❻ self.heading -= 90  # sprite is traveling tail-first
❼ self.distance = math.hypot(dist_x, dist_y)
```

Listing 14-5: Defines the `locate()` *method for the* `Satellite` *class*

To locate the satellite, you need to pass the `locate()` method the `satellite` (`self`) and `planet` objects ❶. First, determine the distance between the objects in x-y space. Get the planet's x- and y-attributes ❷; then subtract them from the satellite's x- and y-attributes ❸.

Now, use these new distance variables to calculate the angle between the satellite's heading and the planet so you can rotate the satellite dish toward the planet. The `math` module uses radians, so assign a local variable called `planet_dir_radians` to hold the direction in radians and pass `dist_x` and `dist_y` to the `math.atan2()` function to calculate the arc tangent ❹. Since `pygame` uses degrees (sigh), convert the angle from radians to degrees using the standard formula; alternatively, you could use `math` to do this, but sometimes it's good to see the man behind the curtain ❺. This should be a sharable attribute of the satellite object, so name it `self.heading`.

In `pygame`, the front of a sprite is to the east by default, which means the satellite sprite is orbiting tail-first (see the satellite icon in Figure 14-13). To get the dish to point toward Mars, you need to subtract 90 degrees from the heading, because negative angles result in *clockwise* rotation in `pygame` ❻. This maneuver will use none of the player's fuel allotment.

Finally, get the Euclidian distance between the satellite and Mars by using the `math` module to calculate the hypotenuse from the x- and y-components ❼. You should make this an attribute of the satellite object since you will use it later in other functions.

NOTE *In real life, there are multiple ways to keep the dish of a satellite pointed toward a planet without expending large amounts of fuel. Techniques include slowly tumbling or spinning the satellite, making the dish end heavier than the opposite end, using magnetic torque, or using internal flywheels—also known as reaction wheels or momentum wheels. Flywheels use electric motors that can be powered by solar panels, eliminating the need for heavy and toxic liquid propellant.*

Rotating the Satellite and Drawing Its Orbit

Listing 14-6 continues the `Satellite` class by defining methods for rotating the satellite dish toward the planet and drawing a path behind it. Later, in the `main()` function, you'll add code that lets the player erase and restart the path by pressing the space bar.

mars_orbiter.py, part 6

```
❶ def rotate(self):
      """Rotate satellite using degrees so dish faces planet."""
    ❷ self.image = pg.transform.rotate(self.image_sat, self.heading)
    ❸ self.rect = self.image.get_rect()

❹ def path(self):
```

```
        """Update satellite's position & draw line to trace orbital path."""
    ❺ last_center = (self.x, self.y)
    ❻ self.x += self.dx
        self.y += self.dy
    ❼ pg.draw.line(self.background, WHITE, last_center, (self.x, self.y))
```

Listing 14-6: Defines the `rotate()` and `path()` methods of the `Satellite` class

The `rotate()` method will use the `heading` attribute, which you calculate in the `locate()` method, to turn the satellite dish toward Mars. Pass `self` to `rotate()` ❶, which means `rotate()` will automatically take the name of the satellite object as an argument when it is called later.

Now, rotate the satellite image using `pygame`'s `transform.rotate()` method ❷. Pass it the original image followed by the `heading` attribute; assign these to the `self.image` attribute so you don't degrade the original master image. You'll need to transform the image with each game loop, and transforming an image rapidly degrades it. So always keep a master image and work off a new copy every time you do a transformation.

End the function by getting the transformed image's `rect` object ❸.

Next, define a method called `path()` and pass it `self` ❹. This will draw a line marking the satellite's path, and since you need two points to draw a line, assign a variable to record the satellite's center location as a tuple prior to moving it ❺. Then increment the x- and y-locations with the `dx` and `dy` attributes ❻. Finish by using `pygame`'s `draw.line()` method to define the line ❼. This method needs a drawing object, so pass it the `background` attribute, followed by the line color and the previous and current x-y location tuples.

Updating the Satellite Object

Listing 14-7 updates the satellite object and completes the class definition. Sprite objects almost always have an `update()` method that is called once per frame as the game runs. Anything that happens to the sprite, such as movement, color changes, user interactions, and so on, is included in this method. To keep them from becoming too cluttered, `update()` methods mostly call other methods.

mars_orbiter.py, part 7

```
❶ def update(self):
        """Update satellite object during game."""
    ❷ self.check_keys()
    ❸ self.rotate()
    ❹ self.path()
    ❺ self.rect.center = (self.x, self.y)
        # change image to fiery red if in atmosphere
    ❻ if self.dx == 0 and self.dy == 0:
            self.image = self.image_crash
            self.image.set_colorkey(BLACK)
```

Listing 14-7: Defines the `update()` method for the `Satellite` class

Start by defining the `update()` method and passing it the object, or `self` ❶. Next, call the methods that you defined earlier. The first of these checks for player interactions made through the keyboard ❷. The second rotates the satellite object so that the dish keeps pointing toward the planet ❸. The final method updates the satellite's x-y location and draws a path behind it so you can visualize the orbit ❹.

The program needs to keep track of the satellite sprite's location as it orbits Mars, so assign a `rect.center` attribute and set it to the satellite's current x-y location ❺.

The final bit of code changes the satellite image in the event the player crashes and burns in the atmosphere ❻. The top of the Martian atmosphere is about 68 miles above its *surface*. For reasons I'll explain later, assume that an altitude value of 68—which is measured in pixels from the *center* of the planet—equates to the top of the atmosphere. If the satellite dips below this altitude during gameplay, the `main()` function will set its velocity—represented by `dx` and `dy`—to `0`. Check that these values are both `0`, and if so, change the image to `image_crash` and set its background to transparent (as you did previously for the main satellite image).

Defining the Planet Class Initialization Method

Listing 14-8 defines the `Planet` class, which you'll use to instantiate a `planet` object.

mars_orbiter.py, part 8

```
❶ class Planet(pg.sprite.Sprite):
      """Planet object that rotates & projects gravity field."""

    ❷ def __init__(self):
          super().__init__()
        ❸ self.image_mars = pg.image.load("mars.png").convert()
          self.image_water = pg.image.load("mars_water.png").convert()
        ❹ self.image_copy = pg.transform.scale(self.image_mars, (100, 100))
        ❺ self.image_copy.set_colorkey(BLACK)
        ❻ self.rect = self.image_copy.get_rect()
          self.image = self.image_copy
        ❼ self.mass = 2000
        ❽ self.x = 400
          self.y = 320
          self.rect.center = (self.x, self.y)
        ❾ self.angle = math.degrees(0)
          self.rotate_by = math.degrees(0.01)
```

Listing 14-8: Begins definition of the `Planet` class

You are probably very familiar with the initial steps to creating the `Planet` class by now. First, you name the class with a capital letter, then pass it the `Sprite` class so it will conveniently inherit features from this built-in `pygame` class ❶. Next, you define an `__init__()`, or initialization, method for your `planet` object ❷. Then you call the `super()` initialization method, as you did for the `Satellite` class.

Load the images as attributes and convert them to `pygame`'s graphic format at the same time ❸. You need both the normal Mars image and the one for mapped soil moisture. You were able to use the satellite sprite at its native size, but the Mars image is too large. Scale the image to 100 pixels × 100 pixels ❹ and assign the scaled image to a new attribute so repeated transformations won't degrade the master image.

Now, set the transformed image's transparent color to black, as you did earlier with the satellite image ❺. Sprites in `pygame` are all "mounted" on rectangular surfaces, and if you don't make black invisible, the corners of the planet surface may overlap and cover the white-colored orbital path drawn by the satellite (see Figure 14-15).

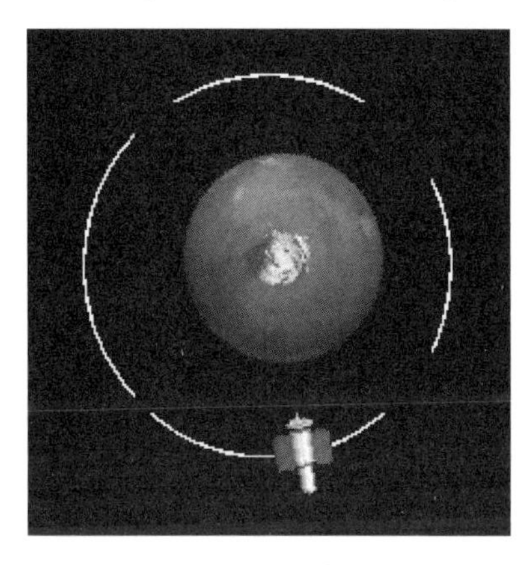

Figure 14-15: Corners of Mars `rect` covering orbital path

As always, get the sprite's `rect` object ❻. There's another transformation to come, so copy the image attribute again and assign it the logical name of `self.image`.

To apply the force of gravity, the planet needs mass, so name a `mass` attribute and assign it a value of `2000` ❼. Earlier, you assigned the satellite a mass of `1`; this means that Mars is only 2,000 times as massive as a satellite! That's okay, because you aren't working in real-world units, and the time and distance scales differ from reality. If you scale distances so that the satellite is only a few hundred pixels from Mars, you have to scale gravity as well. Despite this, the satellite will still behave realistically with respect to gravity.

The planet's mass value was determined through experimentation. To scale the force of gravity, you can either change this mass value or use the gravitational constant (`G`) variable later.

Set the `planet` object's `x` and `y` attributes to the center point of the screen—you'll use a screen size of 800 × 645 in the `main()` function—and assign these values to the `rect` object's center ❽.

Finally, assign the attributes you'll need to slowly rotate Mars about its axis ❾. You'll use the same `transform_rotate()` method you used to turn the satellite, so you need to create an `angle` attribute. Then, use a `rotate_by` attribute to assign the increment—in degrees—by which this rotation angle changes with each game loop.

Rotating the Planet

Listing 14-9 continues the Planet class by defining its rotate() method. This method rotates the planet around its axis, making small changes with each game loop.

mars_orbiter.py, part 9

```
❶ def rotate(self):
       """Rotate the planet image with each game loop."""
     ❷ last_center = self.rect.center
     ❸ self.image = pg.transform.rotate(self.image_copy, self.angle)
       self.rect = self.image.get_rect()
     ❹ self.rect.center = last_center
     ❺ self.angle += self.rotate_by
```

Listing 14-9: Defines a method to rotate the planet around its axis

The rotate() method also takes the object as an argument ❶. As the square Mars image is rotating, the bounding rectangle object (rect) remains stationary and must expand to accommodate the new configuration (see Figure 14-16). This change in size can affect the center point of the rect, so assign a last_center variable and set it to the planet's current center point ❷. If you don't do this, Mars will wobble around its axis as the game runs.

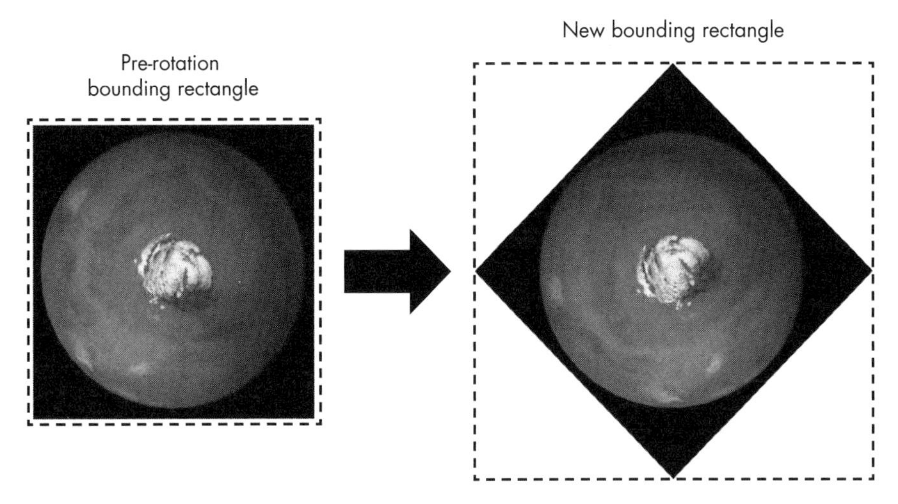

Figure 14-16: The bounding rectangle changes size to accommodate rotating images.

Next, rotate the copied image using pygame's transform.rotate() method and assign it to the self.image attribute ❸; you need to pass the method the copied image and the angle attribute. Immediately after rotating, reset the image's rect attribute and move its center location back to last_center in order to mitigate any shifting of rect that occurred during rotation ❹.

When the planet object is instantiated, the angle attribute will start at 0 degrees, then increase by 0.1—assigned in the rotate_by attribute—with each frame ❺.

Defining the gravity() and update() Methods

Listing 14-10 completes the `Planet` class by defining the `gravity()` and `update()` methods. In Chapter 13, you treated gravity as a constant applied in the y-direction. The method applied here is slightly more sophisticated, because it takes into account the distance between two objects.

mars_orbiter.py, part 10

```
❶ def gravity(self, satellite):
        """Calculate impact of gravity on satellite."""
      ❷ G = 1.0  # gravitational constant for game
      ❸ dist_x = self.x - satellite.x
        dist_y = self.y - satellite.y
        distance = math.hypot(dist_x, dist_y)
        # normalize to a unit vector
      ❹ dist_x /= distance
        dist_y /= distance
        # apply gravity
      ❺ force = G * (satellite.mass * self.mass) / (math.pow(distance, 2))
      ❻ satellite.dx += (dist_x * force)
        satellite.dy += (dist_y * force)

❼ def update(self):
        """Call the rotate method."""
        self.rotate()
```

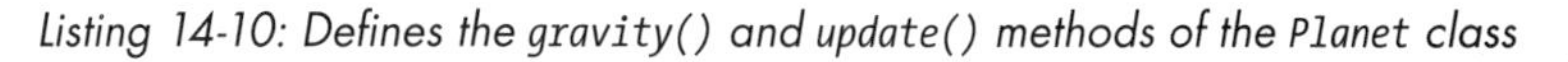

Listing 14-10: Defines the `gravity()` and `update()` methods of the `Planet` class

Define the `gravity()` method and pass it `self` and the satellite object ❶. You're still in the `Planet` class, so `self` here represents Mars.

Start by naming a local variable `G`; an uppercase G is the *universal gravitational constant*, also known as the *constant of proportionality* ❷. In real life, this is a very small, empirically derived number, which is basically a conversion number to get all the units to work out correctly. You're not using real-world units in the game, so set this to `1`; this way, it won't have an impact on the gravity equation. During game development, you can tweak this constant up or down to fine-tune the force of gravity and its effect on orbiting objects.

You need to know how far apart the two objects are, so get their distance in the x-direction and the y-direction ❸. Then, use the `math` module's `hypot()` method to get the Euclidian distance. This will represent the *r* in the gravity equation.

Since you're going to directly address the *magnitude* of the distance between the satellite and Mars in the gravity equation, all you need from the distance vector is *direction*. So, divide `dist_x` and `dist_y` by `distance` to "normalize" the vector to a unit vector with a magnitude of `1` ❹. You are basically dividing the length of each side of a right triangle by its hypotenuse. This preserves the vector's direction, represented by the relative differences in `dist_x` and `dist_y`, but sets its magnitude to `1`. Note that if you don't perform this normalization step, the results will be unrealistic but interesting (see Figure 14-17).

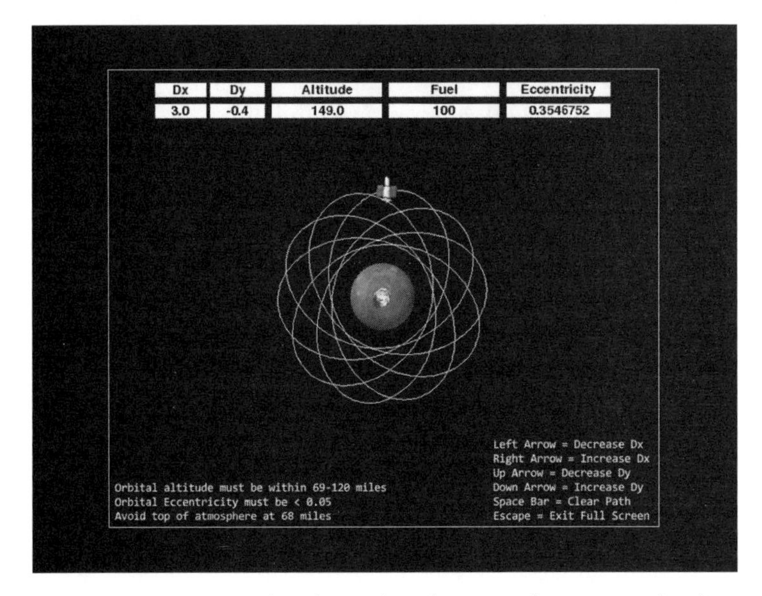

Figure 14-17: "Spirograph" orbit resulting from use of an unnormalized distance vector

Calculate the force of gravity using Newton's equation, which I described in "The Law of Universal Gravity" on page 286 ❺. Finish by multiplying the normalized distances by `force`—to calculate by how much acceleration changes velocity in each step—and add these amounts to the satellite object's `dx` and `dy` attributes ❻.

Note that you don't assign most of these variables as attributes of `self`. These just represent intermediate steps within a method that don't need to be shared with other methods, and you can treat them as you would local variables in procedural programming.

Finally, define a method that will be called every game loop to update the `planet` object ❼. Use it to call the `rotate()` method.

Calculating Eccentricity

You're through defining classes. Now it's time to define some functions that will help with running the game. Listing 14-11 defines a function to calculate the eccentricity of the satellite's orbit. The player will need to achieve a circular orbit within a certain altitude range, and this function will provide the measurement of circularity.

mars_orbiter.py, part 11

```
❶ def calc_eccentricity(dist_list):
      """Calculate & return eccentricity from list of radii."""
    ❷ apoapsis = max(dist_list)
      periapsis = min(dist_list)
    ❸ eccentricity = (apoapsis - periapsis) / (apoapsis + periapsis)
      return eccentricity
```

Listing 14-11: Defines a function to measure orbital eccentricity

Define the calc_eccentricity() function and pass it a list of distances ❶. In the main() function, you'll append the sat.distance attribute—which records the satellite's altitude—to this list during every game loop. To calculate eccentricity, you need to know both the apoapsis and periapsis of the orbit. Get these by finding the maximum and minimum values in this list ❷. Then, calculate eccentricity ❸. Later, in the main() function, you'll display this number to eight decimal places, just to look cool and precise in the readout.

Note that circular orbits will have the same value for both apoapsis and periapsis, and so the calculation will yield 0 for a perfect circle. End the function by returning the eccentricity variable.

Defining Functions to Make Labels

The game will need a fair amount of text for instructions and telemetry readouts. Displaying this text one string at a time can result in a lot of code redundancy, so Listing 14-12 will define two functions—one to post instructions and another for the streams of velocity, altitude, fuel, and eccentricity data you'll need to share with the player.

mars_orbiter.py, part 12

```
❶ def instruct_label(screen, text, color, x, y):
      """Take screen, list of strings, color, & origin & render text to screen."""
    ❷ instruct_font = pg.font.SysFont(None, 25)
    ❸ line_spacing = 22
    ❹ for index, line in enumerate(text):
          label = instruct_font.render(line, True, color, BLACK)
          screen.blit(label, (x, y + index * line_spacing))

❺ def box_label(screen, text, dimensions):
      """Make fixed-size label from screen, text & left, top, width, height."""
      readout_font = pg.font.SysFont(None, 27)
    ❻ base = pg.Rect(dimensions)
    ❼ pg.draw.rect(screen, WHITE, base, 0)
    ❽ label = readout_font.render(text, True, BLACK)
    ❾ label_rect = label.get_rect(center=base.center)
    ❿ screen.blit(label, label_rect)
```

Listing 14-12: Defines functions to make instruction and readout labels

Define a function called instruct_label() for displaying instructions on the game screen ❶. Pass it the screen, a list containing the text, a text color, and the coordinates for the upper-left corner of the pygame surface object that will hold the text.

Next, tell pygame which font to use ❷. The arguments for the font.SysFont() method are the typeface and size. Using None for the typeface invokes pygame's built-in default font, which should work on multiple platforms. Note that the method accepts both None and 'None'.

The introduction and instruction text will take up multiple lines (see the example in Figure 14-14). You'll need to specify the line spacing, in pixels, between the text strings, so assign a variable for this and set it to 22 ❸.

Now, start looping through the list of text strings ❹. Use `enumerate()` to get an index, which you'll use with the `line_spacing` variable to post the strings in the correct locations. The text will need to be placed on a surface. Name this surface `label`, pass the `font.render()` method the line of text you want to display, set antialiasing to `True` for smoother text, color the text, and set the background color to black. Finish by blitting the surface to the screen. Pass the method the `label` variable and the upper-left-corner coordinates, with `y` defined as `y + index * line_spacing`.

Next, define a function called `box_label()` for the data readout labels that will appear as gauges at the top of the screen (see Figure 14-18) ❺. Parameters for this function are the screen, some text, and a tuple containing the dimensions of the rectangular surface that will form the gauge.

Dx	Dy	Altitude	Fuel	Eccentricity
0.1	-3.4	158.7	100	0.20803277

Figure 14-18: Readout labels at the top of the game window (header label above and data label below)

The surfaces made by the `instruct_label()` function will automatically change size to accommodate the amount of text being displayed. This works fine for static displays, but the readout data will change constantly, causing your gauges to expand and shrink as they adjust to fit the text inside them. To mitigate this, you'll use a stand-alone `rect` object of a specified size to form a base for your text object.

Start the function by setting the font, as you did in ❷. Assign a variable called `base` to a `pygame rect` object; use the `dimensions` argument for the size ❻. This argument lets you precisely place the position of the box by specifying the left and top coordinates of the rectangle, followed by its width and height. The resulting rectangle should be wide enough to handle the longest possible readout the game will produce for the data type being displayed.

Now, draw the `base` using the `draw_rect()` method ❼. The arguments are the drawing surface, a fill color, the name of the `rect`, and a width of `0`, which fills the rectangle rather than drawing a border. You'll post your text object on top of this white rectangle.

Repeat the code that renders the text ❽, then get the `rect` for the `label` ❾. Note that in the `get_rect()` method there's a parameter that sets the center equal to the center of `base`. This lets you place the text label on top of the white base rectangle. Finally, blit to the screen, specifying the source and destination rects ❿.

Mapping Soil Moisture

Listing 14-13 defines functions that allow the player to "map" Mars if the game's winning conditions have been met. When the player presses the M key, these functions will be called by the `main()` function, and the planet's image will be replaced with a colorful overlay we'll pretend represents soil moisture content. When the player releases the key, the normal view of Mars will return. The key checks will also be performed in the `main()` function.

mars_orbiter.py, part 13

```
❶ def mapping_on(planet):
      """Show soil moisture image of planet."""
    ❷ last_center = planet.rect.center
    ❸ planet.image_copy = pg.transform.scale(planet.image_water, (100, 100))
    ❹ planet.image_copy.set_colorkey(BLACK)
      planet.rect = planet.image_copy.get_rect()
      planet.rect.center = last_center

❺ def mapping_off(planet):
      """Restore normal planet image."""
    ❻ planet.image_copy = pg.transform.scale(planet.image_mars, (100, 100))
      planet.image_copy.set_colorkey(BLACK)
```

Listing 14-13: Defines functions to let the player make a soil moisture map of Mars

Start by defining a function that takes as an argument the `planet` object ❶. Start by assigning a `last_center` variable as you did in Listing 14-9; this will be used to keep the planet from wobbling on its axis ❷.

Next, scale the water image of Mars to the same size as the normal image and assign this to the planet's `image_copy` attribute, because transformations degrade an image if used repeatedly ❸. Set the image's background to transparent ❹, get its `rect`, and set the center of the `rect` equal to the `last_center` variable; that way Mars will stay put at the center of the screen.

Now, define another function for when the player stops actively mapping Mars ❺. It also takes the `planet` object as an argument. All you need to do is reset the planet image to the original version ❻. Because you're still using the `image_copy` attribute, you don't need to get the `rect` again, but you do need to set the transparent color.

Casting a Shadow

Listing 14-14 defines a function that gives Mars a "dark side" and casts a shadow behind the planet. The shadow will be a black, semitransparent rectangle with its right edge coincident with the center of the planet sprite (see Figure 14-19). This assumes the sun is to the right of the screen and that it is either the vernal or autumnal equinox on Mars.

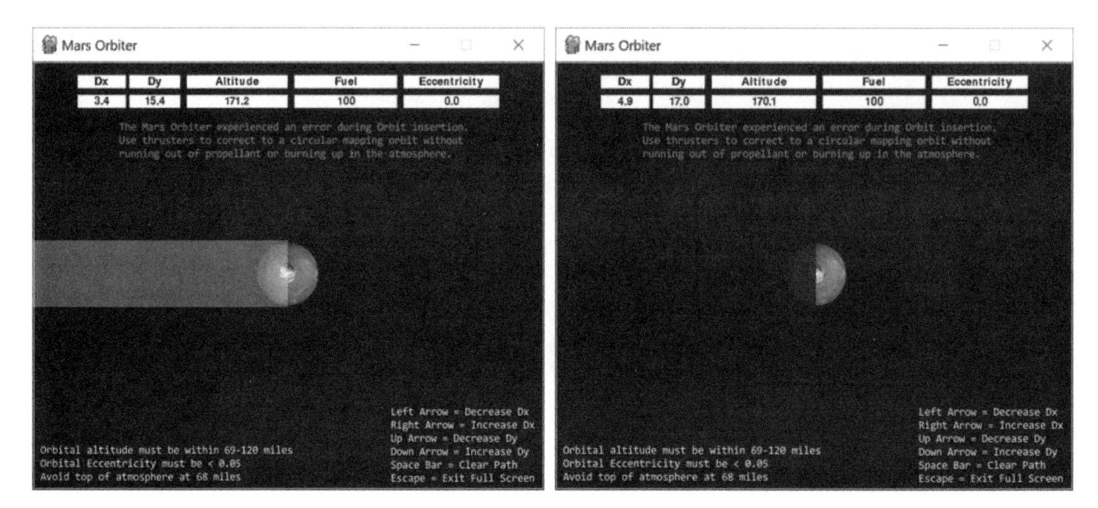
Mars Orbiter
Dx
Dy
Altitude
Fuel
Eccentricity
3.4
15.4
171.2
100
0.0
The Mars Orbiter experienced an error during Orbit insertion.
Use thrusters to correct to a circular mapping orbit without
running out of propellant or burning up in the atmosphere.
Left Arrow = Decrease Dx
Right Arrow = Increase Dx
Up Arrow = Decrease Dy
Down Arrow = Increase Dy
Space Bar = Clear Path
Escape = Exit Full Screen
Orbital altitude must be within 69-120 miles
Orbital Eccentricity must be < 0.05
Avoid top of atmosphere at 68 miles
Mars Orbiter
Dx
Dy
Altitude
Fuel
Eccentricity
4.9
17.0
170.1
100
0.0
The Mars Orbiter experienced an error during Orbit insertion.
Use thrusters to correct to a circular mapping orbit without
running out of propellant or burning up in the atmosphere.
Left Arrow = Decrease Dx
Right Arrow = Increase Dx
Up Arrow = Decrease Dy
Down Arrow = Increase Dy
Space Bar = Clear Path
Escape = Exit Full Screen
Orbital altitude must be within 69-120 miles
Orbital Eccentricity must be < 0.05
Avoid top of atmosphere at 68 miles

Figure 14-19: Shadow rectangle in semitransparent white (left) and final semitransparent black (right)

mars_orbiter.py, part 14

```
❶ def cast_shadow(screen):
       """Add optional terminator & shadow behind planet to screen."""
    ❷ shadow = pg.Surface((400, 100), flags=pg.SRCALPHA)  # tuple is w,h
    ❸ shadow.fill((0, 0, 0, 210))  # last number sets transparency
       screen.blit(shadow, (0, 270))  # tuple is top left coordinates
```

Listing 14-14: Defines a function to give Mars a dark side and let it cast a shadow

The `cast_shadow()` function takes the `screen` object as an argument ❶. Assign a 400 pixel × 100 pixel `pygame` surface to an object named `shadow` ❷. Use `pygame`'s `SRCALPHA` flag—for "source alpha"—to indicate you will use per pixel alpha (transparency). Fill the object with black and set alpha—represented by the last number—to `210` ❸. Alpha is part of the RGBA color system and has valid values of 0 through 255, so this is very dark but not completely opaque. Finally, blit the surface to the screen, along with the coordinates for its top-left corner. To turn off the shadow, just comment out the function call in `main()` or set the alpha value to `0`.

Defining the main() Function

Listing 14-15 begins the definition of the `main()` function that runs the game. The `pygame` package and the sound mixer are initialized, the game screen is set up, and instructions for the player are stored as lists.

mars_orbiter.py, part 15

```
def main():
    """Set up labels & instructions, create objects & run the game loop."""
 ❶ pg.init()  # initialize pygame

    # set up display:
 ❷ os.environ['SDL_VIDEO_WINDOW_POS'] = '700, 100'  # set game window origin
 ❸ screen = pg.display.set_mode((800, 645), pg.FULLSCREEN)
```

```
❹ pg.display.set_caption("Mars Orbiter")
❺ background = pg.Surface(screen.get_size())

❻ pg.mixer.init()  # for sound effects

❼ intro_text = [
       ' The Mars Orbiter experienced an error during Orbit insertion.',
       ' Use thrusters to correct to a circular mapping orbit without',
       ' running out of propellant or burning up in the atmosphere.'
       ]

   instruct_text1 = [
       'Orbital altitude must be within 69-120 miles',
       'Orbital Eccentricity must be < 0.05',
       'Avoid top of atmosphere at 68 miles'
       ]

   instruct_text2 = [
       'Left Arrow = Decrease Dx',
       'Right Arrow = Increase Dx',
       'Up Arrow = Decrease Dy',
       'Down Arrow = Increase Dy',
       'Space Bar = Clear Path',
       'Escape = Exit Full Screen'
       ]
```

Listing 14-15: Starts the `main()` *function by initializing* `pygame` *and the sound mixer and by setting up the game screen and instructions*

Start the `main()` function by initializing `pygame` ❶. Then, use the `os` module's `environ()` method to assign the coordinates of the upper-left corner of the game window ❷. This step is not strictly necessary, but I wanted to demonstrate that you have control over where windows appear on the desktop.

Next, assign a variable to hold the `screen` object and set the display mode to full screen ❸. Use the tuple `(800, 645)` to specify the screen size to use if the player escapes from full-screen mode.

Now use `pygame`'s `display.set_caption()` method to name the game window "Mars Orbiter" ❹. Then, use `pygame`'s `Surface` class to create a background object for the game that's the same size as the screen ❺.

Initialize `pygame`'s sound mixer so you can play the thruster sound effect ❻. You defined this sound earlier in the satellite's initialization method.

The game will start with a short introduction that will vanish after 15 seconds. Permanent legends describing keyboard controls and win conditions occupy the bottom corners of the screen. Enter the text for these as lists ❼. Later, you will pass these lists to the `instruct_label()` function you wrote in Listing 14-12. Each item in the list, delineated by a comma, will appear as a separate line in the game window (see Figure 14-19).

Instantiating Objects, Setting Up Orbit Verification, Mapping, and Timekeeping

Listing 14-16, still in the main() function, instantiates the planet and satellite objects, assigns some useful variables for determining orbital eccentricity, prepares the game clock within the function, and assigns a variable to track the state of the mapping functionality.

mars_orbiter.py, part 16

```
    # instantiate planet and satellite objects
❶  planet = Planet()
❷  planet_sprite = pg.sprite.Group(planet)
❸  sat = Satellite(background)
❹  sat_sprite = pg.sprite.Group(sat)

    # for circular orbit verification
❺  dist_list = []
❻  eccentricity = 1
❼  eccentricity_calc_interval = 5  # optimized for 120 mile altitude

    # time keeping
❽  clock = pg.time.Clock()
    fps = 30
    tick_count = 0

    # for soil moisture mapping functionality
❾  mapping_enabled = False
```

Listing 14-16: Instantiates objects and assigns useful variables in main()

Continue the main() function by creating a planet object from the Planet class ❶, then place it in a sprite group ❷. Remember from Chapter 13 that pygame manages sprites using containers called *groups*.

Next, instantiate a satellite object, passing the Satellite class's initialization method the background object ❸. The satellite needs the background for drawing its path.

After creating the satellite, put it in its own sprite group ❹. You should generally keep radically different sprite types in their own containers. This makes it easy to manage things like display order and collision handling.

Now, assign some variables to help with calculating eccentricity. Start an empty list to hold the distance values calculated in each game loop ❺, then assign an eccentricity variable a placeholder value of 1 ❻, indicating a noncircular starting orbit.

You'll want to update the eccentricity variable regularly to evaluate any changes the player makes to the orbit. Remember, you need the orbit's apoapsis and periapsis to calculate eccentricity, and for large, elliptical orbits, it may take a while to actually sample these. The good news is that you only need to consider "winning" orbits between 69 and 120 miles. So, you can optimize the sampling rate for orbits below 120 miles, which generally take the satellite sprite less than 6 seconds to complete. Use 5 seconds and assign this value to an eccentricity_calc_interval variable ❼. This means that, for orbits with altitudes above 120 miles, the calculated eccentricity may not be technically correct, but it will be good enough considering the orbit doesn't satisfy the winning conditions at that altitude.

Address timekeeping next. Use a `clock` variable to hold `pygame`'s game clock, which will control the speed of the game in frames per second ❽. Each frame will represent one tick of the clock. Assign a variable named `fps` a value of `30`, which means the game will update 30 times per second. Next, assign a `tick_count` variable that you'll use to determine when to clear the introduction text and when to call the `calc_eccentricity()` function.

Finish the section by naming a variable to enable the mapping functionality and set it to `False` ❾. If the player achieves the winning conditions, you'll change this to `True`.

Starting the Game Loop and Playing Sounds

Listing 14-17, still in the `main()` function, starts the game clock and `while` loop, also referred to as the *game loop*. It also receives events, such as a player firing thrusters using the arrow keys. If the player fires the thrusters, the Ogg Vorbis audio file plays, and the player hears a satisfying hiss.

mars_orbiter.py, part 17

```
❶ running = True
  while running:
    ❷ clock.tick(fps)
      tick_count += 1
    ❸ dist_list.append(sat.distance)

      # get keyboard input
    ❹ for event in pg.event.get():
        ❺ if event.type == pg.QUIT:  # close window
              running = False
        ❻ elif event.type == pg.KEYDOWN and event.key == pg.K_ESCAPE:
              screen = pg.display.set_mode((800, 645))  # exit full screen
        ❼ elif event.type == pg.KEYDOWN and event.key == pg.K_SPACE:
              background.fill(BLACK)  # clear path
        ❽ elif event.type == pg.KEYUP:
            ❾ sat.thrust.stop()  # stop sound
              mapping_off(planet)  # turn off moisture map view
        ❿ elif mapping_enabled:
              if event.type == pg.KEYDOWN and event.key == pg.K_m:
                  mapping_on(planet)
```

Listing 14-17: Starts the game loop, gets events, and plays sounds in `main()`

First assign a `running` variable for use with the `while` loop that runs the game ❶, then start the loop. Set the game speed using the clock's `tick()` method and pass it the `fps` variable you named in the previous listing ❷. If the game feels slow to you, set the speed to 40 fps. For each loop—or frame—increment the clock-based counter by 1.

Next, append the satellite object's `sat.distance` value to `dist_list` ❸. This is the distance between the satellite and the planet, calculated each game loop by the satellite's `locate()` method.

Now, gather player input made through the keyboard ❹. As described in the previous chapter, `pygame` records every user interaction—called an *event*—in an event buffer. The `event.get()` method creates a list of these events that you can evaluate, in this case, with `if` statements. Start by checking if the player closed the window to quit the game ❺. If this is `True`, set running to `False` to end the game loop.

If the player presses ESC, they are exiting full-screen mode, so reset the screen size to 800 × 645 pixels using the `display.set_mode()` method that you called at the start of `main()` ❻. If the player presses the space bar, fill the background with black, which will erase the white orbital path of the satellite ❼.

When the player presses an arrow key, the satellite object plays the hissing sound, but nothing in its `check_keys()` method tells it to stop. So, pass `pygame` any `KEYUP` events ❽; when `pygame` reads that the player has released the arrow key, call the `stop()` method on `thrust` to stop the sound from playing ❾.

To map Mars, the player will have to hold down the M key, so use the same `KEYUP` event to call the `mapping_off()` function. This will reset the planet image to its normal, nonmapped state.

Finally, check whether the `mapping_enabled` variable is `True`, meaning the player has achieved the winning conditions and is ready to map Mars ❿. If they press the M key, call the `mapping_on()` function to show the soil moisture overlay in place of the normal view of the planet.

Applying Gravity, Calculating Eccentricity, and Handling Failure

Listing 14-18 continues the `while` loop of the `main()` function by exerting a gravity force on the satellite and then calculating the eccentricity of its orbit. The eccentricity value will determine whether the orbit is circular or not, one of the game's winning conditions. The listing also blits the background and responds to the fail conditions of running out of fuel or burning up in the atmosphere.

mars_orbiter.py, part 18

```
    # get heading & distance to planet & apply gravity
❶   sat.locate(planet)
    planet.gravity(sat)

    # calculate orbital eccentricity
❷   if tick_count % (eccentricity_calc_interval * fps) == 0:
        eccentricity = calc_eccentricity(dist_list)
      ❸ dist_list = []

    # re-blit background for drawing command - prevents clearing path
❹   screen.blit(background, (0, 0))

    # Fuel/Altitude fail conditions
❺   if sat.fuel <= 0:
      ❻ instruct_label(screen, ['Fuel Depleted!'], RED, 340, 195)
        sat.fuel = 0
        sat.dx = 2
❼   elif sat.distance <= 68:
        instruct_label(screen, ['Atmospheric Entry!'], RED, 320, 195)
```

```
        sat.dx = 0
        sat.dy = 0
```

Listing 14-18: Applies gravity, calculates eccentricity, and addresses fail conditions

Call the satellite's `locate()` method and pass it the `planet` object as an argument ❶. This method computes the heading and distance to Mars, which you use to point the dish, calculate orbital eccentricity, and apply gravity. Then, to apply the force of gravity, call the planet's `gravity()` method and pass it the satellite object.

If the modulus of the `tick_count` and the `eccentricity_calc_interval * fps` is `0` ❷, call the function that calculates eccentricity and pass it the `dist_list` variable. Then, reset the `dist_list` variable to `0` to restart the distance sampling ❸.

Next, call the screen's `blit()` method and pass it the background and coordinates for the upper-left corner ❹. The placement of this statement matters. For example, if you move it after the code that updates the sprites, you won't see the satellite or Mars on the game screen.

Now, handle the case where the player runs out of fuel before achieving a circular orbit. First, get the current fuel level from the satellite object's `fuel` attribute ❺. If the level is at or below `0`, use the `instruct_label()` function to announce that the fuel is spent ❻, then set the satellite's `dx` attribute to `2`. This will cause the satellite sprite to quickly fly off the screen and into the depths of space, with the altitude readout getting larger and larger. Though unrealistic, this ensures the player knows they have failed!

The last failure case is when the player burns up in the atmosphere. If the satellite's `distance` attribute is less than or equal to `68` ❼, make a label near the center of the screen that lets the player know they have entered the atmosphere and then set the satellite's velocity attributes equal to `0`. This will cause gravity to lock the sprite against the planet (Figure 14-20). Also, when `dx` and `dy` are `0`, the satellite's `update()` method (Listing 14-7) will switch the satellite's image to the red "crashed" version.

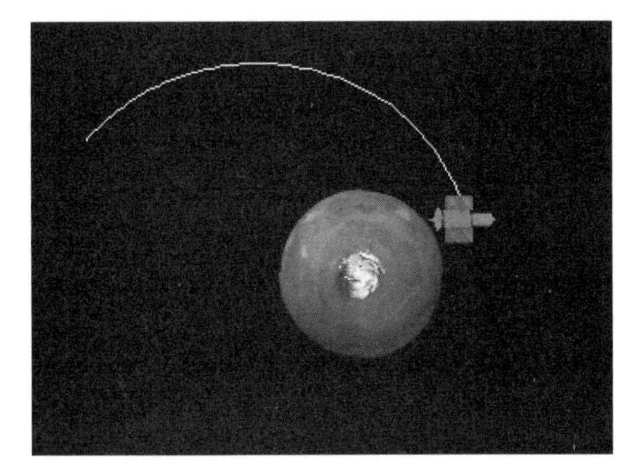

Figure 14-20: Satellite in crash configuration

The altitude parameter is a bit of a cheat, as altitude equates to the `distance` attribute, which is measured from the *centers* of the planet and satellite sprites, rather than from the *surface* of the planet to the satellite. It all comes down to scale. Planetary atmospheres are very thin veneers—at the scale of the game, the Martian atmosphere would be less than 2 pixels thick! As the game is designed, when the tip of the satellite dish scrapes the planet, the satellite will burn up, but since the size of the satellite sprite is unrealistically large, the sprite's 68-mile center point must be pushed farther out.

Rewarding Success and Updating and Drawing Sprites

Listing 14-19, still in the `while` loop of the `main()` function, rewards the winning player by enabling functionality that lets them map the moisture content in the Martian soil. In real life, this might be accomplished with radar or microwave resonators, which can remotely measure moisture in bare soil down to a depth of a few inches. The listing also updates the planet and satellite sprites and draws them to the screen.

mars_orbiter.py, part 19

```
    # enable mapping functionality
❶ if eccentricity < 0.05 and sat.distance >= 69 and sat.distance <= 120:
  ❷ map_instruct = ['Press & hold M to map soil moisture']
     instruct_label(screen, map_instruct, LT_BLUE, 250, 175)
  ❸ mapping_enabled = True
  else:
     mapping_enabled = False

❹ planet_sprite.update()
❺ planet_sprite.draw(screen)
  sat_sprite.update()
  sat_sprite.draw(screen)
```

Listing 14-19: Enables mapping functionality and updates sprites in the game loop

If the orbit is circular and meets the altitude requirements ❶, display a message instructing the player to press the M key to map soil moisture ❷. Put the text in brackets, as the `instruct_label()` function expects a list. Make the text color light blue and place it near the center of the screen.

Next, set the `mapping_enabled` variable to `True` ❸; otherwise, if the orbit strays outside of the target parameters, set it to `False`.

Finish by calling the planet sprite's `update()` method, through the sprite group ❹, then actually draw it to the screen ❺. The argument for the `draw()` method is the `screen`, the object on which to draw the sprites. Repeat these steps for the satellite sprite.

Displaying Instructions and Telemetry and Casting a Shadow

Listing 14-20 completes the `while` loop and the `main()` function by displaying instructions, data readouts, and the planet's shadow. The game introduction text will be shown only for a short time at startup.

mars_orbiter.py, part 20

```
    # display intro text for 15 seconds
❶ if pg.time.get_ticks() <= 15000:  # time in milliseconds
```

```
            instruct_label(screen, intro_text, GREEN, 145, 100)

        # display telemetry and instructions
    ❷ box_label(screen, 'Dx', (70, 20, 75, 20))
        box_label(screen, 'Dy', (150, 20, 80, 20))
        box_label(screen, 'Altitude', (240, 20, 160, 20))
        box_label(screen, 'Fuel', (410, 20, 160, 20))
        box_label(screen, 'Eccentricity', (580, 20, 150, 20))

    ❸ box_label(screen, '{:.1f}'.format(sat.dx), (70, 50, 75, 20))
        box_label(screen, '{:.1f}'.format(sat.dy), (150, 50, 80, 20))
        box_label(screen, '{:.1f}'.format(sat.distance), (240, 50, 160, 20))
        box_label(screen, '{}'.format(sat.fuel), (410, 50, 160, 20))
        box_label(screen, '{:.8f}'.format(eccentricity), (580, 50, 150, 20))

    ❹ instruct_label(screen, instruct_text1, WHITE, 10, 575)
        instruct_label(screen, instruct_text2, WHITE, 570, 510)

        # add terminator & border
    ❺ cast_shadow(screen)
    ❻ pg.draw.rect(screen, WHITE, (1, 1, 798, 643), 1)

    ❼ pg.display.flip()

❽ if __name__ == "__main__":
    main()
```

Listing 14-20: Displays text and planet's shadow and calls the `main()` *function*

The text summarizing the game should hover near the middle of the screen just long enough to be read, then vanish. Control this using an `if` statement and the `pygame` `tick.get_ticks()` method, which returns the number of milliseconds that have elapsed since the game started. If fewer than 15 seconds have passed, use the `instruct_label()` function to display the list of text strings from Listing 14-15 in green.

Next, make the gauges for the data readouts, starting with the header boxes. Use the `box_label()` function and call it for each of the five readout gauges ❷. Repeat this for the data readouts ❸. Note that you can use the string format method when you pass the function the text.

Use the `instruct_label()` function to place the instructions made in Listing 14-15 in the bottom corners of the screen ❹. Feel free to change the text color if you want to distinguish between those that describe the winning conditions and those that define the key functions.

Now, call the function that displays the planet's shadow ❺ and then, as a finishing touch, add a border using `pygame`'s `draw.rect()` method ❻. Pass it the `screen` object, the border color, the corner coordinates, and a line width.

Finish the `main()` function and its game loop by flipping the display ❼. As described in the preceding chapter, the `flip()` method blits everything from the screen object to the visual display.

Finally, call `main()` in the global space, using the standard syntax for running it stand-alone or as a module ❽.

Summary

In this chapter, you used pygame to build a 2D, arcade-style game with image sprites, sound effects, and keyboard game controls. You also created a fun, heuristic method for learning orbital mechanics. All of the techniques shown in "Astrodynamics for Gamers" on page 286 should work in the game. In the following section, "Challenge Projects," you can continue to improve both the game and the player experience.

Challenge Projects

Make the Mars Orbiter game your own by improving it and adding new challenges based on the following suggestions. As always, no solutions are provided to challenge projects.

Game Title Screen

Copy and edit the *mars_orbiter.py* program so that a title screen appears for a short time before the main game screen. Have the title screen display a NASA-type mission patch, like the one for the *Mars Global Surveyor* (Figure 14-21), but make it unique to the Mars Orbiter in the game. You can see some other NASA patches, in color, at *https://space.jpl.nasa.gov/art/patches.html.*

Figure 14-21: Mars Global Surveyor mission patch

Smart Gauges

Copy and edit the *mars_orbiter.py* program so that the altitude and eccentricity readouts use either a red background or red text color when their values are outside of the target ranges. But be careful: a circular eccentricity value should stay red until the altitude value is in range!

Radio Blackout

Copy and edit the *mars_orbiter.py* program so that keyboard controls are locked when the satellite is within the shadow rectangle.

Scoring

Copy and edit the *mars_orbiter.py* program so that it scores the player and keeps the best results in a displayable high-scores list. Highest scores go to those achieving the lowest allowable orbit while using the least amount of fuel in the least amount of time. For example, the fuel component of the score could be the amount of remaining fuel; for the orbit component, the maximum allowable altitude (120) minus the altitude of the circular orbit;

and for the time component, the inverse of the time taken to achieve the circular orbit multiplied by 1,000. Add the three components together for the final score.

Strategy Guide

Copy and edit the *mars_orbiter.py* program so it includes a pop-up strategy guide, or help file, by incorporating some of the figures in "Astrodynamics for Gamers" on page 286. For example, add a line to the instructions telling the player to press and hold the H key for help. This could bring up and cycle through the images of different orbital maneuvers, such as the Hohmann transfer or the One-Tangent Burn. Be sure to include comments on the strengths and weaknesses of each technique and pause the game while the guide is open.

Aerobraking

Aerobraking is a fuel-saving technique that uses atmospheric friction to slow down a spacecraft (Figure 14-22). Copy and edit the *mars_orbiter.py* program to include aerobraking. In the `main()` function, set the lowest winning altitude to 70 miles and the lowest safe altitude to 60 miles. If the satellite's altitude is between 60 and 70 miles, reduce its velocity by a small amount.

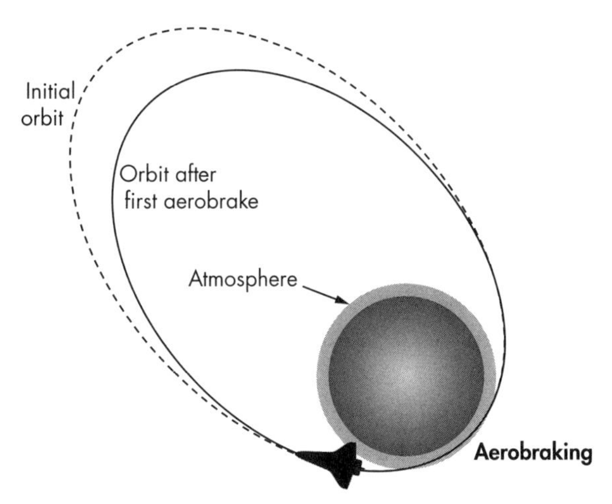

Figure 14-22: Circularizing an orbit using the atmosphere in place of a retrograde burn

Figure 14-23 is an example of using aerobraking in the game to circularize an elliptical orbit. The top of the atmosphere was set at 80 miles. Aerobraking serves the same purpose as a retrograde burn at periapsis, but you have to be cautious and patient and raise the orbit out of the atmosphere before it becomes circular.

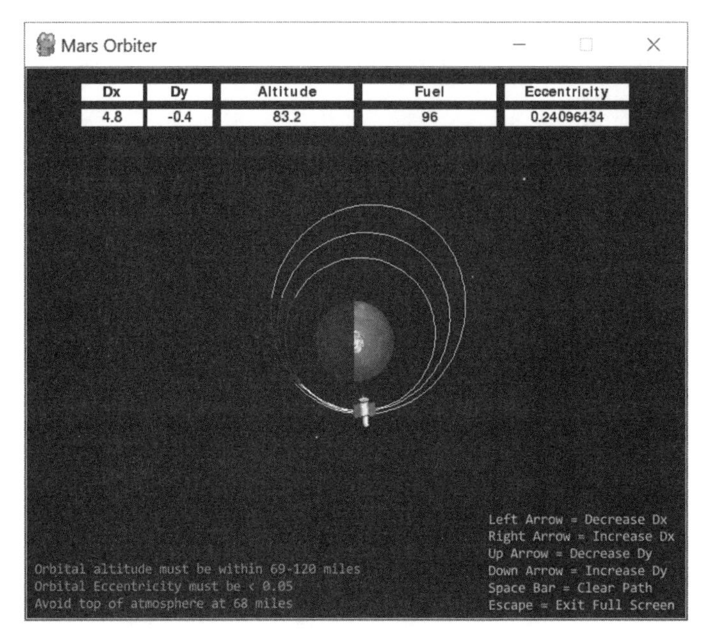

Figure 14-23: Circularizing an orbit using aerobraking. Note the low fuel consumption.

NASA used a similar technique to move the *Mars Global Surveyor* from its elliptical capture orbit to its final mapping orbit. This process took many months to accomplish, because they needed to protect the spacecraft from overheating in the atmosphere.

Intruder Alert!

Copy and edit the *mars_orbiter.py* program so that a new `planet` object is instantiated and flies across the screen, disrupting the satellite's orbit with its gravity. Make a new sprite to represent a comet or asteroid and launch it at random intervals (but not *too* often!). Don't apply Mars's `gravity()` method to the object so that it doesn't enter Martian orbit, but apply the new object's `gravity()` method to the satellite. Play with the new object's mass so that it noticeably perturbs the satellite's orbit from 100 or so pixels away. Allow the object to pass Mars or the satellite without colliding.

Over the Top

The Mars Orbiter currently uses an *equatorial* orbit. This is for easy coding, since you only need to rotate a single Mars image. But true mapping orbits use polar orbits—oriented perpendicular to equatorial orbits—and pass over the planet's poles (Figure 14-24). As the planet rotates beneath the orbit, the satellite can map its entire surface. With equatorial orbits, high latitudes are essentially unmappable due to curvature of the planet's surface (see the dashed line in Figure 14-24).

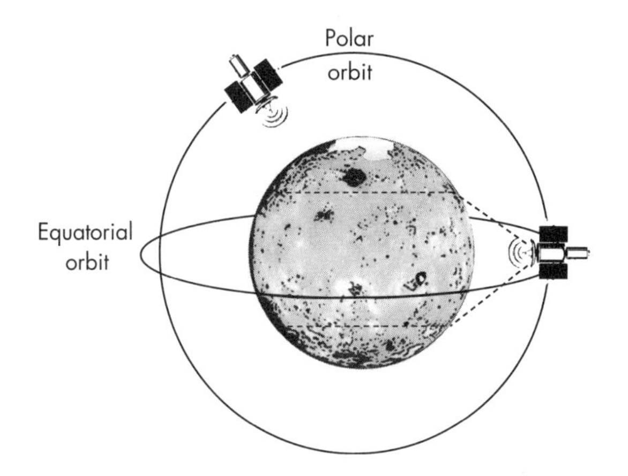

Figure 14-24: Polar versus equatorial orbits; notional north and south mapping limits for an equatorial orbit are represented by the dashed line.

Copy and edit the *mars_orbiter.py* program so that the satellite follows a polar orbit. All this involves is changing the Mars image. But you can't use a single top-down image anymore; the view will need to be perpendicular to the planet's axis of rotation. For a video example, see *https://youtu.be/IP2SDbhFbXk*; for an animated gif of Mars, see *http://gph.is/2caBKKS*. You can't use animated gifs directly in `pygame`, but you can split out and use the individual frames. Tools for splitting out frames can be found online, and in the next chapter, you'll use one of these products to extract images from a video.

15

IMPROVING YOUR ASTROPHOTOGRAPHY WITH PLANET STACKING

If you've ever looked through a telescope at Jupiter, Mars, or Saturn, you were probably a little disappointed. The planets appeared small and featureless. You wanted to zoom in and crank up the magnification, but it didn't work. Anything bigger than about 200x magnification tends to be blurry.

The problem is air turbulence, or what astronomers call *seeing*. Even on a clear night, the air is constantly in motion, with thermal updrafts and downdrafts that can easily blur the pinpoints of light that represent celestial objects. But with the commercialization of the *charge-coupled device (CCD)* in the 1980s, astronomers found a way to overcome the turbulence. Digital photography permits a technique known as *image stacking*, in which many photos—some good, some bad—are averaged together, or stacked, into a single image. With enough photos, the persistent, unchanging features (like a planet's surface) dominate transient features (like a stray cloud). This allows astrophotographers to increase magnification limits, as well as compensate for less-than-optimal seeing conditions.

In this chapter, you'll use a third-party Python module called `pillow` to stack hundreds of images of Jupiter. The result will be a single image with a higher signal-to-noise ratio than any of the individual frames. You'll also work with files in different folders than your Python code and manipulate both the files and folders using the Python operating system (`os`) and shell utilities (`shutil`) modules.

Project #23: Stacking Jupiter

Large, bright, and colorful, the gas giant Jupiter is a favorite target of astrophotographers. Even amateur telescopes can resolve its orange striping, caused by linear cloud bands, and the Great Red Spot, an oval-shaped storm so large it could swallow the Earth (see Figure 15-1).

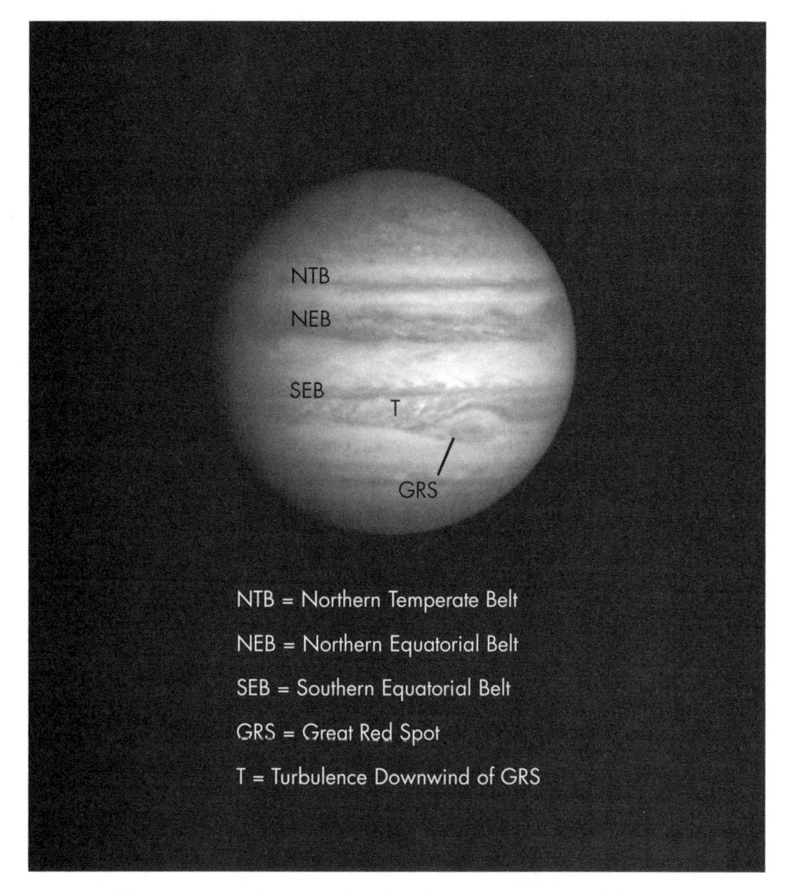

Figure 15-1: Jupiter as photographed by the Cassini spacecraft

Jupiter is a great subject for studying image stacking. Its linear cloud bands and Great Red Spot provide the eye with calibration points for judging improvements in edge definition and clarity, and its relatively large size makes it easy to detect noise.

Noise manifests itself as "graininess." Each color band has its own artifacts, resulting in colored speckles across an image. The main sources of noise are the camera (electronic readout noise and thermal signal) and photon noise from the light itself, as a variable number of photons strike the sensor over time. Noise artifacts are fortunately random in nature and can be largely canceled out by stacking images.

THE OBJECTIVE

Write programs that crop, scale, stack, and enhance images to create a clearer photograph of Jupiter.

The pillow Module

To work with images, you'll need a free third-party Python module called `pillow`. It's the successor project to the Python Imaging Library (PIL), which was discontinued in 2011. The `pillow` module "forked" the PIL repository and upgraded the code for Python 3.

You can use `pillow` on Windows, macOS, and Linux, and it supports many image formats including PNG, JPEG, GIF, BMP, and TIFF. It offers standard image-manipulation procedures, such as altering individual pixels, masking, handling transparency, filtering and enhancing, and adding text. But the real strength of `pillow` is its ability to edit many images with ease.

Installing `pillow` is easy with the pip tool (for more about pip, see "Manipulating Word Documents with `python-docx`" on page 110). From the command line, enter **`pip install pillow`**.

Most major Linux distributions include `pillow` in packages that previously contained PIL, so you may already have `pillow` on your system. Regardless of your platform, if PIL is already installed, you'll need to uninstall it before installing `pillow`. For more installation instructions, see *http://pillow.readthedocs.io/en/latest/installation.html.*

Working with Files and Folders

In all the previous projects in this book, you've kept supporting files and modules in the same folder as your Python code. This was handy for simple projects, but not very realistic for broad use, and it's certainly not good when you're dealing with the hundreds of image files you'll generate in this project. Fortunately, Python ships with several modules that can help with this, like `os` and `shutil`. But first, I'll briefly discuss directory paths.

Directory Paths

The directory path is the address to a file or folder. It starts with a root directory, which is designated with a letter (such as *C:*) in Windows, and a forward slash (/) in Unix-based systems. Additional drives in Windows are assigned a different letter than *C*, those in macOS are placed under */volume*, and those in Unix under */mnt* (for "mount").

NOTE *I use the Windows operating system for the examples in this chapter, but you can achieve the same result on macOS and other systems. And as is commonly done, I use the terms* directory *and* folder *interchangeably here.*

Pathnames appear differently depending on the operating system. Windows separates folders with a backslash (\), while macOS and Unix systems use a forward slash (/). Also, in Unix, folder and file names are case sensitive.

If you're writing your program in Windows and type in pathnames with backslashes, other platforms won't recognize the paths. Fortunately, the `os.path.join()` method will automatically ensure your pathname is suitable for whatever operating system Python is running on. Let's take a look at this, and other examples, in Listing 15-1.

```
❶ >>> import os
❷ >>> os.getcwd()
  'C:\\Python35\\Lib\\idlelib'
❸ >>> os.chdir('C:\\Python35\\Python 3 Stuff')
  >>> os.getcwd()
  'C:\\Python35\\Python 3 Stuff'
❹ >>> os.chdir(r'C:\Python35\Python 3 Stuff\Planet Stacking')
  >>> os.getcwd()
❺ 'C:\\Python35\\Python 3 Stuff\\Planet Stacking'
❻ >>> os.path.join('Planet Stacking', 'stack_8', '8file262.jpg')
  'Planet Stacking\\stack_8\\8file262.jpg'
❼ >>> os.path.normpath('C:/Python35/Python 3 Stuff')
  'C:\\Python35\\Python 3 Stuff'
❽ >>> os.chdir('C:/Python35')
  >>> os.getcwd()
  'C:\\Python35'
```

Listing 15-1: Working with Windows pathnames using the os module

After importing the `os` module for access to operating system–dependent functionality ❶, get the *current working directory*, or *cwd* ❷. The cwd is assigned to a process when it starts up; that is, when you run a script from your shell, the cwd of the shell and the script will be the same. For a Python program, the cwd is the folder that contains the program. When you get the cwd, you're shown the full path. Note that you must use extra backslashes in order to escape the backslash characters used as file separators.

Next, you change the cwd using the `os.chdir()` method ❸, passing it the full path in quotes, using double backslashes. Then you get the cwd again to see the new path.

If you don't want to type the double backslash, you can enter an `r` before the pathname argument string to convert it to a *raw string* ❹. Raw strings use different rules for backslash escape sequences, but even a raw string can't end in a single backslash. The path will still be displayed with double backslashes ❺.

If you want your program to be compatible with all operating systems, use the `os.path.join()` method and pass it the folder names and filenames without a separator character ❻. The `os.path` methods are aware of the system you're using and return the proper separators. This allows for platform-independent manipulation of filenames and folder names.

The `os.path.normpath()` method corrects separators for the system you are using ❼. In the Windows example shown, incorrect Unix-type separators are replaced with backslashes. Native Windows also supports use of the forward slash and will automatically make the conversion ❽.

The full directory path—from the root down—is called the *absolute path*. You can use shortcuts, called *relative paths*, to make working with directories easier. Relative paths are interpreted from the perspective of the current working directory. Whereas absolute paths start with a forward slash or drive label, relative paths do not. In the following code snippet, you can change directories without entering an absolute path—Python is aware of the new location because it is *within* the cwd. Behind the scenes, the relative path is joined to the path leading to the cwd to make a complete absolute path.

```
>>> os.getcwd()
'C:\\Python35\\Python 3 Stuff'
>>> os.chdir('Planet Stacking')
>>> os.getcwd()
'C:\\Python35\\Python 3 Stuff\\Planet Stacking'
```

You can identify folders and save more typing with dot (`.`) and dot-dot (`..`). For example, in Windows, `.\` refers to the cwd, and `..\` refers to the parent directory that holds the cwd. You can also use a dot to get the absolute path to your cwd:

```
>>> os.path.abspath('.')
'C:\\Python35\\Python 3 Stuff\\Planet Stacking\\for_book'
```

Dot folders can be used in Windows, macOS, and Linux. For more on the `os` module, see *https://docs.python.org/3/library/os.html.*

The Shell Utilities Module

The shell utilities module, `shutil`, provides high-level functions for working with files and folders, such as copying, moving, renaming, and deleting. Since it's part of the Python standard library, you can load `shutil` simply by typing **`import shutil`**. You'll see example uses for the module in this chapter's code sections. Meanwhile, you can find the module's documentation at *https://docs.python.org/3.7/library/shutil.html.*

The Video

Brooks Clark recorded the color video of Jupiter used in this project on a windy night in Houston, Texas. It consists of a 101 MB *.mov* file with a runtime of about 16 seconds.

The length of the video is intentionally short. Jupiter's rotation period is about 10 hours, which means still photos may blur with exposure times of only a minute, and features you want to reinforce through stacking video frames can change positions, greatly complicating the process.

To convert the video frames to individual images, I used Free Studio, a freeware set of multimedia programs developed by DVDVideoSoft. The Free Video to JPG Converter tool permits the capture of images at constant time or frame intervals. I set the interval to sample frames across the full length of the video, to improve the odds of capturing some images when the air was still and the seeing good.

A few hundred images should be enough for stacking to show demonstrable improvement. In this case, I captured 256 frames.

You can find the folder of images, named *video_frames*, online with the book's resources at *https://www.nostarch.com/impracticalpython/*. Download this folder and retain the name.

An example frame from the video, in grayscale, is shown in Figure 15-2. Jupiter's cloud bands are faint and fuzzy, the Great Red Spot isn't apparent, and the image suffers from low contrast, a common side effect of magnification. Noise artifacts also give Jupiter a grainy appearance.

Figure 15-2: Example frame from the video of Jupiter

In addition to those issues, the wind shook the camera, and imprecise tracking caused the planet to drift laterally to the left-hand side of the frame. You can see an example of *lateral drift* in Figure 15-3, in which I have overlaid five randomly chosen frames with the black background set to transparent.

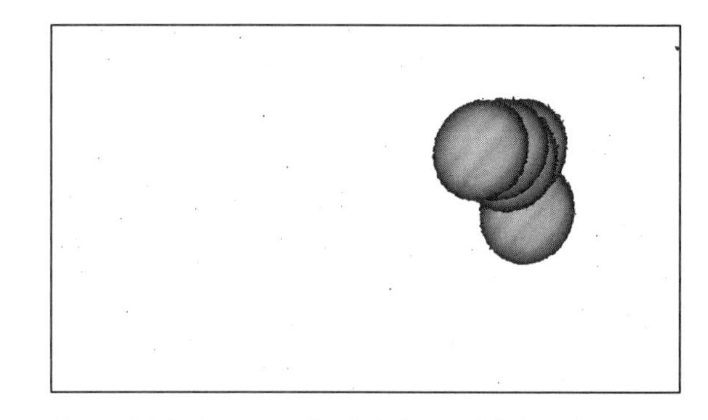

Figure 15-3: An example of shake and drift in the Jupiter video based on five randomly chosen frames

Movement isn't necessarily a bad thing, because shifting the image around can smooth defects associated with the CCD sensor surface, dust on the lens or sensor, and so on. But the key assumption in image stacking is that the images perfectly align so that persistent features, like Jupiter's cloud bands, reinforce each other as you average the images. For the signal-to-noise ratio to be high, the images must be registered.

Image registration is the process of transforming data to the same coordinate system so that it can be compared and integrated. Registration is arguably the hardest part of image stacking. Astronomers typically use commercial software—such as RegiStax, RegiStar, Deep Sky Stacker, or CCDStack—to help them align and stack their astrophotos. You'll get your hands dirty, however, and do this yourself using Python.

The Strategy

The steps required to stack the images are as follows (the first one has already been completed):

1. Extract images from video recording.
2. Crop images around Jupiter.
3. Scale cropped images to the same size.
4. Stack images into a single image.
5. Enhance and filter the final image.

The Code

You can incorporate all the steps into one program, but I chose to distribute them across three programs. This is because you generally want to stop and check results along the way, plus you may want to run later processes, such as enhancement, without having to completely rerun the whole workflow. The first program will crop and scale the images, the second will stack them, and the third will enhance them.

The Cropping and Scaling Code

First, you need to register the images. For large, bright objects like the moon and Jupiter, one approach in astrophotography is to crop each image so that its four borders are tangent with the surface of the body. This removes most of the sky and mitigates any shake and drift issues. Scaling the cropped images will ensure they are all the same size and will smooth them slightly to reduce noise.

You can download *crop_n_scale_images.py* from *https://www.nostarch.com/impracticalpython/*. Keep it in the directory that holds the folder of captured video frames.

Importing Modules and Defining the main() Function

Listing 15-2 performs imports and defines the `main()` function that runs the *crop_n_scale_images.py* program.

crop_n_scale_images.py, part 1

```
❶ import os
  import sys
❷ import shutil
❸ from PIL import Image, ImageOps

  def main():
      """Get starting folder, copy folder, run crop function, & clean folder."""
      # get name of folder in cwd with original video images
    ❹ frames_folder = 'video_frames'

      # prepare files & folders
    ❺ del_folders('cropped')
    ❻ shutil.copytree(frames_folder, 'cropped')

      # run cropping function
      print("start cropping and scaling...")
    ❼ os.chdir('cropped')
      crop_images()
    ❽ clean_folder(prefix_to_save='cropped')  # delete uncropped originals

      print("Done! \n")
```

Listing 15-2: Imports modules and defines the `main()` function

Start by importing both the operating system (`os`) and system (`sys`) ❶. The `os` import already includes an import of `sys`, but this feature may go away in the future, so it's best to manually import `sys` yourself. The `shutil` module contains the shell utilities described earlier ❷. From the imaging library, you'll use `Image` to load, crop, convert, and filter images; you'll also use `ImageOps` to scale images ❸. Note you must use PIL, not `pillow`, in the `import` statement.

Start the `main()` function by assigning the name of the starting folder to the `frames_folder` variable ❹. This folder contains all the original images captured from the video.

You'll store the cropped images in a new folder named *cropped*, but the shell utilities won't create this folder if it already exists, so call the `del_folders()` function that you'll write in a moment ❺. As written, this function won't throw an error if the folder doesn't exist, so it can be run safely at any time.

You should always work off a copy of original images, so use the `shutil.copytree()` method to copy the folder containing the originals to a new folder named *cropped* ❻. Now, switch to this folder ❼ and call the `crop_images()` function, which will crop and scale the images. Follow this with the `clean_folder()` function, which removes the original video frames that were copied into the *cropped* folder and are still hanging around ❽.

Note that you use the parameter name when you pass the argument to the clean_folder() function, since this makes the purpose of the function more obvious.

Print Done! to let the user know when the program is finished.

Deleting and Cleaning Folders

Listing 15-3 defines helper functions to delete files and folders in *crop_n_scale_images.py*. The shutil module will refuse to make a new folder if one with the same name already exists in the target directory. If you want to run the program more than once, you first have to remove or rename existing folders. The program will also rename images once they have been cropped, and you'll want to delete the original images before you start stacking them. Since there will be hundreds of image files, these functions will automate an otherwise laborious task.

crop_n_scale_images.py, part 2

```
❶ def del_folders(name):
      """If a folder with a named prefix exists in directory, delete it."""
    ❷ contents = os.listdir()
    ❸ for item in contents:
        ❹ if os.path.isdir(item) and item.startswith(name):
            ❺ shutil.rmtree(item)

❻ def clean_folder(prefix_to_save):
      """Delete all files in folder except those with a named prefix."""
    ❼ files = os.listdir()
      for file in files:
        ❽ if not file.startswith(prefix_to_save):
            ❾ os.remove(file)
```

Listing 15-3: Defines functions to delete folders and files

Define a function called del_folders() for deleting folders ❶. The only argument will be the name of a folder you want to remove.

Next, list the contents of the folder ❷, then start looping through the contents ❸. If the function encounters an item that starts with the folder name and is also a directory ❹, use shutil.rmtree() to delete the folder ❺. As you'll see in a moment, a different method is used to delete a folder than to delete a file.

NOTE *Always be careful when using the* rmtree() *method, as it* permanently *deletes folders and their contents. You can wipe much of your system, lose important documents unrelated to Python projects, and break your computer!*

Now, define a helper function to "clean" a folder and pass it the name of files *that you don't want to delete* ❻. This is a little counterintuitive at first, but since you only want to keep the last batch of images you've processed, you don't have to worry about explicitly listing any other files in the folder. If the files don't start with the prefix you provide, such as *cropped*, then they are automatically removed.

The process is similar to the last function. List the contents of the folder ❼ and start looping through the list. If the file doesn't start with the prefix you provided ❽, use `os.remove()` to delete it ❾.

Cropping, Scaling, and Saving Images

Listing 15-4 registers the frames captured from the video by fitting a box around Jupiter and cropping the image to the box (Figure 15-4). This technique works well with bright images on a field of black (see "Further Reading" on page 343 for another example).

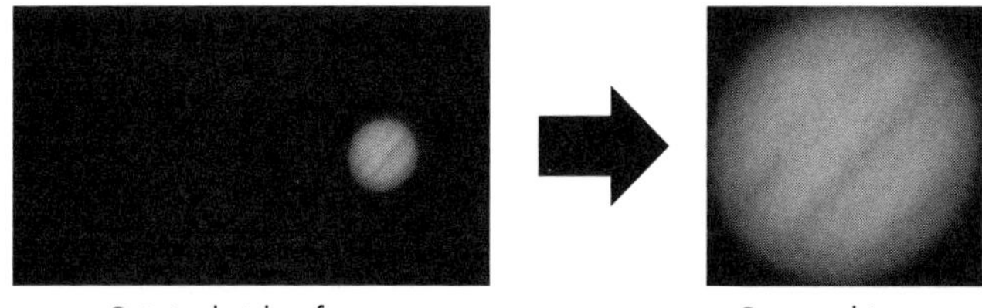

Figure 15-4: Cropping the original video frame to Jupiter to align the images

By cropping the images tightly around Jupiter, you resolve all of the drift and shake issues.

Each cropped image is also scaled to a larger and consistent size and smoothed slightly to reduce noise. The cropped and scaled images will be kept in their own folder, which the `main()` function creates, later.

crop_n_scale_images.py, part 3

```
❶ def crop_images():
      """Crop and scale images of a planet to box around planet."""
    ❷ files = os.listdir()
    ❸ for file_num, file in enumerate(files, start=1):
        ❹ with Image.open(file) as img:
            ❺ gray = img.convert('L')
            ❻ bw = gray.point(lambda x: 0 if x < 90 else 255)
            ❼ box = bw.getbbox()
              padded_box = (box[0]-20, box[1]-20, box[2]+20, box[3]+20)
            ❽ cropped = img.crop(padded_box)
              scaled = ImageOps.fit(cropped, (860, 860),
                                    Image.LANCZOS, 0, (0.5, 0.5))
              file_name = 'cropped_{}.jpg'.format(file_num)
            ❾ scaled.save(file_name, "JPEG")

if __name__ == '__main__':
    main()
```

Listing 15-4: Crops initial video frames to a box around Jupiter and rescales

The `crop_images()` function takes no argument ❶ but will ultimately work on a copy—named *cropped*—of the folder containing the original video frames. You made this copy in the `main()` function prior to calling this function.

Start the function by making a list of the contents of the current (*cropped*) folder ❷. The program will number each image sequentially, so use `enumerate()` with the `for` loop and set the `start` option to `1` ❸. If you haven't used `enumerate()` before, it's a handy built-in function that acts as an automatic counter; the count will be assigned to the `file_num` variable.

Next, name a variable, `img`, to hold the image and use the `open()` method to open the file ❹.

To fit the borders of a bounding box to Jupiter, you need all the non-Jupiter parts of an image to be black `(0, 0, 0)`. Unfortunately, there are stray, noise-related, nonblack pixels beyond Jupiter, and the edge of the planet is diffuse and gradational. These issues result in nonuniform box shapes, as shown in Figure 15-5. Fortunately, you can easily resolve these by converting the image to black and white. You can then use this converted image to determine the proper box dimensions for each color photo.

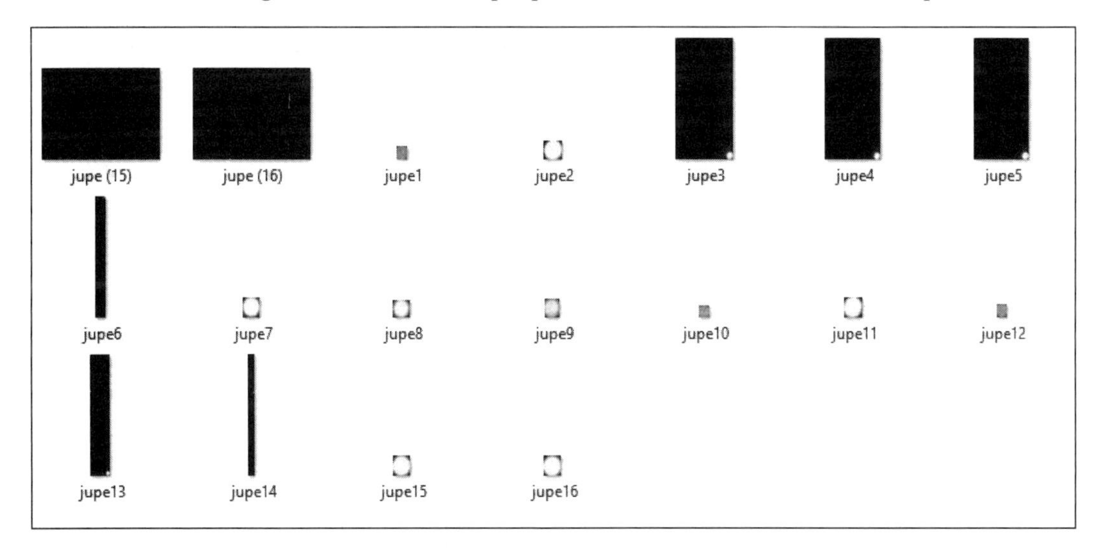

Figure 15-5: Irregularly sized cropped images due to problems defining the bounding box dimensions

To eliminate the noise effects that compromise the bounding-box technique, convert the loaded image to the "L" mode—consisting of 8-bit black and white pixels—and name the variable gray, for grayscale ❺. With this mode there is only one channel (versus the three channels for RGB color images), so you only need to decide on a single value when thresholding—that is, setting a limit above or below which an action occurs.

Assign a new variable, called `bw`, to hold a true black-and-white image ❻. Use the `point()` method, used to change pixel values, and a lambda function to set any value below 90 to black (`0`) and all other values to white (`255`). The threshold value was determined through trial and error. The `point()` method now returns a clean image for fitting the bounding box (Figure 15-6).

Figure 15-6: Screen capture of one of the original video frames converted to pure black and white

Now, call the `Image` module's `getbox()` method on `bw` ❼. This method prunes off black borders by fitting a bounding box to the nonzero regions of an image. It returns a tuple with the left, upper, right, and lower pixel coordinates of the box.

If you use `box` to crop the video frames, you get an image with borders tangent to Jupiter's surface (see the middle image in Figure 15-7). This is what you want, but it's not visually pleasing. So, add some black padding by assigning a new box variable, named `padded_box`, with its edges extended 20 pixels in all four directions (see the rightmost image in Figure 15-7). Because the padding is consistent and applied to all images, it doesn't compromise the results of cropping.

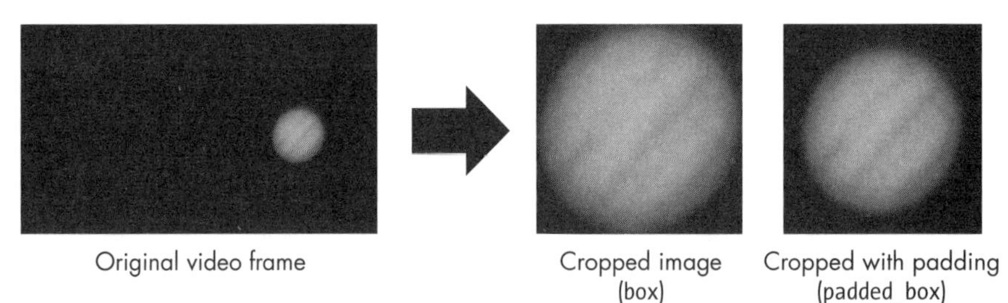

Figure 15-7: Initial crop tangent to Jupiter's surface (box) and final crop with padding (padded_box)

Continue by cropping each image with the `crop()` method ❽. This method takes `padded_box` as an argument.

To scale the image, use the `ImageOps.fit()` method. This takes the image, a size as a pixel width-and-height tuple, a resampling method, a border (`0` = no border), and even cropping from the center, designated by the tuple `(0.5, 0.5)`. The `pillow` module has several algorithm choices for resizing an image, but I chose the popular *Lanczos* filter. Enlarging an image tends to reduce its sharpness, but Lanczos can produce *ringing artifacts* along strong edges; this helps increase *perceived* sharpness. This unintended edge enhancement can help the eye focus on features of interest, which are faint and blurry in the original video frames.

After scaling, assign a `file_name` variable. Each of the 256 cropped images will start with *cropped_* and end with the number of the image, which you pass to the replacement field of the `format()` method. End the function by saving the file ❾.

Back in the global scope, add the code that lets the program run as a module or in stand-alone mode.

NOTE *I save the files using JPEG format because it is universally readable, handles gradations in color well, and takes up very little memory. JPEG uses "lossy" compression, however, which causes a tiny bit of image deterioration each time a file is saved; you can adjust the degree of compression at the expense of storage size. In most cases, when working with astrophotographs, you'll want to use one of the many lossless formats available, such as TIFF.*

At this point in the workflow, you've cropped the original video frames down to a box around Jupiter; then you scaled the cropped images to a larger, consistent size (Figure 15-8).

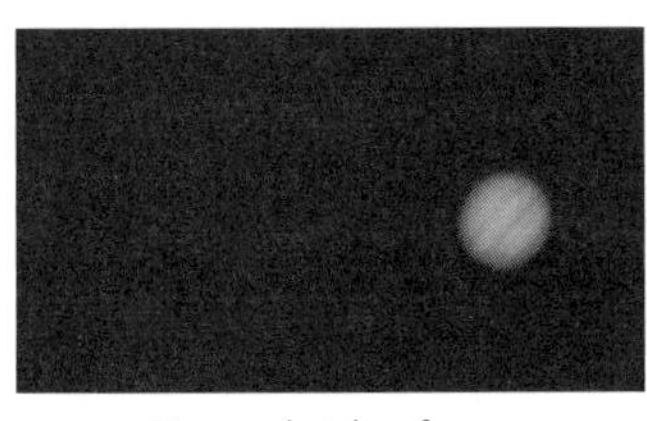

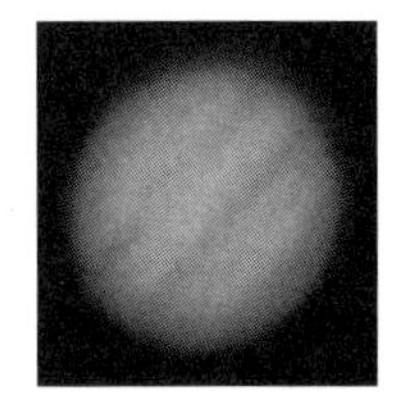

Figure 15-8: Relative sizes of images after cropping and scaling

In the next section, you write the code that stacks the cropped and scaled images.

The Stacking Code

The *stack_images.py* code takes the images produced by the last program and averages them so that a single stacked image is produced. You can download it from the book's resources at *https://www.nostarch.com/impracticalpython/*. Keep it in the same folder as the *crop_n_scale_images.py* program.

Listing 15-5 imports modules, loads images, creates lists of color channels (red, blue, green), averages the channels, recombines the channels, and creates and saves the final stacked image. It's simple enough that we won't bother with a `main()` function.

stack_images.py

```
❶ import os
  from PIL import Image

  print("\nstart stacking images...")

  # list images in directory
❷ os.chdir('cropped')
  images = os.listdir()

  # loop through images and extract RGB channels as separate lists
❸ red_data = []
  green_data = []
  blue_data = []
❹ for image in images:
      with Image.open(image) as img:
          if image == images[0]:  # get size of 1st cropped image
              img_size = img.size  # width-height tuple to use later
        ❺ red_data.append(list(img.getdata(0)))
          green_data.append(list(img.getdata(1)))
          blue_data.append(list(img.getdata(2)))

❻ ave_red = [round(sum(x) / len(red_data)) for x in zip(*red_data)]
  ave_blue = [round(sum(x) / len(blue_data)) for x in zip(*blue_data)]
  ave_green = [round(sum(x) / len(green_data)) for x in zip(*green_data)]

❼ merged_data = [(x) for x in zip(ave_red, ave_green, ave_blue)]
❽ stacked = Image.new('RGB', (img_size))
❾ stacked.putdata(merged_data)
  stacked.show()

❿ os.chdir('..')
  stacked.save('jupiter_stacked.tif', 'TIFF')
```

Listing 15-5: Splits out and averages color channels, then recombines into a single image

Start by repeating some of the imports you used in the previous program ❶. Next, change the current directory to the *cropped* folder, which contains the cropped and scaled images of Jupiter ❷, and immediately make a list of the images in the folder using `os.listdir()`.

With `pillow`, you can manipulate individual pixels or groups of pixels, and you can do this for individual color channels, such as red, blue, and green. To demonstrate this, you'll work on individual color channels to stack the images.

Create three empty lists to hold the RGB pixel data ❸, then start looping through the images list ❹. First, open the image. Then, get the width and height of the first image, in pixels, as a tuple. Remember, in the previous program, you scaled all the small cropped images to a larger size. You'll need these dimensions later for creating the new stacked image, and `size` automatically retrieves this info for you.

Now use the `getdata()` method to get the pixel data for the selected image ❺. Pass the method the index of the color channel you want: `0` for red, `1` for green, and `2` for blue. Append the results to a data list, as appropriate. The data from each image will form a separate list in the data lists.

To average the values in each list, use list comprehension to sum the pixels in all the images and divide by the total number of images ❻. Note that you use `zip` with the splat (*) operator. Your `red_data` list, for example, is a list of lists, with each nested list representing one of the 256 image files. Using `zip` with * unpacks the contents of the lists so that the first pixel in image1 is summed with the first pixel in image2, and so on.

To merge the averaged color channels, use list comprehension with `zip` ❼. Next, create a new image, named `stacked`, using `Image.new()` ❽. Pass the method a color mode (`'RGB'`) and the `img_size` tuple containing the desired width and height of the image in pixels, which was obtained earlier from one of the cropped images.

Populate the new `stacked` image using the `putdata()` method and pass it the `merged_data` list ❾. This method copies data from a sequence object into an image, starting at the upper-left corner (`0, 0`). Display the final image using the `show()` method. Finish by changing the folder to the parent directory and saving the image as a TIFF file named *jupiter_stacked.tif* ❿.

If you compare one of the original video frames to the final stacked image (*jupiter_stacked.tif*), as in Figure 15-9, you'll see a clear improvement in edge definition and the signal-to-noise ratio. This is best appreciated in color, so if you haven't run the program, take the time to download *Figure 15-9.pdf* from the website. When the image is viewed in color, the benefits of the stacking include smoother, "creamier" white bands, better-defined red bands, and a more obvious Great Red Spot. There is still room for improvement, however, so next you'll write a program to enhance the final stacked image.

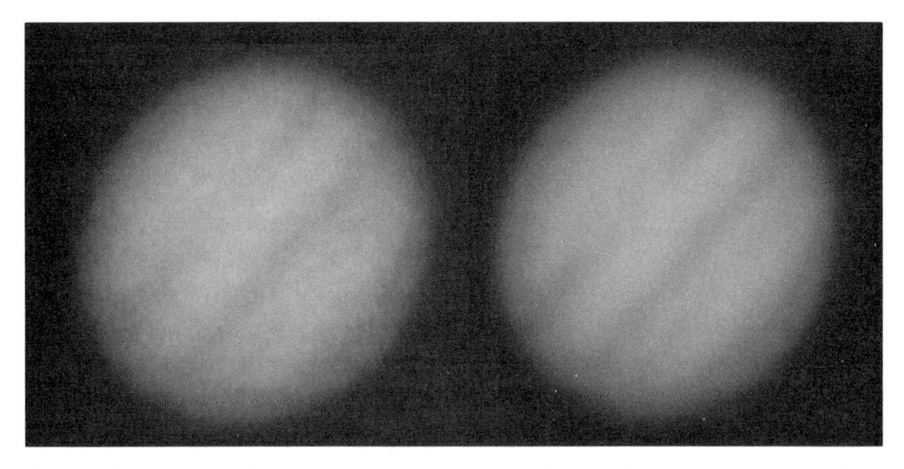

Figure 15-9: An original video frame compared to final stacked image (jupiter_stacked.tif)

NOTE *If the Great Red Spot looks pinkish to you in the stacked image, that's because it is! It fades from time to time, and many published pictures of Jupiter have exaggerated colors due to processing, so this subtle coloration gets lost. This is probably for the best, as "Great Pink Spot" just doesn't have the same ring to it.*

The Enhancing Code

You've successfully stacked all the video frames, but Jupiter is still crooked, and its features are faint. You can further improve the stacked image using filters, enhancers, and transforms found in `pillow`. As you enhance images, you get further and further from the "ground truth" raw data. For this reason, I chose to isolate the enhancement process in a separate program.

In general, the first steps after stacking are to enhance details, using high-pass filters or an unsharp mask algorithm, and then to fine-tune brightness, contrast, and color. The code will use `pillow`'s image enhancement capability to apply these steps—though in a different order. You can download the code as *enhance_image.py* from *https://nostarch.com/impracticalpython/*. Keep it in the same folder as the previous Python programs.

NOTE *The processing of astronomical images can be quite involved, and whole books have been written on the subject. Some of the standard steps have been omitted in this workflow. For instance, the original video was not calibrated, and distortion effects due to turbulence were not corrected. Advanced software, such as RegiStax or AviStack, can prevent blurring by warping individual images so that distorted features, like the edges of cloud bands, overlap properly in all images.*

Listing 15-6 imports `pillow` classes and opens, enhances, and saves the stacked image generated by the previous code. Because there are many possible options for enhancing images, I chose to modularize this program despite its small size.

enhance_image.py

```
❶ from PIL import Image, ImageFilter, ImageEnhance

❷ def main():
      """Get an image and enhance, show, and save it."""
    ❸ in_file = 'jupiter_stacked.tif'
      img = Image.open(in_file)
    ❹ img_enh = enhance_image(img)
      img_enh.show()
      img_enh.save('enhanced.tif', 'TIFF')

❺ def enhance_image(image):
      """Improve an image using pillow filters & transforms."""
    ❻ enhancer = ImageEnhance.Brightness(image)
    ❼ img_enh = enhancer.enhance(0.75)  # 0.75 looks good

    ❽ enhancer = ImageEnhance.Contrast(img_enh)
      img_enh = enhancer.enhance(1.6)
```

```
    enhancer = ImageEnhance.Color(img_enh)
    img_enh = enhancer.enhance(1.7)

❾  img_enh = img_enh.rotate(angle=133, expand=True)

❿  img_enh = img_enh.filter(ImageFilter.SHARPEN)

    return img_enh

if __name__ == '__main__':
    main()
```

Listing 15-6: Opens an image, enhances it, and saves it using a new name

The import is familiar except for the last two ❶. These new modules, `ImageFilter` and `ImageEnhance`, contain predefined filters and classes that can be used to alter images with blurring, sharpening, brightening, smoothing, and more (see *https://pillow.readthedocs.io/en/5.1.x/* for a full listing of what's in each module).

Start by defining the `main()` function ❷. Assign the stacked image to a variable named `in_file`, then pass it to `Image.open()` to open the file ❸. Next, call an `enhance_image()` function and pass it the image variable ❹. Show the enhanced image and then save it as a TIFF file, which results in no deterioration in image quality.

Now, define an enhancement function, `enhance_image()`, that takes an image as an argument ❺. To paraphrase the `pillow` documentation, all enhancement classes implement a common interface containing a single method, `enhance(factor)`, that returns an enhanced image. The `factor` parameter is a floating-point value controlling the enhancement. A value of `1.0` returns a copy of the original; lower values diminish color, brightness, contrast, and so on; and higher values increase these qualities.

To change the brightness of an image, you first create an instance of the `ImageEnhance` module's `Brightness` class, passing it the original image ❻. Mimic the `pillow` docs and name this object `enhancer`. To make the final, enhanced image, you call the object's `enhance()` method and pass it the `factor` argument ❼. In this case, you decrease brightness by 0.25. The `# 0.75` comment at the end of the line is a useful way to experiment with different factors. Use this comment to store values you like; that way, you can remember and restore them if other test values don't yield pleasing results.

Continue enhancing the image, moving to contrast ❽. If you don't want to adjust the contrast manually, you can take a chance and use `pillow`'s automatic contrast method. First, import `ImageOps` from PIL. Then, replace the two lines starting with step ❽ with the single line: `img_enh = ImageOps.autocontrast(img_enh)`.

Next, punch up the color. This will help to make the Great Red Spot more visible.

No one wants to look at a tilted Jupiter, so transform the image by rotating it to a more "conventional" view, where the cloud bands are horizontal and the Great Red Spot is to the lower right. Call the `Image` module's `rotate()` method on the image and pass it an angle, measured counterclockwise in degrees, and have it automatically expand the output image to make it large enough to hold the entire rotated image ❾.

Now, sharpen the image. Even on high-quality images, sharpening may be needed to ameliorate the interpolation effects of converting data, resizing and rotating images, and so on. Although some astrophotography resources recommend placing it first, in most image-processing workflows, it comes last. This is because it is dependent on the final size of the image (viewing distance), as well as the media being used. Sharpening can also increase noise artifacts and is a "lossy" operation that can remove data—things you don't want to happen prior to other edits.

Sharpening is a little different from the previous enhancements, as you use the `ImageFilter` class. No intermediate step is needed; you can build the new image with a single line by calling the `filter()` method on the image object and passing it the predefined `SHARPEN` filter ❿. The `pillow` module has other filters that help define edges, such as `UnsharpMask` and `EDGE_ENHANCE`, but for this image, the results are indiscernible from `SHARPEN`.

Finish by returning the image and applying the code to run the program as a module or in stand-alone mode.

The final enhanced image is compared to a random video frame and the final stacked image in Figure 15-10. All the images have been rotated for ease of comparison.

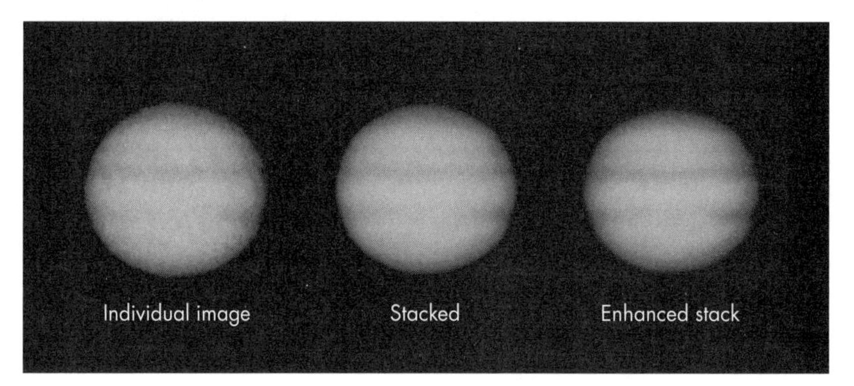

Figure 15-10: A random video frame, the results of stacking 256 frames, and the final enhanced image

You can see the improvement best when you view it in color. If you want to see a color version prior to running the program, view or download *Figure 15-10.pdf* from the website.

NOTE *If you're familiar with `pillow`, you may be aware that you can use the `Image.blend()` method to stack images with only a few lines of code. To my eye, however, the resulting image is noticeably noisier than that obtained by breaking out and averaging the individual color channels, as you did with the* stack_images.py *program.*

Summary

The final image in Figure 15-10 will never win any awards or be featured in *Sky & Telescope* magazine, but the point was to take on a challenge. And the result is a marked improvement over a single image captured from the video. The colors are brighter, the cloud bands sharper, and the Great Red Spot better defined. You can also make out the turbulent zone downwind of the Great Red Spot (refer to Figure 15-1).

Despite starting with rough input, you were able to register the images, remove noise through stacking, and enhance the final image using filters and transforms. And all these steps were accomplished with the freely available `pillow` fork of the Python Imaging Library. You also gained experience with the Python `shutil` and `os` modules, which you used to manipulate files and folders.

For more advanced image processing, you can use OpenSource Computer Vision (OpenCV), which you implement by installing and importing the `cv2` and `NumPy` modules. Other options involve `matplotlib`, `SciPy`, and `NumPy`. As always with Python, there's more than one way to skin a cat!

Further Reading

Automate the Boring Stuff with Python: Practical Programming for Total Beginners (No Starch Press, 2015) by Al Sweigart includes several useful chapters on working with files, folders, and `pillow`.

Online resources for using Python with astronomy include Python for Astronomers (*https://prappleizer.github.io/*) and Practical Python for Astronomers (*https://python4astronomers.github.io/*).

If you want to learn more about the OpenCV-Python library, you can find tutorials at *https://docs.opencv.org/3.4.2/d0/de3/tutorial_py_intro.html.* Note that knowledge of `NumPy` is a prerequisite for the tutorials and for writing optimized OpenCV code. Alternatively, SimpleCV lets you get started with computer vision and image manipulation with a smaller learning curve than OpenCV but only works with Python 2.

Astrophotography (Rocky Nook, 2014) by Thierry Legault is an indispensable resource for anyone interested in serious astrophotography. A comprehensive and readable reference, it covers all aspects of the subject, from equipment selection through image processing.

"Aligning Sun Images Using Python" (LabJG, 2013), a blog by James Gilbert, contains code for cropping the sun using the bounding-box technique. It also includes a clever method for realigning rotated images of the sun using sunspots as registration points. You can find it at *https://labjg.wordpress.com/2013/04/01/aligning-sun-images-using-python/.*

A Google research team figured out how to use stacking to remove watermarks from images on stock photography websites and how the websites could better protect their property. You can read about it at *https://research.googleblog.com/2017/08/making-visible-watermarks-more-effective.html.*

Challenge Project: Vanishing Act

Image-stacking techniques can do more than just remove noise—they can remove anything that moves at a photo site, including people. Adobe Photoshop, for example, has a stack script that makes nonstationary objects magically vanish. It relies on a statistical average known as the *median*, which is simply the "middle" value in a list of numbers arranged from smallest to largest. The process requires multiple photos—preferably taken with a tripod-mounted camera—so that the objects you want to remove change positions from one image to the next, while the background remains constant. You typically need 10 to 30 pictures taken about 20 seconds apart, or similarly spaced frames extracted from a video.

With the mean, you sum numbers and divide by the total. With the median, you sort numbers and choose the middle value. In Figure 15-11, a row of five images is shown with the same pixel location outlined in each. In the fourth image, a blackbird has flown by and ruined the splendid white background. If you stack with the mean, the bird's presence lingers. But do a median stack on the images—that is, sort the red, green, and blue channels and take the middle values—and you get the background value for each channel (255). No trace of the bird remains.

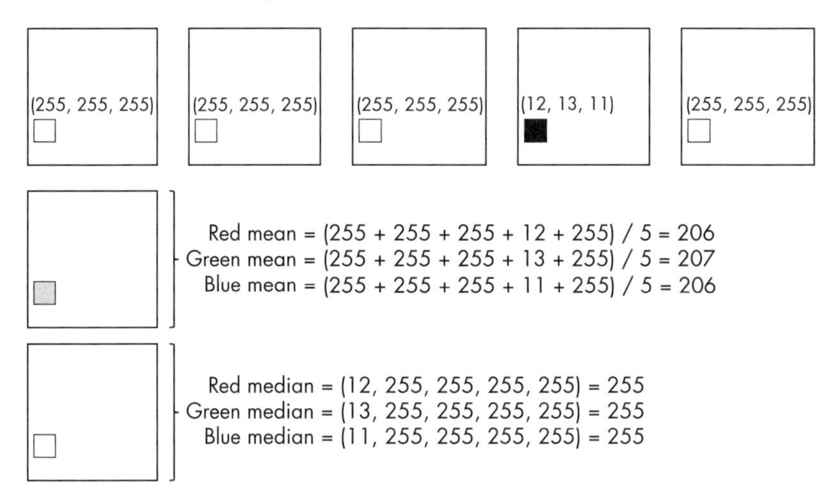

Figure 15-11: Five white images with the same pixel highlighted and its RGB values displayed. Median-stacking removes the black pixel.

When you average using the median, spurious values get pushed to the ends of the list. This makes it easy to remove outliers, such as satellites or airplanes in astrophotos, so long as the number of images containing the outlier is less than half the number of images.

Armed with this knowledge, write an image-stacking program that will remove unwanted tourists from your vacation happy snaps. For testing, you can download the *moon_cropped* folder from the website, which contains five synthetic images of the moon, each "ruined" by a passing plane (see Figure 15-12).

Figure 15-12: Synthetic moon photos for testing the median averaging approach

Your final stacked image should contain no evidence of the plane (Figure 15-13).

Figure 15-13: Result of stacking the images in the moon_cropped *folder using median averaging*

As this is a challenge project, no solution is provided.

16

FINDING FRAUDS WITH BENFORD'S LAW

Prior to the invention of electronic calculators, if you needed to take the log of a number, you looked it up in a table. Astronomer Simon Newcomb used such tables, and in 1881, he noticed that the pages in the front, used for numbers beginning with the lowest digits, were more worn than those in the back. From this mundane observation, he realized that—at least for measurements and constants in nature—the leading digits were much more likely to be small than large. He published a short article about it and moved on.

For decades, this statistical curiosity, like Tolkien's One Ring, "passed out of all knowledge." Then, in 1938, physicist Frank Benford rediscovered and confirmed the phenomenon by collecting over 20,000 samples of real-world numbers, using data sources as diverse as the measurements of rivers, street addresses, numbers contained in *Reader's Digest* magazine, molecular weights, baseball statistics, death rates, and more. As the person who popularized this scientific discovery, he got all the credit.

According to *Benford's law*, also known as the *first-digit law*, the frequency of occurrence of the leading digits in naturally occurring numerical distributions is predictable and nonuniform. In fact, a given number is six times more likely to start with a 1 than a 9! This is very counterintuitive, as most people would expect a uniform distribution, with each number having a one in nine (11.1 percent) chance of occupying the first slot. Due to this cognitive disconnect, Benford's law has become a useful tool for fraud detection in financial, scientific, and election data.

In this chapter, you'll write a Python program that compares real-life datasets to Benford's law and determines whether they appear fraudulent or not. You'll also dust off `matplotlib` one last time to add a useful visual component to the analysis. For a dataset, you'll use votes cast in the contentious 2016 US presidential election.

Project #24: Benford's Law of Leading Digits

Figure 16-1 depicts a bar chart of the leading significant digits in a set of numbers following Benford's law. Surprisingly, scale doesn't matter. A tabulation of the length of Australian roads will follow Benford's law whether it is in miles, kilometers, or cubits! As a statistical principle, it is *scale invariant*.

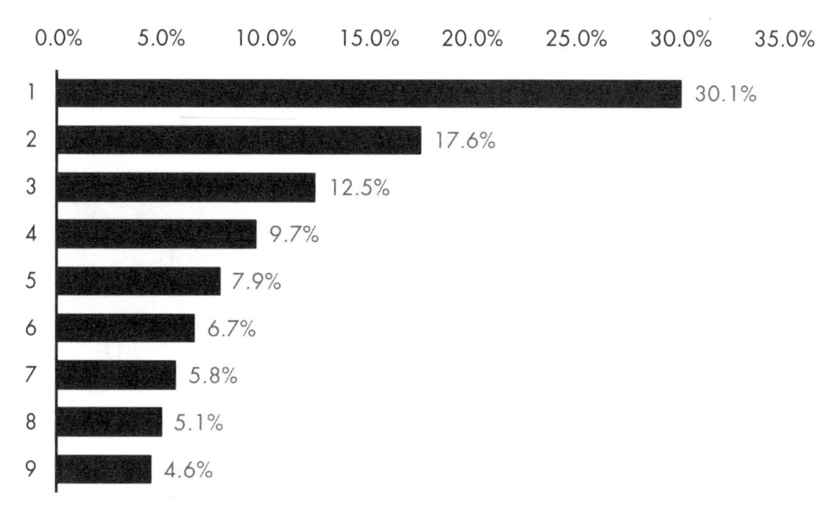

Figure 16-1: The frequency of occurrence of leading digits according to Benford's law

It took mathematicians about a hundred years to come up with an explanation for Benford's law that *they* found satisfactory. For the rest of us, let's just say that there are more little things in the universe than large things. Frank Benford used the analogy that owning *one* acre of land is easier than owning *nine* acres. In fact, you can closely duplicate the frequency produced by Benford's law by simply assuming that there are twice as many 1s as 2s, three times as many 1s as 3s, and so on. You just take the inverse of each of the nine digits (1 / *d*) and divide by the sum of all the inverses (2.83). Then multiply the results by 100 to get the percentage (see Figure 16-2).

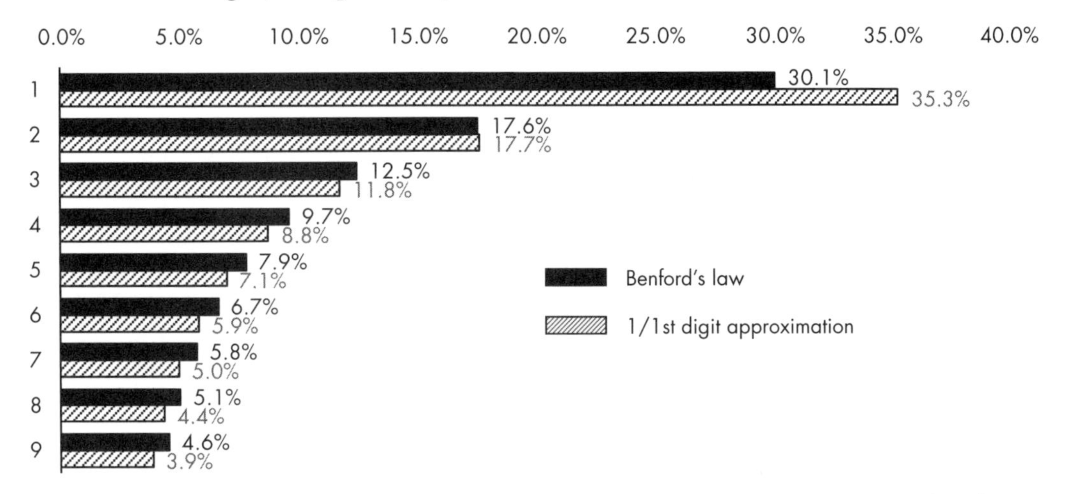

Figure 16-2: Comparison of Benford's law with an approximation proportional to the inverse of the first digit

Because of the size relationships just discussed, Benford's law can be visualized with a *logarithmic* scale, which is used to graph data that are related according to an exponential relationship. In *semilogarithmic* ("semilog") plots, one variable tends to be restricted, like the set of leading digits (1–9), while the other covers a wide range of values that includes several orders of magnitude.

On semilog graph paper, the horizontal x-axis values are log values, and the vertical y-axis values, represented by horizontal lines, are not (see Figure 16-3). On the x-axis, the horizontal divisions aren't regular, and this nonlinear pattern repeats with powers of 10. For every *decade* on the log paper, such as 1 through 10 or 10 through 100, the *width* of the divisions between numbers is proportional to the *length* of the bars in Figure 16-1. For example, the distance between the 1 and 2 in Figure 16-3 is 30.1 percent of the distance between 1 and 10. As one author put it, you could derive Benford's law by simply throwing darts at a piece of log paper!

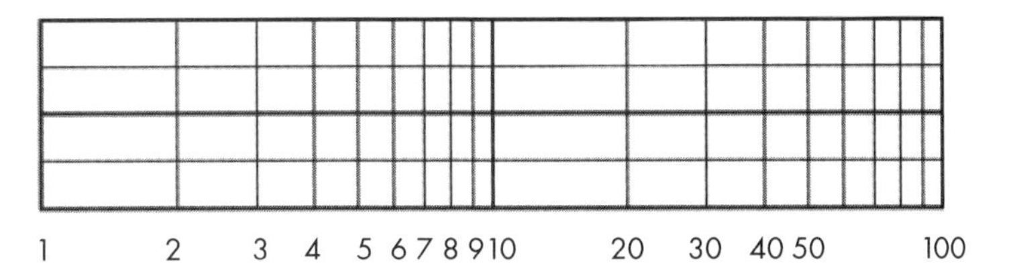

Figure 16-3: Example of two-decade semilogarithmic graph paper

For a collection of numeric data to conform to Benford's law, certain conditions have to be met. The numbers need to be random and not assigned, with no imposed minimums or maximums. The numbers should cover several orders of magnitude, and the dataset should be large; recommendations in the literature call for 100 to 1,000 samples as a minimum, though Benford's law has been shown to hold true for datasets containing as few as 50 numbers. Examples of distributions that won't follow Benford's law are the heights of professional basketball players, US telephone numbers (for which only the last four digits are truly random), prices influenced by psychological barriers ($1.99 versus $2.00), and medical copayments.

Applying Benford's Law

Most financial and accounting data conform to naturally occurring numbers and are thus subject to Benford's law. For example, assume you own a stock mutual fund with a value of $1,000. For your fund to reach $2,000 in value, it would have to double by growing 100 percent. To increase from $2,000 to $3,000, it would only need to grow by 50 percent. For the first digit to be a 4, it needs to grow by another 33 percent. As Benford's law predicts, for the leading digit 1 to become 2, there needs to be more growth than for the 3 to become 4, and so on. Because a Benford distribution is a "distribution of distributions," financial datasets tend to conform, as they result from combining numbers—though exceptions do occur.

Because people are generally unaware of Benford's law, they don't account for it when falsifying numerical records. This gives forensic accountants a powerful tool for quickly identifying datasets that may be fraudulent. In fact, comparisons to Benford's law are legally admissible as evidence in US criminal cases at the federal, state, and local levels.

In the 1993 case of *State of Arizona v. Nelson*, the accused diverted nearly $2 million to bogus vendors in an attempt to defraud the state. Despite taking care to make the fake checks look legitimate, the first-digit distribution clearly violated Benford's law (Figure 16-4), leading to a conviction.

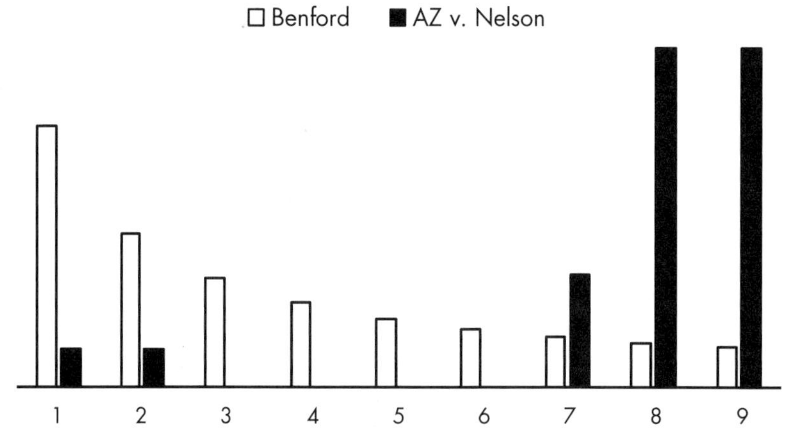

Figure 16-4: Comparison of the frequency of first digits in fraudulent checks to anticipated Benford's law frequency, State of Arizona v. Wayne James Nelson (CV92-18841)

Benford's law is also useful for internal business audits. Imagine a case where any travel and entertainment expenses over $10,000 must be approved by the company vice president. This type of financial threshold can tempt employees to do things like split invoices to game the system. Figure 16-5 is based on a group of expenses ranging from $100 to $12,000, where all values greater than $9,999 were split into two equal halves. As you can guess, there is a spike in first-digit frequencies around 5 and 6, in clear violation of Benford's law.

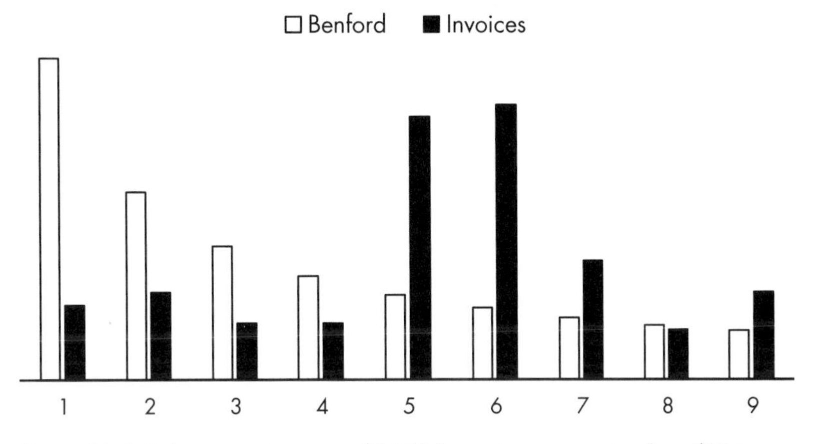

Figure 16-5: Splitting invoices over $9,999 for a dataset ranging from $100 to $12,000 violates Benford's law.

On a grander scale, Benford's law has revealed irregularities in the financial data—such as revenue numbers—of large corporations. An example from Enron, which practiced institutionalized accounting fraud, is shown in Figure 16-6. Enron's bankruptcy in 2001 was the largest in history at the time, and it resulted in the jailing of several top executives. The scandal also brought about the dissolution of Arthur Andersen, a "Big Five" accounting firm and one of the world's largest multinational corporations.

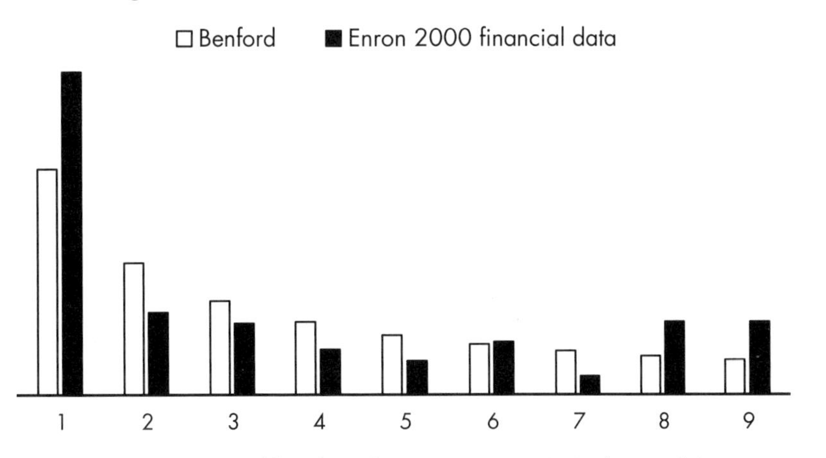

Figure 16-6: Frequency of first digits from Enron's year 2000 financial data versus anticipated frequency based on Benford's law (after the Wall Street Journal*)*

Obviously, Benford's law works best for fraud detection when the criminals are unaware of it. If you know how the law works, you can fool it, which we'll do in a practice project at the end of this chapter. As a result, you can use Benford's law to flag datasets that might be fraudulent, but you can't use it to prove the opposite.

Performing the Chi-Square Test

Auditors and investigators use multiple statistical methods to verify that a dataset obeys Benford's law. In this project, you'll use the *chi-square goodness-of-fit test,* which is a commonly used method for determining whether an empirical (observed) distribution differs significantly from a theoretical (expected) distribution. A significance level, or p-*value,* is used as the discriminator. The most common significance level is 0.05, but other common ones include 0.01 and 0.10. A significance level of 0.05 indicates a 5 percent risk of erroneously concluding that a difference exists when it doesn't.

Here are the steps for performing a chi-square goodness-of-fit test:

1. Find the *degrees of freedom* (df), defined as the number of categories (k) minus 1:

$$df = k - 1$$

   For Benford's law, the categorical levels are the first digits (1–9), so $df = 8$.

2. Calculate the expected frequency count at each level by multiplying the sample size by the theoretical proportions at each level:

$$E_i = np_i$$

   where E is the expected frequency at the ith level, n is the sample size, and p is the theoretical probability at the ith level. For 1,000 samples, the number of samples expected to start with 1 in a Benford's law distribution would be 1,000 × 0.301 = 301 (see Figure 16-1).

3. Calculate the chi-square random variable (X^2), also known as the *test statistic,* which will allow you to judge whether the two distributions are the same:

$$X^2_{df} = \sum_{i=1}^{n} \frac{(O_i - E_i)^2}{E_i}$$

   where O is the observed frequency count for the ith level of the categorical variable, E is the expected frequency count for the ith level of the categorical variable, and df represents the *degrees of freedom.*

4. Refer to the *chi-square distribution table* (Table 16-1), reading across the row corresponding to the calculated degrees of freedom. If the test statistic is *less than* the value shown in the p-value column considered significant, then you can't reject the hypothesis that the observed and theoretical distributions are the same.

Table 16-1: Chi-Square Distribution Table

Degrees of freedom	Probability of exceeding the critical value								
	0.99	0.95	0.90	0.75	0.50	0.25	0.10	0.05	0.01
1	0.000	0.004	0.016	0.102	0.455	1.32	2.71	3.84	6.63
2	0.020	0.103	0.211	0.575	1.386	2.77	4.61	5.99	9.21
3	0.115	0.352	0.584	1.212	2.366	4.11	6.25	7.81	11.34
4	0.297	0.711	1.064	1.923	3.357	5.39	7.78	9.49	13.28
5	0.554	1.145	1.610	2.675	4.351	6.63	9.24	11.07	15.09
6	0.872	1.635	2.204	3.455	5.348	7.84	10.64	12.59	16.81
7	1.239	2.167	2.833	4.255	6.346	9.04	12.02	14.07	18.48
8	1.647	2.733	3.490	5.071	7.344	10.22	13.36	15.51	20.09
9	2.088	3.325	4.168	5.899	8.343	11.39	14.68	16.92	21.67
10	2.558	3.940	4.865	6.737	9.342	12.55	15.99	18.31	23.21
	Not significant							Significant	

In Table 16-2, the critical value for a *p*-value of 0.05—at 8 degrees of freedom—is 15.51. If your calculated test statistic is less than 15.51, then the corresponding *p*-value is greater than 0.05, and you would conclude that there is *no statistically significant difference* between the observed distribution and the one predicted by Benford's law. The *p*-value here is the probability that a test statistic having 8 degrees of freedom is more extreme than 15.51.

Note that you should perform the chi-square test on *counts*. If your data is in percentages, averages, ratios, or so on, then you'll need to convert the values to counts before running the test.

THE OBJECTIVE

Write a Python program that loads numerical data, records the frequency of occurrence of the first digits, compares these to Benford's law using the chi-square goodness-of-fit test, and presents the comparison in both tabular and graphical form.

The Dataset

The 2016 US presidential election was rife with allegations of voter fraud. Most famously, the Russians were accused of supporting Donald Trump, and the Democratic National Committee was accused of favoring Hillary Clinton over Bernie Sanders in that party's nomination process. President Trump also alleged that 5 to 6 million people voted illegally, and in May 2017, he signed an executive order that launched a commission to review voter fraud and voter suppression.

For this project, you'll use a dataset of voting records from the 2016 presidential election. This consists of the final *by-county* votes for the

102 counties in the state of Illinois, which was won by Hillary Clinton. Starting in June 2016, the Illinois Voter Registration System database was the victim of a malicious cyberattack of unknown origin. Illinois election officials confirmed that hackers had accessed thousands of records but apparently didn't alter any data.

There were a surprising number of candidates on the Illinois ballot for president, so the dataset has been parsed to include only Hillary Clinton, Donald Trump, Gary Johnson, and Jill Stein. Votes for these candidates have been lumped together in a 408-line text file, with these first 5 lines:

```
962
997
1020
1025
1031
```

You can find the complete tally of candidates and votes online at *https://www.elections.il.gov/ElectionInformation/DownloadVoteTotals.aspx.*

For this project, you need only the votes, which can be downloaded from *https://www.nostarch.com/impracticalpython/* as *Illinois_votes.txt*. You'll need to keep this file in the same folder as your Python code.

The Strategy

Let's pretend you're an investigator looking into allegations of voter fraud in the 2016 presidential election and you've been assigned the state of Illinois. Before doing a deep dive into the data, you'll want to flag any obvious anomalies. Benford's law can't help you determine whether people are voting illegally, but it's a good place to start for detecting vote *tampering*—that is, changing votes after they are cast.

In cases like this, the ability to communicate the results is every bit as important as the quantitative analysis. Voting commissions don't just include experts but also many laypeople with limited knowledge of statistics. And juries probably will not include a single expert. To convince yourself—and others—that the vote counts are valid (or not), you'll want to show multiple comparisons, like a table, a graph, and the quantitative chi-square variable (test statistic).

The individual steps involved in the analysis lend themselves well to encapsulation in functions. So, instead of pseudocode, let's look at what functions you may need:

`load_data()` Load the data as a list.

`count_first_digits()` Tabulate the first digits in each county's observed vote total.

`get_expected_counts()` Determine the counts for each first digit as predicted by Benford.

`chi_square_test()` Run a chi-square goodness-of-fit test on the observed versus expected counts.

bar_chart() Generate a bar chart to compare observed first-digit percentages to those expected.

main() Get the dataset filename, call the functions, and print the statistics.

The Code

You'll use the *benford.py* code in this section to investigate voter fraud, but it's flexible enough to be used on *any* dataset where categorical values have been counted, such as medical test results, income tax revenues, or customer refunds. Non-fraud-related applications are also possible, such as detecting process inefficiencies caused by a large number of low-value transactions; problems with data collection and handling, such as missing data, truncated values, or typos; and bias in measurement strategies or surveys, such as favoring best-case or worst-case sampling.

You can download the code from *https://www.nostarch.com/impractical python/*. You'll also need the *Illinois_votes.txt* text file described in "The Dataset" on page 353.

Importing Modules and Loading Data

Listing 16-1 imports modules and defines a function to load data. For this project, you'll use data in the form of a tab-delimited text file exported from Microsoft Excel, which you load as a list of strings.

benford.py, part 1

```
import sys
import math
❶ from collections import defaultdict
❷ import matplotlib.pyplot as plt

# Benford's law percentages for leading digits 1-9
❸ BENFORD = [30.1, 17.6, 12.5, 9.7, 7.9, 6.7, 5.8, 5.1, 4.6]

❹ def load_data(filename):
    """Open a text file & return a list of strings."""
  ❺ with open(filename) as f:
        return f.read().strip().split('\n')
```

Listing 16-1: Imports modules and defines a function for loading data

Most of the imports should be familiar at this point. The `collections` module provides specialized alternatives to standard Python containers like sets, tuples, lists, and dictionaries ❶. For counting first-digit frequencies, you'll need `defaultdict`, which is a `dict` subclass that calls a factory function to supply missing values. With `defaultdict`, you can build a dictionary using a loop, and it will automatically create new keys rather than throwing an error. It returns a dictionary object.

The final import is for plotting with `matplotlib` ❷. For more information on `matplotlib` and how to install it, see "The Probability-of-Detection Code" on page 194.

Now, assign a variable to a list containing the Benford's law percentages, ordered from 1 to 9 ❸. Then, define a function to read a text file and return a list ❹. As you've done before, use `with`, as it will automatically close the file when done ❺.

Counting First Digits

Listing 16-2 defines a function to count the first digits and store the results in a dictionary data structure. The final counts, and the frequency of each count as a percentage, are returned as lists to use in subsequent functions. The function will also run quality control on the data and, if it encounters a bad sample, will alert the user and close the program.

benford.py, part 2

```
❶ def count_first_digits(data_list):
      """Count 1st digits in list of numbers; return counts & frequency."""
    ❷ first_digits = defaultdict(int)  # default value of int is 0
    ❸ for sample in data_list:
        ❹ if sample == '':
              continue
          try:
              int(sample)
          except ValueError as e:
              print(e, file=sys.stderr)
              print("Samples must be integers. Exiting", file=sys.stderr)
              sys.exit(1)
        ❺ first_digits[sample[0]] += 1
    ❻ data_count = [v for (k, v) in sorted(first_digits.items())]
      total_count = sum(data_count)
      data_pct = [(i / total_count) * 100 for i in data_count]
    ❼ return data_count, data_pct, total_count
```

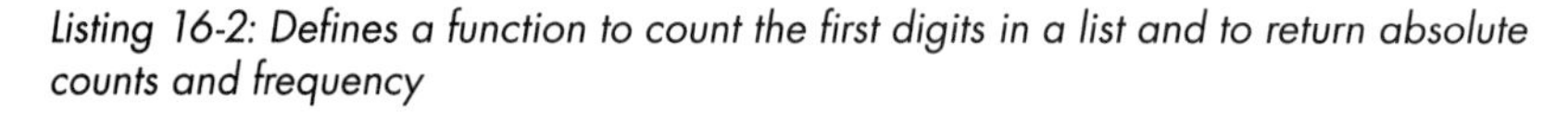

Listing 16-2: Defines a function to count the first digits in a list and to return absolute counts and frequency

The `count_first_digits()` function takes the list of strings returned from the `load_data()` function as an argument ❶. You'll call both functions in `main()`.

Start a dictionary, named `first_digits`, using `defaultdict` ❷. This step just sets up the dictionary for later population. The first argument for `defaultdict` is any callable (with no arguments). In this case, the callable is the type constructor for `int`, as you want to count integers. With `defaultdict`, whenever an operation encounters a missing key, a function named `default_factory` is called with no arguments, and the output is used as the value. Any key that doesn't exist gets the value returned by `default_factory`, and no `KeyError` is raised.

Now start a `for` loop and go through the samples in `data_list` ❸. If the sample is empty—that is, if the text file contains a blank line ❹—skip it with `continue`. Otherwise, use `try` to convert the sample to an integer. If an exception occurs, the sample isn't a proper count value, so let the user know and exit the program. In the following output example, the input file contains a float value (`0.01`) and the `main()` function prints the filename.

```
Name of file with COUNT data: bad_data.txt
invalid literal for int() with base 10: '0.01'
Samples must be integers. Exiting.
```

If the sample passes the test, make its first element (leading digit) the dictionary key and add 1 to the value ❺. Because you used defaultdict with int, the key is initially assigned a default value of 0 on the fly.

Like all Python dictionaries, first_digits is unordered. To compare the counts to a Benford's law distribution, you need the keys listed in numerical order, so use list comprehension and sorted to make a new version of first_digits, named data_count ❻. This will yield the values sorted by key, as shown here:

```
[129, 62, 45, 48, 40, 25, 23, 21, 15]
```

Next, sum the counts, then make a new list and convert the counts to percentages. End the function by returning these two lists and the summed counts ❼. Because the counts in the lists are sorted from 1 to 9, you don't need the associated first digit—it is implicit in the ordering.

Getting the Expected Counts

Listing 16-3 defines the get_expected_counts() function that takes the observed data and calculates what the expected counts should be for the leading digits, based on Benford's law. These expected counts are returned as a list that you'll use later with the chi-square goodness-of-fit test to see how well the observed data conform to Benford's law.

benford.py, part 3

```
❶ def get_expected_counts(total_count):
      """Return list of expected Benford's law counts for a total sample count."""
    ❷ return [round(p * total_count / 100) for p in BENFORD]
```

Listing 16-3: Defines a function to calculate expected Benford's law counts for a dataset

The argument for this function is the summed count that you returned from the count_first_digits() function in Listing 16-2 ❶. To get the counts you would expect for Benford's law, you'll need to use the frequency *probability* of each digit, so convert the percentages in the BENFORD list by dividing by 100. Then multiply the total_count variable by this probability. You can do all this with list comprehension as part of the return statement ❷.

Determining Goodness of Fit

Listing 16-4 defines a function to implement the chi-square test described in "Performing the Chi-Square Test" on page 352. This test calculates the goodness of fit of the observed counts to the expected counts predicted by Benford's law. The function will first calculate the chi-square test statistic, then compare it to the chi-square distribution table entry at a p-value of 0.05 for 8 degrees of freedom. Based on the comparison, the function returns either True or False.

benford.py, part 4

```
❶ def chi_square_test(data_count, expected_counts):
      """Return boolean on chi-square test (8 degrees of freedom & P-val=0.05)."""
    ❷ chi_square_stat = 0  # chi-square test statistic
    ❸ for data, expected in zip(data_count, expected_counts):
        ❹ chi_square = math.pow(data - expected, 2)
          chi_square_stat += chi_square / expected
    ❺ print("\nChi Squared Test Statistic = {:.3f}".format(chi_square_stat))
      print("Critical value at a P-value of 0.05 is 15.51.")

    ❻ return chi_square_stat < 15.51
```

Listing 16-4: Defines a function to measure goodness of fit of observed data versus Benford's law

The chi-square test works on counts, so the function needs the lists of data counts and expected counts that the `count_first_digits()` and `get_expected_counts()` functions returned ❶. Assign a variable, named `chi_square_stat`, to hold the chi-square test statistic, and assign it a value of `0` ❷.

Use `zip` to loop through the nine values in `data_count` and `expected_counts`; `zip` will pair the first item in one list with the first item in the second list, and so on ❸. To calculate the chi-square statistic, first subtract the counts for each digit and square the result ❹. Then, divide this value by the expected count for the digit and add the result to the `chi_square_stat` variable. Then print the result to three decimal places ❺.

Return the boolean test for the `chi_square_stat` variable versus 15.51, which is the critical value corresponding to a *p*-value of 0.05 at 8 degrees of freedom (see Table 16-1) ❻. If `chi_square_stat` is less than this value, the function will return `True`; otherwise, it will return `False`.

Defining the Bar Chart Function

Listing 16-5 defines the first part of a function to display the observed count percentages as a `matplotlib` bar chart. You used similar code in Chapter 12 to graph the outcomes of the retirement nest-egg simulations. This function will also plot the Benford's law percentages as red dots, so you can visually estimate how well the observed data fit the expected distribution.

The `matplotlib` website contains many code examples for building a wide variety of plots. This code is partly based on the demo example at *https://matplotlib.org/examples/api/barchart_demo.html.*

benford.py, part 5

```
❶ def bar_chart(data_pct):
      """Make bar chart of observed vs expected 1st-digit frequency (%)."""
    ❷ fig, ax = plt.subplots()

    ❸ index = [i + 1 for i in range(len(data_pct))]  # 1st digits for x-axis

      # text for labels, title, and ticks
    ❹ fig.canvas.set_window_title('Percentage First Digits')
    ❺ ax.set_title('Data vs. Benford Values', fontsize=15)
    ❻ ax.set_ylabel('Frequency (%)', fontsize=16)
```

```
❼ ax.set_xticks(index)
   ax.set_xticklabels(index, fontsize=14)
```

Listing 16-5: Defines the first part of the bar_chart() function

Define the `bar_chart()` function that takes as an argument the list of frequencies—as percentages—of the first digits in the observed data ❶. The `plt.subplots()` function returns a tuple of figure and axes objects; unpack this tuple into variables named `fig` and `ax` ❷.

Next, use list comprehension to make a list of digits from 1 to 9 ❸. This `index` variable will define the x-axis location of each of the nine vertical bars in the chart.

Set up the plot's title, labels, and so on. Name the plot *window* `'Percentage First Digits'` ❹, then display a title *within* the plot ❺. I am using generic titles, but you can customize these to be more specific. Use the `fontsize` keyword argument to set the text size to `15`. Note that the window title is an attribute of `fig`, but the other labels will be attributes of `ax`.

Use `set_ylabel()` to name the y-axis "Frequency (%)" ❻, then set the x-axis tick marks based on the `index` variable ❼. The tick labels will be the numbers 1 through 9, so use the index variable again and set the font size to `14`.

Completing the Bar Chart Function

Listing 16-6 completes the `bar_chart()` function by defining the bars, annotating the top of each bar with its frequency value, and plotting the Benford distribution values as red-filled circles.

benford.py, part 6

```
   # build bars
❶ rects = ax.bar(index, data_pct, width=0.95, color='black', label='Data')

   # attach a text label above each bar displaying its height
❷ for rect in rects:
     ❸ height = rect.get_height()
     ❹ ax.text(rect.get_x() + rect.get_width()/2, height,
                '{:0.1f}'.format(height), ha='center', va='bottom',
                fontsize=13)

   # plot Benford values as red dots
❺ ax.scatter(index, BENFORD, s=150, c='red', zorder=2, label='Benford')

   # Hide the right and top spines & add legend
❻ ax.spines['right'].set_visible(False)
   ax.spines['top'].set_visible(False)
❼ ax.legend(prop={'size':15}, frameon=False)

❽ plt.show()
```

Listing 16-6: Completes the function for generating a bar chart

Name a variable, called rects, for rectangles, and use it to hold the bars for the bar chart ❶. You generate these with the `bar()` method, which returns a container with all the bars. Pass it the index variable and list of frequency counts as percentages, set the width of each bar to 0.95, fill them with black, and set the `label` argument to `'Data'`. The last parameter is a very handy way to autogenerate a legend. You'll take advantage of this near the end of the function.

I'm a fan of plotting the actual bar value just above the bar so you don't have to squint over at the y-axis and try to guess it. To do this, start by looping through each bar (`rect`) in `rects` ❷ and get its height ❸, which is its y-axis value. Then, call the `ax` object's `text()` method ❹ and pass it the x-location of the left-hand side of the bar—obtained with the `get_x()` method—and add to it half the width of the bar in order to center the label over the bar. Because you use the `get_width()` method, you only have to assign the bar width once, which you did in step ❶. Next comes the bar height—formatted to one decimal place—followed by the horizontal and vertical alignments. Set these to the center and the bottom of the text bounding box, respectively. Finish by assigning the text size.

Now, start building the `matplotlib` "markers"—in this case, dots—that will flag the location of the Benford distribution frequencies for each first digit. Do this using the `scatter()` method, which builds scatterplots ❺.

The first two arguments for `scatter()` are the x-y locations for each marker, represented by consecutive pairs from the `index` and `BENFORD` lists. Next is the marker size, set at `150`, followed by a color. Both `red` and `DodgerBlue` work well. You want the markers to post on top of the bars, so set the `zorder` to `2`. Elements in the figure are referred to as `matplotlib` "artists," and artists with higher `zorder` values will plot over those with lower values. Finish with the `label` argument used to make a legend.

The next two statements are for aesthetics. By default, `matplotlib` will draw a box around the interior of the plot, and the upper border may interfere with the labels posted at the top of each bar. So, remove the top and right borders by setting their visibility to `False` ❻.

Use `legend()` to build a legend for the plot ❼. This will work with no arguments, but set its size property to `15` and turn off the frame around the legend for an arguably more attractive result. End by calling `plt.show()` to display the chart ❽. An example bar chart is shown in Figure 16-7.

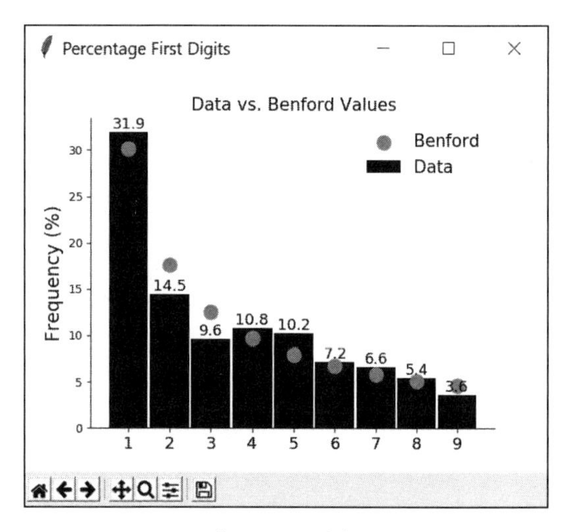

Figure 16-7: Example output of the `bar_chart()` *function*

In the `main()` function, you will display additional information as text in the interpreter window. This will include the value of the chi-square test statistic.

Defining and Running the main() Function

Listing 16-7 defines the `main()` function and runs the program as a module or stand-alone. Since most of the work is done in the individual functions, `main()` "mainly" calls these functions and prints some statistics.

benford.py, part 7

```
def main():
    """Call functions and print stats."""
    # load data
    while True:
     ❶ filename = input("\nName of file with COUNT data: ")
        try:
            data_list = load_data(filename)
        except IOError as e:
            print("{}. Try again.".format(e), file=sys.stderr)
        else:
            break
 ❷ data_count, data_pct, total_count = count_first_digits(data_list)
 ❸ expected_counts = get_expected_counts(total_count)
    print("\nobserved counts = {}".format(data_count))
    print("expected counts = {}".format(expected_counts), "\n")

 ❹ print("First Digit Probabilities:")
 ❺ for i in range(1, 10):
        print("{}: observed: {:.3f}  expected: {:.3f}".
              format(i, data_pct[i - 1] / 100, BENFORD[i - 1] / 100))

 ❻ if chi_square_test(data_count, expected_counts):
        print("Observed distribution matches expected distribution.")
    else:
        print("Observed distribution does not match expected.",
              file=sys.stderr)

 ❼ bar_chart(data_pct)

❽ if __name__ == '__main__':
    main()
```

Listing 16-7: Defines the `main()` function and runs the program as a module or stand-alone

Start by asking the user to input the name of the file with the count data to be analyzed ❶; embed this request in a `while` loop that will continue until the user enters a valid filename or closes the window. The user can enter a filename or a full pathname if they want to load a dataset that isn't stored in the current working directory. For example, in Windows:

```
Name of file with COUNT data: C:\Python35\Benford\Illinois_votes.txt
```

Use a `try` statement to call the `load_data()` function you built earlier and pass the function the filename. If the filename is valid, the returned list is assigned to the `data_list` variable. If an exception occurs, catch it and print the error. Otherwise, `break` from the `while` loop.

Next, pass the returned list of data counts to the `count_first_digits()` function and unpack the results as the variables `data_count`, `data_pct`, and `total_count`, which are lists of the first-digit counts, percentages, and total number of counts, respectively ❷. Then, generate a list of the counts expected for a Benford's law distribution by calling the `get_expected_counts()` function and passing it the `total_count` variable ❸. Print the lists of observed and expected counts.

Now, make a table that compares the first-digit frequency in the data with the expected values. Use probabilities, as decimal values are easy to keep attractively aligned in the shell. Start with a header `print` statement ❹, then loop through the numbers 1 to 9, printing the results for the observed counts (data), followed by the expected counts, each to three decimal places ❺. Note that the indexes in the two lists start with zero, so you have to subtract 1 from `i`.

Pass the two count lists to the `chi_square_test()` function in order to calculate how well the observed data fit the expected distribution ❻. If the function returns `True`, use a `print` statement to let the user know the observed distribution matches Benford's law (or, more technically, *there is no significant difference* between the two). Otherwise, report that they don't match, and for shell users, color the font red.

The `chi_square_test()` function will display its results in the interpreter window, so call the `bar_chart()` function to generate a bar chart ❼. Pass it the list of data counts as percentages.

Back in the global space, end the program with the code for running it as a module or in stand-alone mode ❽.

If you run the program on the *Illinois_votes.txt* dataset, you will see the output shown in Figure 16-8. There is no apparent anomaly in the voting results, based on Benford's law.

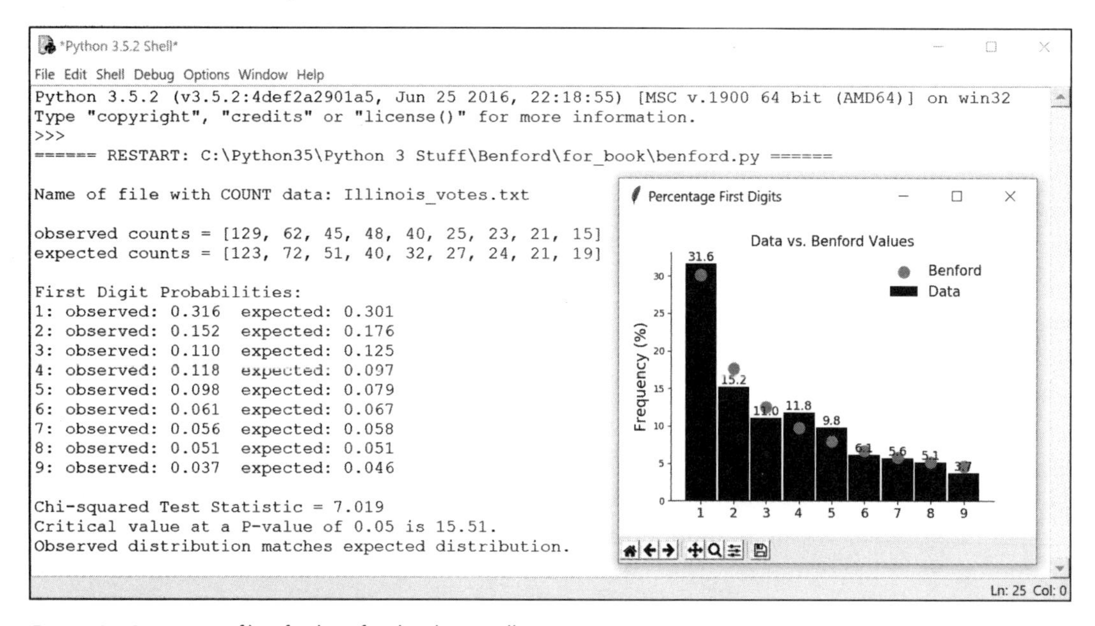

Figure 16-8: Output of benford.py *for the dataset* Illinois_votes.txt

If you run the program using only the Trump votes, then only the Clinton votes, you get the results shown in Figure 16-9. Trump's distribution, with a test statistic of 15.129, barely passes the chi-square test.

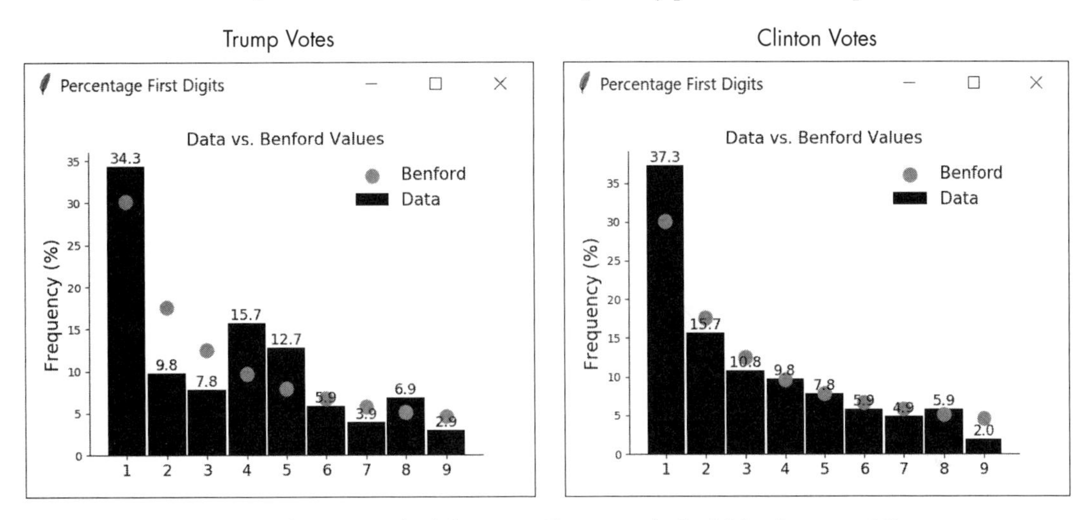

Figure 16-9: Comparison of Trump results (left) versus Clinton results (right) for the state of Illinois

In cases like this, you should be careful about drawing immediate conclusions. The dataset is small—only 102 samples per candidate—and the results may be influenced by things like demographic and voter turnout differences between rural and urban areas. An interesting article on this urban-rural divide can be found at *http://www.chicagotribune.com/news/data/ct-illinois-election-urban-rural-divide-2016-htmlstory.html.*

In "Practice Project: Beating Benford" on page 364, you'll get a chance to tamper with the Illinois vote counts and alter the outcome. You'll then use the preceding code to see how well the results conform to Benford's law.

Summary

Way back in Chapter 1, we used the "Poor Man's Bar Chart" practice project on page 15 and the "Poor Foreign Man's Bar Chart" challenge project on page 16 to look at how the frequency of occurrence of letters in a language is both irregular and predictable. This provides a powerful tool for cryptanalysis. Here at the end of the book, we've come full circle and found that even numbers share this trait, resulting in a powerful tool for fraud detection. With a short and simple Python program, you can shake the very pillars of heaven and bring the high and mighty crashing down to earth—all because someone noticed that the front pages of a book were dirty.

Well, that does it for *Impractical Python Projects.* I hope you had fun, learned something new, and were inspired to create your own set of impractical projects!

Further Reading

Benford's Law: Applications for Forensic Accounting, Auditing, and Fraud Detection (John Wiley & Sons, 2012) by Mark Nigrini covers the mathematics, theory, and testing of Benford's law together with example applications, including fraud, tax evasion, and Ponzi schemes.

Practice Project: Beating Benford

Test your skill at rigging an election using this practice project. You can find a solution, *beat_benford_practice.py*, in the appendix or download it from *https://www.nostarch.com/impracticalpython/*.

A dataset shouldn't be considered valid just because it follows Benford's law. The reason is simple: if you know about Benford's law, then you can beat it.

To prove this, pretend you're a high-level hacker for a nefarious foreign government with access to all the voting records in the state of Illinois. Write a Python program that tampers with county-wide votes so that Donald Trump wins the state, but the vote counts still obey Benford's law. Be careful; Illinois is a "blue" state, so you don't want to engineer a landslide victory (loosely defined as a 10–15 percentage point advantage in the popular vote). To avoid suspicion, Trump should squeak by with a few percentage points.

NOTE *States have rules regarding the recount of votes. Before manipulating an election, a fraudster would want to be aware of these to avoid the scrutiny a recount would bring. The actual statutory rules for each state are no fun to read, but the Citizens for Election Integrity Minnesota provides approachable summaries. The one for Illinois can be found at* https://ceimn.org/searchable-databases/recount-database/illinois/.

Your program should steal votes from the other candidates, while preserving the by-county totals; that way, the total number of votes cast doesn't change. As a quality-control step, print out the old and new vote totals by county for Trump and Clinton, as well as their old and new statewide totals. Then, write out a text file that you can input into *benford.py* so you can check how you did with respect to Benford's law.

Datasets for each candidate are already prepared and listed here; you can download them from *https://www.nostarch.com/impracticalpython/*. Each of these datasets is just a column of numbers, representing votes, that has been sorted alphabetically by county (so don't change the order!).

Clinton_votes_Illinois.txt

Johnson_votes_Illinois.txt

Stein_votes_Illinois.txt

Trump_votes_Illinois.txt

Figure 16-10 shows the results of running *benford.py* on the output from my attempt, *beat_benford_practice.py*, which used the preceding datasets. The distribution passes the chi-square test and yields a visually convincing—but plausibly imperfect—fit to the values predicted by Benford's law.

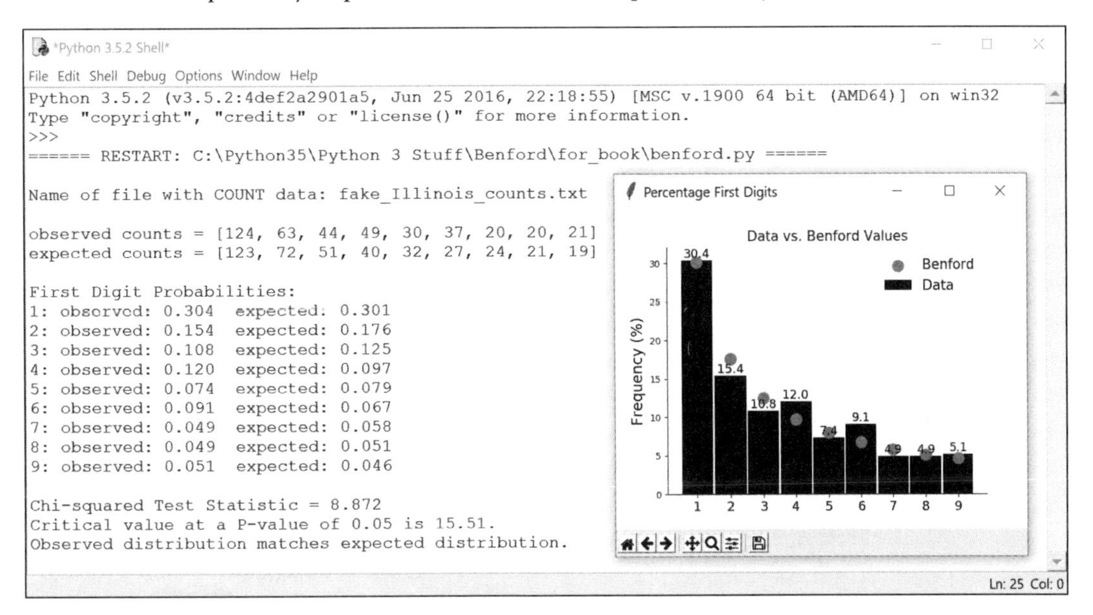

Figure 16-10: Results of running the distribution from beat_benford_practice.py *in* benford.py. *Mischief managed!*

Shown here are a few lines of output from *beat_benford_practice.py*, with the old and new vote totals by county:

```
old Trump: 12412       new Trump: 13223       old Clinton: 3945       new Clinton: 3290
-----------------------------------------------------------------------------------------
old Trump: 13003       new Trump: 14435       old Clinton: 7309       new Clinton: 6096
-----------------------------------------------------------------------------------------
old Trump: 453287      new Trump: 735863      old Clinton: 1611946    new Clinton: 1344496
-----------------------------------------------------------------------------------------
old Trump: 6277        new Trump: 6674        old Clinton: 1992       new Clinton: 1661
-----------------------------------------------------------------------------------------
old Trump: 4206        new Trump: 4426        old Clinton: 1031       new Clinton: 859
-----------------------------------------------------------------------------------------
```

The third line from the top represents Cook County, which contains Chicago. Note that Clinton still wins here, but by a lower margin. For Trump to win this blue county outright would be a tremendous red flag that vote tampering had occurred, even if he won the whole state by only a small margin!

Challenge Projects

Try your hand at these challenge projects. No solutions are provided.

Benfording the Battlegrounds

No candidate needs to cheat in a state they're guaranteed to win. If you're an investigator looking into voter fraud, you would most likely start with the battleground states. These could swing either way, and candidates spend much of their war chest—and time—on these places. According to Ballotpedia (*https://ballotpedia.org*), Trump's battleground states in 2016 were Arizona, Iowa, Michigan, Wisconsin, Ohio, Pennsylvania, North Carolina, and Florida. Clinton's were Colorado, Nevada, New Hampshire, and Virginia.

The online voting records for states are commonly provided in a number of formats, such as Microsoft Excel spreadsheets. Gather the ones for the battleground states, convert them to text files, and run them through *benford.py*. To get you started, you can find the Ohio records here: *https://www.sos.state.oh.us/elections/*.

While No One Was Looking

Former Speaker of the US House of Representatives Tip O'Neill was famous for saying, "All politics is local." Take this to heart and use the *benford.py* program to check out some of your local area races, such as for judges, mayors, county supervisors, sheriffs, and city council members. These events generally attract less scrutiny than do races for Senate seats, governor, or president. If you find an irregularity, make sure the voting dataset is a valid application for Benford's law before raising a stink!

PRACTICE PROJECT SOLUTIONS

This appendix provides the solutions to the practice projects in each chapter. Digital versions are available on the book's website at *https://www.nostarch.com/impracticalpython/*.

Chapter 1: Silly Name Generator

Pig Latin

pig_Latin_practice.py

```
"""Turn a word into its Pig Latin equivalent."""
import sys

VOWELS = 'aeiouy'

while True:
    word = input("Type a word and get its Pig Latin translation: ")

    if word[0] in VOWELS:
        pig_Latin = word + 'way'
```

```
    else:
        pig_Latin = word[1:] + word[0] + 'ay'
    print()
    print("{}".format(pig_Latin), file=sys.stderr)

    try_again = input("\n\nTry again? (Press Enter else n to stop)\n ")
    if try_again.lower() == "n":
        sys.exit()
```

Poor Man's Bar Chart

EATOIN_practice.py

```
"""Map letters from string into dictionary & print bar chart of frequency."""
import sys
import pprint
from collections import defaultdict

# Note: text should be a short phrase for bars to fit in IDLE window
text = 'Like the castle in its corner in a medieval game, I foresee terrible \
trouble and I stay here just the same.'

ALPHABET = 'abcdefghijklmnopqrstuvwxyz'

# defaultdict module lets you build dictionary keys on the fly!
mapped = defaultdict(list)
for character in text:
    character = character.lower()
    if character in ALPHABET:
        mapped[character].append(character)

# pprint lets you print stacked output
print("\nYou may need to stretch console window if text wrapping occurs.\n")
print("text = ", end='')
print("{}\n".format(text), file=sys.stderr)
pprint.pprint(mapped, width=110)
```

Chapter 2: Finding Palingram Spells

Dictionary Cleanup

dictionary_cleanup_practice.py

```
"""Remove single-letter words from list if not 'a' or 'i'."""
word_list = ['a', 'nurses', 'i', 'stack', 'b', 'cats', 'c']

permissible = ('a', 'i')

# remove single-letter words if not "a" or "i"
for word in word_list:
```

```
    if len(word) == 1 and word not in permissible:
        word_list.remove(word)

print("{}".format(word_list))
```

Chapter 3: Solving Anagrams

Finding Digrams

count_digrams_practice.py

```
"""Generate letter pairs in Voldemort & find their frequency in a dictionary.

Requires load_dictionary.py module to load an English dictionary file.

"""
import re
from collections import defaultdict
from itertools import permutations
import load_dictionary

word_list = load_dictionary.load('2of4brif.txt')

name = 'Voldemort'  #(tmvoordle)
name = name.lower()

# generate unique letter pairs from name
digrams = set()
perms = {''.join(i) for i in permutations(name)}
for perm in perms:
    for i in range(0, len(perm) - 1):
        digrams.add(perm[i] + perm[i + 1])
print(*digrams, sep='\n')
print("\nNumber of digrams = {}\n".format(len(digrams)))

# use regular expressions to find repeating digrams in a word
mapped = defaultdict(int)
for word in word_list:
    word = word.lower()
    for digram in digrams:
        for m in re.finditer(digram, word):
            mapped[digram] += 1

print("digram frequency count:")
count = 0
for k in mapped:
    print("{} {}".format(k, mapped[k]))
```

Chapter 4: Decoding American Civil War Ciphers

Hacking Lincoln

Code word	Plaintext
WAYLAND	captured
NEPTUNE	Richmond

Plaintext: correspondents of the Tribune captured at Richmond please ascertain why they are detained and get them off if you can this fills it up

Identifying Cipher Types

identify_cipher_type_practice.py

```
"""Load ciphertext & use fraction of ETAOIN present to classify cipher type."""
import sys
from collections import Counter

# set arbitrary cutoff fraction of 6 most common letters in English
# ciphertext with target fraction or greater = transposition cipher
CUTOFF = 0.5

# load ciphertext
def load(filename):
    """Open text file and return list."""
    with open(filename) as f:
        return f.read().strip()

try:
    ciphertext = load('cipher_a.txt')
except IOError as e:
    print("{}. Terminating program.".format(e),
          file=sys.stderr)
    sys.exit(1)

# count 6 most common letters in ciphertext
six_most_frequent = Counter(ciphertext.lower()).most_common(6)
print("\nSix most-frequently-used letters in English = ETAOIN")
print('\nSix most frequent letters in ciphertext =')
print(*six_most_frequent, sep='\n')

# convert list of tuples to set of letters for comparison
cipher_top_6 = {i[0] for i in six_most_frequent}

TARGET = 'etaoin'
count = 0
for letter in TARGET:
    if letter in cipher_top_6:
        count += 1

if count/len(TARGET) >= CUTOFF:
```

```
    print("\nThis ciphertext most-likely produced by a TRANSPOSITION cipher")
else:
    print("This ciphertext most-likely produced by a SUBSTITUTION cipher")
```

Storing a Key as a Dictionary

key_dictionary_practice.py

```
"""Input cipher key string, get user input on route direction as dict value."""
col_order = """1 3 4 2"""
key = dict()
cols = [int(i) for i in col_order.split()]
for col in cols:
    while True:
        key[col] = input("Direction to read Column {} (u = up, d = down): "
                         .format(col).lower())
        if key[col] == 'u' or key[col] == 'd':
            break
        else:
            print("Input should be 'u' or 'd'")

    print("{}, {}".format(col, key[col]))
```

Automating Possible Keys

permutations_practice.py

```
"""For a total number of columns, find all unique column arrangements.

Builds a list of lists containing all possible unique arrangements of
individual column numbers, including negative values for route direction
(read up column vs. down).

Input:
-total number of columns

Returns:
-list of lists of unique column orders, including negative values for
route cipher encryption direction

"""
import math
from itertools import permutations, product

#------BEGIN INPUT-----------------------------------------------------------

# Input total number of columns:
num_cols = 4

#------DO NOT EDIT BELOW THIS LINE------------------------------------------



# generate listing of individual column numbers
```

```
columns = [x for x in range(1, num_cols+1)]
print("columns = {}".format(columns))

# build list of lists of column number combinations
# itertools product computes the Cartesian product of input iterables
def perms(columns):
    """Take number of columns integer & generate pos & neg permutations."""
    results = []
    for perm in permutations(columns):
        for signs in product([-1, 1], repeat=len(columns)):
            results.append([i*sign for i, sign in zip(perm, signs)])
    return results

col_combos = perms(columns)
print(*col_combos, sep="\n")  # comment-out for num_cols > 4!
print("Factorial of num_cols without negatives = {}"
      .format(math.factorial(num_cols)))
print("Number of column combinations = {}".format(len(col_combos)))
```

Route Transposition Cipher: Brute-Force Attack

This practice project uses two programs. The second, *perms.py*, is used as a module in the first program, *route_cipher_hacker.py*. It was built from the *permutations_practice.py* program previously described in "Automating Possible Keys" on page 371.

route_cipher_hacker.py

route_cipher_hacker.py

```
"""Brute-force hack a Union route cipher (route_cipher_hacker.py).

Designed for whole-word transposition ciphers with variable rows & columns.
Assumes encryption began at either top or bottom of a column.
Possible keys auto-generated based on number of columns & rows input.
Key indicates the order to read columns and the direction to traverse.
Negative column numbers mean start at bottom and read up.
Positive column numbers means start at top & read down.

Example below is for 4x4 matrix with key -1 2 -3 4.
Note "0" is not allowed.
Arrows show encryption route; for negative key values read UP.

  1   2   3   4
 ___ ___ ___ ___
| ^ | | | ^ | | | MESSAGE IS WRITTEN
|_|_|_v_|_|_|_v_|
| ^ | | | ^ | | | ACROSS EACH ROW
|_|_|_v_|_|_|_v_|
| ^ | | | ^ | | | IN THIS MANNER
|_|_|_v_|_|_|_v_|
| ^ | | | ^ | | | LAST ROW IS FILLED WITH DUMMY WORDS
|_|_|_v_|_|_|_v_|
START        END
```

```
Required inputs - a text message, # of columns, # of rows, key string
Requires custom-made "perms" module to generate keys
Prints off key used and translated plaintext
"""
import sys
import perms

#==============================================================================
# USER INPUT:

# the string to be decrypted (type or paste between triple-quotes):
ciphertext = """REST TRANSPORT YOU GODWIN VILLAGE ROANOKE WITH ARE YOUR IS JUST
SUPPLIES FREE SNOW HEADING TO GONE TO SOUTH FILLER
"""

# the number of columns believed to be in the transposition matrix:
COLS = 4

# the number of rows believed to be in the transposition matrix:
ROWS = 5

# END OF USER INPUT - DO NOT EDIT BELOW THIS LINE!
#==============================================================================



def main():
    """Turn ciphertext into list, call validation & decryption functions."""
    cipherlist = list(ciphertext.split())
    validate_col_row(cipherlist)
    decrypt(cipherlist)

def validate_col_row(cipherlist):
    """Check that input columns & rows are valid vs. message length."""
    factors = []
    len_cipher = len(cipherlist)
    for i in range(2, len_cipher):  # range excludes 1-column ciphers
        if len_cipher % i == 0:
            factors.append(i)
    print("\nLength of cipher = {}".format(len_cipher))
    print("Acceptable column/row values include: {}".format(factors))
    print()
    if ROWS * COLS != len_cipher:
        print("\nError - Input columns & rows not factors of length "
              "of cipher. Terminating program.", file=sys.stderr)
        sys.exit(1)

def decrypt(cipherlist):
    """Turn columns into items in list of lists & decrypt ciphertext."""
    col_combos = perms.perms(COLS)
    for key in col_combos:
        translation_matrix = [None] * COLS
        plaintext = ''
        start = 0
```

```
        stop = ROWS
        for k in key:
            if k < 0: # reading bottom-to-top of column
                col_items = cipherlist[start:stop]
            elif k > 0: # reading top-to-bottom of columnn
                col_items = list((reversed(cipherlist[start:stop])))
            translation_matrix[abs(k) - 1] = col_items
            start += ROWS
            stop += ROWS
        # loop through nested lists popping off last item to a new list:
        for i in range(ROWS):
            for matrix_col in translation_matrix:
                word = str(matrix_col.pop())
                plaintext += word + ' '
        print("\nusing key = {}".format(key))
        print("translated = {}".format(plaintext))
    print("\nnumber of keys = {}".format(len(col_combos)))

if __name__ == '__main__':
    main()
```

perms.py

perms.py

```
"""For a total number of columns, find all unique column arrangements.

Builds a list of lists containing all possible unique arrangements of
individual column numbers including negative values for route direction

Input:
-total number of columns

Returns:
-list of lists of unique column orders including negative values for
route cipher encryption direction

"""
from itertools import permutations, product

# build list of lists of column number combinations
# itertools product computes the Cartesian product of input iterables
def perms(num_cols):
    """Take number of columns integer & generate pos & neg permutations."""
    results = []
    columns = [x for x in range(1, num_cols+1)]
    for perm in permutations(columns):
        for signs in product([-1, 1], repeat=len(columns)):
            results.append([i*sign for i, sign in zip(perm, signs)])
    return results
```

Chapter 5: Encoding English Civil War Ciphers

Saving Mary

save_Mary_practice.py

```
"""Hide a null cipher within a list of names using a variable pattern."""
import load_dictionary

# write a short message and use no punctuation or numbers!
message = "Give your word and we rise"
message = "".join(message.split())

# open name file
names = load_dictionary.load('supporters.txt')

name_list = []

# start list with null word not used in cipher
name_list.append(names[0])

# add letter of null cipher to 2nd letter of name, then 3rd, then repeat
count = 1
for letter in message:
    for name in names:
        if len(name) > 2 and name not in name_list:
            if count % 2 == 0 and name[2].lower() == letter.lower():
                name_list.append(name)
                count += 1
                break
            elif count % 2 != 0 and name[1].lower() == letter.lower():
                name_list.append(name)
                count += 1
                break

# add two null words early in message to throw off cryptanalysts
name_list.insert(3, 'Stuart')
name_list.insert(6, 'Jacob')

# display cover letter and list with null cipher
print("""
Your Royal Highness: \n
It is with the greatest pleasure I present the list of noble families who
have undertaken to support your cause and petition the usurper for the
release of your Majesty from the current tragical circumstances.
""")

print(*name_list, sep='\n')
```

The Colchester Catch

colchester_practice.py

```
"""Solve a null cipher based on every nth letter in every nth word."""
import sys

def load_text(file):
    """Load a text file as a string."""
    with open(file) as f:
        return f.read().strip()

# load & process message:
filename = input("\nEnter full filename for message to translate: ")
try:
    loaded_message = load_text(filename)
except IOError as e:
    print("{}. Terminating program.".format(e), file=sys.stderr)
    sys.exit(1)

# check loaded message & # of lines
print("\nORIGINAL MESSAGE = {}\n".format(loaded_message))

# convert message to list and get length
message = loaded_message.split()
end = len(message)

# get user input on interval to check
increment = int(input("Input max word & letter position to \
                      check (e.g., every 1 of 1, 2 of 2, etc.): "))
print()

# find letters at designated intervals
for i in range(1, increment + 1):
    print("\nUsing increment letter {} of word {}".format(i, i))
    print()
    count = i - 1
    location = i - 1
    for index, word in enumerate(message):
        if index == count:
            if location < len(word):
                print("letter = {}".format(word[location]))
                count += i
            else:
                print("Interval doesn't work", file=sys.stderr)
```

Chapter 6: Writing in Invisible Ink

Checking the Number of Blank Lines

elementary_ink_practice.py

```
"""Add code to check blank lines in fake message vs lines in real message."""
import sys
import docx
from docx.shared import RGBColor, Pt

# get text from fake message & make each line a list item
fake_text = docx.Document('fakeMessage.docx')
fake_list = []
for paragraph in fake_text.paragraphs:
    fake_list.append(paragraph.text)

# get text from real message & make each line a list item
real_text = docx.Document('realMessageChallenge.docx')
real_list = []
for paragraph in real_text.paragraphs:
    if len(paragraph.text) != 0:  # remove blank lines
        real_list.append(paragraph.text)

# define function to check available hiding space:
def line_limit(fake, real):
    """Compare number of blank lines in fake vs lines in real and
    warn user if there are not enough blanks to hold real message.

    NOTE:  need to import 'sys'

    """
    num_blanks = 0
    num_real = 0
    for line in fake:
        if line == '':
            num_blanks += 1
    num_real = len(real)
    diff = num_real - num_blanks
    print("\nNumber of blank lines in fake message = {}".format(num_blanks))
    print("Number of lines in real message = {}\n".format(num_real))
    if num_real > num_blanks:
        print("Fake message needs {} more blank lines."
              .format(diff), file=sys.stderr)
        sys.exit()

line_limit(fake_list, real_list)

# load template that sets style, font, margins, etc.
doc = docx.Document('template.docx')

# add letterhead
doc.add_heading('Morland Holmes', 0)
```

```
subtitle = doc.add_heading('Global Consulting & Negotiations', 1)
subtitle.alignment = 1
doc.add_heading('', 1)
doc.add_paragraph('December 17, 2015')
doc.add_paragraph('')

def set_spacing(paragraph):
    """Use docx to set line spacing between paragraphs."""
    paragraph_format = paragraph.paragraph_format
    paragraph_format.space_before = Pt(0)
    paragraph_format.space_after = Pt(0)

length_real = len(real_list)
count_real = 0  # index of current line in real (hidden) message

# interleave real and fake message lines
for line in fake_list:
    if count_real < length_real and line == "":
        paragraph = doc.add_paragraph(real_list[count_real])
        paragraph_index = len(doc.paragraphs) - 1

        # set real message color to white
        run = doc.paragraphs[paragraph_index].runs[0]
        font = run.font
        font.color.rgb = RGBColor(255, 255, 255)  # make it red to test
        count_real += 1

    else:
        paragraph = doc.add_paragraph(line)

    set_spacing(paragraph)

doc.save('ciphertext_message_letterhead.docx')

print("Done"))
```

Chapter 8: Counting Syllables for Haiku Poetry

Syllable Counter vs. Dictionary File

test_count_syllables_w_dict.py

```
"""Load a dictionary file, pick random words, run syllable-counting module."""
import sys
import random
from count_syllables import count_syllables

def load(file):
    """Open a text file & return list of lowercase strings."""
    with open(file) as in_file:
        loaded_txt = in_file.read().strip().split('\n')
        loaded_txt = [x.lower() for x in loaded_txt]
        return loaded_txt
```

```
try:
    word_list = load('2of4brif.txt')
except IOError as e:
    print("{}\nError opening file. Terminating program.".format(e),
          file=sys.stderr)
    sys.exit(1)

test_data = []
num_words = 100
test_data.extend(random.sample(word_list, num_words))

for word in test_data:
    try:
        num_syllables = count_syllables(word)
        print(word, num_syllables, end='\n')
    except KeyError:
        print(word, end='')
        print(" not found", file=sys.stderr)
```

Chapter 10: Are We Alone? Exploring the Fermi Paradox

A Galaxy Far, Far Away

galaxy_practice.py

```
"""Use spiral formula to build galaxy display."""
import math
from random import randint
import tkinter

root = tkinter.Tk()
root.title("Galaxy BR549")
c = tkinter.Canvas(root, width=1000, height=800, bg='black')
c.grid()
c.configure(scrollregion=(-500, -400, 500, 400))
oval_size = 0

# build spiral arms
num_spiral_stars = 500
angle = 3.5
core_diameter = 120
spiral_stars = []
for i in range(num_spiral_stars):
    theta = i * angle
    r = math.sqrt(i) / math.sqrt(num_spiral_stars)
    spiral_stars.append((r * math.cos(theta), r * math.sin(theta)))
for x, y in spiral_stars:
    x = x * 350 + randint(-5, 3)
    y = y * 350 + randint(-5, 3)
    oval_size = randint(1, 3)
    c.create_oval(x-oval_size, y-oval_size, x+oval_size, y+oval_size,
                  fill='white', outline='')
```

```
# build wisps
wisps = []
for i in range(2000):
    theta = i * angle
    # divide by num_spiral_stars for better dust lanes
    r = math.sqrt(i) / math.sqrt(num_spiral_stars)
    spiral_stars.append((r * math.cos(theta), r * math.sin(theta)))
for x, y in spiral_stars:
    x = x * 330 + randint(-15, 10)
    y = y * 330 + randint(-15, 10)
    h = math.sqrt(x**2 + y**2)
    if h < 350:
        wisps.append((x, y))
        c.create_oval(x-1, y-1, x+1, y+1, fill='white', outline='')

# build galactic core
core = []
for i in range(900):
    x = randint(-core_diameter, core_diameter)
    y = randint(-core_diameter, core_diameter)
    h = math.sqrt(x**2 + y**2)
    if h < core_diameter - 70:
        core.append((x, y))
        oval_size = randint(2, 4)
        c.create_oval(x-oval_size, y-oval_size, x+oval_size, y+oval_size,
                      fill='white', outline='')
    elif h < core_diameter:
        core.append((x, y))
        oval_size = randint(0, 2)
        c.create_oval(x-oval_size, y-oval_size, x+oval_size, y+oval_size,
                      fill='white', outline='')

root.mainloop()
```

Building a Galactic Empire

empire_practice.py

```
"""Build 2-D model of galaxy, post expansion rings for galactic empire."""
import tkinter as tk
import time
from random import randint, uniform, random
import math

#=============================================================================
# MAIN INPUT

# location of galactic empire homeworld on map:
HOMEWORLD_LOC = (0, 0)

# maximum number of years to simulate:
MAX_YEARS = 10000000
```

```
# average expansion velocity as fraction of speed of light:
SPEED = 0.005

# scale units
UNIT = 200

#=============================================================================

# set up display canvas
root = tk.Tk()
root.title("Milky Way galaxy")
c = tk.Canvas(root, width=1000, height=800, bg='black')
c.grid()
c.configure(scrollregion=(-500, -400, 500, 400))

# actual Milky Way dimensions (light-years)
DISC_RADIUS = 50000

disc_radius_scaled = round(DISC_RADIUS/UNIT)

def polar_coordinates():
    """Generate uniform random x,y point within a disc for 2-D display."""
    r = random()
    theta = uniform(0, 2 * math.pi)
    x = round(math.sqrt(r) * math.cos(theta) * disc_radius_scaled)
    y = round(math.sqrt(r) * math.sin(theta) * disc_radius_scaled)
    return x, y

def spirals(b, r, rot_fac, fuz_fac, arm):
    """Build spiral arms for tkinter display using Logarithmic spiral formula.

    b = arbitrary constant in logarithmic spiral equation
    r = scaled galactic disc radius
    rot_fac = rotation factor
    fuz_fac = random shift in star position in arm, applied to 'fuzz' variable
    arm = spiral arm (0 = main arm, 1 = trailing stars)
    """
    spiral_stars = []
    fuzz = int(0.030 * abs(r))  # randomly shift star locations
    theta_max_degrees = 520
    for i in range(theta_max_degrees):  # range(0, 700, 2) for no black hole
        theta = math.radians(i)
        x = r * math.exp(b*theta) * math.cos(theta + math.pi * rot_fac)\
            + randint(-fuzz, fuzz) * fuz_fac
        y = r * math.exp(b*theta) * math.sin(theta + math.pi * rot_fac)\
            + randint(-fuzz, fuzz) * fuz_fac
        spiral_stars.append((x, y))
    for x, y in spiral_stars:
        if arm == 0 and int(x % 2) == 0:
            c.create_oval(x-2, y-2, x+2, y+2, fill='white', outline='')
        elif arm == 0 and int(x % 2) != 0:
            c.create_oval(x-1, y-1, x+1, y+1, fill='white', outline='')
        elif arm == 1:
            c.create_oval(x, y, x, y, fill='white', outline='')
```

```
def star_haze(scalar):
    """Randomly distribute faint tkinter stars in galactic disc.

    disc_radius_scaled = galactic disc radius scaled to radio bubble diameter
    scalar = multiplier to vary number of stars posted
    """
    for i in range(0, disc_radius_scaled * scalar):
        x, y = polar_coordinates()
        c.create_text(x, y, fill='white', font=('Helvetica', '7'), text='.')

def model_expansion():
    """Model empire expansion from homeworld with concentric rings."""
    r = 0 # radius from homeworld
    text_y_loc = -290
    x, y = HOMEWORLD_LOC
    c.create_oval(x-5, y-5, x+5, y+5, fill='red')
    increment = round(MAX_YEARS / 10)# year interval to post circles
    c.create_text(-475, -350, anchor='w', fill='red', text='Increment = {:,}'
                  .format(increment))
    c.create_text(-475, -325, anchor='w', fill='red',
                  text='Velocity as fraction of Light = {:,}'.format(SPEED))

    for years in range(increment, MAX_YEARS + 1, increment):
        time.sleep(0.5) # delay before posting new expansion circle
        traveled = SPEED * increment / UNIT
        r = r + traveled
        c.create_oval(x-r, y-r, x+r, y+r, fill='', outline='red', width='2')
        c.create_text(-475, text_y_loc, anchor='w', fill='red',
                      text='Years = {:,}'.format(years))
        text_y_loc += 20
        # update canvas for new circle; no longer need mainloop()
        c.update_idletasks()
        c.update()

def main():
    """Generate galaxy display, model empire expansion, run mainloop."""
    spirals(b=-0.3, r=disc_radius_scaled, rot_fac=2, fuz_fac=1.5, arm=0)
    spirals(b=-0.3, r=disc_radius_scaled, rot_fac=1.91, fuz_fac=1.5, arm=1)
    spirals(b=-0.3, r=-disc_radius_scaled, rot_fac=2, fuz_fac=1.5, arm=0)
    spirals(b=-0.3, r=-disc_radius_scaled, rot_fac=-2.09, fuz_fac=1.5, arm=1)
    spirals(b=-0.3, r=-disc_radius_scaled, rot_fac=0.5, fuz_fac=1.5, arm=0)
    spirals(b=-0.3, r=-disc_radius_scaled, rot_fac=0.4, fuz_fac=1.5, arm=1)
    spirals(b=-0.3, r=-disc_radius_scaled, rot_fac=-0.5, fuz_fac=1.5, arm=0)
    spirals(b=-0.3, r=-disc_radius_scaled, rot_fac=-0.6, fuz_fac=1.5, arm=1)
    star_haze(scalar=9)

    model_expansion()

    # run tkinter loop
    root.mainloop()

if __name__ == '__main__':
    main()
```

A Roundabout Way to Predict Detectability

rounded_detection_practice.py

```
"""Calculate probability of detecting 32 LY-diameter radio bubble given 15.6 M
randomly distributed civilizations in the galaxy."""
import math
from random import uniform, random
from collections import Counter

# length units in light-years
DISC_RADIUS = 50000
DISC_HEIGHT = 1000
NUM_CIVS = 15600000
DETECTION_RADIUS = 16

def random_polar_coordinates_xyz():
    """Generate uniform random xyz point within a 3D disc."""
    r = random()
    theta = uniform(0, 2 * math.pi)
    x = round(math.sqrt(r) * math.cos(theta) * DISC_RADIUS, 3)
    y = round(math.sqrt(r) * math.sin(theta) * DISC_RADIUS, 3)
    z = round(uniform(0, DISC_HEIGHT), 3)
    return x, y, z

def rounded(n, base):
    """Round a number to the nearest number designated by base parameter."""
    return int(round(n/base) * base)

def distribute_civs():
    """Distribute xyz locations in galactic disc model and return list."""
    civ_locs = []
    while len(civ_locs) < NUM_CIVS:
        loc = random_polar_coordinates_xyz()
        civ_locs.append(loc)
    return civ_locs

def round_civ_locs(civ_locs):
    """Round xyz locations and return list of rounded locations."""
    # convert radius to cubic dimensions:
    detect_distance = round((4 / 3 * math.pi * DETECTION_RADIUS**3)**(1/3))
    print("\ndetection radius = {} LY".format(DETECTION_RADIUS))
    print("cubic detection distance = {} LY".format(detect_distance))

    # round civilization xyz to detection distance
    civ_locs_rounded = []

    for x, y, z in civ_locs:
        i = rounded(x, detect_distance)
        j = rounded(y, detect_distance)
        k = rounded(z, detect_distance)
        civ_locs_rounded.append((i, j, k))

    return civ_locs_rounded
```

```
def calc_prob_of_detection(civ_locs_rounded):
    """Count locations and calculate probability of duplicate values."""
    overlap_count = Counter(civ_locs_rounded)
    overlap_rollup = Counter(overlap_count.values())
    num_single_civs = overlap_rollup[1]
    prob = 1 - (num_single_civs / NUM_CIVS)

    return overlap_rollup, prob

def main():
    """Call functions and print results."""
    civ_locs = distribute_civs()
    civ_locs_rounded = round_civ_locs(civ_locs)
    overlap_rollup, detection_prob = calc_prob_of_detection(civ_locs_rounded)
    print("length pre-rounded civ_locs = {}".format(len(civ_locs)))
    print("length of rounded civ_locs_rounded = {}".format(len(civ_locs_rounded)))
    print("overlap_rollup = {}\n".format(overlap_rollup))
    print("probability of detection = {0:.3f}".format(detection_prob))

    # QC step to check rounding
    print("\nFirst 3 locations pre- and post-rounding:\n")
    for i in range(3):
        print("pre-round: {}".format(civ_locs[i]))
        print("post-round: {} \n".format(civ_locs_rounded[i]))

if __name__ == '__main__':
    main()
```

Chapter 11: The Monty Hall Problem

The Birthday Paradox

birthday_paradox_practice.py

```
"""Calculate probability of a shared birthday per x number of people."""
import random

max_people = 50
num_runs = 2000

print("\nProbability of at least 2 people having the same birthday:\n")

for people in range(2, max_people + 1):
    found_shared = 0
    for run in range(num_runs):
        bdays = []
        for i in range(0, people):
            bday = random.randrange(0, 365)  # ignore leap years
            bdays.append(bday)
        set_of_bdays = set(bdays)
        if len(set_of_bdays) < len(bdays):
            found_shared += 1
    prob = found_shared/num_runs
```

```
    print("Number people = {} Prob = {:.4f}".format(people, prob))

print("""
According to the Birthday Paradox, if there are 23 people in a room,
there's a 50% chance that 2 of them will share the same birthday.
""")
```

Chapter 13: Simulating an Alien Volcano

Going the Distance

practice_45.py

```
import sys
import math
import random
import pygame as pg

pg.init()  # initialize pygame

# define color table
BLACK = (0, 0, 0)
WHITE = (255, 255, 255)
LT_GRAY = (180, 180, 180)
GRAY = (120, 120, 120)
DK_GRAY = (80, 80, 80)

class Particle(pg.sprite.Sprite):
    """Builds ejecta particles for volcano simulation."""

    gases_colors = {'SO2': LT_GRAY, 'CO2': GRAY, 'H2S': DK_GRAY, 'H2O': WHITE}

    VENT_LOCATION_XY = (320, 300)
    IO_SURFACE_Y = 308
    GRAVITY = 0.5  # pixels-per-frame
    VELOCITY_SO2 = 8  # pixels-per-frame

    # scalars (SO2 atomic weight/particle atomic weight) used for velocity
    vel_scalar = {'SO2': 1, 'CO2': 1.45, 'H2S': 1.9, 'H2O': 3.6}

    def __init__(self, screen, background):
        super().__init__()
        self.screen = screen
        self.background = background
        self.image = pg.Surface((4, 4))
        self.rect = self.image.get_rect()
        self.gas = 'SO2'
        self.color = ''
        self.vel = Particle.VELOCITY_SO2 * Particle.vel_scalar[self.gas]
        self.x, self.y = Particle.VENT_LOCATION_XY
        self.vector()
```

```
    def vector(self):
        """Calculate particle vector at launch."""
        angles = [65, 55, 45, 35, 25]  # 90 is vertical
        orient = random.choice(angles)
        if orient == 45:
            self.color = WHITE
        else:
            self.color = GRAY
        radians = math.radians(orient)
        self.dx = self.vel * math.cos(radians)
        self.dy = -self.vel * math.sin(radians)  # negative as y increases down

    def update(self):
        """Apply gravity, draw path, and handle boundary conditions."""
        self.dy += Particle.GRAVITY
        pg.draw.line(self.background, self.color, (self.x, self.y),
                     (self.x + self.dx, self.y + self.dy))
        self.x += self.dx
        self.y += self.dy
        if self.x < 0 or self.x > self.screen.get_width():
            self.kill()
        if self.y < 0 or self.y > Particle.IO_SURFACE_Y:
            self.kill()

def main():
    """Set up and run game screen and loop."""
    screen = pg.display.set_mode((639, 360))
    pg.display.set_caption("Io Volcano Simulator")
    background = pg.image.load("tvashtar_plume.gif")

    # Set up color-coded legend
    legend_font = pg.font.SysFont('None', 26)
    text = legend_font.render('White = 45 degrees', True, WHITE, BLACK)


    particles = pg.sprite.Group()

    clock = pg.time.Clock()

    while True:
        clock.tick(25)
        particles.add(Particle(screen, background))
        for event in pg.event.get():
            if event.type == pg.QUIT:
                pg.quit()
                sys.exit()

        screen.blit(background, (0, 0))
        screen.blit(text, (320, 170))

        particles.update()
        particles.draw(screen)

        pg.display.flip()
```

```
if __name__ == "__main__":
    main()
```

Chapter 16: Finding Frauds with Benford's Law

Beating Benford

beat_benford_practice.py

```
"""Manipulate vote counts so that final results conform to Benford's law."""

# example below is for Trump vs. Clinton, Illinois, 2016 Presidental Election

def load_data(filename):
    """Open a text file of numbers & turn contents into a list of integers."""
    with open(filename) as f:
        lines = f.read().strip().split('\n')
        return [int(i) for i in lines]  # turn strings to integers

def steal_votes(opponent_votes, candidate_votes, scalar):
    """Use scalar to reduce one vote count & increase another, return as lists.

    Arguments:
    opponent_votes - votes to steal from
    candidate_votes - votes to increase by stolen amount
    scalar - fractional percentage, < 1, used to reduce votes

    Returns:
    list of changed opponent votes
    list of changed candidate votes

    """
    new_opponent_votes = []
    new_candidate_votes = []
    for opp_vote, can_vote in zip(opponent_votes, candidate_votes):
        new_opp_vote = round(opp_vote * scalar)
        new_opponent_votes.append(new_opp_vote)
        stolen_votes = opp_vote - new_opp_vote
        new_can_vote = can_vote + stolen_votes
        new_candidate_votes.append(new_can_vote)
    return new_opponent_votes, new_candidate_votes


def main():
    """Run the program.

    Load data, set target winning vote count, call functions, display
    results as table, write new combined vote total as text file to
    use as input for Benford's law analysis.

    """
    # load vote data
    c_votes = load_data('Clinton_votes_Illinois.txt')
```

```
    j_votes = load_data('Johnson_votes_Illinois.txt')
    s_votes = load_data('Stein_votes_Illinois.txt')
    t_votes = load_data('Trump_votes_Illinois.txt')

    total_votes = sum(c_votes + j_votes + s_votes + t_votes)


    # assume Trump amasses a plurality of the vote with 49%
    t_target = round(total_votes * 0.49)
    print("\nTrump winning target = {:,} votes".format(t_target))

    # calculate extra votes needed for Trump victory
    extra_votes_needed = abs(t_target - sum(t_votes))
    print("extra votes needed = {:,}".format(extra_votes_needed))

    # calculate scalar needed to generate extra votes
    scalar = 1 - (extra_votes_needed / sum(c_votes + j_votes + s_votes))
    print("scalar = {:.3}".format(scalar))
    print()

    # flip vote counts based on scalar & build new combined list of votes
    fake_counts = []
    new_c_votes, new_t_votes = steal_votes(c_votes, t_votes, scalar)
    fake_counts.extend(new_c_votes)
    new_j_votes, new_t_votes = steal_votes(j_votes, new_t_votes, scalar)
    fake_counts.extend(new_j_votes)
    new_s_votes, new_t_votes = steal_votes(s_votes, new_t_votes, scalar)
    fake_counts.extend(new_s_votes)
    fake_counts.extend(new_t_votes)  # add last as has been changing up til now

    # compare old and new vote counts & totals in tabular form
    # switch-out "Trump" and "Clinton" as necessary
    for i in range(0, len(t_votes)):
        print("old Trump: {} \t new Trump: {} \t old Clinton: {} \t " \
              "new Clinton: {}".
              format(t_votes[i], new_t_votes[i], c_votes[i], new_c_votes[i]))
        print("-" * 95)
    print("TOTALS:")
    print("old Trump: {:,} \t new Trump: {:,} \t old Clinton: {:,}  " \
          "new Clinton: {:,}".format(sum(t_votes), sum(new_t_votes),
                                     sum(c_votes), sum(new_c_votes)))

    # write out a text file to use as input to benford.py program
    # this program will check conformance of faked votes to Benford's law
    with open('fake_Illinois_counts.txt', 'w') as f:
        for count in fake_counts:
            f.write("{}\n".format(count))


if __name__ == '__main__':
    main()
```

INDEX

D

E

F

G

H

I

J

K

L

M

N

O

P

Q

R

S

T

RESOURCES

Visit *https://www.nostarch.com/impracticalpythonprojects/* for resources, errata, and more information.

More no-nonsense books from **NO STARCH PRESS**

PYTHON FLASH CARDS
Syntax, Concepts, and Examples
by ERIC MATTHES
WINTER 2019, 101 CARDS, $27.95
ISBN 978-1-59327-896-0
full color

PYTHON PLAYGROUND
Geeky Projects for the Curious Programmer
by MAHESH VENKITACHALAM
OCTOBER 2015, 352 PP., $29.95
ISBN 978-1-59327-604-1

CRACKING CODES WITH PYTHON
An Introduction to Building and Breaking Ciphers
by AL SWEIGART
JANUARY 2018, 424 PP., $29.95
ISBN 978-1-59327-822-`9

MATH ADVENTURES WITH PYTHON
Fractals, Automata, 3D Graphics, and More!
by PETER FARRELL
FALL 2018, 304 PP., $29.95
ISBN 978-1-59327-867-0
full color

SERIOUS PYTHON
Black-Belt Advice on Deployment, Scalability, Testing, and More
by JULIEN DANJOU
FALL 2018, 300 PP., $34.95
ISBN 978-1-59327-878-6

PYTHON CRASH COURSE
A Hands-On, Project-Based Introduction to Programming
by ERIC MATTHES
NOVEMBER 2015, 560 PP., $39.95
ISBN 978-1-59327-603-4

PHONE:
1.800.420.7240 OR
1.415.863.9900

EMAIL:
SALES@NOSTARCH.COM

WEB:
WWW.NOSTARCH.COM

The Electronic Frontier Foundation (EFF) is the leading organization defending civil liberties in the digital world. We defend free speech on the Internet, fight illegal surveillance, promote the rights of innovators to develop new digital technologies, and work to ensure that the rights and freedoms we enjoy are enhanced – rather than eroded – as our use of technology grows.

EFF.ORG